JEWISH LITURGY
as a
SPIRITUAL SYSTEM

JEWISH LITURGY
—— as a ——
SPIRITUAL SYSTEM

A PRAYER-BY-PRAYER
EXPLANATION OF THE
NATURE AND MEANING
OF JEWISH WORSHIP

ARNOLD S. ROSENBERG

JASON ARONSON INC.
Northvale, New Jersey
London

This book was set in 10 pt. Berkeley Oldstyle by Alabama Book Composition of Deatsville, Alabama, and printed and bound by Book-mart Press of North Bergen, New Jersey.

Library of Congress Cataloging-in-Publication Data

Rosenberg, Arnold, 1951–
    Jewish Liturgy as a spiritual system : a prayer-by-prayer explanation of the nature and meaning of Jewish worship / by Arnold Rosenberg.
      p.   cm.
    Includes bibliographical references and index.
    ISBN 1–56821–971–7 (alk. paper)
    1. Siddur.   2. Judaism—Liturgy.   3. Prayer—Judaism.   4. Spiritual life—Judaism.   I. Title.
BM674.39.R67   1997
296.4′5—dc21   96–39696

Manufactured in the United States of America. Jason Aronson Inc. offers books and cassettes. For information and catalog write to Jason Aronson Inc., 230 Livingston Street, Northvale, New Jersey 07647.

Contents

Acknowledgments

This book is dedicated to my wife, Nelly Reyes, and my children, Julian and Nina Rosenberg, whose love and patience have made many late nights of writing bearable.

Rabbi Joseph Tabory of Bar Ilan University has been an invaluable help in reviewing the manuscript and ensuring its accuracy. I am deeply grateful to him. I am also grateful to Rabbi David Wolpe, Assistant to the Chancellor of the Jewish Theological Seminary, Professors Abraham J. Karp and Raymond Scheindlin of the Jewish Theological Seminary, Cantor Samuel Rosenbaum, Rabbi Alan Lew, Professor Steven Fine of Baltimore Hebrew University, Nama Frenkel, and Richard Fabian, Convener of the Seminar on Problems in the Early History of the Liturgy of the North American Academy of Liturgy, for their comments and assistance. Finally, my thanks to Arthur Kurzweil and Anthony Rubin at Jason Aronson Inc., for their profound interest in, and prompt attention to, the preparation and editing of this book.

Preface: Jewish Prayer, a Technique for Spiritual Transformation

Deepening the prayer experience is essential to Jewish renewal. . . .
Without an infusion of Jewish spiritual fervor in prayer and blessings
and observances, the reason to stay Jewish, the 'juice,' will be
lost. . . . If . . . Judaism is now facing a crisis as great as the first
century, then, too, like the first-century rabbis, we must renew to
preserve.

> Roger Kamenetz, *The Jew in the Lotus* (New York:
> HarperCollins, 1994), p. 287

My conclusion, after conducting the research for this book, is that the
crisis Judaism now faces, while genuine, is due not to a lack of depth in the
traditional Jewish prayer service but to a profound and almost universal
lack of understanding of that prayer service that pervades all segments of
the Jewish community. The traditional Jewish liturgy, if properly understood, *is* a deep experience, a powerful technique for spiritual transformation.

In their origin and structure, the words and rituals of the Jewish prayer
service are merely prods to move the mind of the worshipper through an

odyssey of the mind, a sequence of visualizations and mental transformations that, in the end, leave the worshipper mentally fortified to do good works and resist the temptation toward evil until he or she prays again, and is fortified again. Rather than writing a new liturgy, what we as Jews really need, if Judaism is to be renewed, is to understand the liturgy we have as possessing an underlying spiritual current, and the details and words of the prayers as merely the boats and oars with which we guide ourselves through that current.

Jewish prayer services in many contemporary synagogues lack spiritual fervor because the link between word and ritual on the one hand, and the mental transformation on the other, that would generate such fervor is not generally known to Jewish adults and is not taught to Jewish children. Unfortunately, the prayer service regularly degenerates into a race through words and gestures that are divorced from the sequence of mental states and visualizations through which these words and gestures were intended to lead us.

It is no wonder that many of those Jews who, in the 1960s, were exposed to "wisdom" traditions of the East, such as Buddhism, have rejected traditional Jewish prayer as lacking in spiritual fervor. Neither they, nor many Jews who remained observant, really understand it.

There are numerous popular books on Jewish mysticism and on the Jewish prayer service, but none on the link between the two. Some books on Jewish mysticism discuss meditation, visualization, and other techniques used to achieve an altered state of consciousness, and almost all books on prayer discuss the words and derivations of the prayers. Yet, no book previously written analyzes the prayers as signposts on a mental journey that leads to *devekut* (literally, "attachment [to the divine]"), a state of mind in which we find it easier to perform God's commandments and to resist the daily temptation to break them.

This is intended as that book.

A NOTE ON TRANSLITERATION AND TRANSLATION

In transliterating Hebrew and Aramaic words, I have used *ch* to signify the guttural "h" of the Hebrew letters *chaf* and *chet*, as the English sound *ch* (as in "child") does not exist in classical Hebrew and Aramaic.

Transliterations of Hebrew and Aramaic words are italicized, except where the transliterated words have achieved general usage in English (*e.g.*, the word "Torah"["Pentateuch"]) or are names of people or places.

Biblical translations have been taken from Harry M. Orlinsky, et al., eds., *Tanakh: the Holy Scriptures* (Philadelphia: Jewish Publication Society, 1985).

The Traditional Jewish Prayer Service: A Sequence of Visualizations and Meditations Aided by Prayer

The average synagogue worshipper will probably be surprised to read the following "bird's-eye" summary of the traditional Jewish morning service.

After lengthy preparation of the mind by reciting the morning blessings and singing the psalms in *P'sukei D'Zimra* (Verses of Song), we form a spiritual community with the other worshippers present that is solidified in *Barchu*, the convocation of public worship.

We then share with this community a vision of being at Mount Sinai and listening to God's words in the *Shema*. This is a powerful visualization technique.[1] We are to listen to God so well that we transform our minds sufficiently to make changes in our behavior in our daily lives. Through this transformation we make ourselves worthy of God's attention, and we as a spiritual community proceed to approach God in the first three blessings of the *Amida* (the Standing Prayer).

If we approach God with the proper frame of mind in the first three blessings of the *Amida*, we draw God's attention. Only then can we ask God to do things for us, in the middle blessings of the *Amida* and, later, in *Tachanun* (Supplications), and have our requests answered.

As a spiritual community, and as members of the world community, our obligation is to the community first. If our minds have been prepared properly, we will address our communal requests to God before we make our own individual requests.

1

These communal requests are made, in the weekday *Amida*, through two other visualizations. First, in the fourth through ninth blessings, we visualize ourselves undergoing a collective spiritual transformation, and, through it, attaining God's forgiveness and relief from all suffering. Second, having achieved this pure state in our visualization, we then, in the tenth through fifteenth blessings, visualize our own transformation having worldwide impact through the revival of a spiritually united Jewish people that assumes a central role in the world structure, as in the days of King David. Finally, we pray for our prayers to be accepted by God, and then we visualize ourselves taking our leave of God as if departing from a ruler.

After our communal visualizations, we have individual ones. The traditional service provides many special times for our individual silent prayers to God. We meditate first before public prayer, during the morning blessings and the Verses of Song. We pray silently after the sixteenth blessing of the weekday *Amida* (the petition for acceptance of our prayers), after the Peace Blessing that concludes the *Amida* both on weekdays and on the Sabbath and Festivals, and in *Tachanun* (Supplications), which follows the *Amida* on weekdays.

We remain in our transformed state through our study of the Torah. Unlike some other religions, in Judaism, spiritual transformation does not mean emptying the mind of all thoughts or withdrawing from daily life. Critical thinking and living in this world are part of Judaism. However, the quiet state of mind that comes from being spiritually transformed gives the student of the Torah a special receptiveness and attentiveness. Glowing in our altered mind-state, we are more open to new ideas in a sermon after prayer than at any other time of the day or week—and the Torah reading and the reading from the Prophets (*Haftarah*), as will be seen, originated out of the sermon.

Because group study of the Torah and the Prophets, strictly speaking, is not prayer, it became the time for celebrating community events, such as *b'nai mitzvah*. Although important, these events are really interruptions in the service, for which permission traditionally had to be sought from the congregation.

On the Sabbath and Festivals, after studying Torah, we renew our visualization of a transformed spiritual community and a transformed world in the *Musaf* (Additional) *Amida*. Finally, we close the service with *Aleinu*, a kind of Jewish "pledge of allegiance" that cements our bond with the community until the next time we pray together. As our first public act in our transformed state of mind, we comfort mourners by responding as a congregation while they recite the Mourner's *Kaddish*, and then sing songs, particularly *Adon Olam*, to cheer them.

If you are a Jew who has sat through dozens or hundreds or thousands of prayer services and never knew about the *Shema* being a visualization of receiving the Torah, or the *Amida* being a sequence of visualizations of collective spiritual transformation leading to world peace, or the end of the *Amida* being the time to address God through silent meditation about our personal needs and requests, or the response to the Mourner's *Kaddish* being our first public act in a transformed mental state, you are not alone. Read this book and find out more.

The Objective of Jewish Prayer: Achieving an Altered State of Consciousness (Devekut) That Will Aid Us in Living a Good Life

Jewish prayer is a means to an end. That end is achieving an altered state of mind and, by doing so, reinforcing ourselves in resisting evil and doing good in our daily lives. Judaism recognizes that we are human, that we make mistakes, and that we desperately need help in performing God's commandments and resisting temptation to break them. Judaism delivers that help through prayer.

Judaism not only builds in a mechanism for delivering help through prayer, but requires us to avail ourselves of that device. Daily prayer is mandatory. Moreover, the *Mishna*, the oldest part of the Talmud, requires us to pray with the proper state of mind: "One may not commence praying unless one is mentally attuned."[2] The *Mishna* gives the example of the "*Chasidim* of old," who used to spend an hour in contemplation before praying so that their "heart would be directed to their Father in heaven."[3]

There are at least two different states of mind through which prayer leads us: *kavana* and *devekut*.

KAVANA

Kavana is deep, focused concentration and comprehension. This is the state of mind we attempt to reach during the early part of the prayer service, so that we have already achieved it by the time we recite the *Shema*. It is the mind-state that enables prayer to be effective. Accordingly, both the Talmud and Maimonides declare that if one is able to recite only one part of a prayer with *kavana*, he or she should employ that part, and will thereby satisfy the basic precondition for worship.[4]

Kavana requires not only concentration, but complete comprehension. This means knowledge of the deeper strata of allusion and association that underlie the Jewish prayer service—or, at least, those parts to be employed as a springboard for one's "odyssey of the mind."[5]

The *Shulchan Aruch*, Rabbi Joseph Caro's classic sixteenth-century codification of rabbinic law, describes *kavana* as follows:

> When a person prays he must think deeply about the meaning of the words he is expressing. He should imagine that the Divine Presence is close to him, and he should consequently banish from his mind all distracting thoughts, so that his concentration and intentions are clear and pure.
>
> Let him consider well that if he was addressing an earthly monarch he would rehearse his words perfectly in order not to become confused. How much more should he do so when in the presence of the King of all kings, the Holy One, blessed be He, who probes all our thoughts.
>
> Pious and holy men in the past would sit in solitary meditation, focusing their minds so sharply upon the prayers they were about to utter that they were able to divest themselves of any self-awareness, to achieve a mental, spiritual, and emotional state which was almost at the level of the prophetic.[6]

DEVEKUT

Devekut, literally "attachment" or "clinging," has been defined as "the adhering to God that is so intense as to be an annihilation of self into God."[7] "A person should be so absorbed in prayer that he is no longer aware of his own self. . . . He who still knows how intensely he is praying has not yet overcome the bonds of self."[8] Going beyond *kavana* in the course of the prayer service to achieve a mental state of *devekut* is crucial, because it is *devekut* that lasts beyond prayer to affect our daily behavior.

Through *devekut* we become able to conduct our daily activities with the same focus and intensity with which we pray. The objective, as explained in the early writings of Chasidism in the late eighteenth century, is *avoda b'gashmiut*, serving God in the midst of ordinary life.[9] This idea was poetically put by one Chasidic writer:

> Through everything you see,
> become aware of the divine.
> If you encounter love, remember the love of God.
> If you experience fear, think of the fear of God.
> And even in the bathroom, you should think—
> "Here I am separating bad from good,
> and the good will remain for His service."[10]

The Chasidim did not invent *devekut*; it was an ancient rabbinic concept, and both Rabbi Akiva and the Babylonian talmudic scholar Rav discussed it. Rav said that the cleaving together of the worshipper and God through *devekut* was so close, it was like the cleaving together of "two [palm] dates."[11] The concept was alluded to by Maimonides[12] and was developed by the thirteenth-century Spanish Rabbi Moses ben Nachman (Nachmanides) in his commentary on Deuteronomy 11:22: "If, then, you faithfully keep all this instruction that I command you, loving the Lord your God, walking in all His ways and holding fast to Him. . . ." Nachmanides said of this verse:

> It warns man not to worship God and somebody beside Him; he is to worship God alone in his heart and his actions. And it is plausible that the meaning of "holding fast" is to remember God and His love constantly, not to divert your thought from Him in all your earthly doings. *Such a man may be talking to other people, but his heart is not with them since he is in the presence of God.* And it is further plausible that those who have attained this rank *do, even in their earthly life, partake of the eternal life,* because they have made themselves a dwelling place of the Shekhinah[13] (emphasis added).

Imagine sitting in a car in the middle of a clogged freeway, in a hurry to get somewhere, and yet being able to maintain the quiet intensity of mind of a person who has achieved *devekut*. Though assaulted by the sound of blaring horns from other automobiles, one is able, in this state of mind, to maintain equanimity, perceive the divine despite the distraction, and resist the temptation to curse or gesture at the other drivers. This is a small but concrete example of the human result that Jewish prayer is intended to achieve.

STYLES OF PRAYER WITH *DEVEKUT*

The two different styles of prayer with *devekut* have been characterized as "meditative" or "tumultuous,"[14] or as "contemplative" or "ecstatic."[15] As its name suggests, meditative or contemplative prayer is outwardly sedate. *Devekut* is achieved inwardly by praying with *kavana*, and thereby gaining *bina* (literally, "understanding" of the divine).

Tumultuous or ecstatic prayer, too, is what it sounds like: turbulent and boisterous. *Devekut* is achieved through, and expressed by, body movements, shouts, and song. This form of passion, commonly displayed in Chasidic prayer, is sometimes called *hitlahavut* (enthusiasm).

OTHER WAYS OF ACHIEVING *DEVEKUT*

Participation in the traditional prayer service was not the only technique available for achieving *devekut*. Several devices were used in antiquity and in the Middle Ages to enhance prayer for this purpose. These included, among others, weeping as a means of attaining revelations, mostly of a visual character, or inducing a divine response; visualizing the ascent of the soul, as if riding on or in view of the heavenly chariot envisioned by the prophet Ezekiel,[16] to perceive the heavens and to receive divine secrets; meditation on and repetition of the divine Name or the letters of the divine Name, in a manner analogous to the Buddhist use of a mantra; and visualizing colors, or colored letters of the name of God, as symbols for the *sefirot*, the different kabbalistic attributes of God.[17]

SIYACH, HITBONENUT, AND OTHER "ADVANCED" MEDITATIVE STATES OF MIND IN JUDAISM

Although it is the first objective of Jewish prayer, *devekut* was not the only mind-state that ancient and medieval Jews sought to attain. The ancient Judaism that created the core of the Jewish liturgy was highly mystical, was deeply aware of the subtle changes in mind-states, and was replete with meditative practices for achieving them. The Talmud describes a variety of mystical experiences achieved through meditation, such as Rabbi Akiva's vision of the "pillars of pure marble."[18] The *Heichalot* literature of the same period describes the "vision of the *Merkava* [literally 'chariot,' like the fiery chariot observed in the vision of Ezekiel]" and a secretive organization of Jewish mystics dedicated to ascetic and meditative practices.[19] Some of the Dead Sea Scrolls, particularly those called the Songs of the Sabbath Sacrifice, contain references to "the image of the throne-chariot," the "glory of the perfect light," "the colors of the light of the spirit of the holy of holies," and other similar descriptions evocative of mystical visions.[20]

Rabbi Aryeh Kaplan, in his book *Meditation and the Bible,* points out that the Hebrew Bible contains several groups of words that talmudic and medieval sources understood as signifying different techniques and mind-states associated with meditation:

1. *suach/siyach/sicha* (in Kaplan's view, referring to "inner directed, unstructured meditation, whether verbal or nonverbal, around one central point"[21]);
2. *higayon/hagig/hagut/haga* (in Kaplan's words, "the purifying and clearing of the mind [as by repetition of a mantra, so as to direct it toward one goal"; a "preparation for *Siyach*-meditation."[22]);
3. *ranan/rina* ("building up ecstasy and explosive emotions" through contemplation of the divine "until the soul breaks free to commune with God," a phenomenon that can accompany *haga*-meditation[23]);
4. *shasha* ("rapt attention, where one is oblivious to all outside influence"[24], an intense form of *kavana*); and
5. *hitbonenut/bina* ("contemplating something so deeply and completely that one makes himself understand it in all its aspects"; "to gaze and stare at something, either visually or mentally, until one understands it thoroughly"; a reference to visualization[25]).

The average Jew may attain *devekut* through prayer, but the spiritually advanced Jew may aspire to the higher realm of *siyach* through these more intensive meditational techniques. Prayer can serve as a *higayon*, a kind of mantra to clear the mind, or as a *ranan*, a channel for ecstatic emotion. In particular, *hitbonenut*, deep understanding through visualization and contemplation, is fundamental to Jewish prayer as practiced by the Chasidim.

HITKALELUT, REVELATION, AND PROPHECY

The ultimate purpose of "cleaving" to God through the mind-state of *devekut*, achieved through prayer, and thereby inclining oneself to perform good works, is to approach God so closely as to become integrated into the divine. This integration is known in *Chabad* Chasidism as *hitkalelut*, from the root *k-l-l*, which refers to that which is "universal, comprehensive, or general." Professor Moshe Idel of Hebrew University has observed that in the work of Rabbi Shneor Zalman, founder of *Chabad* Chasidism, "the penetration of the human into the divine realm is portrayed as a profound metamorphosis that makes the soul an inseparable element in the bosom of divinity . . . Moreover, the meaning of the term *hitkalelut* implies an interpenetration of the two elements involved in the process as well as the emergence of a different entity combining the previously separate components of the synthesis."[26]

Why become integrated into the divine? The answer is apparent: by being integrated into the divine, the individual becomes able to hear the still, small voice of God, to perceive the divine revelation that is within ourselves. In antiquity people who reached this point, and became able to hear God's voice, were called *n'vi'im*, "prophets."

Today, Jews do not call any modern person a "prophet." A frequently-heard question from Jewish children is, "Why are there no prophets today?" The answer suggested by the function of prayer in Judaism is that, in a sense, in Judaism every person has the capacity to be his or her own prophet. Through prayer, study, and good works, we are able to achieve revelation ourselves. Anyone can aspire to prophecy; one need not be anointed with oil to achieve it. The still, small voice within us can be heard if one enters the proper frame of mind and performs the commandments. Prayer is the device Judaism gives the worshipper to enter that frame of mind and to incline himself or herself to perform the commandments.

SPIRITUAL COMMUNITY VERSUS SECLUSION

One of the peculiarities of *devekut* is that it is supposed to be achieved through prayer in the presence of others, in a spiritual community formed by a *minyan* of ten adults. However, prayer in a spiritual community was not the only form of spiritual practice in ancient and medieval Judaism. Professor Moshe Greenberg of the Hebrew University has shown that prayer in the Bible was primarily extemporaneous individual prayer that, for the most part, followed ordinary patterns of human speech in expressing need, confessing wrongdoing, and offering thanksgiving.[27] The fact that the Bible records very few fixed prayers but a variety of distinct mind-states suggests that ancient Israelites believed that these expressions of need, confession, and thanksgiving would only be effective if offered in a particular frame of mind.

In the Middle Ages, Judaism borrowed from Sufism (an Islamic mystical movement) the concept of *hitbodedut*, or "seclusion," a special form of *kavana* intended to make the use of meditative techniques like combining the letters of God's name possible in the absence of a spiritual community.[28] There were two types of *hitbodedut*: external (physical isolation) and internal (mental isolation).[29] Following what were interpreted as biblical examples, physical isolation was practiced as a form of preparation for mental isolation.[30] The primary methods of medieval Jewish meditation in physical isolation were contemplation of nature and music, leading to the restraint of all ego and sensation.[31]

The word "seclusion" should not be misinterpreted as meaning that the practitioner should withdraw from the world, as is demanded in some other religions. While one could engage in silent meditative prayer on one's own if no other worshippers were available, or after group prayer had been completed, companionship in prayer was required by Jewish law when possible and certain prayers could not be recited without a *minyan*, based on a talmudic interpretation of Psalms 82:1 ("God stands in the congregation of God").[32] The rationale for requiring one to pray with others as explained by Rabbi Shem Tov ben Abraham ibn Gaon in the late thirteenth or early fourteenth century was to have someone with whom to aid him or her in conceptualizing the experience and to alleviate the burden of it.[33] In other words, the experience of achieving *devekut* could be confusing or frightening, and it was best to have others present for one's assistance.[34]

Some medieval commentators regarded meditative seclusion, *hitbodedut*, as a step following attachment to God, *devekut*, on the path toward prophecy, a step one could take only if one was ready for it. The average Jew needed to pray in a spiritual community to develop *devekut*, but the spiritually advanced Jew was ready, after communal prayer, to meditate in seclusion to ascend to a higher realm in which the *chashmal*, the divine "voice in the silence," could be heard. For example, Rabbi Isaac Abarbanel (1437–1508) stated that the first step in prophecy is to attain a strong level of desire to bind oneself to God, which must then be followed by intense meditation.[35]

Views of the Development of the Jewish Liturgy

That the Jewish liturgy developed as an aid to altering the consciousness of the worshipper is neither a new concept nor one that has ever been uniformly accepted. The medieval Spanish rabbi and poet Yehuda Ha'Levi espoused this idea in *The Kuzari*, but his idea was not pursued by other medieval writers. Medieval commentators on the prayers, such as David Abudraham of Spain, and numerous later rabbinic authorities stressed the obligatory nature of prayer and the effect of prayer and Torah study on God and God's view of the worshipper.

Of course, most medieval scholarly discussions of Jewish liturgy were necessarily ahistorical. Writers like Abudraham lived far from Babylonia and the land of Israel, where the prayers had been canonized, and possessed little accurate information about their historical development. Even the early medieval commentators on the liturgy, such as Rav Amram ben Sheshna and Saadya Gaon of Babylonia, lived several hundred years after the basic structure of the Jewish prayer service took shape and after core prayers such as the *Amida* and the *Shema* had been formalized.

The *Haskalah* ("Enlightenment") among European Jewry in the nineteenth century brought momentous progress in the critical study of Jewish liturgy. However, the pioneer liturgical scholars, such as Leopold Zunz, focused their efforts on proving the supposedly traditional Jewish prayers to be corrupted versions of a hypothetical original Ur-text. Like many in the classical Reform movement, these scholars often regarded the traditional liturgy as an embarrassing relic. Even if this Ur-text could be reconstructed, it was seen as an even more ancient relic by many of the early critical

11

scholars of Jewish liturgy—something of purely academic interest for what it might reveal about ancient Jewish practice and history.

Beginning with Ismar Elbogen, a German Reform scholar in the early twentieth century, it was eventually recognized that the "Ur-text" was a fiction. The search for an Ur-text of the Jewish prayers was replaced in the 1950s and 1960s by the "form-critical" approach of an Orthodox Israeli scholar, Rabbi Joseph Heinemann, and his colleagues. These scholars demonstrated that the Jewish liturgy had been patched together from diverse texts that had developed in a variety of different contexts, and had then been edited and re-edited over several hundred years. Heinemann and his school looked to the form of a prayer as evidence of the context in which it arose, and categorized prayers accordingly.[36]

However, Heinemann and his followers failed to ask what should have been the next set of questions: If the Jewish prayer service developed as a patchwork job, what were the guiding principles by which the patches were stitched together, and what do these principles mean for the modern Jewish worshipper? In other words, whether or not the words of the early prayers were diverse and different from those of today, was there something peculiarly Jewish, something recognizable to the modern Jew, in the way they were structured, in the sequence of functions those words were intended to perform? Can the modern Jewish worshipper learn anything meaningful from the history of her or his liturgy about why we pray in the manner that we do?

Some modern scholars, such as Moshe Greenberg, have attempted to answer some of these questions by dividing prayers into categories of petition, confession, and thanksgiving, depending on the words they employ.[37] Such categories tend to emphasize the impact of prayers on God rather than their impact on the worshipper. If a prayer is petitionary, it works if God grants the petition. If a prayer is confessional, it works if God grants forgiveness. If a prayer is offered in thanksgiving, it works if God is pleased with our gratitude.

Greenberg's focus is on biblical prayer, particularly before and during the First-Temple period. While Greenberg's view may be a valid analysis of the role of individual personal prayer at the time of the First Temple, it does not explain (nor, in fairness, does Greenberg purport it to explain) the much greater complexity of the Jewish communal liturgy that emerged.

Another group of modern scholars, particularly in the United States, led by Rabbi Lawrence A. Hoffman, a Reform liturgiologist, and Professor Tzvee Zahavy of the University of Minnesota, have essentially answered the foregoing question in the negative. To them, prayers merely reflect the culture, ideas, and politics of those who composed them.[38] In this view, prayer may be a cultural artifact, a clue to "the way a group's religious ritual encodes their universe,"[39] or it may have originated as a rallying cry for a political or social faction, a tool of an "elite [that] propagat[ed] liturgy to serve their political and social interests."[40] Zahavy, who was trained at Yeshiva University, identifies the two central prayers in Judaism, the *Shema* and the *Amida*, as competing products of the rival scribal and priestly factions at the time of the Second Temple, and calls the *Amida* the "civic prayer for Jerusalem."[41]

Whether or not Zahavy is correct about the *Shema* and the *Amida*, there is doubtless some validity in his approach. Jewish liturgy did not arise according to a master plan with a single purpose, and some versions of some prayers may at one time have been political rallying cries. Yet, to conclude that the traditional liturgy is merely a collection of cultural artifacts or ancient political slogans is to make it scarcely more meaningful to the modern worshipper than a collection of old presidential campaign buttons. Such a conclusion has drastic implications for the Jewish worshipper and should not be accepted without question unless the evidence for it is overwhelming, which it is not.

It is submitted that the search for meaning in the origins and history of Jewish liturgy is not a lost cause. The texts of the prayers did vary throughout their history, and frequently they are not meaningful in themselves, but there is an overriding flow of mind-state evident in the structure of the Jewish liturgy. As prayers were incorporated into the liturgy, they tended to be inserted in a form and a manner that promoted or preserved this flow. The objective of this flow is to fortify the mind of the worshipper and the minds of the assembled community of worshippers to do good and resist evil—i.e., to achieve *devekut*.

The History of Spiritual Transformation as an Objective of Jewish Worship

PRAYER AND MIND-STATE IN THE RELIGIONS
OF THE ANCIENT NEAR EAST

Altered states of mind played a role in religious ritual in many ancient Middle Eastern religions. The Jews were presumably exposed to the traditions of their conquerors and of the areas in which they lived, and perhaps even the traditions of areas further to the east.[42] However, the role of mind-state in Jewish prayer was novel and distinct from its role in these indigenous religions.

Egypt. In ancient Egypt, silent contemplation and prayer played such a large role in priestly worship that priests would spend as much as half their day in silent meditation.[43] Contemplating the deity was, however, a privilege theoretically reserved to the pharoah. Only the highest-ranking priests were permitted to contemplate it as a substitute for the sovereign.[44]

Babylonia. Babylonian religion featured sacrifice, soothsaying and magic. Soothsayers were consulted continually.[45] "[T]here was hardly an occurrence in the private life of the Babylonian which did not provide an occasion for some form of ritual."[46] Babylonian religious practice included prayers for the individual to do good and resist evil, as well as exorcisms which sound as though they were intended to work the victim of an illness into an ecstatic state of mind.[47] One could become reconciled with the gods by honestly confessing one's sins and leading a pure and clean life.[48] However, altered mind-states in Babylonian popular religion, while perhaps

14

a mass phenomenon, were merely ancillary to magic and the consultation of oracles and seers.

Canaan. Canaanite religion before the Exodus was based on sacrifice. The Canaanites are believed to have conceived of the gods as a kind of upward extension of the theocratic bureaucracy that governed them, and perhaps thought of the many sacrifices to their gods such as El and Asherah as a form of tribute similar to what was exacted from them by their human leaders.[49]

Persia. Persia and Israel shared the same political fortunes from the sixth century B.C.E. until about the time of the destruction of the Second Temple, and retained close contacts thereafter.[50] The Zoroastrian religion that emerged in Persia in the sixth and seventh centuries B.C.E. included such practices as the wearing of knotted ritual cords, the *kusti*, around the waist as a constant reminder of one's obligation to do good and resist evil. This practice perhaps gave rise to the wearing of the *tzitzit*, or knotted Jewish ritual fringe, as a ritual device for maintaining a proper state of mind in daily life.[51] Zoroastrianism also utilized readings of holy texts as a method of aiding the worshipper in the battle between the god of light and the god of darkness for dominance of the mind and the body, conceivably a practice which influenced the use of the Torah in ancient Jewish religion.[52] If Zoroastrianism had influence on ancient Judaism, however, it occurred more through opposition than imitation.

Greece and Rome. Prayer and altered state of mind appear to have played little role in ancient Greek and Roman popular religion until a relatively late time. Instead, the early Greeks and the pre-Christian Romans offered sacrifices to their gods incessantly as propitiation and as a *quid pro quo* for favors desired or received.[53]

While Greek religion in general was sacrificial in nature, the Greek "Mystery religions" which took root in Rome as well as Greece appear to have been far more oriented toward alteration of mind-state as an objective of worship. The Mystery religions shared three features: "(1) a rite of initiation or purification by which the individual is rendered worthy of participation in the activity of the Mystery; (2) a sense of personal relationship with a deity or group of deities whom the initiate claimed as his or her own; and (3) the hope of life beyond death."[54] The Mystery rites were secret. Membership in the Mystery "included the promise of release from earthbound concerns and of life beyond death."[55] Both Cicero and the Roman Emperor Augustus were initiated into the Eleusian Mystery; Cicero described the initiation ceremonies by saying, "We have gained from them the way of living in happiness and dying with a better hope."[56] Even the Dionysian Mystery, with its orgiastic Bacchanalia, used intoxication, at least in theory, as a device for altering the mind and thereby achieving immortality.[57]

PRAYER AND MIND-STATE IN ANCIENT JUDAISM

Ancient Jewish popular prayer was largely spontaneous and focused on the mind-state of the worshipper. The Israeli scholar Ezra Fleischer has recently argued that prior to the destruction of the Second Temple, all Jewish prayer outside the Temple was "a personal expression of religious feelings [with] no fixed form and no appointed time."[58] While this is an extreme view,[59] the synagogue liturgy does appear to have arisen out of personal prayers, prayers adopted as a response to community emergencies, prayers of small tableside prayer groups called *chavurot*, and prayers that developed as incidents to study sessions and sermons given by charismatic scholars and "men of God" in community gathering places called *Bet Ha'Midrash* (House of Study).[60] All of these sources of prayer involve an altered state of mind on the part of the worshipper; these are prayers that arose out of spontaneous emotion, collective fear, joyous celebration, and the fervor engendered by charismatic leaders.

Moreover, the *Bet Ha'Midrash*, which acted as a crucible for the early Jewish prayer service, was itself a focus of ancient Jewish mysticism, dedicated to "inquiry into the secret meaning of the Torah [so as to] experientially discove[r] the divine within the text [through] various forms of intense reading and studying the details of the revealed book."[61] The purpose of this activity, called *derisha*, was to achieve *bina*, a "prophetic enlightenment" that was a "prerequisite for mystical experience."[62]

Ancient Judaism before the fall of the Second Temple in 70 C.E. obviously centered on the sacrificial cult at the Temple. However, the meaning of Temple sacrifice changed over time from paying tribute and giving an anthropomorphic God a cooked meal and other human necessities, as in ancient Canaanite religion, to an emphasis on altering the state of mind of the priest giving the offering.

Yohanan Muffs of the Jewish Theological Seminary has pointed out that in ancient Judaism, as in ancient Babylonian religion, a sacrifice was valid only if the offerer of the sacrifice possessed the proper donative mental state.[63] In the Temple in Jerusalem, as Nehama Leibowitz has observed, the sacrificial offering was ineffective unless the priest or Levite conducting the sacrifice was in the proper "spirit of generosity or willingness."[64] The emphasis was on the state of mind of the person who performed the work of the sacrifice, not the one who contributed the offering to the Temple[65]; but in the latter part of the Second-Temple period, the Festival of Passover became a time when people slaughtered their own sacrificial offerings in the Temple, and therefore had to assume the necessary state of mind in order for it to be effective.[66] While the sacrificial ritual of the Temple had grown out of the earlier anthropomorphic idea of the gods as being in daily need of food, shelter, incense (to eliminate the foul odor left by food), and light, the Temple priests had long ago ceased to conceive of God in these terms.[67] Existing forms and conventions of pre-biblical culture such as the outer sacrificial rites, circumcision, the Sabbath, the New Moon, and Passover were adapted to new purposes in the Temple and were imbued with a new spiritual meaning.[68]

Judaism, too, had what might be called its "mystery" traditions in that much was kept secret. Moshe Idel has written, "[T]he Book and its secrets oftenly [sic] play in Jewish spirituality a paramount role, similar in some respects to that the Christ and his mysteries play in Christianity and its mysticism."[69] It has been speculated by scholars of the view that the Torah merged a number of different documents that at least one of those, the so-called "P" Document, was kept secret by the priests.[70] The Oral Law of the Talmud was handed down through a system of professional memorizers, who were given the title *tanna* or *roveh*, a system that began as early as Joshua, who is described in the Torah as the official memorizer for Moses, and lasted until about 1000 C.E.[71] Jacob Neusner points out that this system was a deliberate anachronism adopted despite the availability of written materials, a method of "ritualizing" the process of formulating and handing down the law.[72] It also was a means of keeping the law a closely held secret accessible only by those with access to the rabbis, priests, and their official memorizers.

Similarly, Jewish liturgy was transmitted predominantly through memorization at least until the ninth century C.E.; in fact, the general rule, according to Rabbi Johanan, was "that which was given orally you may not put into writing, and that which is given in writing you cannot recite by heart."[73] The tradition of singing the prayers, like the system of Torah cantillation, may have arisen as an aid to memorizing them.[74]

Ancient Israel thus occupied a crossroads between two archetypes of religious traditions. Emerging from an Egypt whose religion appears to have included an emphasis on prayer and altered mind-states as a means of connecting to and influencing the divine, the Hebrews conquered a territory where the indigenous religions downplayed prayer and mind-state and instead emphasized sacrifices as a method of propitiating the gods and obtaining divine favor. Exiled from that territory to the cosmopolitan city of Babylon, and then coming under the rule of the Persians, they were exposed to Zoroastrianism, in which altering the worshipper's state of mind was central, as it had been in Egypt. The Jews who returned from Babylon to build the Second Temple may well have brought this idea with them. They were conquered a couple of centuries later by the Greeks and then the Romans, whose religious practice was more like the sacrificial cult of the Canaanites, but whose society encompassed a myriad of religious societies with secret rites that sometimes were intended to transform the mind of the practitioner.[75]

PRAYER IN THE SECOND TEMPLE

Consistent with this exposure of the ancient Jews to divergent religious traditions, both sacrificial ritual and altered states of consciousness played a prominent role in worship in the Temple in Jerusalem. The fundamental task of the priests was the constant service of God with both mind and body; they were called *mesharte Yahweh* (servants of God).[76] We know that prayer was prevalent in the Temple courts outside the priestly circle, and while there is no evidence that the priests themselves engaged in prayer during the First-Temple period,[77] prayer became a function of the priests as well as the Levites during the Second-Temple period.[78]

Morning prayers in the Second Temple included recital by the priests of the Ten Commandments and the *Shema*, including *Va 'Y'hi Im Shamoa* (from Deuteronomy) and *Va'Yomer* (from Numbers), a blessing after the *Shema* beginning *Emet V'Yatziv*, the *Avoda*, and the Priestly Blessing.[79] On *Shabbat*, the priests recited an additional blessing for the outgoing *mishmar* (the priestly shift, of which a total of twenty-four alternated during the year). The Levites would sing psalms during and after the sacrifices, including a Psalm of the Day, as well as special psalms on holidays (such as Psalm 30 on Chanuka). On pilgrimage festivals they would sing Psalms 120 to 134 while ascending the fifteen steps that led from the Women's Court to the Men's Court, where the altar was situated.[80]

EARLY DEVELOPMENT OF THE SYNAGOGUE LITURGY

During or soon after the Second Temple period the synagogues developed,[81] based perhaps on prayer services originally held at the Temple by the *ma'amadot*, rotating delegations of citizens sent to monitor the priests in the performance of their duties, or more likely based on prayers developed in the houses of study and in *chavurot*.[82] Distanced from the Temple hierarchy and much less confined by ritual requirements, the nascent synagogue liturgy was, perhaps, more powerfully influenced by the "wisdom" traditions and was devised with spiritual transformation as one of its apparent goals. After the destruction of the Second Temple, various Temple prayers and substitutes for Temple rituals were mingled with the prayers developed in other contexts, but with the evident purpose of maintaining a flow of mind-state.

There is evidence that mystical activity was an integral part of this development. It was in this time frame that *Merkava* mysticism, the mysticism of the wheeled chariot that bore the throne of God in Ezekiel's vision, developed. The Reform liturgiologist Lawrence Hoffman has written, "[T]here is no reason to limit the *merkavah* influence on the liturgy to fringe elements, a prayer here or a line there. Nor need we assume their influence to stem from people outside the mainstream of Judaism . . . More likely it is that the *merkavah* tendency is evident in many places in the prayers. . . ."[83] The mystics of the *Merkava* devised prayers, particularly the *Kedusha*, that were believed to have the power to assist the worshipper in ascending to heaven. This power consisted not in the words of the prayers, but in the manner in which they were recited. "Like mantras, they were a means by which a worshipper could transfer his mind from cognitive considerations to effective alteration of one's total perspective."[84] Why make this ascent? To achieve divine revelation.

Indeed, this was a possible response of the Jewish mystics to the early Christians and the Muslims: that for Jews, there was no need for further prophets, because every Jew had the capacity to achieve divine revelation personally through prayer and mystical experience. It is a fair assumption that when prayers were added and modified during those periods, the intention of those who were responsible for adding and modifying them was, at least in part, to improve the performance of the service as a vehicle to achieving this state of mind. It is also fair, therefore, to ask ourselves as we read a prayer, "How was this prayer intended to affect our state of mind?"

THE BABYLONIAN ACADEMIES

The early function of prayer as an aid to reaching a higher state of mind went into decline during the period of the *Amoraim* and *Saboraim*, the rabbis in Babylonia from about 200 to 1100 c.e. Babylonia was the largest center of Jews in the early Diaspora, and its scholarly life was organized around the academies at Sura and Pumbedita. The synagogue service, already largely formed, crystallized in the Babylonian academies, and also became sclerotic.[85] Where prayer had previously retained a degree of spontaneity, with certain points in the service intended for deep individual meditation, it became customary for students in the academies to parrot a prayer or discourse given by the Gaon or scholar who led the service. So, for example, the meditation following the *Amida*, originally intended for personal private reflection, was replaced by a prayer composed by the fifth-century Babylonian scholar Mar ben Ravina.

THE MIDDLE AGES

As Jews wandered through the Diaspora during the early Middle Ages, settling in places as distant from the land of Israel as Spain, France, and Germany, the level of Jewish knowledge declined. Many Jews could not read or understand Hebrew. The associations with biblical sources and historical events that many prayers were intended to evoke were forgotten, or were known to only a few. Efforts were made to put the prayers into writing so that they would not be completely forgotten, but under these circumstances the synagogue service could not be as effective in helping the worshipper to reach a higher mind-state. Also, this void of information was filled, in some instances, particularly in medieval Germany, by the notion that the prayers were divinely inspired and that, therefore, every word was important and had to be recited and searched for hidden meaning. Rote recitation replaced *devekut* in the value system of Jewish prayer.

There were, of course, exceptions. Maimonides stressed the need for intense concentration of the mind, *kavanat ha'lev*,[86] during prayer. Ehud Ben-Or, in his book on Maimonides' concept of prayer, *Worship of the Heart* (Albany: State University of New York Press, 1995), says that Maimonides' conception of prayer "transcends the prevailing distinction between supplication and meditation. Maimonides saw prayer primarily not as a manner of communicating with God or of contemplating eternal truths but as a pure act of worship. He saw it as an act that brings a person to realize the true nature of God, to experience God's presence, and to inculcate this realization in all dimensions of life. Maimonides[s] characteriz[ed] statutory Jewish prayer as a sustained effort to conform the mind to a proper worshipful stance. . . ."[87]

There also were exceptions among the mystics. While the German mystics, the *Chasidei Ashkenaz*, promoted the idea that the words of the prayers had to be recited in a precise manner and lengthened the service in the belief that more prayer was better prayer, the kabbalists of thirteenth-century Spain transformed prayer into an "elaborate vehicle for the contemplation of God and for cleaving with one's soul to the sefirotic world."[88] The Lurianic kabbalists of Safed in the 1570s developed new meditative techniques and revived the function of traditional prayer as an aid to achieving *devekut*.[89]

CHASIDISM

The function of prayer as an aid to reaching a higher mind-state, with the ultimate objective of fortifying the worshipper to do good and resist evil, again went into eclipse with the decline of Jewish mysticism after the debacle of the "false Messiah," Sabbatai Zevi, in the seventeenth century.[90] It was temporarily revived in the second half of the eighteenth century with the founding of Chasidism.

The early Chasidim regarded prayer as an exercise in transcending the self and achieving *devekut*.[91] Early Chasidism expected the worshipper, through prayer, to reach a state described as *bittul ha'yesh*, the "annihilation of somethingness."[92] The petitionary nature of the words of many prayers was held to be a request for God not to satisfy man's needs, but to satisfy the needs of the *Shechina*, God's Presence. The benefits of petitionary prayer would be felt by the community, not necessarily by the individual worshipper.[93] Rabbi Jacob Joseph of Pulnoye, a disciple of the Baal Shem Tov, the founder of Chasidism, wrote that prayers had to be recited aloud rather than merely thought in one's mind because "when a man gives verbal expression to his prayers he provides a 'vessel' through which the divine grace can flow to the material world, otherwise it would only be capable of flowing into the spiritual 'vessels' provided by thought."[94] In the purely spiritual matter of achieving *devekut*, said Rabbi Jacob Joseph, a prayer for man to cleave to God requires no verbal expression.[95]

The opponents of Chasidism, the *Mitnagdim* (literally, the "Opponents"), led by Elijah ben Solomon Zalman, the Gaon of Vilna, however, fostered the idea of prayer as an intellectual exercise, a kind of study session organized around reading the Torah and the Talmud. Even Chasidism, in the second half of the nineteenth century, lost its focus on state of mind and, in fighting the secularization of Eastern European Judaism, became increasingly rigid in its insistence on conformity in prayer, as in other aspects of daily life, and its resistance to spontaneity and change.[96]

This tension between a scholarly ideal and the application of religious practice to the realities of Jewish life permeates Jewish history and still exists today. It has a corollary in divergent views on the relative priority of strict adherence to Torah principles and Jewish social cohesion. Norman Lamm, president of Yeshiva University, commented in 1985:

> The tension between these two values, Torah and Israel, has lain dormant for centuries. Thus, in the High Middle Ages we find divergent approaches by R. Saadia Gaon and by R. Yehuda Halevi. The former asserts the undisputed primacy of Torah [while] Halevi maintains the reverse position . . . [In modern times] the attitude

most prevalent [among Orthodox Jews] has been that Torah takes precedence—witness the readiness of our fellow Orthodox Jews to turn exclusivist, to the extent that psychologically, though certainly not halakhically, many of our people no longer regard non-Orthodox Jews as part of *Kelal Yisrael*.[97]

Women and the Origins of Jewish Prayer

There is strong evidence that women participated in ancient synagogue services along with men in both Israel and various parts of the Diaspora, served as heads of synagogues in both Israel and southern Europe, and even may have served as priests at the Jewish temple founded by Onias, heir to the Jerusalem high priesthood, in Egypt between 160 B.C.E and 73 C.E. In her pathbreaking Harvard Ph.D thesis, *Women Leaders in the Ancient Synagogue* (Brown Judaic Studies, published by Chicago: Scholars' Press, 1982), Bernadette Brooten analyzed this evidence. She found no persuasive evidence for separation of the sexes in ancient synagogues; the majority did not have galleries or separate rooms that could have been designated for women's use, and evidence from the New Testament and other writings of the period summarized in her work indicates that women participated along with men, including reading of the Torah.

The only prayer requirements from which women were specifically exempted were recital of the *Shema* and putting on *tefillin* (phylacteries). These were considered time-bound, and women were exempted from all commandments that had to be performed at a specific time. However, women were not exempted from reciting the Grace After Meals (*Birkat Ha'Mazon*) or from praying for God's forgiveness.[98] Whether women were covered by other prayer obligations, notably the recital of the *Amida*, is not specified in the Mishna.

The *Amida* was included in the liturgy as a substitute for Temple sacrifices, which were a time-bound obligation from which women were exempt, although the weekday *Amida* includes prayers for forgiveness of the prayer community.

23

However, *Tachanun* (Supplications), including prayers for God's forgiveness, followed the *Amida* in the synagogue service and was called the People's Prayer. As will be discussed in detail later, this was a time for personal, private prayer. Women clearly were not exempted, and, accordingly, they participated freely.

Women's prayers "remained essentially private, personal and spontaneous supplication."[99] In the early post-Exilic period, women increasingly came to be excluded from communal prayer. They were not counted as part of a *minyan*, on the theory that only those obligated to perform a *mitzvah* counted toward the required quorum for its performance. Use of the *mechitza*, the physical separation of women from men in the synagogue, became the norm, to the extent that in medieval Europe a synagogue had to possess a women's gallery. In Babylonia, women came to be forbidden to read the Torah, to preserve what the Talmud calls *k'vod ha'tzibbur*, the "honor of the community," probably a euphemism for avoiding embarrassment to uneducated men whose wives would have to read the Torah for them.[100]

Excluded from formal community prayer, women informally created their own communities and their own prayers, called *techinnot*. In the women's gallery, behind the *mechitza*, the assembled women would intersperse *techinnot* with the prayers of the regular daily service.[101] Particularly in the sixteenth through the nineteenth centuries, prayer manuals of Yiddish-language *techinnot* were published in Eastern Europe.

Because the role of women in prayer tended to focus on personal and private supplications, the historical tendency of Jewish liturgy to substitute fixed texts where, in ancient Judaism, personal and private prayer and meditation were the rule has tended to write women out of the liturgy. Most synagogues today allot no time for personal prayer following the *Amida*. There is no time for *techinnot*. Even on Mondays and Thursdays, when *Tachanun* is still included in the Orthodox and Conservative liturgies, it is thrust into a formalized text containing, in large part, what were once the meditations of male rabbis in Babylonia.

Attempts to Renew the Jewish Liturgy

THE REFORM MOVEMENT

With the advent of the Reform movement in the early nineteenth century, Jews rethought the purpose of the liturgy. This rethinking, however, did not lead to an infusion of spiritual fervor into Jewish prayer; quite the contrary. Prayers originally intended as vehicles for spiritual feelings and the achievement of a higher state of consciousness, in many cases already ossified by a thousand years of prayer-by-rote, were reduced to dour sequences of "theologically correct" but joyless statements.

For example, taking literally the blessing of the *Amida* that refers to God as the Reviver of the dead, the leaders of the Reform movement deleted it. "We don't believe that God revives the dead," they reasoned, "so why say that He does?" More than half of the *Shema* was deleted. The middle paragraph of the Torah excerpts that make up the *Shema* emphasizes that God rewards those who keep the commandments and punishes those who do not, and the Reform movement rejected the doctrine of reward and punishment on theological grounds, so that paragraph was deleted. The first part of the last paragraph of the *Shema* also was omitted; it recites the commandment to wear the ritual fringes (*tzitzit*) and the Reform movement rejected this practice as well, so the offending language was removed.

Many segments of the traditional liturgy pay lip service to the restoration of sacrificial worship in Jerusalem, and the restoration of the Jews to Israel. Though these segments are really aids to visualization of national unity and world peace, they were deleted by the Reform movement as being contrary to its theological doctrine. For the same reason, the

25

Reform movement removed from its liturgy all references to angels and supernatural creatures, and virtually all vestiges of mysticism.[102]

Because Reform theology rejected the authority of rabbinic law and left greater room for differing opinions than traditional Judaism, several different versions of the *Tefilla* (an ancient name for what is called the *Amida*, the Standing Prayer, or *Shemoneh Esrei*, the Eighteen Blessings, in other movements of Judaism[103]) were authorized. Virtually all prayers were recited in the vernacular; it was felt that if the purpose of liturgy was to make a theological statement, there was no point to praying in a language not readily understood. The concept of liturgy as an agent to altering the consciousness of the worshipper was alien to classical Reform doctrine.

THE CONSERVATIVE MOVEMENT

These liturgical changes came under attack as going too far, to the point where religious services ceased to be recognizably Jewish. In the 1870s, Conservative Judaism broke off from the Reform movement. Conservative Judaism essentially preserved Orthodox liturgy, but made some limited revisions for theological reasons. In particular, Conservative Judaism joined Reform in rejecting the goal of restoring sacrificial worship. In 1927 certain blessings of the *Amida* were rephrased to convert requests for the restoration of the sacrificial rite of the Temple to "remembrances" of that rite as practiced in the past.[104] The Sacrificial Readings, or *Korbanot*, included in the Orthodox liturgy as part of the preparation for formal public worship in the Morning Service were deleted. Conservative Judaism also rejected the *mechitza*, the separation of women and men in the synagogue, but until recently preserved the Orthodox practice of reserving Torah reading, rabbinic ordination, and prayer leadership for men. Some Conservative synagogues, based on a new-found commitment to equality of the sexes in worship, have recently joined the Reform movement in renaming the *Avot* (Forefathers) blessing of the *Amida* as *Avot* and *Imahot* (Forefathers and Foremothers).[105]

"TRADITIONAL REFORM"

The Reform movement, too, experienced a trend, beginning in about 1940, of restoring some portions of the traditional liturgy and ritual that had been deleted by the classical Reform movement, and adding more Hebrew to the liturgy.[106] This trend is sometimes called "Traditional Reform." The articulated purpose of these changes was not, however, to return to the concept of liturgy as an aid to an altered state of consciousness, but to diminish the damage to Jewish unity in the face of evidence that discarding too many distinctively Jewish practices had not resulted in acceptance of the Jews into the larger society in either Europe or the United States.[107] The introduction in 1975 of a revised Reform liturgy, *The Gates of Prayer,* resulted in greater opportunity for congregational participation, as a "respon[se] to the popular urge to recapture the spontaneity and fervor that have traditionally been characteristic of Jewish worship."[108] However, the notion of liturgy as a technique for achieving an altered state of consciousness continues to be largely absent in the Reform movement.

THE RECONSTRUCTIONIST MOVEMENT

The Reform and Conservative movements were not alone in editing the liturgy to reflect theology. The followers of Reconstructionism, a movement founded by Rabbi Mordecai Kaplan (a Conservative Jew) in the 1920s, in their prayerbook *Kol Ha'Neshamah* (Wyncote, Penn.: Reconstructionist Press, 1994), rewrote most of the major prayers, making many of the same changes as the Reform movement, but leaving in more Hebrew and giving more opportunity within the service than either the official Reform or Conservative liturgies for personal prayer and meditation. For example, references in *Aleinu* to the Jews as the "chosen people" have been omitted, based on the Reconstructionists' position rejecting this concept. Unlike the other movements, Reconstructionism gives local congregations the authority to edit their own liturgies.

THE JEWISH RENEWAL MOVEMENT

A mystically oriented backlash against this trend toward theologizing prayer has developed in the "Jewish Renewal" movement that was founded by Rabbi Zalman Schachter. The Jewish Renewal movement has not developed a uniform liturgy, but many adherents to it have downplayed prayer in favor of spiritual techniques such as meditation, or have taken steps to rewrite prayerbooks and substitute new prayers, on the erroneous premise that the traditional liturgy is lacking in spirituality.[109] "Reb Zalman," as he is affectionately known, is himself a knowledgeable Jewish mystic trained in the Chasidic tradition. The Jewish Renewal movement within the American Jewish community has been influential in the recent tendency toward greater traditionalism in Reform Judaism, in the rapid growth of the Reconstructionist movement, and in the resurgence of Jewish mysticism within Conservative Judaism.

The Need for a Guide to the Jewish Liturgy as a Method of Spiritual Transformation

As this book will demonstrate, the traditional liturgy does not lack spirituality. Rather, over its two-thousand-year history, it has been progressively sapped of the spirituality with which it was originally infused. Prayer-by-rote has gradually replaced the visualizations, allusions, and meditations that form the core of Jewish worship. Today, one has to engage in a kind of liturgical archeology to reconstruct the associations between prayer and mind-state that originally were so powerful.

This effort is laborious, but by no means impossible. The associations between the words of the prayers and the worshipper's state of mind are reconstructed later in this book. This reconstruction reveals a spiritual flow to the Jewish prayer service that is merely helped along by reciting prayers, a sequence of changes of mind in which one could engage even without uttering a word.

It is crucial to observe that this sequence of spiritual transformation is not random, nor is it simple. It has a structure that is central to Jewish worship. Jewish worship cannot be reduced to an amorphous set of breathing exercises and mantras. If liturgy is to change, the changes must be evaluated by whether they maintain and strengthen this structure of spiritual transformation.

The notion underlying this book—that the liturgy has an overriding structure and purpose, a spiritual flow—is not self-evident. It is easy for a casual student of the Jewish liturgy to conclude, erroneously, that the helter-skelter origins of the individual prayers preclude any overriding logic to the service. Many prayers began as rites of a theocracy led by priests, preserved by the Pharisees after the destruction of the theocratic capital, the Second Temple in Jerusalem, to hold together a nation in exile. Some, such as the *Haftarah* and its blessings, began as homiletic practices of ancient preachers. Others originated as poems written to substitute for prayers on the same themes, to circumvent attempts by foreign rulers to ban Jewish ritual observance. Some, like *Aleinu*, were taken out of their original context to commemorate historical events—in the case of *Aleinu*, the martyrdom of Jews in Blois (France) during the First Crusade.

This perspective was promoted during the late nineteenth and early twentieth centuries by a number of scholars[110] who wrote books showing that the traditional Jewish religious service developed piecemeal in response to historical conditions. The purpose of most of these efforts was to justify the early Reform movement's drastic revisions in the Jewish liturgy. If the *Amida* of the Orthodox prayerbook (*siddur*) had changed so many times, for example, why couldn't it be changed again, or even deleted in response to new conditions?

More recent popular works, such as *To Pray as a Jew* by Rabbi Haim Halevy Donin and *Entering Jewish Prayer* by Rabbi Reuben Hammer, have suffered from the opposite tendency. As rabbis committed to traditional Judaism, these authors tend to assume that the reader shares this commitment and will not cast a critical eye at the many traditions that they point out but fail to coherently explain in a way that makes sense today. As one example, Rabbi Donin notes the tradition of standing at certain points in the service, which he enumerates. He makes no attempt to explain to the reader, however, why we stand at those points and not at others, a question that is no doubt prominent in the minds of many worshippers as they struggle repeatedly to their feet. Perhaps reflecting their lack of attention to the underlying structure, neither rabbi discusses the reasons for the order of the prayers in the service. Why does the *Shema* precede the *Amida*? Why does the Torah service follow the *Amida*? Why is *Aleinu* at the end of the service?

Surprisingly few popular works on the Jewish liturgy have been published in English. Those books that exist on the subject are hard-to-read scholarly works, such as Elbogen's *Jewish Liturgy* (recently translated from the German by Professor Raymond Scheindlin of the Jewish Theological Seminary), Idelsohn's *Jewish Liturgy and Its Development*, Heinemann's *Prayer in the Talmud*, and Hoffman's *The Canonization of the Synagogue Service*; or "how-to" books such as Donin's *To Pray as a Jew*; or history books, such as Stefan Reif's *Judaism and Hebrew Prayer*, and Millgram's *Jewish Worship*; or books written in archaic English about outdated versions of the *siddur*, such as Abrahams' 1922 *A Companion to the Daily Prayer*

Book. None is written as a companion to the prayerbooks currently in use in America; few are organized in a way that tracks the order of the service, and those that are (e.g., B.S. Jacobson, *The Weekday Siddur: An Exposition and Analysis of Its Structure, Contents, Language and Ideas*) are difficult to read and rely predominantly on fanciful interpretations by medieval rabbis that ignore the historical contexts in which prayers developed. Some works on the subject also suffer from a tendency to follow a "party line," perhaps reflecting their authorship by rabbis who are obligated to find meaning that corresponds to the official views of their denomination.

Without an intelligent analysis of the structure and development of the traditional Jewish prayer service, the risk is great that modification will result in the loss of irreplaceable elements of the service, and that the functions those elements performed will be left unserved. It is impossible to tell what is essential in the liturgy, and to ascertain what ought to be preserved in the process of modifying it to meet contemporary needs, if one doesn't really understand it. If essential elements are lost, the Jewish people will have lost through the prevailing ignorance an essential part of what binds it together.

My ambition in this book is to write a more historically accurate, realistic, and readable account of where the prayers came from and what they are doing in their place in the traditional service than has heretofore been available, an account that does not regard the spirituality, meditation, and visualization that are basic elements of the service as an embarrassment. Armed with this information, the average worshipper will be able to make sense of the structure of the liturgy, utilize it for spiritual growth, and judge for himself or herself whether modified versions of the prayers fulfill the same purposes.

There is an overriding structure and spiritual flow to the traditional service. This flow of the service consists not of words, but of a sequence of changes in the mind-state of the worshipper. The words of the prayers are merely aids to facilitate those changes. This fact has been overlooked in scholarly writings on the subject. While the pieces of that structure have diverse origins, the manner in which they were fitted together, albeit piecemeal, possesses a logic that still can hold meaning for us today. Each part of the traditional service has an intended function. The prayers and practices that were strung together over thousands of years in thousands of different places—and often "restrung" again and again—form the liturgical structures that fulfill those functions.

Reading a translation of the Jewish prayerbook, the *siddur*, without any explanation of the prayers can be boring. Much seems, at first blush, repetitious or trite. Take, for example, the *Shema*, one of the key prayers of the service and one that most Jews learn at an early age: "Hear, O Israel, the

Lord our God, the Lord is One!" These words are hardly profound to the modern Jew. We all know that Judaism is a monotheistic religion, and, unlike our ancient ancestors, we live in a predominantly monotheistic society. To proclaim today that there is one God is like loudly announcing that the voting age is eighteen, or that a red light means Stop. It is to vociferously state the obvious.

Take another example: the *Amida*, the Standing Prayer. The *Amida* is recited no fewer than four times on Saturday morning. Twice it is read silently, and each time is then repeated aloud. Most of the time is spent standing uncomfortably erect. On the High Holidays, the *Amida* is repeated numerous times, with lengthy additions and insertions that make it an endurance contest. Yet, to read a translation of the *Amida* without an understanding of its structure, development, and context is not a philosophically revealing experience. It consists largely of seemingly redundant praises of God.

Not unexpectedly, many Jewish sons and daughters in America become non-observant, or cease to consider themselves religiously Jewish at all. Why should they attend synagogue services and pray, when they have been given no idea of what they are saying when they pray or why they are saying it? They will not glean this idea from their parents, who recite the prayers by rote out of nostalgia or obedience to community norms. They will not acquire it from their Hebrew school; they will be fortunate if they learn enough Hebrew in two or three afterschool sessions each week to be able to pray at all. Hebrew school curricula, and even Jewish day-school curricula, typically include Torah, Jewish history, basic Hebrew, and the text of the major prayers, but they give little or no information about why we pray, where the prayers came from, or what they mean.

This information gap about the Jewish liturgy is a principal factor in Jewish assimilation, and results in the loss of what may be the best opportunity to attract the unaffiliated to traditional Judaism. The average American Jew knows little Hebrew, rarely—if ever—reads the Torah, has never seen a Talmud, and hardly ever attends weekday *minyan*, but will occasionally go to a synagogue on *Shabbat*—most often to attend a *bar* or *bat mitzvah*—and usually goes at least once on the High Holidays. These sporadic, brief attendances represent the entire contact of a large segment of American Jewry with organized religious observance. If the services these Jews attend turn them off because the liturgy is not made comprehensible to them, they or their children will be lost to organized Judaism.

This book differs from past works on the subject. It discusses the liturgies of all major branches of American Judaism, not just the Orthodox liturgy. It tracks the order of the service, and includes the additions to the service for *Shabbat* and the High Holidays, the services most frequently attended by the average Jewish worshipper, as well as home rituals. It is written to be comprehensible and interesting to the casual reader. The occasional attendee at *Shabbat* services can pick up this book in the middle of the service and learn what he or she is reading, and why, without undue difficulty.

It also differs from earlier works in its approach to the prayers. It looks for meaning in the structure and flow of the service and in the historical context in which that structure emerged, rather than through a literal reading of the prayers themselves. The meaning of prayers is sought by asking what must have been intended by their authors and by those who put them into their present form and place in the liturgy. Where quotations from and allusions to biblical and rabbinic texts appear in prayers, the reasons that these particular texts may have been deemed pertinent by whoever decided to use them in the liturgy are discussed. Where medieval superstitions played a role in the development of a prayer, this is discussed, but ways are suggested in which the prayer makes sense as a vehicle for religious experience without getting bogged down in the superstitions.

I have not climbed on the bandwagon of rewriting prayers to make their words "relevant." The words in themselves have little significance; their import lies in their context and use. What should be more meaningful to the knowledgeable worshipper is the structure of the prayers, where the words came from, what purpose they serve, and what associations they bring to mind. Where prayers are rewritten, what is crucial is that the new words adequately serve the same spiritual purposes as the old words. Prayer is not an intellectual exercise, but an aid to spiritual experience.

For example, *Aleinu* came into daily use, as will be seen, during the persecutions of the Crusades, as a pledge of loyalty to Judaism recited by Jewish martyrs while they were being burned at the stake. Is *Aleinu* part of the Jewish service because the wording of the quotations from Isaiah is theologically correct, or because those words recall the martyrs' use of them to declare their undying loyalty to Judaism? I submit that it is the latter, although the casual worshipper unfamiliar with the history of *Aleinu* can do nothing more than read the words in the *siddur*. Changing those words will not make them materially more comprehensible or meaningful to someone ignorant of why *Aleinu* is part of the liturgy.[111]

As an analogy, imagine someone who has never heard of segregation or the civil rights movement reading the text of Martin Luther King's "I Have a Dream" speech. Dr. King's dream of black children and white children playing together would hold no significance for someone unaware of the tensions between the races. Changing the words of the speech to refer to Asian children or Hispanic children to make it relevant to those who live where these groups are predominant would add nothing for our hypothetical ignorant listener.

The Jewish liturgy is like a field of flowers strewn with monuments to historical and biblical events. Those monuments, and even the flowers in the field, are arranged in a particular order, and there is meaning in that order. If worshippers had a guidebook to enable them to navigate that liturgical field, recognize its landmarks, and understand why they are there and what order they follow, there would be less incentive to tear them down, and more incentive to dust off the monuments and make the flowers bright and beautiful, the better to dazzle us and enhance our spiritual experience in worship. This text is intended as such a guidebook.

The Preliminary Service

The first two sections of the morning liturgy, *Birchot Ha'Shachar* (literally, Sunrise Blessings) and *P'sukei D'Zimra* (Verses of Song), are said for the purpose of achieving the necessary level of concentration (*kavana*; literally, "focused intention") for saying the central prayers of the service, the *Shema* and the *Amida*. The Mishna tells us that, prior to the destruction of the Second Temple, this was done through silent meditation:

> One should not stand to recite [the *Amida*] unless one is in a serious frame of mind. The pious men of old would pause for an hour and then pray so that they might direct their hearts toward God. Even if a king greeted them, they would not respond, nor would they stop if a serpent was coiled at their heels (*Ber.* 5:1).

Over the years this silent meditation was replaced with the blessings called *Birchot Ha'Shachar*, and readings from Psalms and other books of the Bible, called *P'Sukei D'Zimra*. The blessings originally were said by individuals at home, but during the Middle Ages, they were incorporated into the service in Babylonia and Spain to assist those unable to say them on their own.[112] The main readings from the psalms included in *P'sukei D'Zimra* had been sung by the Levites during or after Temple sacrifices, but were adopted for use in synagogue worship after the Second Temple was destroyed.[113]

The Ashkenazic tradition is to have the leader sing the first few lines and last few lines of most prayers in the preliminary service, with the congregation reading the middle portion silently or in a hushed voice. The melodies are stirring, but it is important to remember that they are sung as a means to achieving a state of deep concentration, *kavana*. These prayers are not mandatory, and, if preferred, silent meditation may be substituted for any of them. The Reform movement omits them altogether, except for a truncated version that may be recited on *Shabbat*.

BIRCHOT HA'SHACHAR: SUNRISE BLESSINGS

Ma Tovu: Entering a House of Prayer

The theme of this prayer is coming before God. Found in some versions of the *Seder Rav Amram* (nineth century c.e.), the earliest known complete written prayer code,[114] it is composed of a verse from Numbers and verses from three different psalms. The first verse was uttered in the Torah by the prophet of the nations, Balaam, who had been hired to curse Israel and wound up blessing it instead (Num. 24:5):

> How good are your tents, Jacob,
> Your dwellings, Israel!

The Talmud (*B. Sanh.* 105b) equates the "tents of Jacob" and "dwellings of Israel" with the synagogues and houses of study.

The second verse, beginning with *Va'ani b'rov chas-d'cha*, has ten words. Recited on entering the synagogue, it was used to count the *minyan* of ten required for a public service.[115]

Ma Tovu is said upon entering a synagogue. In a sense, it is the descendant of the "entrance liturgies" of ancient Israel, which paralleled those of ancient Egypt.[116] It marks a transition. Like Balaam, we are capable of changing our state of mind. Within the words of *Ma Tovu* there is another transition, too: from *ohel* (tent) to *mishkan* (sanctuary, like the one carried by the Israelites in the desert), to *bayit* (house), to *heichal* (palace). As our minds are altered, as we enter a higher state of consciousness, even the most rudimentary surroundings can become palatial.

Blessing on Donning the Tallit (L'Hit'atef Ba'Tzitzit)

This blessing, which is dictated by the Talmud (*B. Men.* 43a), is actually a blessing on wearing a garment with *tzitzit*, the four knotted fringes found at the corners of the *tallit*. Wearing *tzitzit* on garments with corners is a commandment found in the Torah; they serve as a constant reminder of the presence of, and one's obligations to, God. The *tzitzit* contain thirteen sets of knots, which, when combined with the numeric value of the Hebrew word *tzitzit* (600), symbolize the 613 *mitzvot* in the Torah.

In ancient Israel, *tzitzit* were worn on all garments with corners, not just on one worn specially for prayer. *Tzitzit* could be worn by both men and women.[117]

The *tallit* itself originated in talmudic times as a garment somewhat resembling the Bedouin *abayah*, or striped blanket, still seen in the Middle East, and the *kittel* worn today on the High Holidays. An *atifa* ("wrapping") in the nature of a *tallit*, covering the body and the head, was required in ancient Israel on all solemn occasions, in the same manner in which the Roman toga was worn covering the back of the head and the shoulders on such occasions. For example, a judge wore an *atifa* during a trial.[118] Mourners were required to wear one,[119] and an *atifa* was required of prayer leaders,[120] one who said the Grace After Meals in the company of others,[121] and one who visited the sick.[122] It was worn by the prayer leader and the rabbis in the medieval Babylonian academies, and came to be customary garb for the synagogue.[123]

By the thirteenth century, garments with corners were no longer customarily worn in daily dress, so *tzitzit* were no longer mandatory features on them. However, possibly in response to the edict of Pope Innocent III in 1215 compelling the Jews to wear a degrading badge, the wearing of a *tallit* on top of one's clothes became a sign of protest, and therefore it was preserved as the uniform of Jewish worship.[124]

Numbers 15:39, where God commands the wearing of *tzitzit* "that you may look at it, and remember all the commandments of the Lord, and do them," was held to imply that the *tzitzit* were only required to be worn for worship during daylight; if they cannot be seen, they cannot serve as a reminder. The sole exception is *Yom Kippur*, when the *tallit* is worn at the *Kol Nidrei* service in the evening. This is because *Kol Nidrei* is a formal court session that is supposed to be convened and concluded before sunset.[125]

The *tzitzit* of old included a doubled thread on each corner dyed deep blue (some think that it was royal purple) in accordance with a biblical commandment. The blue thread was ascribed mystical significance,[126] but in reality it was an example of the ancient Middle Eastern practice, not unique to Jews, of using elaborate hems on garments that ascribed a social status to the wearer according to their color and intricacy.[127] The blue color was the same as that used in the garments worn by the priests, so it elevated the wearer to the same status as the priests. This practice evokes the principle that every Jew has an equal capacity to have a direct relationship with God, and that Judaism, unlike some other religions, does not consider religious leaders to be intermediaries between man and God or blessed with special powers by virtue of their position.

Because the blue dye, from a snail (possibly the murex) found on the northern coast of Israel, was rare and costly, the blue thread eventually fell out of use, and *tzitzit* came to be made of white wool.[128] The sixteenth-century kabbalist, Rabbi Isaac Luria, asked his followers in Safed to visualize a blue thread on their *tzitzit* as a means of helping the soul rise to divine heights.[129]

The *tallit* is part of our prayer uniform, which we don to focus our minds on the divine, and is a visible symbol of our forming our spiritual community with other Jews. In our still-torpid state in the early morning, we are being reminded of something important: our responsibility to keep the commandments. As we put on the *tallit* we visualize ourselves for a moment as being intimately connected with our ancient ancestors, who wore the fringes as proof of their tribal membership. A tribe exists not only across space, but across time.

The *Kippa*

Another part of our prayer uniform is the skullcap or *kippa*, called in Yiddish a *yarmulke*. The *kippa*, unlike the *tzitzit*, is not required by the Torah, nor is there unanimous opinion that it is required by rabbinic law. It originated in the hats, or turbans, worn by the priests at the Second Temple.[130] Certain rabbis adopted the custom of imitating the head-covering of the priests after the destruction of the Temple, as a constant reminder of the *Shechina*, the Divine Presence, above their heads, and the *kippa* was later adopted by all rabbis in Babylonia as a mark of piety.[131]

The *kippa* was a practice of not only the priests, but also other important personages. While Assyrian reliefs depict Hebrew captives in the eighth century B.C.E. as going bareheaded, ambassadors from King Jehu to the Assyrian ruler Shalmaneser are shown with covered heads.[132] Turban-like head-coverings made of coiled cords were used by men, and women wore veils on certain occasions, though not as a general practice.[133] The Talmud provides a blessing to say when putting a "kerchief" (probably similar to the modern Arabic *kaffiyeh*) on one's head in the morning, so it can be assumed that this was the usual practice.[134]

Like the *tallit*, the *kippa* is not mandatory in Reform services. Orthodox Jews wear both *kippa* and *tzitzit* all the time, not just in prayer, as a constant reminder that God is with us, watching us, and judging our conduct. Conservative Jews wear the *kippa* and *tzitzit* while praying.

Rabbi Alan Lew, a one-time Buddhist who became a Conservative rabbi, recounts that when he is driving, on occasion he wants to swear at another driver who has done something discourteous or careless, but he can't: The *kippa* on his head makes him a representative of the Jewish people and compels him to control himself. Such is the utility of a uniform in maintaining *devekut*, our connection with the Divine Presence, in our daily life.

Blessing on Putting on *Tefillin* (Weekdays Only)

The *tefillin* constitute another biblically mandated reminder to use to observe the commandments and, more specifically, to recall the Exodus from Egypt. "Bind them as a sign on your hand, and let them serve as a symbol on your forehead" (Deut. 6:8, 11:18). In reality, this injunction—in Moses' second discourse to the Israelites, delivered east of the Jordan River soon before his death—referred to binding on one's hand "these words which I command you this day." The words Moses commanded the Jews that day encompass several chapters of Deuteronomy. They include not only the *Shema* and the Ten Commandments, but the entire biblical code of laws, including *kashrut*; the rules concerning the sanctuary; the laws on debts; tithing for the poor; the release of slaves; the laws of the three pilgrimage Festivals; laws relating to crime; laws pertaining to the priests and Levites; laws concerning judges; the laws of welfare; laws of marriage and divorce; laws of purity; laws on treatment of workers; laws of kindness; and various other laws.

It is not possible to "wear" all of these laws—at least, not in any way that would be a meaningful reminder. Accordingly, we wear, inside the *tefillin*, scrolls containing four biblical passages that refer to the wearing of *tefillin*: the first two paragraphs of the *Shema*, and two passages from Exodus (13:1–10 and 13:11–16) that refer to the *tefillin* as a "sign" and "memorial" of the redemption of the Israelites from slavery in Egypt.

There are two blessings on putting on *tefillin*: *L'haniach tefillin* (who commanded us on laying *tefillin*) and *Al mitzvat tefillin* (who commanded us on the precept of the *tefillin*) both taken from the Talmud (*Ber.* 60b). These are followed by the same prayer that is said by a bride and a groom (in the Orthodox ritual, by the groom only) at their wedding: *V'airastich li* (and I will betroth you forever). The *tefillin* are compared with the flowers worn by a bride, as a symbol of Israel's devotion to God, the same motif found in the Friday-night prayer *Lecha Dodi*. This prayer was inserted by Rabbi Nathan Shapira of Krakow, one of the mystics who followed the Ari, Rabbi Isaac Luria, in the early 1600s.[135]

The conspicuousness of *tefillin* suggests that their purpose is to be seen and felt. We wear them with pride, a feeling much like a bride's about wearing her flowers. Putting on *tefillin* in public is like a "coming out" as a Jew.

Introductory Hymns

Adon Olam (Lord of the World)

Two *piyyutim*, or poetic hymns, follow the donning of the *tallit*. The first, *Adon Olam*, dates from the eleventh century and is said to have been written by the poet Solomon ibn Gabirol of Spain. More information about *Adon Olam* is found on pages 142–143.

Adon Olam originated as a bedtime hymn or poem recited to ask God's protection during the night. Saying it again in the morning is a happy occasion; we made it through the night and can start another day.

Yigdal (Exalt God)

The second *piyyut*, *Yigdal*, was written by Daniel ben Judah, *dayan* (judge) of the Jewish community of Rome in the fourteenth century.[136] It is based on Maimonides' Thirteen Articles of Faith (though not an entirely accurate rendition of them); it consists of thirteen verses, each representing one of the Articles. *Yigdal* is a relatively late addition to the service, first appearing in *siddurim* in Poland in the seventeenth and early eighteenth centuries.[137] Chasidic and Sephardic authorities objected to this attempt to condense the 613 *mitzvot* into thirteen principles, so *Yigdal* is found in neither the Chasidic nor the Sephardic liturgy.[138]

PRIVATE MORNING BLESSINGS

Blessing on Lifting the Hands After Washing:
The Purification Blessing (Al N'tilat Yadayim)

This blessing, literally a blessing on the "lifting of the hands," comes from the same talmudic passage (B. Ber. 60b) as most of the *Birchot Ha'Shachar*. It reminds us that in the ancient Temple service, the *kohen* (priest) was required to wash his hands before beginning the daily ritual (Exod. 30:20).[139] This custom became part of the synagogue service after the fall of the Second Temple in 70 C.E. It was one of many rules of purity developed in ancient Israel.

Washing is a normal act of hygiene, but as a procedure preparatory to prayer, it also is a *mitzva* for which a blessing is recited.[140] Washing, like other purity rituals, "lifts" us to a higher plane and shows respect for God.[141] We have put on the uniform to pray; now we purify ourselves for daily renewal in the same manner as the ancient priests.[142]

The custom of lifting the hands after washing is prescribed in the

Gemara (Sotah 4b): "Whoever washes his hands must raise them aloft so that the water below the joint should not flow back and render the hands unclean."

Blessing of Gratitude for the Gift of Our Body
(*Rofei kol basar u'mafli la'asot*)

This is a talmudic blessing for the physical health of the body (*B. Ber.* 60b). Like the rest of *Birchot Ha'Shachar*, it originally was said at home before going to the synagogue, while performing the normal actions connected with getting up. The specific activity after which this blessing was intended to be performed—excretion—is obvious from the graphic reference in the blessing to orifices of the body. We meditate, even after we go to the bathroom, on the perfection of God's work in creating the human body and on the omnipresence of the *Shechina*, God's presence in the world.

With blessings, "the simple acts of waking up, opening our eyes, rising, dressing, and preparing to meet a new day"—even the act of going to the bathroom—"are transformed into a recognition of God's gift of life to us."[143]

Blessings of Gratitude for the Torah (*La'asok b'divrei Torah*)

This is a blessing of thanksgiving for the commandment to study the holy teachings. It may have originated with Rav Shemuel (third century C.E.)[144] It is followed by a reading from the Talmud, beginning *V'ha'arev'na*, that mentions the importance of regular synagogue attendance and Torah study and contains a second Torah blessing. A third blessing on the Torah follows.

Why are there three blessings on the Torah? In the *Gemara (B. Ber.* 11b), three third-century rabbis had three different opinions on which blessing should be used as an introduction to daily Torah study. Rabbi Papa (fourth century), in accordance with a characteristic means of resolving disputes, combined them.[145]

Having said blessings on Torah study, we should study Torah, in keeping with the talmudic rule against reciting blessings idly and the talmudic principle that one is obligated to study Torah and Talmud daily, so we read the three-part Priestly Blessing (commanded by God, in Numbers 6:24–26, to be recited by Aaron and his sons to bless the children of Israel), which begins: *Y'varech'cha Adonai v'yishm'recha*. The importance of what we have just done is reinforced by a talmudic quotation that the study of the Torah is "equivalent to all" of the other *mitzvot* (of which "a man enjoys their fruit in this life while the principal remains for him to all eternity)." With this quotation, we have now fulfilled our obligation to study Torah and Talmud, even if we die the next moment or are unable to pray any further during the day.

Blessing of Gratitude for the Gift of Our Soul (*Elohai N'Shama*)

This is another talmudic blessing (*B. Ber.* 60b) to be recited upon rising. It is a thanksgiving for the return of the soul to the body and a profession of belief in the immortality of the soul. When we go to sleep, there is no way to be sure we will awaken in the morning. To wake up is "to experience a foretaste of resurrection."[146]

The order of these blessings—body, Torah study, soul—parallels our daily reality. As we awaken in the morning, we first are aware of our bodies. Then our cognitive abilities, those used in study, come to us. Finally, our spiritual capacity, our soul, awakens.

Sunrise Blessings of Thanksgiving: Converting Routine Acts into Reminders of God's Beneficence

This series of blessings is recited every morning, including weekdays. Except for the fourteenth one (eleventh, in the Reform liturgy), "who gives strength to the weary," which probably originated with Rashi,[147] they all are based on sayings found in the Talmud and in the *Tosefta*, a fourth-century compendium of material from the mishnaic period. The custom of reciting this series of blessings in the synagogue service dates back to the Babylonian academies and ninth-century Spain.[148] Maimonides opposed including them in public worship, but people had trouble remembering them all by heart, so in the course of time they were incorporated into the morning service.[149]

One can follow in these blessings the sequence of events involved in getting up in the morning. The first originally was said upon hearing the cock crow: "who gave the rooster the ability to distinguish between night and day." The fifth, "who gives sight to the blind," was said when first opening one's eyes. The sixth, "who clothes the naked," was said while getting dressed.[150] The last, "who removes sleep from my eyes and slumber from my eyelids," was said when one was ready to rub the sleep from one's eyes and get to the daily chores.

The Talmud (*Ber.* 60b) makes explicit this relationship of the blessings to our daily routine of getting up in the morning:

> When he wakes he says: "My God, the soul which Thou hast placed in me is pure. Thou has fashioned it in me, Thou didst breathe it into me, and Thou preservest it within me and Thou wilt one day take it from me and restore it to me in the time to come. So long as the soul is within

me I give thanks unto Thee, O Lord, my God, and the God of my fathers, Sovereign of all worlds, Lord of all souls. Blessed art Thou, O Lord, who restorest souls to dead corpses." When he hears the cock crowing he should say: "Blessed is He who has given to the cock understanding to distinguish between day and night." When he opens his eyes he should say: "Blessed is He who opens the eyes of the blind." When he stretches himself and sits up he should say: "Blessed is He who looseneth the bound." When he dresses he should say: "Blessed is He who clothes the naked." When he draws himself up he should say: "Blessed is He who raises the bowed." When he steps on to the ground he should say. "Blessed is He who spread the earth on the waters." When he commences to walk he should say: "Blessed is He who makes firm the steps of man." When he ties his shoes he should say: "Blessed is He who has supplied all my wants." When he fastens his girdle, he should say: "Blessed is He who girds Israel with might." When he spread a kerchief over his head he should say: "Blessed is He who crowns Israel with glory." When he wraps himself with the fringed garment he should say: "Blessed is He who hast sanctified us with His commandments and commanded us to enwrap ourselves in the fringed garment." When he puts the tefillin on his arm he should say: "Blessed is He who has sanctified us with His commandments and commanded us to put on tefillin." [When he puts it] on his head he should say: "Blessed is He who has sanctified us with His commandments and commanded us concerning the commandment of tefillin." When he washes his hands he should say: "Blessed is He who has sanctified us with His commandments and commanded us concerning the washing of hands." When he washes his face he should say: "Blessed is He who has removed the bands of sleep from mine eyes and slumber from mine eyes. And may it be Thy will O Lord, my God, to habituate me to Thy law and make me cleave to Thy commandments, and do not bring me into sin, or into iniquity, or into temptation, or into contempt, and bend my inclination to be subservient unto Thee, and remove me far from a bad man and a bad companion, and make me cleave to the good inclination and to a good companion in Thy world, and let me obtain this day and every day grace, favour, and mercy in Thine eyes, and in the eyes of all that see me, and show lovingkindness unto me. Blessed art Thou, O Lord, who bestowest lovingkindness upon Thy people Israel."

The fifteen blessings were not the original set of blessings of thanksgiving used in the daily service. Eleven of the blessings are found in the Talmud (primarily, B. Ber. 60b), but the Talmud also records three others (B.

Men. 43b): "who made me a Jew," "who has not made me a woman," "who has not made me an ignoramus." The first benediction elsewhere was given as "who has not made me a Gentile" (*T. Ber.* 7:18, *Y. Ber.* 9:2, 12b), and the third as "who has not made me a slave." "Who made me a Jew" is retained in modern *siddurim*, including those of the Conservative and Reform movements. "Who has not made me a woman," however, was replaced in the Conservative liturgy with "who made me in His image," and was omitted in the Reform liturgy.[151] In the Orthodox liturgy, a separate blessing was adopted to be recited by women: "who has made me according to His will."

During the first eight hundred years C.E., these three blessings—or blessings closely resembling them—were the only ones used in the daily service. This was the practice of Saadya Gaon in the ninth century, and Maimonides, in the twelfth century, still advocated their use.[152]

The three blessings may have originated in an emulation of an ancient Persian prayer to the god Ormuzd, which blessed the Creator for making the worshippers Iranian, adherents to the good religion, free men and not slaves, and men and not women.[153] The blessings are also found in ancient Greek sources.[154] However, the motivation for including them in the service may have been in response to the early Christian view, expressed in the Epistle of Paul to the Galateans, that because of the death of Jesus all distinction between Jews and Greeks, slaves and free men, and men and women had become void.[155] In this historical context, rather than being an expression of Jewish jingoism and male chauvinism, the original three morning blessings of thanksgiving were a rejection of the theological significance of the death of Jesus.[156]

The Sunrise Blessings can be employed meaningfully with the following activities:

Blessing	*Activity*
Who enables the rooster [literally, "morning bird"] to distinguish between night and day.	We hear the birds begin to sing in the morning.
Who made me in God's image. Who made me a Jew. Who made me free. [In the Orthodox version: Who did not make me a woman, Who did not make me a Gentile, Who did not make me a slave.	As we gain consciousness, we become aware—and proud—of who we are.[157]

Who gives sight to the blind.	We open our eyes.
Who clothes the naked.	We become aware of our night garment.
Who releases the bound.	We stretch and sit up.
Who raises the downtrodden.	We draw ourselves up to get out of bed, and throw off the covers.
Who spreads out the land upon the waters.	We step onto the floor, walk to the window, and look outside.
Who provides for all my needs.	We tie our shoes.
Who guides us on our path.	We think about what we are to do today.
Who strengthens the people Israel with courage [literally, "girds the people Israel with might"].	We put on our day garments.
Who crowns the people Israel with glory.	We put on a *kippa*; we put on the finishing touches, such as a jacket or cosmetics.
Who restores vigor to the weary.	We exercise and attend to our health needs.
Who removes sleep from my eyes and slumber from my eyelids.	We wipe the sleep from our eyes and prepare for the daily activities and chores.

Personal Meditations: Examples from the Rabbis; the *Korbanot* (Sacrificial Readings)

As our *kavana*—our focus on prayer—increases, we graduate from waking up to studying, and now we are ready to pursue spiritual and moral concerns by personal meditation. We are getting our minds ready for public prayer. Two paragraphs each beginning with *Y'hi Ratzon Mil'fanecha* follow the fifteen blessings. Both are from Tractate *Berachot* of the Talmud. They remind us of our duty to God to conduct ourselves properly during the day that is beginning, and pray for God's assistance in fulfilling this duty. The first paragraph was part of the sequence of blessings set forth in *B. Berachot* 60b. The second, from *B. Berachot* 16b, probably was added because it begins with the same words and has the same theme.[158]

Many of the great rabbis of antiquity had personal confessions and meditations they would recite after the *Amida*, in the place in the daily service now occupied on Mondays and Thursdays by the *Tachanun* prayers. Some are included in the potpourri of miscellaneous talmudic quotations that come next, beginning with the introductory words *L'Olam Y'hei Adam.* Owing to a difference of opinion over whether or not the introductory words were to be recited as part of the service, they normally appear in small print. These quotations were initially compiled in the *Midrash, Tana Deve Eliyahu,* 118 (ch. 19–end), from which they were added to the service.

The first verse of these quotations, *Ribon Kol-Ha'Olamim,* was the personal confession of Rabbi Yohanan ben Zakkai. The succeeding paragraphs, beginning *Ma Anu? Ma Chayeinu* (What are we? What is our life?) were the personal confession of the Babylonian scholar Mar Samuel.[159]

The Orthodox liturgy includes not only meditations at this point in the service, but the study of a lengthy series of biblical and talmudic excerpts regarding sacrifice, called *Korbanot* (Sacrifices). After a meditation in which we invoke the merits of our ancestors as a plea for God's mercy, the biblical description of the *Akeida* (Abraham's near-sacrifice of his son Isaac) is read. Then comes a detailed description of the daily *Tamid* (Continual) offering in the Second Temple in Jerusalem, including excerpts from Exodus 30:17–21 describing the laver for washing the hands and feet of the priests in preparation for the sacrificial ritual; from Leviticus 6:1–6 describing the taking of ashes from the previous day's sacrifices in preparation for the *Tamid* offering; and from Numbers 28:1–8 describing the rules concerning the *Tamid* offering. The theory underlying this recounting of the *Tamid* offering is that the morning synagogue service originated as a substitute for the offering after the destruction of the Second Temple.

A reading from Exodus 30:34–36 and 7–8 describing the incense that was burned on the Golden Altar in the Second Temple is then added in the Orthodox liturgy, though it does not relate directly to the *Tamid* offering. This insertion is based on a medieval mystical view that recounting the laws regarding incense would "remove impurity from the world prior to the prayers [i.e., the morning service] that take the place of offerings."[160]

Next, in the Orthodox service, came lengthy quotations from the *Mishna* explaining the biblical passages just read. *On Shabbat* and *Rosh Chodesh,* further biblical passages are added that describe the *Musaf* (Additional) offerings for those days, together with further excerpts from the *Mishna* on the same subject.

The Orthodox custom is to preface the morning service with study of Torah and Talmud. By so doing, the Orthodox liturgy reinforces the concept that rabbinic law is the divinely inspired Oral Torah, and is just as binding on Jews as the Five Books of Moses. What has been selected for use in the service is the introduction to *Sifra,* a tannaitic midrash that is a *baraita* (literally, "outside"), one of the talmudic teachings that was left out of the

Mishna but was, because of its antiquity, regarded equally as binding as those that were included in the *Mishna*. This *baraita* sets forth the rules of construction articulated by Rabbi Yishmael that were accepted by the rabbis in interpreting the Torah. This section of the service in the Orthodox liturgy concludes with a personal meditation in which the worshipper prays for the restoration of the Temple in Jerusalem and the return of sacrificial worship.

The excerpts from the Talmud generally describe the preparations for the daily sacrifice in the Second Temple. These preparations were a means of purifying the body and focusing the mind. We do the same through meditation and prayer.

Kaddish D'Rabbanan: Kaddish After Study (Scholar's Kaddish)

Kaddish punctuates the traditional service. Whenever a *Kaddish* is said, it means that a major section of the service is ending. Here it marks the end of the *Birchot Ha'Shachar*. We depart the mundane and prepare to form a spiritual community for public prayer.

There are four principal versions of *Kaddish*: the Complete *Kaddish* (*Kaddish Shalem* or *Kaddish Titkabal*), the Half (*Chatzi*) *Kaddish*, the Mourner's *Kaddish* (*Kaddish Yatom*), and the Scholar's *Kaddish* (*Kaddish D'Rabbanan*). The Scholar's *Kaddish* is the *Kaddish* recited after a Talmud lesson or a recitation of part of the Talmud, particularly by mourners. Because the fifteen blessings previously recited are derived from sayings in the Talmud, and because of the other readings from the Talmud that are included in the *Birchot Ha'Shachar*, it is considered that a Talmud lesson or recitation has just been completed, so recitation of the Scholar's *Kaddish* is appropriate here.

Though it appears in Hebrew characters and contains some Hebrew words, *Kaddish* is written mostly in Aramaic, the everyday language of Jews in talmudic times. *Kaddish*, which means "holy" in Aramaic, originated in Israel in the first century B.C.E. as a prayer that marked the end of a study session in a house of study.[161] The institution of the synagogue may have had its inception in the houses of study where the common people of Israel at the time of the Second Temple learned the Oral tradition. With the destruction of the Temple and the end of sacrificial ritual, the synagogue became the focus of public worship.

It was natural for *Kaddish*, which must have been widely known, to be accorded the same function in the synagogue liturgy—marking endings—as it had had in the earlier study sessions.[162]

The different types of *Kaddish* reflect different functions and possess a logical structure. The so-called Half-*Kaddish* is the basic *Kaddish*. When it is not followed by another section of prayer—i.e., when it concludes a service—requests for the blessing of peace are added both in Aramaic and in Hebrew, beginning, *Y'hei shlama rabba min sh'maya* and *Oseh shalom bi'm'romav*. When *Kaddish* is recited after an *Amida*—the prayer in which we make our requests of God—a request is added to it, beginning *Titkabel*, which asks that the preceding prayer be accepted by God. When it follows a section of Torah study, a sentence is added asking for a blessing for the scholars of Torah.[163]

At an early date in Germany and France, it became customary to honor deceased scholars with a learned discourse at the end of the seven days of mourning. The discourse would conclude with the *Kaddish D'Rabbanan* recited by the assembled mourners. The decision whether or not to recite *Kaddish D'Rabbanan* came to be a touchy one, because its omission implied a lack of learning on the part of the deceased. To avoid embarrassment, it became the rule that a discourse or study session, followed by *Kaddish*, would take place during the mourning period of every deceased Jew.[164] The study sessions disappeared, but *Kaddish D'Rabbanan* remained.

Preparing for Collective Prayer

The Psalm of the Day

It was customary in the Temple in Jerusalem for the Levites, each day after cleaning the altar at sunrise, to recite a special psalm designated as the psalm for that day.[165] Recitation of this Psalm of the Day marked the onset of collective worship; the Temple was now open for business. Psalm 92 was the Psalm of the Day for *Shabbat*, and its reading is another link between the synagogue and the Temple in Jerusalem. In the Conservative liturgy on weekdays, other "psalms of the day" are recited, a different one for each day of the week, in accordance with the practice of the Levites. Psalm 27 is added as a special psalm morning and night from the beginning of the penitential period in the month of *Ellul* through the end of *Sukkot*.

Consistent with its rejection of practices that suggest a desire for restoration of Temple worship, the Reform movement deleted this part of the service. The Psalm of the Day, however, may be viewed as using raw materials from the Temple to solidify the sense of community as we begin true collective worship.

Shir Ha'Kavod (Song of Glory)

This prayer, beginning *An'im Z'mirot* (I will chant hymns), was actually the end of a longer mystical hymn called *Shir Ha'Yichud* (the Song of Unity), which was written by Rabbi Judah He'Chasid (Judah the Pious), who, with his father Samuel, founded the mystical movement called Chasidei Ashkenaz in Regensburg, Germany, in the twelfth century. The twelfth-century German mystics were not content with achieving *kavana* (deep concentration) in prayer, their goal was *devekut*, a spiritual transformation that induced a feeling of closeness to God.[166]

In 1569, about four hundred years after the Chasidei Ashkenaz, another mystical movement arose in Safed, (Israel), led by Rabbi Isaac Luria. The Lurianic kabbalists inserted part of the *Shir Ha'Yichud* into the daily liturgy. For the Lurianic kabbalists, *yichudim* (unifications) were the manner in which a particular occurrence of the name of God in the context of a prayer was supposed to be emphasized and pronounced.[167] The objective of the kabbalists was to achieve a unification of the tetragrammaton *Y-H-W-H* with the word *Adonai* (literally, "our Lord") so that they became a single divine name. By thus unifying the divine Essence that had been damaged upon the expulsion of Adam and Eve from the Garden of Eden, the kabbalists believed that they could hasten the coming of the Messiah and achieve the redemption of Israel.[168] The custom of opening the Ark reflects the importance of this prayer to the mystics.

Consistent with its origin, this prayer can serve as an exhortation to us to not just concentrate on prayer, but allow it to transform us.

Psalm 30: Bridge to a Higher World

This psalm is a transition to the next part of the service, the reading of psalms of praise called "*P'sukei D'Zimra.*" It is a relatively recent addition to the service, having been added to the Sephardic liturgy in the seventeenth century and to the Ashkenazic liturgy in the nineteenth century.[169]

Psalm 30 was believed by the mystics to be a bridge between the material world and the heavens. In Kabbalah, the four parts of the morning prayers are equated to four worlds: the material world (*Olam Ha'Asiya*), the heavens and firmaments (*Olam Ha'Yetzira*), the world of the angels (*Olam Ha'B'riya*), and the world of the divine, which is beyond human comprehension (*Olam Ha'Atzilut*). As we progress through the morning prayers, in the kabbalistic view, we elevate the sparks of holiness to higher worlds, thus liberating them from the *kelipot*—the shells that entrap them—with the ultimate goal of *tikkun olam*—repairing the world—by reuniting the sparks of holiness that were dispersed when Adam and Eve were expelled from the Garden of Eden.[170]

The psalm is King David's personal and impassioned declaration of his gratitude to God, written (it says) for the dedication of the Temple in Jerusalem. King David died before the Temple was ever built, so the psalm cannot have been meant literally. The Temple was not merely a place of worship, but served as the center of justice, legislative activity, priestly training, scholarly inquiry, and distribution of charity. In a theocracy, all governmental and economic activity had a spiritual dimension. King David's vision of a Temple was a vision of a world organized around spirituality.

By forming a prayer group and collectively allowing prayer to transform our minds, we achieve the purpose of the Temple, which was the unification of the Jewish people as a spiritual force. "[T]he Temple's purpose is best achieved when each individual Jew recognizes God's presence and help in his personal life."[171]

Mourner's *Kaddish*

Just as it marked the end of a segment of the synagogue service, *Kaddish* also came, in the Middle Ages in France and Germany, to mark the end of life, as the Mourner's Prayer. The Mourner's *Kaddish* first appeared around 1200 C.E. in Germany, during the great persecutions that accompanied the Crusades, and at first was called *Kaddish Yatom*, the Orphan's *Kaddish*.[172] Life is, in a sense, a study session that ends only in death; we can and, ideally, do continue learning new things each day of our lives.

The Mourner's *Kaddish* originated as a preliminary to *Barchu*, the call to prayer.[173] At first it consisted of only two or three lines and was said by orphans, who were given priority in its recitation during their period of mourning as a means of alleviating the severity of any possible punishment being inflicted on their dead relative, and particularly during the evening hour following the Sabbath.[174]

In other words, orphans were given the privilege of calling the public to prayer, lest someone else forget to convene the prayer community and the orphans lose the ability to have the congregation give the crucial response that would come to the aid of the deceased. *Kaddish Yatom* gradually lengthened to include a majority of *Kaddish D'Rabbanan*, and became a separate prayer.

Kaddish is an expression of yearning for the coming of the Messiah and the rebuilding of Jerusalem. Though *Kaddish* has no express connection with death or mourning, these thoughts of optimism must have been soothing to Jews suffering through the horrors of the Crusades and other medieval persecutions, and, hence, appropriate for those recovering from the loss of a loved one.[175]

The power of *Kaddish* as a means of aiding a deceased loved one was attributed to the congregation's response, *Y'hei shmei rabba m'vorach*, which, according to legend, could in effect reach into the afterlife to assist the deceased. Since talmudic times a superstition has existed that responding to *Kaddish* with "*y'hei sh'mei rabba m'vorach l'olam u'l'olmei olmaya,*" would nullify heavenly decrees against a person.[176] A legend grew that Rabbi Akiva had helped to redeem the soul of a deceased man by teaching his son to recite *Kaddish* at a congregational service.[177] Saying *Kaddish* for a decedent was understood in the Middle Ages to be particularly crucial on the afternoon of the Sabbath, when the plight of the deceased was believed to be especially severe, since even the dead were thought to gain respite on the Sabbath.

The twelfth century was also a time when the beliefs of a group of mystics called the Chasidei Ashkenaz, the Pious Ones of Germany, affected the liturgy. The Chasidei Ashkenaz developed what one commentator called a "cult of the prayer book, which fondled its every phrase, counted every word, played kabbalistic games with the letters, and left a library of some seventy-three volumes of commentaries [on the prayer book]."[178] The Chasidei Ashkenaz found that the congregation's response in the middle of the *Kaddish* contained the same number of words and letters as the first verse of the Torah. They developed the superstitious belief that one who responded to *Kaddish* with these words would become God's partner in the creation of the world, and, hence, empowered to change the fate of the departed.[179] For some, then, the Mourner's *Kaddish* was an attempt to change the fate of the deceased through participation in an act of creation.

The most significant aspect of this history of the Mourner's *Kaddish* is that, whichever theory one accepts of its origins, the congregation's response is required for *Kaddish* to have the desired effect. The Mourner's *Kaddish* is the opportunity for the congregation to assist and comfort the mourner. The legend that the response of the congregation ameliorates the fate of the deceased in the afterlife no doubt was comforting to the mourner, who thereby felt that he or she could still do something to help the loved one by appearing in synagogue and making sure that the congregation gave the appropriate response. By comforting the mourners among us, we as congregants perform a *mitzva* (religious duty).

The only difference between *Kaddish Shalem*, (Full *Kaddish*) and the Mourner's *Kaddish* is the omission in the latter of the verse that begins *Titkabel*, (May He receive [the prayers of all Israel]). This omission has been explained as being due to the fact that, to the mourner, God does not appear to have received his or her prayers to spare the life of a loved one. In *Kaddish D'Rabbanan*, the Scholar's *Kaddish*, a long paragraph praying for God's blessings for students of the Torah appears in lieu of *Titkabel*, and is also omitted in the Mourner's *Kaddish*. One can speculate that this paragraph in the Scholar's *Kaddish* was rewritten to make it more generally applicable to worshippers when the *Kaddish* entered the synagogue liturgy.

P'SUKEI D'ZIMRA (VERSES OF SONG): WE PREPARE OUR MINDS FOR PRAYER

The Talmud says that praises should precede prayer.[180] P'sukei D'Zimra (literally, Verses of Song) consists of psalms and excerpts from psalms that praise God. They are said in public worship for purpose of getting into the proper frame of mind to recite the obligatory morning prayers, the Shema, and, most of all, the Amida.[181] Blessings precede and follow the psalms.

This custom originally stemmed from the Levites' practice of reciting certain psalms, particularly a version of Psalm 105, during the morning sacrifices.[182] On Festivals, the Levites recited Psalms 120 to 134 while ascending the fifteen steps to the altar,[183] one psalm per step, making the act of climbing the steps a lengthy processional, perhaps symbolic of ascending to heaven and bringing the mind closer to divine revelation. After the destruction of the Second Temple, it came to be the custom of some of the talmudic rabbis in the second century c.e. to prepare for prayer not only by silent meditation, but by the regimen of reciting either the entire book of Psalms or collections of representative verses from the psalms and Psalm 134,[184] perhaps adopting the former practice of the Levites as something analogous to a mantra to prepare the mind for communication with God.

The collections of verses, particularly those called by their first words, Hodu, Va'y'varech David, and Y'hi ch'vod, are organized in ways that either parallel or reverse the order of mind-states in the blessing formula: beracha, from the Hebrew word berech for bending the knee, a sign of humility;[185] Haz'Karat Ha'shem, "remembrance" (or visualization) of the name of God; and malchut, a sense of awe at God's kingship.[186]

The psychological underpinnings of this rapid mental leap from the solitary individual on bended knee to the mystery and majesty of God are similar to those underlying the blessings before and after the Shema, as described by Tzvee Zahavy:

> A more pliant mode of consciousness better accommodates the sweeping scope of such liturgy. Within this frame of mind the participant senses an increased feeling of factuality and truth. Partici-pation in the rituals of prayer helps to foster this attitude. The praying-person assumes the ability to see the "true meaning" of the wide sweep of history and destiny through the texts of the liturgy in the experience of praying.[187]

Because reciting all 150 psalms is impractical for most people, the concluding psalms (145 to 150), which form the core of P'sukei D'Zimra, together with the collections of verses from various other psalms,[188] were eventually chosen, probably in post-talmudic times, to symbolize the earlier practice, thought to be the ideal, of completing the entire book. By reciting P'sukei D'Zimra, we symbolically "finish" the book daily, even though we have not completed it.[189]

The purpose of P'sukei D'Zimra must not be forgotten: to collectively prepare the minds of the worshippers for intense concentration during the Shema and the Amida. We ascend mentally toward God and awaken our capacity for receiving and perceiving divine revelation within ourselves by going through a series of mind-states prompted by psalms and excerpts from psalms. This program generally follows the three-part format of the beracha: first, awakening our humility by allowing us to experience being saved from an emergency; second, making us remember what the name of God stands for, both the beauty and danger of God's works, and how they fit into a divine plan; and third, causing us to emotionally accept God's kingship.

There are other ways to prepare one's mind besides reciting prayers; silent meditation on breathing, as in Zen Buddhism, and engaging in ritualized movements, as in T'ai Chi, are two examples. There is nothing to preclude such methods from being used in Jewish worship, so long as the mental preparation is done through concerted group activity. In Jewish prayer, we prepare our minds as a group whenever possible. It is important to achieving the purposes of prayer for the worshippers to develop cohesiveness as a group, and this means acting in concert rather than on one's own.

Baruch She'Amar: Praise God, the Source of All Being

This poetic introduction to the morning psalms begins the morning service proper. With this prayer, the private benedictions have ended and we begin public worship. Traditionally, after Baruch She'Amar, worshippers are forbidden from speaking to or interrupting others until the conclusion of the Amida, in order to avoid interfering with their intense concentration (kavana).[190] The prayer serves as a cue to us to enter a state of kavana.

Baruch She'Amar is probably talmudic in origin. It appeared in the prayer code of Rav Amram in the ninth century, and is actually a combination of two separate prayers.[191] From Ha'm'hu-lal b'fi amo to the end, it is a prayer unit culminating in the blessing said before the psalms, in keeping with the tradition of reciting blessings before and after biblical readings. The first part is a hymn of praise to God, derived from several blessings in the Mishna, which was interpreted by medieval kabbalists as an exposition of the various meanings of God's name.[192]

Collected Excerpts from the Psalms and Related Biblical Passages, in Lieu of Reciting Psalms 1 to 144

Hodu: *David's Song to Be Sung on the Return of the Ark to Jerusalem*

Rom'Mu *and* P'sukei D'Rachmei *(Verses of Mercy): Excerpts from the Psalms Arranged as a Dialogue Between God and Man*

One would expect psalms to immediately follow *Baruch She'Amar*, the introduction to the psalms, but this is not the case. In lieu of the first 144 psalms, we recite a collection of excerpts from various psalms and from Chronicles that, in the Talmud or *Midrash*, were given special significance.[193] This collection is commonly called by its first word: *Hodu*. The custom of saying *Hodu* dates from the Middle Ages, when it was part of the festival liturgy.[194]

This apparent inconsistency—saying a blessing on reading psalms and then reading something else—does not exist in the Sephardic liturgy, in which *Hodu* is placed before *Baruch She'Amar*. It is explained by the fact that *Hodu*, though mostly from Chronicles rather than Psalms, was a song of King David.

The excerpts begin with 1 Chronicles 16:8–36, starting with *Hodu L'Adonay Kir'u Vi'shmo*. This is a song that was written by King David to be sung when the Holy Ark was returned to Jerusalem by the Philistines.[195] It can be used as a focus for visualization; we enhance our *kavana* by visualizing ourselves in Jerusalem, singing, as the Ark is returned. This is a foreshadowing of, and practice for, the *Shema*, in which we visualize ourselves receiving the Torah at Mount Sinai, a visualization that must be experienced with sufficient intensity, a sensation sufficient that we are actually witnessing the event, to achieve the necessary mental state to address God in the *Amida* and merit His attention to our requests.

The excerpts continue with a pastiche of verses from Psalms that begin with *Rom'mu*. Rabbi Profiat Duran, a refugee from the Spanish massacres of 1391,[196] called them *P'sukei D'Rachmei* (Verses of Mercy) because they were pleas for God's mercy that were successful in invoking it. They had been compiled ingeniously in Babylonia by the *Saboraim*,[197] successors to the *Amoraim* (the rabbis who compiled the *Gemara*), sometime during the preceding couple of centuries, without adding or changing any words, to create a dialogue between man and God on the theme of God's mercy, asking for salvation from our oppressors.[198]

Other Psalms, Psalm Excerpts, and Related Passages: Psalm 100 (*Y'hi Ch'vod*), and Psalms 19, 34, 90, 91, 92, and 135

In the Orthodox and Conservative weekday morning service, Psalm 100 follows, beginning *Mizmor L'Todah* (Song for the Thanksgiving Offering). The thanksgiving offering was made in Temple times when one survived a life-threatening situation, such as serious illness or a long journey. In reciting this psalm, we meditate upon the many potential dangers we incur in our daily lives we never even are aware of, and our dependence on God to avert those dangers. Because the thanksgiving offering was not made on *Shabbat*, Festivals, and certain other days, Psalm 100 is not recited on those days.[199]

Next in the weekday morning service comes another collection of biblical verses, mainly verses from Psalms, beginning *Y'hi Ch'vod* (May the Glory). These originally were meant for holidays, and each verse contains the tetragrammaton, the four-letter Name of God. The Talmud lists *Y'hi Ch'vod* as one of the psalms to be said standing, but it is uncertain whether the *Y'hi Ch'vod* referred to in the Talmud is the same one we recite.[200] The fact that each contains the Name of God suggests that this collection of verses originated with the early mystics, either the *Merkava* mystics of mishnaic times or the medieval kabbalists, both of whom would meditate at length on the various combinations of the letters of the tetragrammaton.[201] The prayer begins with Psalms 104:31, which the Talmud says was the praise proclaimed by an angel when the newly created plant world developed according to God's wishes.[202] Its underlying concept is that every being exists as part of God's plan and is dedicated to His service, and that this is apparent from contemplating the beauty and perfection of nature.[203] *Y'hi Ch'vod* is, thus, an opportunity for us to meditate upon the Name of God and the various permutations of its four letters, and on the beauty and perfection of nature.

On *Shabbat* and Festival mornings, Psalms 19, 34, 90, 91, 92, and 135, in that order, are recited in the Orthodox and Conservative liturgies. These psalms were selected by the kabbalists in accordance with the teaching of the *Zohar* that the prayers of *Shabbat* morning symbolize the special spiritual bliss that adorns Israel on *Shabbat*.[204] According to Kabbalah, elevating ourselves spiritually by reciting these psalms enables the angels themselves to rise to greater heights.[205] These psalms all are recited in some way to the Creation, which we celebrate on *Shabbat*.

In the Reform liturgy, brief excerpts are recited from Psalms 19, 33, and 92.[206] Psalm 33 is not found in the traditional service. The Reform movement eliminated most psalms in *P'Sukei D'Zimra*, in keeping with its general rejection of mystical influences on the liturgy and emphasis on theological statements rather than mental transformation.[207]

Psalm 19 has the same theme as *Y'hi Ch'vod*—nature as a manifestation of God's plan and God's perfection—which may explain why it is substituted for it on *Shabbat* rather than merely added to it. It depicts all of God's creations singing God's praises.

Psalm 34 carries this theme further. It shows how all things created by God have a purpose. David once questioned God as to why He had created insanity. God replied that some day David would need insanity, and even pray for it. A short time later, David had to escape from King Saul to save his own life. He fled to the land of the Philistines, who recognized him as Israel's greatest warrior and threatened to kill him. He pretended to be insane, and was expelled instead of being killed. David was moved by this experience to compose Psalm 34. We meditate, in reading Psalm 34, on the divine purpose of those of God's creations that we perceive as negative, dangerous, and destructive.

Psalms 90 and 91 were the first two of eleven psalms that King David supposedly found written on an ancient scroll in the hand of Moses. Psalm 90 is a prayer for repentance and forgiveness. The Talmud taught that the capacity for repentance was a prerequisite for Creation, because without it man cannot fulfill his purpose.[208] We meditate, in reading Psalm 90, on repentance as a means of saving ourselves from the negative forces we read about in Psalm 34, and what the world would be like without it.

Psalm 91 is about redemption, and the purpose for which the Jews were saved from slavery in Egypt. The Talmud calls it the Song of Plagues because, it says, one who recites it with complete faith in God will be helped in time of danger, as the Jews were in Egypt. According to the *Midrash*, Moses composed Psalm 91 on the day he finished building the Tabernacle—the *Mishkan*—and its beginning refers to Moses' having entered the divine clouds and being enveloped in the "shadow of God."[209] The question arose that day as to how the Tabernacle could contain God. The answer God gave was that He could not be contained by the entire universe, and yet was capable of concentrating His essence into one small spot so that the purpose of the Exodus could be fulfilled. That purpose was to have the people of Israel "serve God upon the mountain" by undertaking to obey the commandments.

Psalm 92, discussed further in connection with the Friday evening service, was, according to legend, composed by Adam after he repented of the sin that caused the expulsion from the Garden of Eden.

Psalm 135 follows Psalm 91 in subject-matter. It goes into more detail on the miracles of the Exodus. God's power reflected in the Creation, celebrated on *Shabbat*, remains manifest through miracles in recorded history.[210]

Psalm 136: The Great *Hallel*

During *P'sukei D'Zimra* on *Shabbat* and Festivals, the congregation rises for the recitation of Psalm 136, which came to be known as the Great *Hallel*, or the *Hallel* of *P'sukei D'Zimra*. The Talmud compared it to *Hallel* because of resemblances to the language of the psalms of *Hallel*, but the name is misleading. Psalms 113 to 118, which constitute the ordinary *Hallel* recited on Festivals after the *Amida*, are actually much more important.

Psalm 136 owes its vast importance to medieval German kabbalists in the twelfth century. The kabbalists believed that the words of God were full of hidden patterns and meanings. One of their techniques for ferreting out these secrets was *gematria*, the manipulation and study of the numerical values of the Hebrew letters in words and passages. Psalm 136 contains the refrain, *Ki l'olam chasdo*, twenty-six times. The kabbalists found that this equaled the numerical value of the letters in the tetragrammaton, the name of God. They considered this a major discovery, and ascribed to Psalm 136 tremendous importance.

Psalms 145–150

Psalm 145: Ashrei (Fortunate Are Those Who Dwell in Your House)

Ashrei is Psalm 145, the most famous of all liturgical psalms, and is found in all liturgies, including Reform. We have read excerpts from many earlier psalms, but Psalms 145 to 150 are read in their entirety. Psalm 145 is written in alphabetical acrostic; the first letters of each sentence form the Hebrew alphabet. The first two verses, however, are not from that psalm, but rather are the final verses of Psalm 144.

A close look at *Ashrei* reveals that the prayer is missing a line beginning with the Hebrew letter *nun*. There is evidence from Greek sources and from one of the Qumran scrolls that a verse beginning with *nun* existed in antiquity, but was later omitted. The Talmud cites Rabbi Yochanan as saying that the letter *nun* was avoided because it is the first letter in the word *nofel* ("to fall"), and that its omission indicated that Israel would not fall—it would not be defeated.[211]

According to the Talmud, whoever recites Psalm 145 daily is "assured of a place in the World to come."[212] *Ashrei* was singled out because the word meaning "dwell" or "sit" (*yoshvei*) in the first sentence—"Happy are they who dwell in Your house"—was interpreted to mean that one should sit for some time in the synagogue prior to prayer, to achieve the proper frame of mind.[213]

Psalms 145 to 150 are supposed to lead us deeper into *kavana*, focused concentration. We have awakened, met our physical needs, ascended to the higher realm, practiced visualization, meditated on God's wonders, both beautiful and deadly, and now we assume the same holy frame of mind as the Levites at the time of the daily sacrifice.

Psalms 146 to 149

These psalms are all on the theme of redemption of the Jewish people. Their presence in the service, however, is due to the need to "complete" the psalms every day to assume the frame of mind of the righteous people of old. See page 48.

Psalm 150: Halleluya, Hallelu El B'Kadsho
(Halleluya, Praise God in His Holiness)

This is the last psalm of David, is short but intense. It begins with *Halleluya*, combining *hallelu* (praise) and *Yah* (God), a command to those listening to praise God. This command is then carried out by reciting the words of the psalm.[214] Its language arouses fervor. One can almost envision the priests saying these words in front of the assembled throng at the time of the First Temple. The last line is repeated, because it is the end of Psalms, and it was an ancient custom to repeat the last line to signal the conclusion of a book of the Bible.[215]

Baruch Adonai L'Olam Amen V'Amen

The reading of Psalms 145 to 150 is in the nature of a daily *Hallel*, the sequence of Psalms 113 to 118 that marks morning services on Festivals. In fact, since Psalms 145 to 150 are recited at a surrogate for reciting all the psalms, including Psalms 113 to 118, symbolically we *have* just read *Hallel*.

As in the case of *Hallel*, a blessing is recited upon completing Psalms 145 to 150. The blessing, in this case, takes the form of the first part of a collection of verses from Psalms that originated as a night prayer in Babylonia.[216] To that collection is appended a series of biblical quotations, beginning, respectively, *Va'y'varech David*,[217] *Ata Hu Adonai*,[218] and *Va'Yosha Adonai Ba'yom Ha'hu*.[219]

This series contains praises of God that were uttered by David, Nehemiah, and Moses. *Va'Y'Varech David* is a prayer said by King David to thank God for allowing him to collect the materials from which the First Temple was to be built in Jerusalem, even though God denied David permission to build the Temple himself. *Ata Hu Adonai* was recited by Ezra, Nehemiah, and the assembled returnees from Exile on *Shemini Atzeret*, at the end of the first Festival season they celebrated after returning to Jerusalem. The final quotation includes the Song at the Sea, which begins, *Az Ya'shir Moshe* (Then Moses sang), recited by Moses when the Israelites were saved by God at the Red Sea. These quotations were included because the fifteen terms of praise of God found in *Yishtabach*, the concluding prayer of *P'sukei D'Zimra*, were all taken from these verses.[220] They represent, in a sense, an unfolding of *Yishtabach*, a prayer that had powerful mystical associations for the kabbalists. For us, they are an opportunity to visualize the events they signify, as we build up to the visualization of receiving the Torah on Mount Sinai that we are to experience during the recitation of the *Shema.*

Nishmat (Let the Soul of Everything That Lives Praise Your Name)

This ancient prayer was part of what was called, in the Talmud, the Blessing of the Song, though it does not contain the standard blessing formula.[221] It is added to the blessings recited after the Song at the Sea on *Shabbat* and Festivals only, including the Passover *seder.* Parts of it were derived from a prayer recited in thanksgiving for rainfall that follows a drought.[222] It is similar to the blessing recited on Festivals after *Hallel*, Psalms 113 to 118, and may well have entered the services as an addition to that blessing.[223]

Again, this is an opportunity to visualize, to feel the relief one experiences after an emergency is over. Rainfall following a drought was a type of relief common to the experience of most Jews in antiquity. Having just visualized miracles that are foreign to our personal experience, the return of the Jews from Exile and the rescue at the Red Sea, we now move our minds to other situations in which we may have personally experienced relief after an emergency.

Shochen Ad: Greatness Expressed Through Praise; Yishtabach

This is the last portion of an ancient hymn, including several Torah passages, that was added to the service in compliance with an opinion of Rabbi Yohanan ben Zakkai in the *Mishna* that the recitation of *Hallel* be followed by a Blessing of the Song.[224] Of course, we have not actually recited *Hallel*, but we have recited Psalms 145 to 150 in place of reciting all the psalms, including those that make up *Hallel*. *Shochen Ad* is really an ending to the psalms, rather than a beginning of the *Shacharit* service.

The final paragraph, beginning with *Yishtabach*, was awarded mystical significance in the *Zohar*. Its thirteen individual praises of God[225] were regarded as activating the thirteen kabbalistic attributes of God.[226] The kabbalistic practice, therefore, was to recite this prayer while standing and to refrain from any conversation and interruption during it.[227]

With *Yishtabach*, we become conscious of our need—that we as a community require the relief God gave to Moses and the people of Israel in their emergency. We experience a sense of urgency that motivates us to take the prayers more seriously than before.

Chatzi Kaddish (Half Kaddish)

Kaddish has already been discussed (see p. 47). Here, the short version, called *Chatzi* (Half) *Kaddish* acts as a divider between *P'sukei D'Zimra* and the *Shacharit* service in the traditional liturgy. This use of *Kaddish* has been eliminated or made optional in the Reform liturgy.

Chatzi Kaddish dates from mishnaic times. It is actually older than the Complete *Kaddish*, which did not appear until the ninth century.[228] The middle sentence recited by the congregation, *Y'hei shmei raba m'vorakh l'olam ul'olmei olmaya* (May His great name be blessed forever and ever), is traditionally the most important. It was used, in the ancient houses of study, at the end of sermons that were conceived of as efforts to understand the secrets of the Bible as a prerequisite for mystical experience.[229] "The rule was that every sermon had to conclude with words of consolation—that is, with references to the messianic age."[230] Some preachers added *Kaddish* as a concluding short prayer because it contains petitions for the sanctification of God's name and for the coming of God's kingdom, of which *Y'hei shmei raba* is the central one. It is an Aramaic translation of the blessing, *Baruch shem k'vod malchuto l'olam va'ed*, which was customary in the Second Temple and is also the second line of the *Shema*.

With the recitation of *Chatzi Kaddish*, we make another transition—this time from mental preparation to forming a spiritual community with our fellow worshippers.

Shacharit: The Morning Service

Having completed the preliminary service, we now ought to be ready to say the required morning prayers with intense concentration (*kavana*).

The *Shacharit* (literally, Sunrise) service originated during the Second-Temple period. Four daily services were instituted among the *ma'amadot* (literally "those who stand"), the delegations of public representatives who were sent in a year-round rotation on one-week missions from outlying areas to Jerusalem to "stand over" the sacrifices.[231] One of those services was held at sunrise.

These services, and the practice of using *ma'amadot*, were devised to enable all Jews to participate in worship. No longer was the purpose of ritual to please or placate God with sacrifices, as it had been at the time of the First Temple. No longer was Jewish ritual dominated by priests. The new spirit "demanded personal piety and the participation of all Jews in religious life, 'the service of the heart.'"[232]

Since the time of the Second Temple, the *Shacharit* service has been built around two central prayers, the *Shema* and the *Amida.*[233] In the *Shema,* we listen to what God said when He spoke to our ancestors. In the *Amida,* we ask God to redeem us as He redeemed them.

BARCHU: THE CALL TO PUBLIC WORSHIP

We now establish our formal prayer community. *Barchu,* the ancient call to public worship, may have originated when Ezra and Nehemiah led the Jews in building the Second Temple.[234] It is an invitation by the leader of the service to say the *Shema*.[235] Originally the first line alone was used to make the announcement.[236] By the second century c.e., because the preliminary service had been added, *Barchu* had become a part of the *Shacharit* service. It was pointless to call people to prayer when they were already at prayer, so the "call to prayer" was made into a prayer, too.

The custom of standing and bowing during *Barchu* is ancient, as shown in a verse in Nehemiah: "Then the Levites said, 'Stand up and bless the Lord your God.'"[237] We bow as if entering the presence of a king.[238] The word *barchu*, like *baruch*, comes from the Hebrew word for knee, and *baruch* originally referred to the bending of the knee in prayer, a sign of humility.[239]

The second line (*Baruch Adonai ham'vorach l'olam va'ed*) originated as the congregational response to the same first line when read by people called to the Torah. It was adopted for use in *Barchu* in the second century when *Barchu* came to be part of the *Shacharit* service.[240] It is repeated by the *chazan* after the congregation finishes saying it, as an acknowledgment that in Judaism the *chazan* joins with, and is part of, the congregation in praising God, rather than being special and apart from it.[241] For this reason, the word *ha'm'vorach* (literally, "the one to whom the knee is bent") was appended to *Barchu Et Adonai* in the first line of *Barchu*. Rabbi Akiva advocated omitting *ha'm'vorach* to remain true to the corresponding phrases in the psalms, but Rabbi Ishmael urged that it be added to demonstrate that the leader was not excluding himself from the congregation in paying homage to God. Rabbi Ishmael's view prevailed.[242]

Originally, *Barchu* was preceded by a Mourner's *Kaddish*, and orphans had priority in calling the worshippers to prayer by reciting *Barchu*. See above, p. 50.

THE *SHEMA* AND ITS BLESSINGS: WE LISTEN TO GOD; WE GLIMPSE THE SWEEP OF TIME

The Blessings Before the *Shema*

The *Yotzer Ohr* (Former of light) blessing after *Barchu* is actually the beginning of a separate prayer, the first of two blessings that precede the *Shema*. Since we have already entered the presence of "the king" during *Barchu*, we may now sit down.

This blessing is taken from a polemic in Isaiah 45:7 against religious dualism, such as prevailed in ancient Persia:[243]

> I form light and create darkness,
> I make peace and create woe.

The talmudic rabbis changed the last words to "Who makes peace and creates everything."[244] The blessings before the *Shema* were determined by the second century C.E. It was the rule among the talmudic rabbis that blessings be recited before and after the ritual recitation of any biblical passage.[245] The blessings serve to "introduce [the passage] as a biblical reading and then to affirm the truth of what has been read."[246]

The importance of this blessing is reflected by the fact that the *Shacharit* service was also called *Yotzer* in midrashic times.[247]

With this blessing, we focus our minds on the unity of God. Light and darkness have the same source; well-being and woe are manifestations of the same Divine Presence. This was a revolutionary concept in the ancient world; it was much easier for ancient peoples to understand forces like light and darkness, wind and sun, and good fortune and bad fortune as separate gods warring with each other. We visualize ourselves ascending Mount Sinai, approaching that Presence, and, from that pinnacle, surveying the sweep of time, from the Creation to the ultimate redemption.

Introductory Hymns of the First Blessing
Before the Shema (Yotzer Ohr, Creator of Light)

El Adon (God the Lord)

This poem, which was inserted into the first blessing before the *Shema* for *Shabbat* and Festivals in the second century C.E., is an alphabetical acrostic; each sentence begins with the succeeding letter of the Hebrew alphabet. It was probably written by a group of mystics called *Yordei Merkava* (literally, "those who go down in the chariot"), who influenced the later development of Jewish mysticism in Europe.[248] The poem praises God for creating the sun, the moon, and the stars.

El Adon is an expansion of an alphabetical prayer said on weekdays. Each of the first four words of the weekday prayer becomes the first word of an entire sentence on *Shabbat* in *El Adon*.[249] This prayer thus highlights the importance of taking extra time on *Shabbat* to develop our deepest thoughts and feelings. We allow ourselves the luxury of time; the freedom to linger as we ascend the mountain to meet the *Shechina*.

The Kedusha (Sanctification) of Yotzer

Kedusha is an insert recited three times during the morning service: in the first blessing before the *Shema*, in the repetition of the *Amida*, and in the repetition of the *Musaf Amida*. The *Kedusha* found in the *Yotzer Ohr* blessing before the *Shema* is called the *Kedusha* of *Yotzer*.

In *Kedusha*, we become, for a moment, winged angels in heaven praising God with the same words Isaiah and Ezekiel heard them use: "Holy, holy, holy is the Lord of hosts; the whole world is filled with His glory," and "Praised be the glory of the Lord throughout the universe."[250] When we say, *Kadosh, kadosh, kadosh* ("Holy, holy, holy"), it is customary to rise to our toes three times, as if the wings of the angels are lifting our heels.[251] Two paragraphs describing the angels preface the *Kedusha* blessing.

Kedusha originated with the *Merkava* mystics sometime before 600 C.E.[252] They believed that it had special powers to help people ascend to the higher realm, and that they were divinely charged to disseminate it and receive recognition from God in return.[253] Consequently, *Kedusha* was inserted into the blessings before the *Shema*, as well as into the *Musaf* (Additional) service after the Torah has been read. This may have been to ensure that those who were unable to stay for the entire service would have the opportunity to say *Kedusha* either early or late in the service.[254]

The connection between the *Kedusha* of *Yotzer* and *Yotzer* is that *Yotzer* speaks of the praise of God by His servants—the sun, the moon, and the stars. These servants praise God silently by fulfilling His commands, while the angels praise God aloud with the words contained in *Kedusha*.

The connecting verse in the *Kedusha* of *Yotzer* differs from the analogous verses of the *Kedusha* found in the *Shacharit* and *Musaf Amidot*. It refers to "wheels" (*ofanim*) and "holy beasts" (*chayot ha'kodesh*). The "wheels" and the "holy beasts" carried the throne of God, according to the "fiery chariot" vision of Ezekiel (Ezek. 1:4–28). It was on these chariot wheels that the *Merkava* mystics thought it possible for man to ascend to heaven.

Yotzer Ohr (Creator of Light): The First Blessing Before the Shema

The two mystical inserts, *El Adon* and the *Kedusha* of *Yotzer*, are found within the first blessing before the *Shema*. This blessing calls God *Yotzer ohr* (literally, Former of light). The opening formula of this blessing, which immediately follows *Barchu* and precedes *El Adon*, praises God as the One who "forms light and creates darkness," and the closing benediction, which comes after the *Kedusha* of *Yotzer*, praises Him for forming the "heavenly lights." This blessing is from the Talmud, and the text was formalized by Saadya Gaon, head of one of the Babylonian academies, in the tenth century C.E.[255]

It is logical to give recognition to God in the morning for creating light. The blessing is worded in the present tense, showing that Creation is an "ongoing process in which the exuberance of God's power can be seen and felt anew each day."[256] We also praise God for creating darkness, however, and, earlier in the service, in the Sunrise Blessings (*Birchot Ha'Shachar*), the first blessing we recite praises God for giving us the capacity to distinguish between light and darkness. This emphasis on God as Creator of both light and darkness may have been a Pharisaic reaction to the dualism of the Sadducees and the Gnostics. The Sadducees, the priestly class with which the Pharisees were in frequent conflict, were likely the authors of the Dead Sea Scrolls, one of which portrays the struggle between the "forces of light" and the "forces of darkness." The Gnostics, a first- and second-century sect, went further; echoing the Zoroastrians of ancient Persia, they believed that separate gods of goodness and evil not only existed, but were in constant conflict. The Gnostics drew many Jewish adherents, but viewed Yahveh, the God of the Jews, as the "evil god." The talmudic rabbis at Yavneh, who were Pharisees, may have worded the *Yotzer Ohr* so as to stress that the same God created and controlled both the "forces of light" and the "forces of darkness."

In the penultimate sentence (*Ohr Chadash Al Tziyon Ta'Ir*) comes a petition for God to bring the Messiah. This was a mystical insertion that was unrelated to the rest of the paragraph, and it was opposed by Saadya Gaon for that reason.

Ahava Rabba (*The Blessing of Torah*): The Second Blessing Before the *Shema*

In our vision we have climbed Mount Sinai to receive the Torah. Now, we bless what we are about to receive.

The *Mishna* required two blessings before the *Shema* in the morning service, and one after it.[257] A blessing on the Torah logically comes before the *Shema*, because the *Shema* we are about to read consists of three readings from the Torah.

The blessing is on the theme of gratitude to God for the revelation of the Torah. It is talmudic in origin, and was adopted at the rabbinic academy in Sura, Babylonia, during the ninth century C.E. as the second blessing to be recited before the *Shema* in the morning service.[258]

Shema: The Confession of Faith

With the *Shema* we visualize ourselves receiving the Torah from God. We stand on a pinnacle from which we can perceive the entire scope of history, from the creation of light discussed in the *Yotzer* blessing before the *Shema*, to the end of time alluded to in *Tzur Yisrael*, the *Ge'ula* (Redeemer) prayer found at the end of the blessing that follows the *Shema*.[259]

The *Shema*, the confession of faith in one God, consists of three passages from the Torah: *Shema* (Deut. 6:4–9), *V'Haya Im Shamoa* (Deut. 11:13–21), and *Va'Yomer* (Num. 15:37–41). We do not merely listen to these passages; we allow them to transform our minds, as if transfixed by the brilliance of the divine Presence before us.

The *Shema* is one of the oldest prayers in the Jewish liturgy. At least as far back as 444 B.C.E., when Ezra the Scribe established the rule of the Torah as the official constitution of the Jewish people newly returned from Babylonian exile, Torah reading (and explaining the Torah) was an integral part of the priestly service.[260] It was impossible to read the entire Torah every day, so four passages were designated to be repeated daily by the priests in the Second Temple in public worship on account of the importance of their teachings: the Ten Commandments, and the three passages that became the *Shema*.[261] The talmudic rabbis taught that saying the *Shema* every morning and evening fulfilled the biblical commandment to study Torah day and night.[262]

That the *Shema* was intended to be recited in an altered mind-state is made explicit in the Talmud. *Mishna Berachot* 2:1 says that a person who recited the *Shema* without *kavana* "did not fulfill his obligation." There is lengthy discussion in *Mishna Berachot* 2:2 and 2:3 about the degree to which the reciter must shut out external distractions. Essentially, the *Shema* must be said with a type of concentration that filters out normal encounters with others, but does not abandon contact with reality.[263]

Consistent with this idea, persons suffering from great distractions or stress, or from other conditions in which they would be unable to undergo the necessary mental transformation, were specifically exempted by the Talmud from saying the *Shema*. For example, newlyweds in their first week of marriage who had not yet consummated the marriage were exempted,[264] as were mourners whose deceased relative was not yet buried.[265]

The Ten Commandments were deleted from the service during mishnaic times as a response to heretics (*minim*), who argued that only the Ten Commandments, and not the rest of the Torah, were the word of God (B. *Ber.*12a).

The *minim* pointed to the prominence of the Ten Commandments in the service as evidence that even the rabbis must agree with them. To avoid giving credence to this argument, and to deny the Ten Commandments any special sanctity, the rabbis eliminated their recitation from the service.

Today, the *Shema* remains. While the rest of the service is us speaking to God, the *Shema* is when we are listening to God speaking to us. For our prayers to be heard, we must first listen and be transformed.

The Proclamation of Faith:
"Shema Yisrael, Adonai Eloheinu, Adonai Echad!"

In ancient times, the first line of the *Shema* was not merely read—it was "proclaimed."[266] The prayer leader assumed the role of Moses when he addressed the people of Israel to give them the Torah.[267] Prior to the destruction of the Second Temple in the year 70 c.e., when the *Shema* was said by the priests in the Temple, the name of God, the tetragrammation (Y-H-V-H), was pronounced.

The purpose of the proclamation was for these words always to appear as if they were being heard for the first time:

> They should not be in your eyes like some antiquated edict to which no one pays any attention, but like a new edict which everyone runs to read.[268]

Rabbi Reuven Hammer comments: "In the ancient town square, a messenger would proclaim an edict of the ruler and affix it to a wall or post. Something that had hung there for a long time grew stale. The *Shema* was to be proclaimed twice each day as if it had never been heard before."[269]

During persecutions after the fall of the Second Temple, the public practice of Judaism was forbidden, and the custom of proclaiming the *Shema* in public ended. Jews continued to read it privately, though, and it continued thereafter as part of the synagogue service.

It is customary to stress the "d" at the end of the word *echad* (one), to avoid saying the word *acher* (another). Sephardic Jews also raise the pitch at the end of *echad* in remembrance of Rabbi Akiva's defiance of the Roman decree against the public teaching of the Torah. This illustrates another function of the *Shema: kiddush Hashem,* the sanctification of God's name at the time of one's death. The Talmud tells the following story:

> When they brought Rabbi Akiva to be executed, it was the time of the recitation of the *Shema.* Although they were raking his flesh with rakes of iron, he took upon himself the yoke of Heaven. His disciples said to him, "Our master—do you go so far?" He said to them, "My entire life I was troubled by the verse 'with all your soul'—even if He takes your soul, I thought, if it comes to that, will I be able to fulfill it? And now that it has come about, shall I not fulfill it?" He prolonged the word "One" until his soul departed while he was saying "One."[270]

It has become general practice for Jews to recite the first verse of the *Shema* on their deathbed. Millions of Jews slain because they were Jews have said the *Shema* when they were about to be killed—from Roman times to the Crusades, from the pogroms to the Holocaust.

Except in the Reform liturgy, the *Shema* is recited while seated. This seems odd for a prayer that is one of the most important in the liturgy, but it is no accident. In the eighth century c.e., a dissident sect, the Karaites, argued that only the *Shema* and the Ten Commandments were actually given by God at Mount Sinai. The Ten Commandments had already been removed from the liturgy to deemphasize them in response to the *minim* several centuries earlier. The Karaites pointed to the prominence of the *Shema* in the liturgy as evidence for their cause, particularly the practice of standing for the *Shema* while remaining seated during other Torah passages that were part of the liturgy. Amram Gaon, head of the Babylonian academies at the time, responded by ruling that one should not stand for the *Shema*, thereby downplaying its importance relative to other Torah passages in the liturgy and refuting the Karaites' argument.[271]

The Reform movement has reinstituted the practice of standing for the *Shema*, and has removed from the liturgy many of the other Torah excerpts recited in the Orthodox and Conservative services. This is ironic, since the Reform movement does not consider all 613 commandments in the Old Testament to be binding, and the passages that make up the *Shema* were selected, in large measure, because they remind us of the obligation to follow all the commandments as a means of showing our love for God. The first part of the third passage of the *Shema*, *Va'Yomer*, was removed from the Reform service because it contains the commandment to wear *tzitzit* as a reminder of the 613 commandments, a commandment not regarded as binding by Reform Jews. The second passage, *V'Haya Im Shamoa*, which says we should show our love for God because God judges our actions, was also omitted, based on the Reform movement's rejection of the concept of divine reward and punishment.

The Response: "Baruch Shem K'Vod Malchuto L'Olam Va'Ed!"

In ancient times, whenever the name of God was proclaimed in public, it was customary for the worshippers to respond: *Baruch shem k'vod malchuto l'olam va'ed* (Blessed be the name of His glorious Majesty forever and ever). It became the customary response to the proclamation of the first line of the *Shema*, although it is an interruption in the reading of the Torah passages that make up the prayer. The ancient response was preserved through the Roman persecutions when public worship was forbidden, but came to be said quietly so as not to interrupt the Torah passages that follow.[272]

V'Ahavta: *Showing Love for God by Our Conduct*

The first Torah passage of the *Shema* is succeeded by the passage that follows it in the Torah: *V'Ahavta*. *V'Ahavta* begins with a command to love

God "with all your heart and with all your soul and with all your might." How are we to achieve this intense dedication to God? Not through faith, as in Christianity, nor through feelings of oneness with the universe, as in Buddhism, but by "cling[ing] to his ways."[273] Following God's commandments in how we behave toward others, and in our relationship with God, is more important than words or feelings in Judaism. What we do ultimately shapes what we think, speak, and feel.

V'Ahavta ends with God's commanding us to study and recite "these words" at all times, to teach them to the next generation, and to place them on our arms and foreheads and on our doorposts and gates. Constant reiteration and study of the words of the Torah—in the *Shema*, in *tefillin*, and in *mezuzot*—serve as daily reminders of the conduct required of us as Jews.

In antiquity, the *Shema* was probably recited as a prompted reading, in which the prayer leader, who was merely one of the worshippers rather than a professional cantor, would say a couple of words at the beginning of each line, and the congregation would chime in with the rest. The leader was called the *poreis al Shema*, the "divider" of the *Shema*. There were no prayerbooks in those days, and the *Shema* was a lot to remember; even a scholar such as Eleazar Chisma is said by the Talmud to have been unable to officiate.[274]

In ancient Jericho, there was another kind of recitation of the *Shema*, called *korech al Shema* (wrapping up the *Shema*). The Jericho custom was for the reader to read the entire section without interruption while the congregation said it quietly with him.[275] It may have been this custom that ultimately prevailed.

V'Haya Im Shamoa: *Why Show Love for God? Because* *God Notices and Judges Our Actions*

The third Torah passage in the *Shema*, *V'Haya Im Shamoa*, is about reward and punishment. This passage is omitted from the Reform version of the *Shema*. After echoing the themes of *V'Ahavta* this passage states that if we love God and serve Him with all our heart and soul, "I will grant the rain for your land in season." Conversely, if we bow to other gods, God will "shut up the skies so that there will be no rain."

The rain is metaphorical. This passage voices a continuing belief in God's justice despite all the injustice present in the world. We cannot explain the suffering of the righteous or the prosperity of the wicked, but we believe that God has reasons for these things—reasons that, from our limited vantage point bound by time and space, we cannot fathom.

Va'Yomer: *What Conduct Shows Love for God?*
Observance of the Mitzvot

There are 613 *mitzvot* (commandments) in the Torah. Reading the fourth and last Torah passage of the *Shema, Va'Yomer,* is a substitute for reading all 613 commandments.[276]

Va'Yomer focuses on *tzitzit,* the ritual fringes, as a symbolic representation and daily reminder of the *mitzvot.* The *tzitzit* contain a total of 613 knots. In biblical times, the *tzitzit* were worn daily on the corners of both men's and women's clothing, where they could easily be seen. In Numbers 15:39, God gave the reason for wearing them:

> That shall be your fringe; look at it and recall all the commandments of the Lord and observe them, so that you do not follow your heart and eyes in your lustful urge.

For theological reasons, owing to the Reform view that wearing the fringes is optional, the foregoing part of *Va'Yomer* is omitted in the Reform version of the *Shema.* The Reform version resumes with a non sequitur: "So that you will remember and keep all of my commandments, and be holy for your God," a verse that refers back to the deleted reference to wearing the fringes.

Va'Yomer concludes with a reference to God as Redeemer, the God who brought the Jews out of the land of Egypt. God brought us out of Egypt "to be your God." God chose us to worship Him, and He entrusted us with the responsibility of observing His commandments.

Blessings After the *Shema: Emet Ve'Emuna* and *Emet V'Yatziv* (Prayers of Redemption)

At Mount Sinai, there were doubters among the Jews; that is why the Golden Calf was fashioned while Moses was atop the mountain. At the Red Sea, however, there were no doubters; everyone saw the miracle of God's parting of the waters. We now attempt to achieve the kind of unity of mind that the Jews achieved only that single time in our history, as a means of the redemption through which our urgent needs may be met.

At the end of *Va'Yomer,* the *chazan* repeats the last two words, *Adonai Eloheichem,* and adds the word *emet. Emet* is actually the first word of the blessing after the *Shema.* There are two versions of the first part of that blessing. *Emet Ve'Emuna* and *Emet V'Yatziv,* both of which begin with *emet* (truth). Their subject is the redemption of the Jewish people.

The talmudic rabbis did not prescribe a specific blessing after the morning *Shema.* The last part of *Va'Yomer* discusses the Exodus and redemption of the Jewish people. The rabbis wanted to continue this theme, but they thought, variously, that one should mention the Exodus in general, God's kingship, the parting of the Red Sea, and the smiting of the firstborn. Unable to resolve the dispute, they decided that one should mention all of them.[277] More than one version developed that fulfilled these requirements. At evening services, Ashkenazic synagogues use the shorter version, *Emet Ve'Emuna.* However, the longer version, *Emet V'Yatziv,* which is included in the morning liturgy in all denominations, was the prayer said at the conclusion of public worship in the most ancient period.[278]

Why say *Adonai Eloheichem emet* (The Lord your God is true) rather than *Adonai Eloheichem* at the end of *Va'Yomer?* The word *emet* is not found in the Torah passage, which ends with *Eloheichem.* The Talmud (*Ber.* 14a) says that it is to form a phrase like one found in Jeremiah 10:10: *Adonai Elohim emet* (The Lord is truly God). However, the real reason probably is different. Until relatively recent history, Jews in most parts of the world had to rely on memory rather than a *siddur* (prayerbook) to say the prayers, because *siddurim* didn't exist or were forbidden by the local ruler. Indeed, in Second Temple times it was forbidden to write down the synagogue prayers, just as it was forbidden to write down the Oral Law. Various explanations are given for this prohibition, which had its analogues among other ancient cultures, but, whatever the reason, it made ancient synagogue prayer far more spontaneous, individual, and fluid than it became in medieval times and remains today. At many places in the service, including this one,[279] verbal prompts have been built into the recitation of the prayers to remind the leader what comes next. The addition of verbal prompts is a reminder that Jews have not always been able to worship freely, and is also, perhaps, an aid to those worshippers who prefer to pray on their own rather than rely on a prayerbook.

Mi Chamocha

After a description of the Exodus, the blessing after the *Shema* includes extensive quotations from The Song at the Sea (Exod. 15:11, 15:18), which the Jews sang after being saved at the Red Sea. These include Mi Chamocha (Who is like you, God, among the mighty? Who is like you, glorious in holiness?). The reason The Song at the Sea is accorded such importance is that its singing at the Red Sea coincided with the Jews' initial acceptance of God's authority, and, indeed, represented the high point of that acceptance. Only then did God appear for the entire Jewish people to see. At no time before or since did the Jews accept God with such unanimity.[280]

Mi Chamocha is a final exhortation before the *Amida* to unite as a spiritual community. Its underlying message is "unity through singing." It was added as part of an expansion of *Emet V'Yatziv* by the talmudic rabbis, who regarded it as obligatory to recall both the suffering of the Egyptians and the joy of the Jews at the time of the Exodus, in order to dramatize God's sovereignty.[281]

Tzur Yisrael: The *Ge'ula* (Redeemer)

At the end of the blessing following the *Shema* is *Tzur Yisrael* (Rock of Israel), which dates, in its present form, from fourth-century Babylonia.[282] Having described the first redemption of the Jewish people, we now petition God to redeem us again.

In *Tzur Yisrael*, we make the transition from praising and listening to God to asking God for something. Because we are now asking the Ruler to do something for us, we stand up.

Tzur Yisrael was inserted in the course of the talmudic expansion of *Emet V'Yatziv* as a bridge between what originally were separate prayer services. In ancient times, before the *Amida* became part of the service, the public service ended with *Emet V'Yatziv*, the blessing after the *Shema*, and the worshippers would then remain standing in private worship, each directing his or her own supplications to God.[283] At some point during the late Second-Temple period, the *Amida* came to be recited, but it originally was recited at different times than the *Shema* and its blessings. Consistent with this early practice, it was still the custom among Jews on the Arabian Peninsula at the time of Mohammed, in the seventh century, to pray five times a day rather than three; they would say the sunrise *Shema*, the morning *Amida*, the afternoon *Amida*, and the evening *Amida*, and the bedtime *Shema*, in that order. This may well have been the origin of the Muslims' practice of praying five times a day.[284]

Both the Babylonian and Jerusalem Talmuds state emphatically that the *Amida* should follow immediately after the blessing after the *Shema*. There is a likely reason for this: it had become a deeply held custom for worshippers to remain after the *Shema* to address God directly with their personal prayers.[285] The expansion of the blessing after the *Shema* to include Mi *Chamocha* and *Tzur Yisrael* was designed to force worshippers to defer personal prayer until after the *Amida*.

Were the *Shema* and the *Amida* originally recited not only at separate times, but by different factions? This is the view of some modern scholars (one of whom is Professor Tzvee Zahavy of the University of Minnesota), who identify the *Shema* with the scribes and the *Amida* with the priests. In this view, the *Shema* was "the primary rite of the scribal brotherhood, . . . a polemic of scribal triumphalism," while the *Amida* was "the main liturgy of the deposed priestly aristocracy" after the destruction of the Temple in 70 c.e., and "the kingship motif served as a justification of priestly and patriarchal authority as postdestruction client rules of the community, implicitly for Rome and explicitly for God."[286] According to these scholars, the synagogue service as we know it was the product of a compromise between these two social groups that occurred sometime between 155 and 220 C.E., avoiding a schism.[287]

This view, carried to its extreme, suggests that the two central prayers of Judaism are merely ancient factional polemics and, therefore, have no relevance to worshippers almost two millennia later. This is a simplistic understanding of the prayers. Even if one assumes liturgical factionalism in ancient Israel, it is necessary to inquire what meaning each prayer had to those who made it central to their ritual. The *Shema* clearly was not perceived as a mere political polemic by Hillel and Shammai, whose debate over the proper time for its recital in the morning is recorded in the Mishna. Nor was the *Amida* understood as a mere "Civic Prayer for Jerusalem," as Zahavy calls it, by Rabbi Yochanan ben Zakkai and Rabban Gamaliel II, for whom it was instead a substitute for the Temple ritual and—critically—was intended to have the same impact on the worshipper and on God that that ritual had. The *Amida* possesses a powerful spiritual flow that makes apparent its intended function: to enable the worshipper in his or her altered state of consciousness to communicate communal and personal needs to God and to derive strength from that communication.

THE *AMIDA*: WE SPEAK TO GOD; WE EXPERIENCE PERSONAL, COMMUNAL, AND NATIONAL REDEMPTION IN "VIRTUAL REALITY"

Purpose

The *Amida* (literally, "standing") is the climax not only of the morning prayers, but of every Jewish service. In it, we finally speak directly to God. Because we are addressing God directly, we approach God as we would approach a king, standing and bowing.

What we ask God for—what we visualize during the *Amida*—is national redemption culminating in world peace.[288] The *Amida* is a time to ask God for things that will benefit humankind and the Jewish people. With all the focused concentration (*kavana*) we have mustered by participating in the preliminary service and the *Shema*, we now ask God as a group to grant our collective requests. "A person who does not take the grief and humiliation of other people into his heart will not be answered. That is why prayers and petitions all are voiced as 'we' and 'our.'"[289]

The nineteen blessings that make up the *Amida* guide us in visualizing the path through which redemption can be achieved, and in appreciating the benefits it would bring. First, we must respect and comprehend ourselves; we visualize our ancestors to engender pride (Blessing 1). Then, we must respect and comprehend the forces of nature (Blessing 2). Third, we must sanctify ourselves and connect with the divine force within ourselves by emulating the angels (Blessing 3). Through these efforts we develop knowledge of good and evil (Blessing 4). By knowing good and evil we develop the capacity to repent (Blessing 5) and to achieve God's forgiveness (Blessing 6). With God's forgiveness, we can be redeemed (Blessing 7) from the adversity that resulted from the bad we have done.

This redemption takes on many forms: being healed from disease and from physical and mental wounds (Blessing 8), being blessed with good harvests (Blessing 9), and being restored to our land (Blessing 10) and our own system of justice (Blessing 11). Redemption also entails having our people reunified in spirit as a nation; this requires that we fortify ourselves to take a strong stand against members of our own people who turn against us (Blessing 12) and that we develop the generosity of spirit to welcome members of other peoples who sincerely wish to become part of us as Jews-by-choice (Blessing 13). Being a Jew is not just a legal matter or a phenomenon of birth; it is a state of mind, a sense of being spiritually united with the Jewish people.

Reunited as a sovereign and prosperous nation, we will be able to rebuild the physical and governmental structures that once formed the heart of that nation—not merely as buildings and bureaucracies, but as lasting structures of peace (Blessing 14 and 15). We pray to God to accept our prayers (Blessing 16), then silently meditate, perhaps adding personal prayers and requests. We then thank God in advance for granting our requests (Blessings 17 and 18).

Finally we recite the Peace Blessing (Blessing 19), in which we pray that, again united as a nation, we will become a force that will bring peace to the entire world and not just benefit ourselves.[290]

The Mishna makes it clear that the Amida is to be said in the deepest state of concentration, even more so than the Shema. For example, a craftsman atop a tree or on a scaffold is permitted to say the Shema, but not the Amida.[291] For the Amida, one must break entirely with the performance of daily activity. It is not merely a drama that the worshipper figuratively watches from a distance, but a visualization in which we place ourselves in the midst of that drama and experience its becoming real. As will appear below, the Passover seder involves much the same technique as the Amida of making something—in the case of the seder, the Exodus and freedom— seem so immanent that the participant experiences it as a kind of virtual reality. In the *Amida*, we experience the process of personal, communal, and national redemption and world peace as virtual reality.

History

Some of the basic elements of the *Amida* may date from the pre-Hasmonean period in Israel, but it is more likely that the *Amida* was compiled after the fall of the Second Temple.[292] Tradition has it that the *Amida* was written by the men of the Great Assembly, an institution that began with the "great assemblies" convened by Ezra the Scribe when the Jews returned from Exile in 444 B.C.E. It was recited at times that originally coincided with the *Tamid* offering in the Temple. However, several parts of the *Amida* are of later origin. The Talmud attributes the formalization, though not the authorship, of the *Amida* to Shimon Ha'Pakuli (Simon the Flaxworker) under the supervision of Rabban Gamaliel II, who lived in Yavneh, the land of Israel, in the early second century C.E.[293]

Before the Roman persecutions of the Jews and the destruction of the Second Temple in 70 C.E., the *Amida* was informal and personal, lacked a fixed text, and was recited with a meditative quality. It was led by a prayer leader acting as *shaliach tzibbur* (representative of the community), and the congregation adopted each blessing as its own by responding Amen.[294] The Talmud relates that the *Chasidim rishonim* ("original righteous ones") took one hour to say the *Amida*, which, if we can take it literally, comes out to one word every seven seconds.[295] The *Amida* was followed by private prayer in which worshippers would petition God to meet their personal needs and desires, and to forgive their transgressions.[296]

This changed after the fall of the Second Temple. At the time of Rabban Gamaliel II, between 70 and 100 C.E., the Jews who had adopted Christianity still worshipped in the synagogue with other Jews, and even served as prayer leaders. These Judeo-Christians regarded the destruction of the Second Temple as a sign that it was God's will that the law of Moses be abrogated. They attempted to use the synagogue as a convenient base for missionary activities, and to introduce changes in the liturgy, such as inserting additional words into blessings to address Jesus as a miracle-worker. Some also curried favor with the Roman authorities by serving as informers against those who violated the Roman proscriptions of Jewish public worship.[297]

To combat this incipient movement, Rabban Gamaliel II of Yavneh and other rabbis of the Sanhedrin, which met there, took numerous steps to formalize the service. One such step was having Shim'on Ha'Pakuli ("the flaxworker," but more likely an indication of his place of origin), apparently a devout congregant, edit the *Amida*. A benediction that previously had been directed at "the wicked" was changed by Samuel Ha'Katan to denounce "sectarians and apostates," and later was changed to denounce *malshinim* (informers). At the time, these terms were employed as euphemisms for Judeo-Christians.

Rather than have the prayer leader say the *Amida* on behalf of the congregation, as before, it was decreed that all worshippers had to say it in its entirety, thereby requiring the Judeo-Christians to denounce themselves or stay away from the synagogue. Also, a rule was adopted that when a Judeo-Christian recited a benediction, one must not answer Amen unless he has heard the benediction in its entirety, in order to avoid inadvertently voicing agreement with a benediction altered to incorporate Christian beliefs. Finally, in about 100 C.E., the Judeo-Christians were formally expelled from the synagogues.[298]

Structure

The *Amida* is also called the *Shemoneh Esrei* (eighteen) because the weekday version used to contain eighteen blessings. A nineteenth blessing was later added, and only seven are recited on *Shabbat* and Festivals (nine on *Rosh Ha'Shana*), but the name *Shemoneh Esrei* has remained.

All of the blessings are worded in the first-person plural. Contrary to what some commentators say, they are all collective blessings of the prayer community, not individual personal prayers, even though some of the blessings pray collectively for the worshippers to be given personal qualities that will enable them to achieve God's forgiveness and redemption.[299] All of the blessings use the format of the *beracha*.[300] These blessings were deliberately formulated as a sequence, in order to broaden and diversify the scope of prayer.[301]

These blessings fall roughly into three categories.[302]

The first three blessings praise God. Medieval commentators likened them to a slave praising his master. As we approach God in our visualizations, we become closer to the divine within ourselves.

The middle blessings are petitions. They have been compared to the pleas of a slave who asks his master for a favor. Now that we are spiritually as close as possible to the divine, we are able to move along the sequence of visualizations that lead ultimately to redemption.

The last three blessings are of thanksgiving. They have been likened to the ingratiations of a slave who has received a favor from his master and is departing.

The first three and last three blessings are recited every day. The middle section consists of thirteen blessings on weekdays, but differs on *Shabbat* and Festivals, when we pray only for the acceptance of our prayers and the purification of our minds to serve God. On *Rosh Ha'Shana* and *Yom Kippur*, the middle section of the *Musaf Amida* consists of three blessings: *Malchuyot* (acknowledgment of God's kingship), *Zichronot* (a reminder of the good deeds of our forefathers, and *Shofarot* (the events that will take place to the sound of the shofar).

Customs

The Amida is said standing, with feet together

The custom of standing was derived, by the talmudic rabbis, from a passage in Psalm 106.[303] The prophet Ezekiel said that the ministering angels stood around God's throne with their feet "straight." (Ezek. 1:7). In reading the *Amida*, we put ourselves in the position assumed by the angels in the presence of God.[304] If it works for the angels, it will work for us.

The Amida is said facing Jerusalem

This custom is based on 1 Kings 8:44–48. On the day that King Solomon declared his intention to build the Temple, he publicly asked God to accept the prayers of reformed sinners if they prayed in the direction of the Temple: "When they sin against You . . . and they repent . . . and then later they turn back to You with all their heart and soul."[305] We turn toward the ancient Temple in Jerusalem as a symbol of our turning back to God with all our heart and soul.

We take three steps forward when beginning the Amida

In antiquity, it was customary when in the presence of a king, to approach him slowly and respectfully. As we spiritually approach God to make our communal requests, we approach Him as we would approach a king.[306] As we take these steps, we close our eyes and are mentally transported to a different realm in which we are spiritually able to communicate with God.

We bow at the beginning and the end of the first (Avot) and the eighteenth (Hoda'ah) blessings

Bowing was also customary, in ancient times, when approaching a king. That is why we bow in the first blessings as we say the words, *Baruch ata Adonai* (Blessed are You, God). The custom of bowing in the eighteenth blessing is based on the second-century Aramaic translation of the Bible, the *Targum Onkelos*. In 2 Samuel 16:4, it is recounted that Ziba, a servant of the House of Saul, provided essential food supplies to King David, and informed him that Mephiboshet, Jonathan's son, had remained in Jerusalem in the hope of regaining the throne. He was rewarded by King David with all of Mephiboshet's property, whereupon he thanked the King by saying, "I bow low. Your majesty is most gracious to me." In Hebrew, "I bow" is *hishtachaveiti*, from the word *hishtachava*. The *Targum* translated this word in Aramaic as *hodaya*, meaning "thank," "confess," or "agree." The eighteenth blessing begins with the word *Modim*, which comes from the same root as *hodaya*, thereby echoing the manner in which Ziba thanked King David according to the vernacular of the first century when the blessing was composed.[307] We thank God, in other words, in the same way that the servant Ziba did when he thanked King David. Bowing is a way to enhance our sense of humility and to make a spiritual connection with our humble ancestors.

The Amida is said silently by all worshippers, then repeated by the prayer leader

Requiring all worshippers, rather than just the prayer leader, to say the *Amida* and formalizing its text were two of several measures instituted by Rabban Gamaliel at Yavneh between 70 and 100 c.e. to dissuade Judeo-Christians who served as prayer leaders from using the synagogues for proselytizing. There were no written prayerbooks at that time, and the *Amida* previously had not been given a fixed wording. It had been customary for the prayer leader always to add something new—a custom that was apparently much abused during that period—and the order of the middle blessings was still left to the individual to decide even after these changes occurred.[308] Therefore, the prayer leader was given time before beginning the *Amida* to gather his thoughts, meditate, and prepare to lead the prayer.

This caused an interruption in the flow of the service. The rabbis at Yavneh decided to have the congregation read the *Amida* silently during this time, followed by a repetition of the *Amida* by the prayer leader.[309] In this decision, they followed the example of Hannah, the mother of the prophet Samuel, whose silent prayers to God were answered.[310]

Rather than just the prayer leader gathering his or her thoughts before the *Amida* is read aloud, we all gather our thoughts. We all meditate. We all emulate Hannah. By doing so, we achieve spiritual transformation, *devekut*. Silent prayer, the silent recitation of the *Amida*, is the heart of the traditional Jewish service.

To sum up: In Judaism, prayers are most effective when they are rendered by an entire community with profound concentration (*kavana*). Through *kavana*, we can enter a mental state of *devekut*, the state in which we are spiritually transformed a way that lasts beyond prayer to influence our daily behavior. *Kavana* can be achieved only through great effort displayed by observance of the *mitzvot*, and silent prayer—the *Amida*—is the most profound and powerful of all.

The Blessings of Praise

Blessing 1: Avot *(Patriarchs): To Merit God's Attention,*
We Must Respect Ourselves

Baruch ata Adonai, Eloheinu v'Elohei avoteinu
Blessed are You, our God and God of our fathers

The first blessing is called *Avot* because it refers to Abraham, Isaac, and Jacob. It is becoming common today in egalitarian congregations, to add the *Imahot* (Matriarchs), Sarah, Rebecca, Rachel, and Leah. Here, we remind ourselves of our proud *yichus*, our lineage, the chain of practice and belief that links us with our ancestors. We visualize our connection with them.

The meaning of the first blessing is that we praise God, but do not grovel to Him. For God to pay attention to us, we must respect ourselves, and our ancestors are role models that engender self-respect. The first blessing features a collection of phrases gleaned from the Bible that glorify God's powers, with emphasis on redemption.[311] Although we glorify God, the Talmud severely prohibited "heaping up" epithets for God, and allowed only certain biblical phrases to be used;[312] this contrasted with other ancient peoples, who had lengthy formulas for praising their various gods as well as their rulers.

Although the praises of God contained in this blessing may seem lengthy by modern standards, their significance lies in how brief they really are in comparison with the rituals of other ancient peoples. The first blessing thus is a time for us to meditate on self-respect as a condition for achieving the mental state in which we will behave as God desires us to behave.

On the High Holidays, the sentence beginning *Zachreinu l'chayim* (Remember us for life) is inserted. This is out of place, since it contains a petition rather than praise for God. This, as well as the numerous other inserts for the High Holidays, were unknown at the time of the Talmud, and first appeared in the *Seder Rav Amram*, the earliest complete written prayer code, in the ninth century.[313]

The purpose of these High-Holiday inserts is discussed elsewhere, but inserts are found in each of the *Amida* blessings. This probably was done in a mystical effort to increase the power of the *Amida* to respond to a national emergency—the writing and sealing of the collective fate of the community for the coming year. These inserts should stimulate us to contemplate the urgency of the situation, and inspire us to spiritually transform ourselves even if we usually cannot do so.

*Blessing 2: Gevurot (Wonders): To Merit God's Attention,
We Must Respect His Power Over Nature*

Ata gibor l'olam Adonai
You are the mighty One [literally, 'hero'] of the world, Lord

This blessing begins with *Ata gibor* (You are the mighty One). The original text probably was shorter and focused on God's power over nature, but was expanded, probably by Rabbi Eliezer in the first century C.E., to include repeated references to the ultimate power over nature, God's power to revive the dead.[314] This expansion occurred because of a dispute between the Pharisees, who believed in resurrection of the dead, and the Sadducees, who did not. By featuring resurrection of the dead in this blessing, the Pharisees made it impossible for Sadducees to lead the service, since they would be unable to say these words.[315]

The Reform movement has eliminated from its service any reference to revival of the dead, substituting *M'chayei ha'col* (Who gives life to everything) for *M'chayei ha'meitim* (who gives life to the dead). Conservative and Modern Orthodox Jews have tried to find new meaning in the old words.[316]

For traditional Jews, this is a time to visualize the cycle of birth and creation, death and renewal. With God's help, we do achieve a measure of immortality, through the birth of our children and the creations of our mind and spirit, and even through the decay of our flesh, which becomes part of the soil from which new life grows.[317]

*Blessing 3: Kedusha (Holiness):
To Merit God's Attention, We Must Feel Holy*

Ata kadosh v'shimcha kadosh
You are holy and Your name is holy

Kedusha is the most mystical of the blessings. During *Kedusha*, we become, for a moment, winged angels in heaven praising God with the same words Isaiah and Ezekiel heard them use: "Holy, holy, holy is the Lord of hosts; the whole world is filled with His glory" (*Kadosh, kadosh, kadosh,*

Adonai tz'va'ot, m'lo chol ha'aretz k'vodo) and "Praised be the glory of the Lord throughout the universe" (*Baruch k'vod Adonai mi'm'komo*).[318]

When we say *Kadosh, kadosh, kadosh,* it is customary to rise to our toes three times, as if the wings of the angels are lifting our heels.[319] From meditating on respect for ourselves in the first blessing, and on our place in the natural cycle of birth and rebirth in the second, we now focus our minds on rising above nature, on reaching for the spark of the divine within ourselves.

The *Kedusha* blessing originated with mystics during the early rabbinic period.[320] Mystical prayers and practices existed in which worshippers would attempt to ascend to heaven and come into the presence of God.[321] Special formulas were recited to help the worshipper progress upward and ward off danger.[322] The words that the prophets heard spoken by the angels, which had been used in the Second-Temple ritual, were considered effective in helping one make the ascent.[323] The early mystics believed that they were divinely charged to disseminate *Kedusha* and receive recognition from God in return.[324]

We cannot ascend to heaven by saying Kedusha, but traditional Jews do believe in following the code of ethical conduct and religious practice (*halacha*) as a means of making ourselves, and our daily lives, holy. Through our conduct, we can emulate some of God's qualities.

The full *Kedusha* is said only during the repetition of the *Amida,* and only if a *minyan* (ten adults; according to medieval interpretation, ten men) is present. This is because it is a public act, a *kiddush Hashem* (sanctification of God's name), which, under talmudic law, is supposed to be said only in public in the presence of a *minyan.* As a result, while *Kedusha* is not the most important blessing of the *Amida* from a theological standpoint (the middle blessings are, for reasons discussed below), it is the one part of the repetition of the *Amida* that the worshipper is required to recite, since it is the one part we have not already read silently.[325]

Most of the *Kedusha* blessing is not actually the third blessing, but a mystical insert. The third blessing during the silent reading of the *Amida* consists of two sentences, beginning with *Ata kadosh* (You are holy). This was the original text, and it remains the only version in the Sephardic ritual. When *Kedusha* is recited during the repetition of the *Amida,* the third blessing in the Ashkenazic ritual is the portion beginning with *L'dor va'dor* and ending with *Ha'El ha-kadosh.*[326]

Kedusha is structured around the two sentences recounted by Isaiah and Ezekiel. There are several connecting sentences in *Kedusha* that differ in the *Shacharit* and *Musaf Amidot.* Between *Kadosh, kadosh, kadosh* and *Baruch k'vod* in *Shacharit,* the connecting verse begins: "Then with the sound of great quaking" (*Az b'kol ra'ash gadol*). This passage probably originated with the *Merkava* mystics; its content is similar to "wheels" and "holy beasts" of the *Kedusha* of *Yotzer*.

During the *Musaf* service, the *Shema*, (Hear O Israel, the Lord is our God, the Lord is One) is inserted in the *Kedusha* blessing. This is done for an interesting reason. When Israel was under Byzantine Christian rule, during the Justinian persecutions from 553 to 636 C.E., the recital of the *Shema* during *Shacharit* was forbidden, since the Christians regarded it as a denial of the trinity. However, *Kedusha* was initially permitted, because the authorities thought that the words *Kadosh, kadosh, kadosh* were an affirmation of the trinity. The Jews circumvented the proscription by inserting the *Shema* into the *Kedusha* of the *Musaf Amida*, at which point the officer posted to make sure the *Shema* wasn't said during *Shacharit* had already left.[327] The *Shema* is retained in the *Kedusha* recited during the repetition of the *Musaf Amida* as a reminder of this history of persecution and defiance.

The Middle Blessings of the *Amida*: We Communicate Our Requests to God

Middle Blessing of the Shabbat *and Festival* Amida

Introduction to the Middle Blessing of the *Shabbat Amida*

Arvit: (Shabbat evening) You made the seventh day holy in Your name
    Ata kidashta et yom ha'sh'vi'i l'shimcha
Shacharit: And Moses rejoiced in the gift of his portion
    Yismach Moshe b'matnat chelko
Musaf: You did establish the Sabbath and did accept its offerings
    Tikkanta shabbat ratzita kor'b'noteha
Mincha (Shabbat afternoon): You are one and Your name is One
Ata echad v'shimcha echad

We now arrive at the most important part of the service: our petitions to God. All of the service to this point has been preparation for making these collective requests.

The middle blessing on *Shabbat* begins with an introduction. The introduction is different in each service, but on Friday night and in the Saturday morning and *Musaf Amidot*, it consists of a quotation from the Torah preceded by a few sentences that point out the significance of the quoted passage.

On Friday night, an introduction begins *Ata kidashta et yom ha'shvi'i li' shmecha,* and includes Genesis 2:1–3 (beginning *V'yachulu ha'shamayim*), the biblical account of the first *Shabbat,* when God rested after the Creation. The introduction to the passage from Genesis dates from the talmudic period[328] and refers to *Shabbat* as the "purpose [*tach'lit*] of the Creation of heaven and earth." The Genesis passage appears to have originally been a proof-text for this point. Why didn't God designate as holy one of the days on which He created something of which He was particularly proud? The Genesis quotation says that God blessed the seventh day "because" He ceased from all the work of Creation that He had done. God didn't rest to reward Himself for finishing His work; God is not like a human being, who needs rest after exertion. Rather, the Creation had a planned objective, and that objective was to make the Sabbath day possible.

In the *Shacharit* service, the introduction begins with *Yismach Moshe,* which recounts Moses' joy on receiving the Ten Commandments from God at Mount Sinai. In ancient times, this may have prefaced the recitation of the Ten Commandments or a poetic hymn.[329] Perhaps because of Roman or Syrian prohibitions on reciting the Ten Commandments, or, more probably, as a response to heretical groups,[330] this recitation was removed and a biblical verse commanding observance of the Sabbath, beginning *V'shamru b'nei yisrael,* was inserted. The following paragraph, *V'lo n'tato,* is a rabbinic explanation of the preceding biblical text—that the Sabbath was given to Israel as God's gift to the people He chose to take on the honor and the obligation of keeping it.[331]

In the *Musaf* (Additional) service, an inverse alphabetical poem, *Tikkanta Shabbat,* is recited,[332] followed by a biblical passage (Num. 28:9–10) containing the command to offer special sacrifices on *Shabbat. Musaf,* in antiquity, was the extra Sabbath sacrifice. This part originally expressed a longing to return to sacrificial worship, but has been changed in the Conservative liturgy to a historical remembrance of what our ancestors did, and has been deleted entirely in the Reform liturgy.[333] When the order of the *Amida* was fixed by Rabban Gamaliel and his assistants soon after the destruction of the Second Temple by the Romans in 70 C.E., the expression of a desire to return to the Temple form of worship must have been linked to the Jews' desire to return also to their former freedom and nationhood, which the Temple had symbolized.[334] The references in the *Amida* to the sacrificial rite can be understood as expressions of longing for the freedom and independence of the Jewish people.[335]

A logical progression is apparent in the order of the blessings. Upon the return of the exiled communities, the first thing they will need is a government.

The Middle Blessing of the *Shabbat Amida*

Eloheinu v'Elohei avoteinu kadsheinu b'mitzvotecha
Our God and God of our fathers, accept our rest

While the first three blessings (praise) and the last three blessings (thanksgiving) are always said, our collective requests of God vary with the occasion. During weekday services, there are no fewer than thirteen middle blessings that contain requests for fulfillment of our shared intellectual, spiritual, and physical needs (knowledge, repentance, forgiveness, redemption, healing, and prosperity) as well as our public or national needs (return of exiles, justice, protection from enemies, righteousness, rebuilding of Jerusalem, and the coming of the Messianic era).[336]

On *Shabbat*, however, our mood should be one of contentment.[337] *Shabbat* was considered by the talmudic rabbis to be a foretaste of the World-to-Come, in which all needs will be met.[338] Therefore, on *Shabbat* we put our worldly needs aside. We request only that God grant our spiritual needs. This request is contained in the paragraph that begins, *Eloheinu ve'Elohei avoteinu.* It asks God to "accept our rest," to "sanctify us through Your commandments," to "grant our portion in Your Torah," to "give us abundantly of Your goodness," to "make us rejoice in Your salvation," and to "purify our hearts (*v'taher libeinu*) to serve You in truth." It goes on to ask that God make the *Shabbat* our heritage and that all Israel should rest on *Shabbat*.

In antiquity, it was believed that the heart was the location of the human mind. We have spent much of the morning working up the necessary intensity of "heart"-mind (*kavana*) to be able to pray. Why? In Judaism, communicating our requests to God in such a way that He will pay attention to them is hard work that can only be done when we are in the proper frame of mind. Yet, at the same time, we recognize that God has the power to know our thoughts and to hear our requests when He chooses to do so. God decides whether we deserve to have our hearts "purified," to achieve the proper state of mind, so that our prayers will merit His attention. God's decision, in turn, depends upon how we act. Through observance of the *mitzvot* (commandments), such as resting on *Shabbat*, through good deeds, and through prayer, we earn God's assistance in achieving the necessary state of mind to claim His attention and have our needs met.

Once we reach that mind-state, *devekut*, we will be fortified in our conduct after prayer until the next time we pray, and through proper conduct we will create the conditions in which our needs will be met.

Mind-alteration through prayer has a self-fulfilling quality: We pray so that our needs will be met, but, in the process of achieving the proper mind-state for prayer, we affect our behavior in such a way that we become better able to meet our own needs.

The Middle Blessing of the Festival *Amida*

Ata v'chartanu mi'kol ha'amim
"You have chosen us from all the peoples"

Sanctification of the Day: *Kedushat Ha'Yom*

The Middle Blessing: *V'Hasieinu*

The middle blessing of the *Amida* on the three pilgrimage Festivals naturally focuses on the Temple. That is where people went on the pilgrimage Festivals. People stayed there the whole day, so the middle blessing of the Festival *Amida* is the same for *Arvit*, *Shacharit*, and *Mincha*.

It begins with the Sanctification of the Day. We reflect first on what is special about the day. The wording of this section, including the paragraph beginning *Ata v'chartanu* and continuing through the next paragraph, *Va'titen lanu*, is taken from the Talmud (*Yoma* 87b) and includes interwoven snippets from various biblical passages, including Deuteronomy 10:15 and 14:2, Psalm 149, Isaiah 66:18, and Jeremiah 14:9.[339]

The middle blessing continues with what the Talmud calls the "synopsis of the event" (*Shab.* 24a), beginning with *Ya'aleh v'yavo*. This paragraph, itself from the Talmud (*Sof.* 19:7), is a vivid listing of the procedures followed during the sacrifices in the Second Temple in Jerusalem:[340]

Go up the steps (*Ya'aleh*)
Come forward (*yavo*)
Approach [the altar] (*Yageea*)
Appear [before the officiating *kohen*] (*Yei'ra-eh*)
Let the gift be accepted (*yeiratzeh*)
Let him be heard [to make his declaration] (*yishama*)
Let the gift be recorded (*yipaked*)
And let this act be remembered [by God] (*Yizacher*).[341]

The final part of the middle blessing of the festival *Amida* begins, *V'ha' sieinu*. First referred to in the Jerusalem Talmud (*Ber.* 9), its beginning literally means: "Cause us to lift up the blessing of your Festivals for life and peace. . . ." Having figuratively performed the sacrifice through prayer, we now make our request that God "cause us to lift up the blessing" of the Festival.

This phrase is unusual. We are regarded as having the power to cause the sacrifice we have just performed to be lifted up to God. If we have that power, then the power is within ourselves to cause our prayers to be accepted. How can we accomplish this? The paragraph tells us: Through the observance of God's commandments, we become worthy of having God "purify our heart-minds" (v'taher libeinu) to serve Him in truth. By achieving this pure mind-state, we fortify ourselves to observe the mitzvot, but by good conduct we become better able to achieve a pure mind-state.

The Middle Blessings of the Weekday Amida

On weekdays, the three opening paragraphs—the blessings of praise—are followed by thirteen petitions (bakashot), which, coming after the initial three blessings, begin with Blessing 4: (4) Knowledge; (5) Repentance; (6) Forgiveness; (7) Redemption; (8) Healing; (9) Blessing of the Years; (10) Ingathering of the Exiles; (11) Judges; (12) "Blessing" of the Heretics; (13) Converts; (14) Rebuilding Jerusalem; (15) Restoring the Line of David; (16) Petition That Our Prayers Be Heard.

These petitions originally had no fixed order, but the order that has developed follows a logical format as a sequence of visualizations.[342] To review the previous discussion of this order (see p.74) By knowing good and evil (Blessing 4), we develop the capacity to repent (Blessing 5) and achieve God's forgiveness (Blessing 6). With God's forgiveness, we can be redeemed (Blessing 7) from the adversity that resulted from the bad we have done.

This redemption takes many forms: being healed from disease and from physical and mental wounds (Blessing 8); being blessed with good harvests (Blessing 9); being restored to our land (Blessing 10) and to our own system of justice (Blessing 11); and having our people unified in spirit as a nation by a strong stand against members of our own people who turn against us and by welcoming members of the other peoples who sincerely wish to become part of us as Jews-by-choice (Blessings 12 and 13).

Reunited as a sovereign and prosperous nation, we will be able to rebuild the physical and governmental structures that once formed the heart of that nation, not merely as buildings and bureaucracies, but as lasting structures for peace (Blessing 14 and 15). Finally, we pray that our prayers be accepted (Blessing 16).

Blessing 4: Knowledge of Good and Evil

Ata chonen l'adam da'at
You grant knowledge to man

The first weekday petition, *Ata chonen l'adam da'at*, is specifically a prayer for knowledge of good and evil as the prerequisite for repentance. In praying for knowledge, we follow the example of King Solomon, who prayed to God for the knowledge to distinguish good from evil, and received it.[343] Just as King Solomon's prayer was answered, we hope that our prayer will be answered, too.

The prayer quotes Jeremiah: "Return O rebel Israel. . . . Only know your sin: For you have transgressed against the Lord" (Jer. 3:12–13). The Second Temple had been destroyed and Israel had been conquered because of the sins of the Jewish people. To regain the Jewish nation, its people must understand what they have done wrong, and repent.[344]

Because of the common theme of discerning between two opposites (good and evil, holy and secular), on Saturday nights and on the nights when Festivals end, the *Havdala* (Separation) prayer is inserted here.

Blessing 5: Repentance

Hashiveinu Avinu l'Toratecha
Return us, our Father, to Your Torah

The second petition is for repentance (*teshuva*). The original text came from Lamentations 5:21: "Return us, O Lord, to You, and we shall return; renew our days as of old." Through knowledge of good and bad, we achieve a repentant state of mind. Repentance, in turn, leads to renewal.

The reference to God as our "Father" is derived from Psalms 103:13: "As a father has compassion for his children, so the Lord has compassion for those who fear Him."[345]

The recital of lamentations to achieve divine forgiveness was not unique to the Jews in the ancient world. What was unique was the idea that reciting them was not enough—that the worshipper had to experience a change of mental state to achieve God's forgiveness. The words of this blessing are a device to facilitate this change of mindset.

Blessing 6: Forgiveness

S'lach lanu avinu ki chatanu
Forgive us, Father, for we have sinned

We cannot take it for granted that because we recite lamentations, we will be forgiven. As the books of Job and Lamentations show, we cannot always know when we have achieved the requisite condition to be forgiven. We often commit unintentional sins,[346] and cannot avoid them even with a repentant mind.

Therefore, the third petition, originating in the Jerusalem Talmud, is for forgiveness.[347] Its beginning will be familiar to Catholics, whose liturgy incorporated the first phrase. It includes paraphrases of excerpts from the psalms. *Ki mochel v'soleach ata* (For You are a forgiving and pardoning God) is a shortened form of Psalms 86:5.[348] The benediction at the end of this blessing, *chanun ha'marbeh li'slo'ach* (Who grants forgiveness abundantly), is adapted from *Midrash Tehillim* 29:2, but was modified in the Ashkenazic liturgy to include the word *chanun* (grantor), paralleling the reference to God in Blessing 4 as Grantor of knowledge. On fast days other than the ninth of *Av*, penitential poems called *Selichot*[349] used to be inserted in this petition.

Blessing 7: Redemption from Suffering

Re'eh na v'an'yeinu v'riva riveinu
Look at our suffering and plead our cause

We have prayed for the capacity to tell good from evil. We have prayed to achieve a repentant frame of mind. We have prayed for forgiveness for those sins that we committed inadvertently, despite our knowledge and our repentant mental state. Now we pray that armed with knowledge of good and evil, a proper mental state, and God's forgiveness, God will grant us a practical benefit: relief from our suffering. According to Rabbi Samson Raphael Hirsch, *riveinu*, literally "our quarrel," connotes a reference to troubles that befall us because of the hostility of others, rather than internal or psychological suffering.[350]

The wording, the first part of which is taken from Psalms 119: 153–154, is in the present tense; it does not refer to the redemption of the Jews from past exile and oppression, but to our current predicaments, whatever they may be. The psalmic wording in the singular has been converted to the plural, reflecting the collective nature of the petitions in the *Amida*.[351]

On fast days, an insert beginning "Answer us" (*Aneinu*) derived from *Mishna Ta'anit* 11b and Isaiah 65:24, follows this blessing. We add an extra prayer for fast days as a response to a public emergency. The paraphrase of Isaiah is particularly interesting, because the verse on which it is based attributes God as saying: "Before they pray, I will answer, while they are still speaking, I will respond." We pray in time of emergency with the hope that our prayers will prove unnecessary.

Blessing 8: Health

R'fa'enu Adonai v'neirafei, hoshieinu v'nivasheia
Heal us, Lord, and let us be healed, save us and let us be saved

We now begin to descend the hierarchy of human needs. We have prayed for redemption from immediate peril. Next, we worry about our physical well-being.

As in Blessing 7, a biblical verse is converted from singular to plural in Blessing 8 to make it a collective, rather than an individual, petition—this time, a quotation from Jeremiah 17:14: "Heal me, Lord, and let me be healed; save me, and let me be saved; for You are my glory." The Jerusalem Talmud ended this blessing with the benediction, "Who heals the sick," but the Babylonian Talmud changed this to read, "Who heals the sick of his nation Israel."[352] The Reform movement has reverted to the original version to be consistent with its rejection of the doctrine of the Jews as the Chosen People.

Blessing 9: Sustenance

Barech aleinu Adonai Eloheinu et ha'shana ha'zot, v'et-kol minei t'vu'ata l'tova
Bless for us, our Lord and our God, this year and every species of its produce

We move further down the hierarchy of needs with the ninth blessing. Blessing 9 is generally considered the blessing for a good harvest, although there is some authority that it referred also to the success of one's livelihood, which in agrarian ancient Israel would have been synonymous with a successful harvest.[353] It is generally called the Blessing of the Years, referring to the progression of the year, i.e., the change of seasons. Following *Mishna Berachot* 5:2, the prayer of rain is inserted in this blessing during the winter, which is the rainy season in Israel.

Blessing 10: Return of the Exiled Communities

T'ka b'shofar gadol l'cheruteinu v'sa nes l'kabetz galuyoteinu
Cause a great ram's horn to sound for our liberation, and hold up a signal to gather our exiles

This beautiful passage is an adaptation of Isaiah 11:12 and 27:13, which prophesied the return of the exiles (the Ten Lost Tribes) from Assyria and Egypt after the fall of the Northern Kingdom of Israel.[354]

With it we make a transition from communal needs to national needs. We have progressed from collective mental and spiritual well-being to physical well-being; now we progress from our small group of worshippers to petition for a larger body, the exiled Jewish communities throughout the world. Another way to view this progression is that, through collective worship, we mend ourselves; once we have done so, our prayer group is empowered to alleviate the suffering of others.

The overarching national need for which we pray is a justly-ruled community of Jews restored to its homeland and at peace with both its neighbors and itself.

Blessing 11: Restoration of Justice

Hashiva shofteinyu k'varishona v'yoatzeinu k'vat'chila
Restore our judges as they were originally, and our advisors as they
were in the beginning

When exiled communities are restored to their homeland, they need a just government, or they will be no better off than they were in Exile. This blessing, taken from Isaiah 1:26,[355] asks for God to "restore our judges." Echoing Proverbs 29:2 ("When the wicked rule, the people sigh"), a phrase probably added by Rashi or his students[256] asks God to "remove from us sorrow and sighing."

In talmudic times, the blessing also asked for judgment to be "executed against the wicked."[357] This phrase may have been interpreted by foreign rulers as a veiled threat directed against them. Perhaps the phrase added by Rashi or his students was intended as an even more veiled replacement.

Blessing 12: God's Protection From Those Who Tear Our Community Apart

V'la'malshinim al t'hi tikvah v'chol-oseh rish'ah k'rega yoveidu
And for the slanderers [informers] let there be no hope, and may all
the doers of evil perish in an instant

An exiled community of Jews, restored to its homeland and possessed of a just government, also needs protection from hostile forces present among it in that land. Restoration of an exiled community implies victory over foreign claimants to the same territory or a settlement with them, but it does not imply unity within that community.

There certainly was no unity within the Jewish community subjugated by the Romans during the first century c.e. As was discussed above at p. 75, the community was torn apart by the schism between the Pharisees and the Judeo-Christians. Many Judeo-Christians, to avoid being persecuted themselves, acted as informers for the Romans against Jews who disobeyed Roman proscriptions against Jewish religious practices. Many also used the synagogue pulpits to preach their gospel to their fellow Jews.

At the behest of Rabban Gamaliel, this blessing, originally directed against the "wicked," was modified to condemn the Christians, in order to drive them away from the synagogues. In that form, it began: "As for the apostates there shall be no hope, the Christians [*notz'rim*] and the sectarians [*minim*, probably a reference to the Essenes[358] or the Gnostics] will perish as in an instant." It came to be known as the Apostates Blessing. At an early date, the first phrase, regarding apostates, was followed by "if they do not return to Your Torah," presumably to appease Christian authorities. The blessing was later amended to delete the reference to the Christians,[359] then to substitute the word *malshinim*, meaning "informers" or "slanderers," for the "sectarians," and finally, in the Middle Ages, to move "the slanderers" to the beginning in place of "the apostates."[360] It is easy to infer that those responsible for these amendments were acting to avoid persecution by Christian rulers, and that their congregants knew quite well what "informers" or "slanderers" really meant.

This blessing has an archaic ring to it. It can have meaning for us only if it is viewed in context. The nineteenth-century Orthodox scholar, Rabbi Samson Raphael Hirsch, said: "National well-being is attained on two levels. In one blessing therefore, we pray for competent leadership and in the other for the detachment and removal of those in our midst who obstruct the attainment of our objectives."[361] Another way of putting it is that the unity of our people is worth praying for.

There are allusions in Blessing 12 to Isaiah 14:5 ("Who has broken the staff of the wicked") and 25:5 ("[and] subdued the heat . . . of the strangers"), and to Psalms 69:29 ("May they be erased from the Book of Life, and not be inscribed with the righteous").

Blessing 13: God's Favor for Those Who Hold Our Community Together

Al-ha 'tzadikim v'al-ha'chasidim v'al-ziknei amcha beit yisrael
To the righteous and the pious and to the elders of Your nation, the
    house of Israel

Having prayed for God to take out of our midst those who tear the community apart, we now pay for God to show favor to those who hold our community together: the righteous, the pious, the elders, the "remnant of the scribes," and the pious proselytes. After condemning Jews who turn against their community, we now pray not only for Jewish community leaders, but for Jews-by-choice who join and sustain the Jewish community.

To put it another way: In Blessings 10 and 11, we pray for the Jews in Exile to be brought back together under a government that would be fair to them, a government of their own. In Blessings 12 and 13, we pray for the Jewish community to be held together, for those who set a proper example to be rewarded and shown compassion, and for the community to be purged of divisive internal forces.

The reference to proselytes dates from the Talmud (*Ber.* 3:25; *Y. Ber.* 3:25), and is found in the medieval prayer codes as well. The ninth-century *Seder Rav Amram* (the earliest complete prayer code) refers not to the "remnant of the scribes," but to the "remnant of the house of Israel." The reference to the remnant of the scribes apparently was adopted at the time of Rashi,[362] but refers back to an historical event mentioned in *Megillat Ta'anit*: "On the seventeenth of [*Adar*] the nations [i.e., the Gentiles] rose up against the remnant of the scribes in the state of Chalcis in the house of Zavdi, and He redeemed them . . . (the incident occurred during the reign of Alexander Jannai)."[363] The persecution of Jews by the Gentiles at the time of the Crusades, in Rashi's time, inspired Jewish scholars to look for an analogy in the sources where Jews were redeemed by God from a gentile uprising, and they found it in the escape of the Pharisaic leaders from persecutions inspired by the tyrannical ruler Alexander Jannai during the first century B.C.E.[364]

The conclusion of this blessing derives from Psalms 22:6 and 25:2 (compare "Nor suffer us to be ashamed, for in You have we put our trust" and "In You I trust, may I not be disappointed"). The benediction at the end comes from *Midrash Tehillim* [the *Midrash* on Psalms] 29:2.

Blessing 14: The Rebuilding of Jerusalem as an Eternal "Structure of the World"

V'li'Yerushalayim ir'cha b'rachamim tashuv v'tishkon b'tocha ka'asher dibarta

And to Jerusalem, Your city, may You return in mercy and dwell in its midst as You said You would

The theme of the second half of the middle blessings is emerging: getting the Jewish people back together, and keeping them together. Once the Jews are returned from Exile, once they have a just administration and the requisite cohesiveness and unity of purpose, then Jerusalem will be rebuilt as the eternal capital of the Jewish people.

The prophet Zechariah, during Babylonian Exile before the building of the Second Temple, predicted the rebuilding of Jerusalem in many of the same words employed in Blessing 14 of the weekday *Amida:* "Thus said the Lord: 'I have returned to Zion, and I will dwell in Jerusalem'" (Zech. 8:3).

Why pray for the rebuilding of Jerusalem today, when Jerusalem has already been rebuilt? Viewed in the broader context of Blessings 10 to 13, the key phrase of Blessing 14 is *binyan olam,* which can mean "eternal structure" or "structure of the world." Jerusalem should be rebuilt—not just as a city, but as an "eternal structure" or a "structure of the world." We pray not for the rebuilding of the physical Jerusalem, but the rebuilding of the "eternal" Jerusalem, a nexus that will bind together the Jewish people forever, and become the hub of a world structure of peace under God's dominion.

Why does the first word of this blessing begin with a *vav* (Hebrew for "and")? This appears to have resulted from a medieval clerical error. The earliest version, in the *Seder Rav Amram,* began: *Al Y'rushalayim* (upon Jerusalem). The first letter, *ayin,* of the word *Al* was inadvertently changed to a *vav* in subsequent versions. This error was facilitated by the fact that medieval manuscripts did not include spaces between words.

On the Ninth of Av, the fast day that commemorates the fall of the First Temple in 586 B.C.E., two passages are added to this blessing in some congregations. One, beginning *Racheim, Adonai Eloheinu, al Yisrael amecha* (Have mercy, God, on Your nation Israel), from the Jerusalem Talmud (*Y. Ber* 4:3, 8a), may have been the original form of Blessing 14.[365] It was substituted in a modified form for Blessing 14 by Maimonides, and is echoed in the Grace After Meals (*Birkat Ha'Mazon*). It is recited in some synagogues in the morning and evening services. The other, beginning *Nacheim, Adonai Eloheinu, et avlei-tzion,* (Console, Lord our God, the mourners of Zion), originated with the tenth-century scholar Saadya Gaon, who prescribed it only for the afternoon service.

Blessing 15: Flourishing of the Jewish Nation

Et tzemach David av'd'cha m'heyra tatz'miach
Let the offspring of David, Your servant, quickly flourish

The Jewish people having been restored to Israel under their own government, with unity of spirit and with Jerusalem rebuilt as the eternal "structure of the world," the *Amida* now places the finishing touch on its vision: The Jewish nation flourishes. The Jewish nation regains the power that it briefly enjoyed during the reign of King David. Moreover, God enhances the power of the nation with His "salvation that we daily hope for."

The language of Blessing 15 is derived from Psalms 132:17: "There [in Zion] I will make a horn sprout for David." The Hebrew word for "sprout" or "offspring" and the Hebrew word for "flourish" come from the same root, *tzemach*. This root normally refers to the sprouts or seeds of plants; here it connotes multiplication. The "offspring of David," the Jewish nation, will multiply and become powerful, with the help of God.

The references to David may have to do with the fact that the Babylonian Exilarch, the head to the government of the Jewish community in Babylonia from the third of the eleventh centuries, was said to be descended from King David. This blessing may have been added to counter the rising tide of Christianity by reinforcing the Jewish belief that the Messianic Age was yet to come. The blessing nowhere mentions the Messiah, although the "offspring of David" may have been intended as a Messianic reference, since the Messiah was to be a descendant of King David. Another theory is that this blessing dates from before the destruction of the Second Temple, and was written in the time of Herod in opposition to the Hasmoneans, a priestly line of rulers who represented a break in the Davidic line.[366]

Because the *Amida* originally had eighteen blessings, it is also called the *Shemoneh Esrei* (Hebrew for "eighteen"). Blessing 12, *Birkat Ha'Minim,*was added later as a nineteenth blessing. When this occurred, Blessing 15 was combined for a time with the preceding blessing to preserve the number of eighteen blessings, and it therefore is altered or missing in some early versions.[367]

Blessing 16: Praying for God to Listen to Our Requests

Shema koleinu Adonai Eloheinu, chus v'racheim aleinu v'kabel
    b'rachamim u'v'ratzon et-t'filateinu
Listen to our voice, Lord our God, have pity and compassion upon us,
    and accept our prayers in mercy and with favor

Blessing 16 is the last of the middle blessings of the weekday *Amida.* We have finished our requests, save one: the request that God listen to us and accept our prayers. Everything else we have prayed for is useless if this final request is not granted. The consummate importance of this request is demonstrated by the fact that the Babylonian Talmud gives this blessing the same name—the *Tefilla*—that given to the entire *Amida*. It also is shown by the fact that the same request, though in a different form, is the only request we make of God on *Shabbat*.

The request that God accept our prayers is derived from the *Targum*, the second-century translation of the Torah into Aramaic. In Deuteronomy 26, Moses instructs the Jews to take the first fruits to the Temple every year and to recite, briefly, the story of the Exodus from Egypt while the fruits are placed on the altar. Part of the story to be told is how the Jews, oppressed by the Egyptians, "cried to the Lord . . . and the Lord heard our plea and saw our plight . . . [and] freed us from Egypt by a mighty hand, by an outstretched arm and awesome power, and by signs and portents . . . [and] brought us to . . . a land flowing with milk and honey." The *Targum* translated "and the Lord heard our plea" (Deut. 26:7) as "and the Lord accepted our prayers," and this language was incorporated into Blessing 16.

Since ancient times, Blessing 16 has been a place where it is permissible to insert private petitions during the silent recitation of the *Amida*.[369] This may be owing to (or may be the cause of) the reference in the blessing to supplications, *tachanunim*, which are private prayers that follow the *Amida*. The kabbalists formulated elaborate private petitions for use at this point, and it became the place where it was acceptable for a worshipper who had omitted additions for particular days, such a *Havdala*, to insert them. On fast days, a penitential petition to God to "answer us on the day of our fasting," beginning *Aneinu, Adonai, aneinu*, came to be inserted here, presumably because of the similarity of the theme.

The Concluding Blessings of the Amida

Blessing 17 (on Shabbat and Festivals, Blessing 5): Avoda

R'tzei Adonai Eloheinu b'amcha Yisrael uvi't'fillatam
Be favorable, Adonai our God, toward Your people Israel and their prayer

According to the Talmud, in the last three blessings of the *Amida*, we are like a servant taking leave of the king who has just given him a gift.[370] Actually, the first of the three, called *Avoda* (the name of the climactic part of the ancient Temple Service) and beginning *R'tzei*, is a further request— that God accept our prayers and restore sacrificial worship in Jerusalem. Some of this paragraph is taken from the original *Avoda*, the petition that was recited by the priests in the Temple while sacrifices were offered; the remainder was modified to reflect that the Temple no longer existed.[371]

Blessing 18: Thanksgiving (Hoda'ah)

Modim anachnu lach
We give thanks [pay tribute] to You

The next blessing *Hoda'ah* (Thanksgiving), was the last part of the *Amida* in ancient times, and, like *Avoda* it was part of the ancient Temple service.[372] It begins *Modim anachnu lach* (We give thanks to You), a biblical phrase from 1 Chronicles 29:13.[373] (The word *Modim* comes from the same Hebrew root as *Hoda'ah*, and also means "to pay tribute.") In the Temple service, *Modim* was recited by the priest after the sacrifice while the congregation prostrated itself, in the manner of a servant bowing to a king while taking his leave to say thank you for favors granted, thus, the custom of bowing at the beginning and the end of this blessing.[374] In the same manner as telling someone, "Thank you in advance," we hope that this expression of gratitude for the granting the requests we have just made—which, of course, have not really been granted yet—will act as a self-fulfilling prophecy and convince God that we deserve to have them granted.

In the Amoraic period (when the Gemara was written, circa 220–500 C.E.), the custom arose in Babylonia that while the *chazan* read *Modim* during the repetition of the *Amida*, the congregation would silently read additional material written by leading rabbis. Various rabbis, most prominently Rav, recommended different sentences for the congregation to read, and they ultimately were put together as *Modim D'Rabbanan* (*Modim* of the Scholars).[375]

The Talmud dictated that special prayers, beginning *Al Ha'Nissim* (On the miracles), be added after the *Modim* on *Chanuka* and *Purim* to thank God for the miracles celebrated on those holidays.[376] These prayers were lengthy and originally included the request that God perform miracles for us as He did our ancestors, a request that the Tosafists, the students of Rashi, considered out of place in the blessings of thanksgiving.[377] An analogous set of requests for God's mercy was inserted in this location for the High-Holiday *Amida*.[378]

Because of the long interruption of *Al Ha'Nissim* and its harkening back to requests otherwise confined to the middle blessings, it was felt necessary to return to the theme of thanksgiving before proceeding further. Therefore, two short sections were added at the end of the *Hoda'ah*, beginning with *V'al kulam* (And for all of them) and *V'chol ha-chayim* (And all the living), which summarize the contents of *Modim*.[379]

Blessing 19: Birkat Kohanim: *Blessing of the Priests (also called* Birkat Shalom, *Blessing of Peace)*

The Priestly Blessing

Eloheinu v'Elohei avoteinu, hu y'varech aleinu ba'b'racha ha'm 'shuleshet
Our God and God of our fathers, He will bless us with the three-part blessing

The final blessing of the *Amida* is called *Birkat Shalom,* the Blessing of Peace. When the *Amida* is recited aloud as a public prayer, this blessing begins with the three-part Priestly Blessing (*Birkat Kohanim*) commanded by God in Numbers 6:24–26 to be recited by Aaron and his sons to bless the children of Israel. The Priestly Blessing is omitted when the *Amida* is said silently.

The Priestly Blessing was one of the most impressive features of the Temple service in Jerusalem, where it was recited by the *Kohanim* (priests) from a special platform (in Hebrew, *duchan*; thus, it is called "duchaning" in its formal form). It was recited after the daily morning and evening sacrifices and at noon during the additional (*Musaf*) service. On fast days and during the services of *ma'amadot* (delegations of laypeople sent to watch and monitor the sacrifices), it was also said toward evening at the time of the Locking of the Gates.[380] It did not originally have any connection to the *Amida*.[381]

The Torah makes it clear that it is really God, not the priests, blessing the congregation. God said: "So shall they put My name upon the children of Israel, and I will bless them" (Num. 6:27). The priests were "merely the channel through which the blessing was conveyed to the Israelites."[382]

This notion of priests as a channel for God's blessings is really foreign to Judaism, in which each worshipper is supposed to stand on an equal footing before God and have a direct relationship with Him. It reflects the fact that the Priestly Blessing is the most ancient of all our prayers, and conceivably could have been derived by the Jews from an ancient Canaanite incantation. Although the Torah indicates that it was to be recited to a group, it is worded entirely in the second-person singular, suggesting that it originally was used as an incantation recited by a priest to a single person, perhaps for healing[383] or ritual purification purposes.

The *Kohanim* would stand with their "hands lifted" so as to emulate Aaron at the dedication of the Tent of Meeting (Lev. 9:22). The words "So shall they put My name upon the children of Israel" were taken as an instruction from God to utter His name, the tetragrammaton, in the Temple when saying the blessing.

As synagogue worship developed prior to the destruction of the Second Temple, the Priestly Blessing came to be performed in the synagogues, but the ritual varied slightly from the Temple ritual so as to draw a distinction between them.[384] In the Temple, the Priestly Blessing was recited without interruption, while in the synagogues it was recited as three blessings punctuated by the congregation's response, Amen.[385] In the Temple, the name of God, the tetragrammaton, was used, but outside it was not.[386] In the Temple, the priests would lift their hands to the level of their heads, while in the synagogues they would lift them only to the level of their shoulders.[387]

Soon after the destruction of the Second Temple, the Priestly Blessing was incorporated into the *Amida*.[388] The rabbis, particularly Yohanan ben Zakkai, set new requirements for the *Kohanim* (who could no longer be Temple priests and were not always prayer leaders anymore) so as to emulate the conditions that had pertained in the Temple. For example, the *Kohanim* were required to remove their shoes and wash their hands before the blessing, to say a special blessing over the performance of the command-ment, and to say silent prayers while going up to say the blessing and while returning to their places.[389] In the Temple, the *Kohanim* had been regarded as purified by the sacrificial offering they had just given; without the offering, a new means of purification was required. The practices also arose of having the *Kohanim* spread their fingers when reciting the blessing,[390] and of having the congregation stand facing them, but not looking at them, while the blessing was being recited.[391]

Also at this time, it became customary for the prayer leader to say the blessing aloud before the *Kohanim* began.[392] This was another logical development, as generations of *Kohanim* ceased to be trained Temple priests and became ordinary, no doubt sometimes illiterate, congregants who might not know when to rise to say the blessing, or how to say it.

Since the congregation did not want to be idle while the *Kohanim* went up, said the blessing, and sat down, certain verses were designated for the worshippers to recite during the blessing apart from the response, Amen.[393] The congregation was supposed to say them only while the *chazan* said the blessings, and to be silent while the *Kohanim* recited them. Unfortunately, the number of these verses got out of hand, to the point where the hubbub drowned out the words of the blessing.[394] Later, under kabbalistic influ-ence, a longer prayer, beginning *Y'hi Ratzon* (May it be Your will), was appended to the blessing.[395] Eventually, these chaotic practices gave way to the simple congregational response, *Kein Y'hi Ratzon* (Thus may it be Your will) to each of the thee parts of the blessing when the *chazan* says it. When *Kohanim* say the blessing, the congregation responds Amen, as in antiquity.

Sim Shalom: The Peace Blessing

Sim shalom, tova u'v'racha
Grant peace, goodness, and blessing

We end the mental journey of the *Amida* with a vision of peace.

The Priestly Blessing ends, *V'yasem l'cha shalom*, a prayer to "grant you peace." *Sim Shalom* (Grant Peace) follows these words. *Sim Shalom* was the ancient response of the congregation to the Priestly Blessing in the Second Temple, where the *Kohanim* did not pause between each of the three parts, as in synagogue worship. With some expansions, it was included in the ninth-century prayer code. *Seder Rav Amram*, and has been essentially unchanged since then.

When the Priestly Blessing is not recited, as in the evening service, *Shalom Rav* (Great Peace), a prayer that originated in eleventh-century Germany, is said by Ashkenazim instead of *Sim Shalom*.[396]

Although the repetition of the *Amida* ends with *Sim Shalom*, the congregation, in reading it silently, adds a prayer: *Elohai n'tzor l'shoni mi'ra* (My God, protect my tongue from evil). This remarkable piece was the private meditation of Mar ben Ravina, one of the Amoraim in Babylonia in the fifth century C.E.[397] Just as we gradually reach the proper frame of mind to connect with God in the *Amida*, we do not abruptly leave that frame of mind when it ends.

Rabbi Yohanan ben Zakkai (first century C.E.) believed that the *Amida* should begin and end with a biblical verse.[398] Accordingly, Psalms 19:15, "May the words of my mouth and the meditations of my heart be acceptable to You," was added at the end, and *Adonai s'fatai tiftach u'fi yagid t'hilatecha*, a Torah verse, was added at the beginning. Perhaps to preserve the theme of peace at the end of the *Amida*, it has been the practice since Rashi's day to close with *Oseh shalom bim'romav* (He Who establishes peace in the heavens), based on Job 25:2.[399]

While the meditation of Mar ben Ravina is beautiful, it also occupies space once dedicated to personal meditations and supplications. This meditation is not part of the *Amida*, and need not be recited. Personal prayer, in one's own words and articulating one's own thoughts, would be more consistent with ancient practice.

This substitution of Mar's meditation for personal prayer exemplifies an unfortunate tendency in Jewish liturgy. What originally were moments of clarity meant for silent meditation and visualization have, over the past two millennia, been scribbled over with prescribed words. Students in the Babylonian religious academies in the early medieval period probably started the trend. In the belief that the prayers of great scholars would be more effective than their own, they stopped meditating and began to copy the prayers of the leading scholars of the academies wherever no words were prescribed. This trend accelerated in the Middle Ages, when the German mystics, among others, taught that longer prayers—more words—would be more effective than short ones.

It is a challenge for modern Jews to peel off the layers of two thousand years of rules and words and to behold the silent core of prayer: collective spiritual transformation.

HIGH-HOLIDAY ADDITIONS TO THE *AMIDA*: AN EMERGENCY PRAYER REGIMEN TO SAVE THE JEWISH PEOPLE

The *Amida* said on the High Holidays is vastly expanded. Much of the increased length of the service is due to additions to the *Amida*. While some of the additions reflect the special purpose of the holiday, many, particularly *piyyutim* (poetic hymns), are inserted for no other reason than to make the service longer. The rabbis lengthened the service, particularly on *Yom Kippur*, so that worshippers would be compelled to elevate themselves above their daily routine and spend the entire day in prayer and meditation.[400] This was done for the High Holidays and not for *Shabbat* because of the urgency of repenting in time to be written and sealed in the Book of Life for the next year; the rabbis created an emergency regimen to save their congregants.

Most, if not all, of the *piyyutim* were written between the destruction of the Second Temple in 70 C.E. and the expulsion of the Jews from Spain in 1492. Many of the *piyyutim* added to the High-Holiday service are early *piyyutim* called *kerovot*, from the Hebrew root *k'rav* (to draw near), so named, according to a leading scholar, Ismar Elbogen, because they were recited by a prayer leader called the *karov* who led the reading of the *Amida* as he "drew near" to the Ark.[401]

What follows is not a comprehensive discussion of the High-Holiday liturgy. Such a discussion would occupy another book. However, it does highlight the key additions to the *Amida*, particularly the *Musaf Amida*. These are the most important liturgical additions to the traditional High-Holiday service.[402] The High-Holiday liturgy is greatly modified in the Reform movement. Unfortunately, an adequate explanation of these modifications is beyond the scope of this book.

Hineni (Here I Am)

Perhaps the most dramatic prayer in the High-Holiday liturgy is *Hineni*, which the *chazan* sings before beginning the repetition of the *Musaf Amida*.

The custom is for the *chazan* to start at the back of the sanctuary and to walk forward while chanting the prayer until he reaches the *bima* (podium) at the front.

Hineni originated in Europe in the Middle Ages.[403] It is the *chazan's* plea to God not to hold the *chazan's* sins against the congregants whom he represents as *shaliach tzibur* (community representative). The *chazan* is approaching God on behalf of the community; that is why he walks forward as he recites *Hineni*.

Why is the *chazan* concerned about his sins being held against the congregation? Doesn't each Jew have his or her own direct relationship to God? The *chazan's* recital of *Hineni*, though addressed to God, is in the nature of a request for the congregation's permission to approach God on its behalf. He is leading the repetition of the *Amida* because the congregation permits him to do so, and because some members of the congregation are unable to recite the *Amida* themselves. The *chazan* pleads with God not to hold his sins against the congregation as a public showing of humility, so that the congregation will feel more comfortable having him as its representative.

Piyyutim Added to the *Avot* and *Gevurot: Zachreinu L'Chaim* and *U'N'taneh Tokef*

The first *piyyut* is inserted in the *Avot* blessing and begins *Zachreinu l'Chaim* (Remember Us for Life). This is probably a very early *piyyut* that originated in ancient Israel but was not inserted in the High-Holiday service until the ninth century.[404] It is out of place in *Avot*, because it contains a petition to God that would have been appropriate for the middle blessings.[405]

Perhaps the most notable of the *piyyutim* is *U'N'Taneh Tokef*, recited between *Gevurot* and *Kedusha* during the repetition of the *Musaf Amida*. This prayer expresses in simple but beautiful words the basic idea of the High-Holidays: that repentance, prayer, and charity "avert the severe decree," and that God grants forgiveness to man, whose life is like "a fleeting shadow, . . . a passing cloud . . . and as a dream that vanishes." It was derived from a very early prayer of ancient Israel but was arranged in its present form by Kalonymus ben Meshullam Kalonymus, an eleventh-century *paytan* (hymn-writer) of Mayence.[406]

Legend has it that the tenth-century martyr Rabbi Amon of Mainz, having been brutally tortured following his refusal to convert to Christianity, was carried into the synagogue on *Rosh Ha'Shana* as *Kedusha* was about to be chanted. He asked the *chazan* to wait while he sanctified God's name by saying *U'N'taneh Tokef*, and then he died.[407] This legend explains the placement of *U'N'taneh Tokef* immediately before *Kedusha* in the *Musaf Amida* on the High Holidays.

The Special Middle Blessings—*Malchuyot, Zichronot*, and *Shofarot*: Our Requests of God on *Rosh HaShana*

In the *Amida* on *Rosh Ha'Shana*, three special middle blessings are substituted for the usual ones, making a total of nine blessings. These special blessings are called *Malchuyot* (Kingship Verses), proclamations of God's power and authority; *Zichronot* (Remembrance Verses), proclamations that God remembers our deeds and rewards or punishes them; and *Shofarot* (Shofar Verses), proclamations that God reveals and redeems as He did at Mount Sinai to the sound of the *shofar*.

These three blessings are separated on *Rosh HaShana* by the sounding of the *shofar*. Ismar Elbogen theorized that, originally, in the Second Temple, the *shofar* was blown early in the morning during *Shacharit*. Once, however, the Romans interpreted these sounds as a call to rebellion, fell upon the Jews, and massacred them.[408] Thereafter, the blowing of the shofar was moved to the *Musaf* service, because by that late hour there could be no doubt about its festive nature.[409] Forcing worshippers to wait for *Musaf* before hearing the *shofar* blown was not desirable, however, so later on, when the Roman oppression of the Jews was temporarily eased, the early sounding of the *shofar* was restored. By that time the blowing of the shofar during *Musaf* had gained acceptance, so it was left in.[410]

Each of the special *Rosh HaShana* middle blessings consists of ten sentences—three from the Torah, three from the Writings, three from the Prophets, and a closing verse from the Torah.[411] These verses were prescribed in a book of the *Mishna* called *Mishna Rosh HaShana*.[412] They were carefully chosen, although the rabbis disagreed on their order, specifically on the placement of the *Malchuyot*,[413] and did not reach a consensus until the Restoration period (circa 140 C.E.). For example, no verse threatening punishment was permitted, owing to the penitential nature of the holiday.[414]

The requests contained in these three special middle blessings are set forth in *Zichronot* and *Shofarot*. The first of the three, *Malchuyot*, is really an additional blessing of praise, while *Zichronot* makes a transition from praise to requests. In *Zichronot* we beg God to remember the good deeds of the Patriarchs, particularly the *Akeida* (the binding of Isaac). In essence, we are saying that even though we may not be worthy of favor based on our deeds of the past year, God should forgive us because of the good deeds of our ancestors. In *Shofarot* we describe the events that took place at Mount Sinai to the sound of the *shofar*, and ask God to make those events happen again to us.

In Galilee, in the second century C.E., *Malchuyot* was treated as part of *Kedusha* (the third blessing) rather than as a separate blessing. In southern Israel it was attached to the fourth blessing, while elsewhere *Zichronot* was attached to *Kedusha*.[415] Later this practice changed, and each of the three special middle blessings was given an introduction and a conclusion in the form of *piyyutim* ascribed to Rav, a Babylonian Jewish scholar who lived in the late second and early third centuries C.E.[416] Each *piyyut* corresponds to the theme of the blessing it accompanies. However, vestiges of the ancient practice of including *Zichronot* in *Kedusha* remain, including *U'V'Chein Tein Pach'd'cha, U'v'chein tein kavod,* and *U'v'chein tzaddikim.*[417]

Aleinu (It Is Our Duty) and *V'Al Kein N'Kaveh* precede *Malchuyot*. *Aleinu* originated as a hymn that introduced *Malchuyot* on the High Holidays, but later became a regular part of the daily and *Shabbat* services as well.[418]

A *piyyut* called *Ata Zocher* (You Remember) introduces *Zichronot;* another, *Ata Nigleita,* precedes *Shofarot.*[419]

The *Avoda* Service

The word *avoda* has two meanings in Hebrew: "prayer service" and "work." For Jews, worshipping God is hard work. Only by making the necessary effort can one achieve the required frame of mind to merit God's attention.

The *Avoda* service recited on *Yom Kippur* during the repetition of the *Musaf Amida* is a description of the sacrificial rite of the same name that was observed in the Second Temple. It differs from the *Avoda* blessing normally recited as the first of the three concluding blessings of the *Amida*. This is because, in the Second Temple ritual, on *Yom Kippur* the High Priest alone would perform the sacrifice and all attendant duties, including prayer, reading the Torah, and confession of sins.[420] *Yom Kippur* also was the only day on which the High Priest entered the Holy of Holies.

The *Avoda* service recited on *Yom Kippur* dates back at least to the fourth century C.E.[421] Originally it followed the text of the *Mishna,* reproducing its account of the order of confessions and sacrifices. Later, it was a popular subject for poets, who embellished the mishnaic account in a variety of ways; numerous versions of the *Avoda* evolved.[422] Although the *Avoda* is said before the conclusion of the middle blessing of the *Musaf Amida* on *Yom Kippur,* it has no internal connection with the rest of the *Amida.*[423] As the Temple was the symbol of independence and the seat of power in ancient Israel, this harkening back to the Second-Temple ritual expresses not merely spiritual nostalgia, but a longing for the restoration of the freedom of the Jewish people. It was also a brave assertion, in the time of the Roman and Byzantine persecutions of the Jews and the rise of Christianity, that, rather than having become moot through the coming of Jesus, the Mosaic law lives on.

SELICHOT: FORGIVENESS THROUGH PRAYER

The *Selichot* prayers are what replaced sacrifices after the fall of the Second Temple as a means of requesting forgiveness for sins. The word *selicha*, which literally means "forgiveness," is used in the singular to refer to a *piyyut* (poetic hymn) whose subject is a plea for forgiveness for sins. *Selichot*, the plural form, refers to a special order of service consisting of additional prayers for forgiveness originally recited on all fast days, including *Yom Kippur, Tisha B'Av*, and the Fast of Esther. *Selichot* later came to be said during the High Holidays from the Sunday before *Rosh Ha'Shana* to *Yom Kippur*.[424]

The central prayer of all *Selichot* services is a biblical verse, the Thirteen Attributes of God (beginning *Adonai, Adonai, El rachum v'chanun*). All *Selichot* services also must include *Vidui* (Confession of Sins).[425] The poetic additions to these verses are grouped in numerous categories, by content and form, and traditions developed by which the categories were required to follow a particular order depending on the occasion.[426]

Selichot apparently were recited on each first day at the Second Temple. They continued to be recited after the fall of the Temple at the urging of Rabbi Yochanan ben Zakkai. The fact that Moses achieved God's forgiveness for the people of Israel at Mount Sinai through prayer, without sacrificing animals, was viewed by the rabbis as proof that the Mosaic law could survive without the Temple, through the medium of prayer. In saying *Selichot* we not only pray for forgiveness, but give testimony to the efficacy of prayer itself.

Some scholars have theorized that *Selichot* actually originated as a prayer for public emergencies. Public fasts were usually proclaimed in mishnaic times during periods of drought.[427] The High Holidays come at a season when, in Israel, rain is critical for the crops that are soon to be harvested. It became customary to read verses from the Bible containing confessions, and these verses came to be called *Selichot*.[428]

Later, the *Selichot* service was embellished with poetic hymns on subjects appropriate to prayers for forgiveness, such as the description of sin, the weakness of man and the transience of life, the vanished glories of the past, oppression and persecution, petition for God's mercy, and requests for redemption of the Jews and the punishment of oppressors.[429] It became customary to write new hymns to commemorate tragedies, such as massacres and expulsions, suffered by the Jewish community. These poetic insertions were placed between the traditional biblical verses and litanies, which were divided into groups.[430]

Selichot came to be said on the High Holidays because of the custom of fasting on the days before *Rosh Ha'Shana*. *Selichot* were said because of the fast, and the custom of saying *Selichot* was later extended through the Ten Days of Repentance to *Yom Kippur*.[431]

Conflicting customs developed regarding when in the service *Selichot* should be recited. In Israel, long poetic hymns called *kerovot* were used on fast days. In the *Mishna* and in Babylonia, however, *Selichot*, which were shorter, were prescribed, and the custom was adopted in the *Mishna* to insert them into the sixth blessing of the *Amida*.[432]

The Thirteen Attributes of God:
Biblical Proof That Prayer Works as Well as Sacrifices

This passage, beginning with *Adonai, Adonai, El rachum v'chanun*, is the central prayer of *Selichot*. It recounts what God said to Moses on top of Mount Sinai, when God gave Moses the Ten Commandments for the second time (Moses had broken the tablets the first time, upon finding the Jews worshipping the Golden Calf). God described Himself to Moses as follows: "The Lord, the Lord, merciful and gracious God, long-suffering, and abundant in goodness and truth; keeping mercy unto the thousandth generation, forgiving iniquity and transgression and sin; and not allowing the guilty to go unpunished; visiting the iniquity of the fathers upon the children, and upon the children's children, to the third and fourth generations."

In other words, God rewards even our remotest descendants for our good deeds by forgiving them their sins, and He rewards us for the good deeds of our remotest ancestors, Abraham, Isaac, and Jacob, by forgiving us our sins.

Rabbi Yochanan ben Zakkai, one of the leading rabbis when the Second Temple was destroyed, cited a Torah passage, Exodus 34:6, as support for the concept that prayers could accomplish the same purpose as sacrifices. Dramatizing the point, he said that at Mount Sinai God "descended from the mist like a *shaliach tzibur*, enveloped in his *tallit*, and stood before the Ark and revealed to Moses the order of *Selichot*.[433]

Significantly, for Rabbi Yochanan's point, Moses responded by bowing and praying to God to forgive the Jews for the Golden Calf incident, and He did so, reestablishing the covenant between God and Israel that had been annulled by the apostasy in connection with the Golden Calf.[434] In other words, when Moses wanted God to forgive the people of Israel, he did not sacrifice animals; he prayed, and it worked. The message of this prayer for Jews in the first century c.e., when the Temple had been destroyed, was: "Don't fear: Even if you can't offer sacrifices anymore, you can pray, and it will work just as well."

Because the Thirteen Attributes passage begins with an excerpt from the Torah, an introduction was provided for it in the fifth or sixth century c.e. that explains its purpose, beginning *El erech apayim ata*.

Eileh Ezkera (Martyrology): Remembrance of the Sacrifices Made by Our Ancestors in the Name of God and the Jewish People

The Martyrology is the portion of *Selichot* into which the poetic works commemorating tragedies that befell the Jewish people, called *gezerot*, were inserted.

The traditional focus of the Martyrology, in the Ashkenazic liturgy, is a poem attributed to Rabbi Yehuda[435] titled *Eleih Ezkera* (These I Remember).[436] *Eileh Ezkera* contains a graphic account of the slaying of the Ten Martyrs—leading talmudic rabbis, including Rabbi Akiva, who defied the Roman decree banning the teaching of the Torah and were brutally murdered during the Hadrianic persecutions following the end of the Bar Kochba Revolt in 135 c.e. This *piyyut* is based on midrashic stories that date from Geonic times (the first millennium c.e. in Babylonia). According to the story, the Roman emperor condemned the ten rabbis to death on account of the ten sons of Jacob who sold their brother Joseph into slavery and were never punished for it. One of the rabbis ascended to heaven and learned that the decree had been irrevocably sealed, so the ten sages accepted their fate.[437] The legend has mystical overtones and served as a model for Jewish martyrs in the Middle Ages, especially at the time of the First Crusade.[438]

Owing to the nineteenth-century Russian pogroms and the Holocaust, the Martyrology segment has been modified in the Conservative movement. Most of *Eileh Ezkera* is missing from the Conservative *machzor* (High-Holiday prayerbook), but it includes Chaim Nachman Bialik's poem "City of Slaughter," commemorating the Kishinev Pogrom of 1903. The martyrs of the Holocaust are commemorated with poems and recitation of the Mourner's *Kaddish*, interspersed with the names of concentration camps and other places where they were killed.

These are by no means all the poetic *Selichot* commemorating disasters that befell the Jewish people. They are as voluminous as the disasters themselves. Individual communities can, and often do, say special *Selichot* for tragedies that affected them in particular.

Shema Koleinu: A Plea to God to Hear Our Prayer for Redemption

The Martyrology segment is a digression from the recitation of selected biblical passages that were in the original *Selichot.* These passages resume in the paragraph beginning *Z'char lanu b'rit.*[439] They invoke God's covenant with our ancestors in pleading with Him for redemption from our sins.

Shema Koleinu follows. This prayer is derived from the prayer of the High Priest in the Second Temple on *Yom Kippur,* when he would enter the Holy of Holies. The first two verses are the same as those that begin the sixteenth benediction of the weekday *Amida.* This is the blessing that pleads for acceptance of our requests to God. When the *Amida* was edited and its text fixed by Shimon Ha'Pakuli, at the behest of Rabban Gamaliel II, in Yavneh shortly after the destruction of the Second Temple by the Romans in 70 C.E., the text of this blessing, beyond the first two verses, was left open for the worshipper to make his or her private requests of God.

In times of public emergency, however, the requests of the community must take precedence over individual requests. The *Selichot* service consists of what were originally the prayers recited at times of public emergency, and the insertions in the *Amida* for *Yom Kippur* are largely taken from the *Selichot* service, since *Yom Kippur* is considered a time of public emergency, the community's last chance for forgiveness. Accordingly, the version of *Shema Koleinu* that appears in the liturgy for *Selichot* and *Yom Kippur* includes biblical passages that were originally in the first person, such as Palms 19:15 (May the words of my mouth and the meditations of my heart be acceptable to You), but in the prayer appear in the first-person plural because they are being said by the entire community together. It is the community that is pleading for forgiveness, not merely one individual.

In the Polish tradition, *Shema Koleinu* is followed by a series of *piyyutim, Al Ta'azeinu* and *S'lach Lanu,* which beautifully express the urgency of the occasion.

Vidui: Communal Confessions of Our Sins

Maimonides taught, consistent with talmudic sources, that one cannot seek forgiveness for one's sins until one confesses having committed them.[440] Therefore, on *Yom Kippur,* both the silent *Amida* and the *Amida,* in every service, include several prayers which are communal confessions of sins written in the first-person plural. This is an expression of the concept of collective responsibility, we acknowledge that "we," not merely "I," have sinned.[441] In biblical terms, we are our brothers' (and sisters') keepers.

These *Yom Kippur* confessions, added at the end of the *Amida,* are called *Vidui* (Confession of Sins). The central confessions are the *Ashamnu* (We are guilty), also called the *Vidui Katan* (Little Confession), and *Al Cheit*

She'Chatanu (On the Sin we committed), also called *Vidui Gadol* (Great Confession).[442] *Ashamnu* probably was put into its present form in the late Amoraic period (fifth century C.E.).[443] It consists of twenty-four or more words in alphabetical order, the last letter of the Hebrew alphabet being repeated three times.[444] *Ashamnu*, in the first-person singular, is also used as a confession at the approach of death, and by the bridegroom and bride before their wedding, which is considered as a kind of judgment day.[445]

Al Cheit is a longer alphabetical list of sins. Its origins are unknown, but traces of it can be found in a second-century Christian prayer, suggesting that some form of it dates from that period.[446] The number of sins in the list gradually expanded, from six in the seventh century, to eight in the ninth century, to twenty-two in the Ashkenazic service today.[447] It is customary to beat one's breast at the mention of each sin.

The types of sins listed in *Al Cheit* are noteworthy for their universality. Murder, robbery, rape, and arson are not on the list. Rather, the sins are those that we all commit or of which we all tolerate the commission, and for which we bear collective responsibility.[448]

Preceding *Vidui* is an introduction, *Tavo l'fanecha t'filateinu* (Hear our prayer). At the end of this introduction are the words *Aval anachnu chatanu* (Indeed we have sinned). The confession was originally just a few words; according to the *Mishna*, the High Priest's confession described in Leviticus 16:21 consisted of three: *Chatanu, avinu, peshanu* (I have erred, I have sinned, I have transgressed).[449] The words *Aval anachnu chatanu* were originally the core of the confession for the common people, but were expanded upon greatly in the post-talmudic period.[450]

Avinu Malkeinu: Adding Extra Power to the *Amida* in a Time of Public Emergency

After the *Amida* has been concluded on *Yom Kippur*, we recite *Avinu Malkeinu* (Our Father, Our King). This part of the service normally is set aside for private prayer in which we direct our personal pleas to God; however, on *Yom Kippur* we relinquish some of our time for private prayer in favor of reciting a communal prayer designed to magnify the power of the *Amida*.

Rabbi Akiva first used this prayer format in a five-line prayer he prepared for a special emergency service that he held in a time of drought. The Talmud tells us that his prayer bore immediate results: It rained.[451] Rabbi Akiva's five lines still form the kernel of *Avinu Malkeinu*.

As *Avinu Malkeinu* evolved, a conscious effort was made to use it to embellish the various blessings of the *Amida*. If the usual *Amida* by itself didn't persuade God to forgive us and extend our lives, then articulating the same ideas in a format that worked for Rabbi Akiva perhaps would work for us.

Thus, a close reading of *Avinu Malkeinu* discloses a parallelism between it and the weekday *Amida*.[452] For example, *Choneinu va'aneinu* (Favor us) in the refrain corresponds in the *Amida* to the blessing *Ata chonein* (You favor man). The second line, *Ein lanu melech ela ata* (We have no King but You), corresponds to part of the first blessing of the *Amida, Melech ozer* (A King Who helps). The fourth line, *Chadesh aleinu shana tova* (Renew for us a good year), corresponds to part of the ninth blessing of the *Amida, Barech aleinu . . . et ha'shana ha'zot . . . l'tova* (Bless this year to us . . . for good). The eleventh line, *Sh'lach r'fu'ah sh'leima* (Send perfect healing) corresponds precisely to a portion of the eighth blessing of the *Amida, V'ha'aleh r'fu'ah sh'leima.*

TACHANUN (SUPPLICATIONS): ON WEEKDAYS, WE PLEAD WITH GOD PRIVATELY, IN SILENCE, TO GRANT OUR INDIVIDUAL REQUESTS

The middle blessings of the *Amida* are an occasion for the community to plead with God to grant our personal redemption and national renewal. However, each worshipper has a plethora of individual needs, too.

Tachanun (Supplications) is a time immediately following the *Amida* when we pray silently and privately, our faces down on our forearms, asking God to grant our individual requests. This is a chance to pray spontaneously, without following a script, to talk to God directly about the most personal and pressing matters. *Tachanun* is our most intimate moment with God.

This custom began in the Second-Temple service. After the daily sacrifice, the Levites would sing psalms. At the end of each section, the *shofar* was blown and the people present would prostrate themselves. They would "fall on their faces" several times, and again after the Priestly Blessing. While prostrate, the worshippers would address their private prayers to God.[453]

This custom was transferred to the synagogue after the destruction of the Second Temple in 70 C.E. The private prayers came to be called *d'varim* (words), and they could be of any length.[454] There was no formula for these prayers. This was the primary occasion in the prayer service for each individual to meditate and to commune with God personally. Having fulfilled one's obligation of communal prayer, it was now time for the individual to indulge his or her own needs and desires in prayer. However, these individual prayers were regarded as optional, a matter of personal choice.

Opinions varied as to the proper place in the prayer service for *Tachanun*. The oldest practice appears to have been to offer personal private requests after Blessing 16 of the *Amida*, the request to God to hear our prayers.[455] The opinion of Rav, an early Babylonian scholar, was that such prayers could be offered after any of the blessings of the *Amida*.[456] The rule came to be, however, particularly in the land of Israel, that the preferred place for personal prayer was after the end of the *Amida*.[457] That has remained the most common custom.

The practice of prostrating oneself was modified in medieval times. Even in the talmudic era, great scholars and men of high rank were permitted to turn their faces to one side rather than to prostrate themselves.[458] It became customary to lean one's face on one's arm. However, *Tachanun* remained a silent prayer, and the prayer leader would sit down, figuratively leaving the congregation to worship on its own.

In early medieval Babylonia, *Tachanun* became a fixed part of the liturgy, and, like almost all parts of the liturgy that originally were spent in silent meditation, it acquired a text. The personal nature of the words of *Tachanun* was destroyed in the Babylonian academies. In place of one's own words, it became the practice to parrot the words of leading scholars. The scholar Solomon Freehof has shown that each of the prayers now part of the *Tachanun* liturgy originated as the personal prayer of one of the Amoraim, the scholars of the Babylonian academies.[459] He also has demonstrated that each of them appears originally to have been composed to be recited after a particular benediction of the *Amida*, in accordance with the view of Rav.[460]

On Monday and Thursday mornings, *Tachanun* is introduced by seven elegies that speak repeatedly of Israel's unending suffering, which, they say, is a just retribution for Israel's unfaithfulness to the covenant. Mondays and Thursdays were the ancient market days when the Torah was read for the benefit of the farmers who could not attend synagogue services on *Shabbat*. These days also evolved, in the late Second-Temple period, into days of fasting. The community was together only on market days, and fasting in times of public emergency was considered a communal activity of the utmost importance.

On other weekdays, *Tachanun* begins with a quotation from 2 Samuel 24:14, which was King David's reply to the prophet Gad. David had committed a serious sin, and Gad had offered him a choice of punishment at the hands of either man or God. In the quotation, David chooses the hand of God, "for His mercies are great; and let me not fall into the hand of man." To medieval Jews, this was highly relevant: If the Jews deserved punishment, it should not be at the hands of the Crusaders or other human beings.[461]

A short confession follows, and then a quotation from Psalms 6:2 "God, do not rebuke me in Your anger."

On Mondays and Thursdays, a medieval *piyyut*, or poetic hymn, comes next. This hymn reads, in part, "Look from heaven and see how we have become a scorn and a derision among the nations; we are accounted as sheep brought to the slaughter, to be slain and destroyed, or to be smitten and reproached. Yet, despite all this, we have not forgotten Your name; we plead to You, do not forget us."

Tachanun concludes on all occasions with another *piyyut, Shomer Yisrael* (Guardian of Israel). This reads, in part, "Guardian of Israel, guard the remnant of Israel, and do not allow Israel to perish, who say, "Hear, O Israel."

We should bear in mind that the prayers found in the prayerbook for *Tachanun* are only suggestions. The essence of *Tachanun* is spontaneity. There is a script today for *Tachanun* in traditional *siddurim* only because medieval students preferred to emulate their teachers' meditations rather than to dare to speak spontaneously to God, thinking that the meditations uttered by great scholars would be more effective than anything they could dream up. Their timidity or superstition should not force us, a millennium later, to forfeit this precious time for spontaneous personal supplications to God, the original *Tachanun.*

HALLEL: ON MAJOR FESTIVALS, WE REMIND OURSELVES OF OUR DEPENDENCE ON GOD EVEN IN THE BEST OF TIMES

Hallel (literally, "praise") consists of Psalms 113 to 118. These psalms came to be recited in the Second Temple by the Levites on all major biblical Festivals while the Festival sacrifice was being slaughtered.[462] This practice was quite ancient, and certainly predated the Hasmonean period;[463] one talmudic source even attributed it, improbably, to Moses. It once may have had an association with warding off potential misfortune, but came to be recited on happy occasions, a sobering reminder of our dependence on God even at the best of times, perhaps analogous in this sense to the groom's breaking the glass at a wedding.[464] It is mental fortification to do the extra things God requires of us on Festivals if we are to have our requests fulfilled.

Hallel originally was recited on the eight days of *Sukkot* and at the sacrifice of the paschal lamb on the first night of Passover. It came to be said on *Chanuka* as well, when that holiday came into existence after the Maccabean revolt in the third century B.C.E.

When the Second Temple was destroyed, *Hallel* passed into the synagogue liturgy. At about that time, it came to be recited on *Shavuot* as a substitute for the pilgrim psalms, Psalms 120 to 134, which used to be chanted when the first fruits were brought to the Temple.[465] Later, at the beginning of the third century or possibly earlier, the Babylonian Jews developed the practice of reciting *Hallel* on the last six days of Passover and on *Rosh Chodesh* (the New Moon).[466] However, to distinguish these occasions from those on which *Hallel* had traditionally been recited, the Babylonian Jews devised the Half-*Hallel* by omitting verses 1 to 11 from Psalms 115 and 116.

The text of these psalms suggest the reason for their association with sacrifice. Psalm 113 begins: "*Halleluya.* O servants of the Lord, give praise. . . ." The Levites were the servants in the Second Temple. They did the "dirty work" involved in preparing the sacrificial offering. This line, calling upon the "servants of the Lord" to "give praise," was a cue for the Levites to begin singing.

Ending *Hallel* with Psalm 118 also makes sense in light of the psalm's wording. Psalm 118 ends: "May he who enters be blessed in the name of the Lord; we bless You from the House of the Lord. The Lord is God; He has given us light; bind the Festival offering to the horns of the altar with cords. You are my God and I will praise You; You are my God and I will extol You. Praise the Lord for He is good, His steadfast love is eternal."[467] The words "bind the Festival offering to the horns of the altar with cords" speak for themselves. One can visualize the Levites doing so on this cue, and the *Kohanim* then slaughtering the sacrificial animal while the Levites sang again the cycle of psalms.

The association of *Hallel* and *Sukkot* and Passover also is logical. Psalm 114, *B'Tzeit Yisrael*, is concerned entirely with the Exodus from Egypt. *Sukkot* and Passover are the two holidays that celebrate the Exodus— Passover, the events up to and including the crossing of the Red Sea, and *Sukkot*, the aftermath in the desert.

Any time groups of psalms are read, they are preceded by and followed by blessings. This is the case with *P'sukei D'Zimra*, which is preceded by *Baruch She'Amar* and followed by the blessing of *Yishtabach*. This is also the case with *Hallel*, which is preceded by a blessing on reading *Hallel*, and followed by a blessing to God, "a King extolled with praises."

KADDISH SHALEM

In the traditional (but not the Reform) service, *Kaddish* punctuates the service, as was discussed earlier. With the *Amida* finished, and, on festivals, when *Hallel* has been recited, the *Shacharit* service is over. Consequently, we say the full *Kaddish* (*Kaddish Shalem*). For explanation of the origins and meaning of the *Kaddish* prayer, see p. 47.

The Torah Service

Public Recitation of the Torah as an Instrument for Understanding

We are in a receptive frame of mind, having prepared our minds through prayer and having made our requests of God. Now, we set out to acquire what the fourth blessing of the daily *Amida* tells us is the first essential prerequisite for our requests to be granted: knowledge (*da'at*) and understanding (*bina*). We do so by studying the Torah as a community.

The Torah reading originated in the fifth century B.C.E. when the Temple in Jerusalem was rebuilt. At first, only brief passages were recited at public assemblies as part of a *d'rasha* (literally, a "search"), or sermon, on pilgrimage Festival days.[468] The brevity was understandable, because, in antiquity, the Torah was recited from memory, not read from a scroll.[469]

The Torah reading thus began not as a ritualistic exercise, but as an aid to learning. It was incidental to a sermon or study session. Unless the Torah reading is understood, its purpose is not accomplished. The Torah reading is subordinate to, and inseparable from, the discussion of what is being read. Without a *d'rasha* or sermon, the Torah service is incomplete.

The ancient *d'rasha* developed a structure of its own. The rule was that the *darshan*, or preacher, had to begin with a verse from the Hagiographa (the *K'tuvim*, or Writings). He would connect it linguistically with verses from the Prophets, which came to be known as the *Haftarah*. Using the *Haftarah* as a bridge, he would recite the excerpt from the Torah that served as a source or foundation for the verses he had discussed.[470]

114

The Torah as a Unifying Force for Jewish Nationhood

When the tradition of Torah-reading began, there was a particular need for public instruction. The Samaritans were a breakaway sect that espoused and preached a different interpretation of the Festivals. The fact that the reading of the Torah originated with Festival readings suggests that it was, at least in part, a campaign in reaction to what was considered the heresy of the Samaritans, and an attempt to avoid the splintering of the Jewish people newly returned from Exile.[471] Rather than the present cyclical reading of the entire Torah, originally only a few brief excerpts were read, presumably excerpts that were considered a rebuttal of the Samaritans' position.

We can draw from this historical fact another principle regarding the Torah reading: The Torah is a unifying force for the Jewish people. Many nations, such as Great Britain, have ceremonial kings or queens that serve a similar function; we have the Torah.

Having a book, rather than a person, as the organizing force for a nation is a remarkable concept. Books are susceptible to interpretation; kings are not. If a king disapproves of the way in which his laws are interpreted, he changes them, or else changes the people responsible for their enforcement. No such easy feedback is available for the Jews. Rather, we are left to our free will to determine how biblical law should be applied to modern conditions.

Torah Reading as an Affirmation That Critical Discourse Is a Public Function

The oldest injunction regarding Torah-reading is found in Deuteronomy 31:10, where we are told to read the Torah at the public assembly on *Sukkot* every seventh year. When Ezra the Scribe led the Jews back to Jerusalem from Babylonian Exile and rebuilt the Temple in 444 B.C.E., he held public meetings to read the Torah. Initially, these were held on the three pilgrimage Festivals, *Sukkot*, Passover, and *Shavuot*, which were the only Festivals when laypeople from all over Israel were present in Jerusalem.[472] Perhaps because of the special commandment in the Torah about reading the Torah on *Sukkot*, Ezra ordered that it be read on each day of that Festival, but on Passover and *Shavuot* there was originally only one Torah reading.[473]

The Torah reading on *Yom Kippur* had a different origin, being derived from the reading performed by the High Priest in the Temple after completing the rites on that day.[474] Logically, there was no reason for a Torah reading on *Rosh Ha'Shana*, which was not a pilgrimage Festival and did not have the tradition of Torah reading in the Temple associated with it;

however, "since each festival had its own reading, the New Year could not be the only exception."[475] Because the Torah reading on *Rosh Ha'Shana* originated as something of an afterthought, it is the shortest of the Festival readings.

The tradition developed of also reading from the Torah on the four special Sabbaths in the spring, between the last Sabbath before the month of *Adar* and the last Sabbath before the month of *Nisan*,[476] perhaps because they came to attract large numbers from outlying areas. Similarly, because large numbers gathered in the towns on Mondays and Thursdays, the ancient market days, it became customary to preview the next week's Torah reading on Mondays and Thursdays for the benefit of those unable to attend. This remains the custom today.

Another principle may be induced from this history: Learning is a public function. We learn collectively. Education is our collective responsibility. We are all responsible for the education of our fellow Jews. Debate of religious and ethical issues is a communal obligation. As shown by the example of the prophets, critical thinking in public discourse is central to Jewish tradition.

Torah Reading as a Means of Organizing the Jewish Year

The custom of reading the Torah every *Shabbat* developed at a somewhat later date than the Festival and special *Shabbat* readings, but was established before the middle of the third century B.C.E.[477] Presumably, the Torah reading on the special Sabbaths proved successful, and was expanded to a weekly event, although a biblical fig leaf was provided for the practice by misinterpreting the phrase *mikra kodesh* (holy assembly) in Isaiah 1:13 to mean a "holy Torah reading."[478] However, the *Mishna* makes it plain that the special *Shabbat* readings were in no way dependent on the regular *Shabbat* readings.

Once the Torah reading became a weekly event, the division of the Torah into weekly portions followed. For a prolonged period after the weekly readings developed, the portions remained short—on *Shabbat*, generally no more than twenty-one lines divided into seven groups of three sentences each.[479] In the land of Israel, the portions remained short; a triennial cycle was adopted for reading the entire Torah that divided it into between 141 and 167 portions, each called a *sidra*, and took almost 3 ½ years to complete.[480] This triennial cycle was not coordinated with the calendar, so that a given reading could come at any time of year.

In contrast, in the academies of Babylonia during the talmudic period, the annual cycle, beginning and ending with the end of *Sukkot*, was adopted,[481] in which Genesis is divided into twelve portions, each called a *parasha*, Exodus and Deuteronomy into eleven each, and Leviticus and Numbers into ten each. The last portion of Deuteronomy is read on *Shemini Atzeret*, the last day of *Sukkot*, leaving fifty-three for regular Sabbath readings. This still exceeds the number of Sabbaths years that are not leap years, so certain *parshiyot* are read as double portions on the same day.

As in most matters of dispute between Babylonia and Israel, the Babylonian talmudic tradition prevailed. The annual cycle had the virtue of permitting coordination between calendar events and Torah readings. For example, sometime prior to 1000 C.E., the holiday of *Simchat Torah* developed in Babylonia and then in eastern Germany to mark the day after *Sukkot*, when the annual cycle begins anew. Had the 3 ½ year cycle of Israel become the custom in the Diaspora, the holiday would not exist.[483]

The disadvantage of the annual cycle was to make the Torah reading on a given day much longer. Reading the entire Torah in one year requires longer *Shabbat* readings than if it were to be read in 3 ½ years. When the Torah recitation consisted of a few memorized verses followed by a *d'rasha*, it wasn't hard to find congregants to recite them. Children were taught the Torah from their earliest years during the Second-Temple period. In Babylonia, however, it became difficult to find people capable of reading an entire *parasha*. Therefore, it became customary for the prayer leader to help the reader—first in an undertone and later more loudly, until finally, by the thirteenth century, prayer leaders became the readers, and members of the congregation were relegated to reciting the blessings before and after the Torah was read.[483]

The adoption of the one-year cycle caused a separation between the Torah reading and the sermon of which it had once been a part. The sermon came to be read in the afternoon, after the customary Sabbath siesta.[484] This divorcing of the Torah reading from the sermon had a profound effect. The Torah reading became increasingly ritualistic, an end in itself rather than a means to understanding. Complex rules developed in Babylonia governing the manner in which the Torah was read.

Initially, the annual cycle was interrupted four times per year for the special *Shabbat* readings. To increase the number of available Sabbaths and to decrease the length of the portion per Sabbath, these interruptions in the cycle were eliminated, and the special *Shabbat* readings became additional readings from a second scroll. To mark other special occasions of equal importance, such as *Rosh Chodesh* (the New Moon) and *Chanuka*, Yehudai Gaon, head of one of the Babylonian academies, added other second-scroll readings from Numbers describing the sacrifice of the day as it had been performed in the Second Temple.[485]

The Language of the Torah

By the first century C.E., Aramaic had long since replaced Hebrew as the common language in the land of Israel. Because the purpose of the Torah reading was pedagogical, it would be defeated if the words were not made comprehensible to the congregation. Therefore, the custom arose of having the *meturgeman* (translator) translate the reading into the vernacular.[486] The *meturgeman* was supposed to translate without looking at the words; it was supposed to be a free-flowing, rather than literal, translation.[487] The advent of the annual cycle and the consequent lengthening of the weekly Torah reading placed a strain on the reader and the *meturgeman*; mistakes doubtless became more common. At the same time, however, the Babylonian academies placed gather emphasis on precision in the Torah reading. Later, in the Middle Ages, a second person in addition to the reader (*ba'al k'riya*) was added to the functionaries on the *bima* during the Torah reading, to avoid mistakes. This was the *gabbai*, whose job was to follow the text and correct the reader and the *meturgeman*.[488]

Perhaps because the Torah reading on the annual cycle prolonged the service so much, the institution of the *meturgeman* gradually faded. Leaving out the translation drastically streamlined the service. The *meturgeman* became nothing more than a second *gabbai* on the *bima*. We still have two *gabbaim* on the *bima* during the Torah reading today.

The *Aliyot* and the Blessings on Reading the Torah

Originally there was one blessing at the beginning of the entire reading and another at the end, in accordance with the general rule of reciting a blessing before and after a quotation from the Torah.[489] One prominent person typically would say the blessings, recite the Torah excerpt, and deliver the *d'rasha* (sermon) in the synagogue. When more than one congregant was called to the Torah, he would read without saying a blessing.

When the Second Temple was destroyed, and the *Kohanim* and Levites were dispersed among the population, they were given priority for Torah reading out of respect for their former status and in the hope that it someday would be restored.[490] The tradition remains that the first *aliya* is reserved for a *Kohen* and the second for a Levite.

During the *Amoraic* period (200–500 C.E.), when the *Gemara*, the second part of the Talmud, was written, separate blessings became customary before and after particular Torah passages of significance, such as the songs, the Ten Commandments, and the curses. In the Babylonian academies, this practice was expanded so that every person who read from the Torah said a blessing before and after the reading. In the Middle Ages, as fewer and fewer people knew how to read the Torah, the use of a *ba'al koreh*, a professional reader, became common, and the congregant called to the Torah said merely the blessings.

The blessing before reading the Torah begins with *Barchu et Adonai ha'm'vorach*, the ancient call to prayer. In effect, we are commencing a new service each time we read the Torah. The congregation responds with *Baruch Adonai ha'm'vorach l'olam va'ed*, the public response from the days of the Second Temple. According to a ruling by Saadya Gaon, a tenth-century Babylonian scholar who compiled one of the earliest prayer codes, the response is then repeated by the person saying the blessing. Consistent with the practice of saying a blessing before and after reading the Torah, *Barchu* is followed by a blessing of ancient origin. After the Torah has been read, the congregant called to the Torah recites another, more recent, blessing.

Why is each Torah reading, each *aliya*, treated as though it were a new and separate service, with the convening of a new spiritual community? Historically, this reflects the facts that the Torah reading developed independently from the prayer service, as a method of public instruction and part of the *d'rasha* (sermon), and that originally there was only one Torah reading, not several *aliyot*.[491] There was no separate liturgy for taking out the Torah; the *Barchu* that begins the blessing convened a new service, which could be termed the "*D'rasha* service" since the sermon was its focal point. Since the Torah was commonly kept in a portable chest or Ark, often in a different room, there was an interruption as the Torah was fetched and taken out, which was used for socializing or meditating. The liturgy for removing the Torah evolved to fill this hiatus.

The medieval kabbalists gave another explanation. The reading of the Torah, to them, was a dramatic reenactment of the giving of the Torah to Moses at Mount Sinai.[492] In this view, each time a person goes up for an *aliya*, he is figuratively ascending Mount Sinai to receive the words of the Torah, as a representative of the assembled community.

They perhaps found support for their view in the example of Ezra, who, according to Nehemiah's description of the first public Torah reading, "stood on a wooden tower made for this purpose" and "opened the scroll in the sight of all the people, for he was above all the people."[493] This emulation of Ezra is why the *bima*, the pulpit, is a raised platform,[494] and why being called to the Torah is referred to as an *aliya*, a "going up."

In the mystical view, the person called to the Torah acts as the representative of the Jews who assembled to receive the Torah. The *gabbai*, in this view, plays the role of Moses overseeing the process, while the reader takes the role of God giving the Torah.[495] Each time we have an *aliya*, we are figuratively ascending Mount Sinai to receive the Torah from God. For this momentous event, we call all the people to pray together.

The blessing after the Torah reading refers to the "Torah of truth" and "eternal life." These were interpreted by the medieval scholar Jacob ben Asher as references to the Written Law and the Oral Law, showing the continuity of one from the other.[496]

REMOVING THE TORAH FROM THE ARK: AROUSING THE COMMUNAL SPIRIT THROUGH PRAYER

The ceremonies for removing the Torah from the Ark and later replacing it in the Ark are not particularly suited to individual spiritual transformation, but they are rousing moments for reinforcing the spiritual community in which we pray. We need to rebuild that community to some degree after we have spent some minutes in mental isolation with God following the *Amida*. Remember that knowledge is the crucial first step on the path to redemption outlined in the *Amida*. We are about to study together in the Torah reading and the sermon, moving forward on that path as a spiritual community. To follow that path, we must strengthen our community's cohesion.

Elaborate ceremonies for taking out and replacing the Torah did not develop until many centuries after the Torah reading was instituted, and they developed for reasons with which most modern Jews would not agree. Gradually, the Torah reading ceased to be an aid to a *d'rasha* and became an end in itself. The Torah itself came to be honored, rather than the words read from it.[497] A ceremony developed that was loosely based on the biblical account of the bringing of the Ark of the Covenant by King David (2 Sam. 6:5; 1 Chron. 13:8), and on the description of Ezra's reading the Torah (Neh. 8:5–6):

> Ezra opened the scroll in the sight of all the people, for he was above all the people; as he opened it, all the people stood up. Ezra blessed the Lord, the great God, and all the people answered, "Amen, amen."[498]

Attendant customs manifesting reverence for the Torah as a holy object also developed, such as kissing the Torah during the procession around the synagogue and not touching the Torah scroll with any part of one's body (hence the use of a pointer, or *yad,* to follow the reading).

There are three parts to the liturgy for removing the Torah on *Shabbat* and Festivals; the liturgy is abbreviated on weekdays because of the time constraints of the worshippers. First, a group of talmudic verses from *Sof.* 14:8, beginning with *Ein Camocha* (There is none like You), precedes the removal of the Torah on *Shabbat* and Festivals, but not on weekdays. These verses, which extol God's kingship, may have become customary in the gaonic period in Israel.[499]

Next the Ark is opened, and we recite a biblical quotation (Num. 10:35), beginning *Va'y'hi binsoa ha'aron,* alluding to how the Israelites carried the Ark through the desert for forty years under Moses' leadership. This is where the Torah service begins on Mondays and Thursdays. A quotation from Isaiah 2:3 follows, beginning with *Ki mitziyon teitzei Torah,* which alludes to the future coming of the Torah "from Zion" in the Messianic era. The message of these verses seems to be eternality of the Torah; the Torah helped the Israelites vanquish their foes in ancient times, and the Torah again will prevail when the Messiah comes. The recitation of these verses is of relatively recent vintage, and has been customary among Eastern European Jews since 1541. The verses first appeared in the Torah service in written form in a *siddur* printed in Vilna in 1699.[500]

The prayer *B'rich Sh'mei* (Blessed Is the Name) follows in many congregations. It is commonly read silently except for the last five sentences, beginning *Bei anna rachetz* (In Him do we trust). This prayer is written in Aramaic and is taken from the *Zohar,* the classic kabbalistic work attributed by legend to Shimon bar Yochai in the second century C.E.[501] *B'rich Sh'mei* was first included in the liturgy in Italy in private prayers, and was made a regular part of the Torah service at the instance of Isaac Luria, also known as the Ari (lion), a sixteenth-century kabbalistic rabbi who lived in Safed, Israel.[502] This excerpt from the *Zohar* is recited at the opening of the Ark because, in the kabbalistic view, "at that moment the gates of heaven are opened and the divine love is aroused."[503] Since *B'rich Sh'mei* is in the form of a blessing, the congregation says Amen at the end.

On Festivals and fast days, the Thirteen Attributes of God are recited, also as a result of kabbalistic influence. This Torah excerpt is discussed more fully in connection with the *Selichot* service, of which it is the core prayer.

Next, the *chazan* takes the Torah from the Ark and recites the *Shema,* an excerpt from the Torah. The congregation repeats it. The *chazan* then recites *Echad Eloheinu,* a verse from the Talmud (*Sof.* 14:8), and the congregation repeats that.

The *chazan* then quotes Psalm 34: *Gadlu la'Adonai iti, u'n'rom'mah sh'mo yachdav* (Exalt the Lord together with me and let us together extol His name). He carries the Torah around the synagogue, giving the congregants an opportunity to show their love of the Torah by using their *tzitzit* or *siddurim* to kiss it. While he is doing so, the congregation sings excerpts from 1 Chronicles 29:11, beginning *L'cha Adonai Ha'G'Dula,* and from Psalm 99, beginning *Rom'Mu,* both of which extol God.

Notice the progression from Talmud to Torah to Prophets to Torah to Talmud to Writings. With the addition of talmudic quotations, we go through the progression of the ancient *d'rasha,* connecting phrases from the Torah, Prophet, and Writings. The liturgy for removing the Torah is designed as a proof of the divinity of all of the parts of the Bible and of the Talmud, the Oral Law; it proclaims this principle in a manner analogous to a cheer at a football game intended to arouse a sense of enthusiasm and commonality of purpose among those present.

The liturgy for taking out the Torah resonates with allusions to the Israelites' carrying the Ark through the desert for forty years. When the prayer leader takes the Torah out of the Ark, he or she says the words Moses said when the Israelites carrying the Ark set forth across the desert. When the Torah is returned to the Ark, the prayer leader says the same words Moses said when the Israelites put down the Ark and rested.

In other words, reading the Torah is a journey. It is a journey of the mind, unbound by space or time. It is a journey that involves effort and sacrifice. As a spiritual community, when we take out the Torah, we proclaim our readiness to undertake that journey, as a first step toward doing what we must if we are to merit God's attention to our urgent communal and personal needs.

INSERTIONS IN THE TORAH SERVICE FOR *SHABBAT, ROSH CHODESH,* AND FESTIVALS: *MI-SHE'BERACH* (HE WHO BLESSED), *Y'KUM PURKAN* (MAY SALVATION ARISE), PRAYER FOR THE GOVERNMENT, BLESSING FOR THE NEW MOON

We have renewed and strengthened our cohesiveness as a spiritual community in removing the Torah from the Ark. During the Torah Service, and particularly right after the Torah reading, we build in various prompts and prods to reinforce the sense of community and also to take advantage of it for practical purposes, particularly raising funds for community needs. Immediately after the Torah has been studied, we take time to reinforce our spiritual community by celebrating the joyous occasions of its members, such as bar mitzvahs and bat mitzvahs, weddings, and births, and by bestowing the community's good wishes on those in need of them, such as those who are sick or those about to go on a dangerous journey.

These prompts and prods originally began as time-fillers. At an early point in the development of the Torah service, it became customary to recite special prayers after the Torah reading to fill the time while the Torah was being rewound and dressed.[504]

These prayers evolved during medieval times into fundraising devices. After the fall of the Second Temple, Jews were at the mercy of the governments of the nations in which they resided. In medieval France and Germany, Jewish communities had the power to tax their members, but the taxes went into government coffers and were unavailable for synagogue use. To raise separate funds for synagogues, various devices arose for honoring members of the congregation, for which honors a donation was expected.[505]

The primary such device was the *mi-she'berach*. A *mi-she'berach* is a prayer that asks God, "Who blessed Abraham, Isaac, and Jacob," also to bless the person who has been called to the Torah for an *aliya*. There is no limit on the number of *mi-she'berachs* that may be recited.

The earliest *mi-she'berachs* may have been in the nature of these special prayers recited between the Torah readings and before returning the Torah to the Ark.[506] Under the pressure of fundraising needs, what originally may have been a time for private meditation after the Torah reading and before the *d'rasha* was converted to a time for bestowing public honors in exchange for pledges of money for the synagogue. With the advent of the annual Torah-reading cycle, the *d'rasha* was moved to the afternoon, after the customary Saturday-afternoon siesta, but the *mi-she'berachs* remained.[507] Indeed, they were expanded, so that the person receiving the *alyia* could request additional *mi-she'berachs* for family and friends in exchange for additional pledges. *Mi-she'berachs* were developed for different occasions: illness, marriage, birth, and bar mitzvah. It even became customary in some places to announce the amount pledged in the midst of the *mi-she'berach*, a custom that mostly has been abolished today.

Another fund-raising prayer, recited on *Shabbat* after the Torah reading, is an Aramaic prayer called *Y'kum Purkan*. This prayer was instituted during the waning years of the Babylonian academies at Sura and Pumbedita, around 1100 c.e. The academies, like Jewish institutions of higher learning in Israel today, were supported by contributions from Jews throughout the Diaspora. These contributions dried up as the Jewish communities of Spain and Western Europe expanded and developed their own institutions while the Babylonian Jewish community declined. Emissaries from the Babylonian academies traveled to Jewish communities elsewhere in search of funds. Still short of money, the Babylonian authorities inserted a prayer, *Y'kum Purkan*, into the service that honored the heads of the academies (*gaonim*), the judges, and the Exilarch (*resh galuta*), the political leader of the Babylonian Jewish community. It was hoped that this prayer would remind worshippers of the academies and their needs, thus prodding them to make donations in honor of the leaders of the community.[508]

A second *Y'kum Purkan* prayer developed in later medieval times in Europe. This *Y'kum Purkan* is a prayer for the well-being of the congregation, also recited only on *Shabbat*. Its addition may have reflected the sense that to pray only for the well-being of community leaders was to ignore the fact that those leaders derived their authority from the congregation.

In the traditional service, there is another prayer for the well-being of the congregation that begins *Mi-she'berach*, but it is not to be confused with the prayer of the same name recited for the honor of an individual called to the Torah. This prayer, of Spanish origin, is to honor philanthropists and patrons of the synagogue.[509]

Along with these fundraising prayers before the Torah is returned to the Ark, in the Orthodox service a prayer may be recited for the government. This prayer is not a modern innovation. In fact, the custom of offering prayers for the ruler goes back at least as far as the prophet Jeremiah and the conquest of Israel by Alexander the Great.[510] The Talmud quotes Rabbi Hanina as saying, "Pray for the welfare of the government, for were it not for the fear thereof, one man would swallow up alive his fellow-man."[511]

The traditional prayer for the government dates, in its present form, at least from the fourteenth century, and was justified on the basis of Jeremiah's letter to the Jewish captives in Babylonia, whom he urged to "pray for the peace of the city."[512] David Abudarham, a fourteenth-century commentator on the prayerbook, observed that to pray for the peace of the city is "to pray that God enable the king to vanquish his enemies."[513] The traditional text of this prayer is derived from Psalms 144:10: "God, I will sing You a new song . . . to You Who give victory to kings, Who rescue His servant David from the deadly sword."

Another set of inserted prayers is included after the Torah reading on *Rosh Chodesh*, the time of the New Moon. In biblical times, the New Moon was a solemn and important occasion, perhaps reflecting practices of other ancient peoples in the Middle East. The date of the New Moon was established by a formal legal proceeding conducted each month by the Sanhedrin that involved testimony of eyewitnesses who had observed the New Moon.[514] A festive meal would be held, and a special Grace After Meals recited.[515] An additional sacrifice was performed in the Temple. The public was informed of the Sanhedrin's findings each month by public proclamations.

After the destruction of the Temple, the recitation of *Musaf* and *Hallel* took the place of the additional sacrifice. Determining the occurrence of the New Moon continued to be an important event, as it would determine whether these prayers needed to be said, though its importance dwindled over time. Meanwhile, however, the Jewish Diaspora developed, and with it the need to communicate the information over long distances as to when the New Moon had occurred in Israel, as this, and not the New Moon in the Diaspora, was determinative of when *Musaf* and *Hallel* had to be recited. To allow leeway for the accuracy of this information and its transmittal, an extra day was added to Festivals in the Diaspora to ensure that they would be observed on the correct day. This is how, in the Diaspora, Passover observance came to entail two seders. *Sukkot* and Passover became eight-day rather than seven-day holidays, with pairs of holy days at their beginning and end rather than single holy days, and *Shavuot* became a two-day festival.

After the fixed calendar was adopted in Babylonia in 360 c.e.,[516] it became predictable when the New Moon would rise, so the proclamation came to be given, in the Aramaic vernacular, at synagogue services on the *Shabbat* preceding the New Moon.[517] It also became the custom to recite, after the proclamation, a prayer for the welfare of the community in the coming month.[518]

Over time, the prayer for the welfare of the community became more important than the function of the *Rosh Chodesh* proclamation as a substitute for a calendar. Hence, it came to be placed after the Torah reading, along with other prayers for the community's well-being.

In the Ashkenazic ritual, a meditative introduction was adopted for the *Rosh Chodesh* prayers during the eighteenth century. The personal meditation of Rav, beginning *Y'hi ratzon mil'fanecha*, which is commonly recited after the *Amida*, was put into plural form and some phrases were added to adapt it as a *Rosh Chodesh* prayer.[519] With this introduction, in a sense, we resume where we left off at the end of the *Amida*.

A brief petition for the gathering of the exiled people and the restoration of Israel follows, beginning, *Mi she'asa nissim*. Since we are making do with a substitute for the original custom of announcing the New Moon at the Temple in Jerusalem, we pray for restoration of the site where this custom could some day be renewed.

What follows is the ancient one-line proclamation of the New Moon, beginning with the words *Rosh Chodesh*. After the proclamation comes the prayer for the welfare of the community, beginning *Y'chad'sheihu ha'kadosh Baruch Hu*.

All of these insertions have been eliminated in the Reform service, except the recitation of *mi-she'berach* by the rabbi or *chazan* for people who are called to the Torah or are being honored.

We should not forget the purpose of forming a cohesive spiritual community. The various prompts and prods toward community cohesion that are built into the Torah service ultimately serve a religious purpose: aiding us in collectively following the path toward national redemption laid out in the *Amida*. Only through community can our nation be rebuilt; only as a community can we achieve God's forgiveness to such a degree that the Jewish nation will become, and remain, a force that brings peace to the world. This is a time to meditate on the connection between our community and world events.

THE *HAFTARAH* (DISMISSAL): READING FROM THE PROPHETS; BAR AND BAT MITZVAH AND OTHER CELEBRATIONS

Haftarah means "dismissal" or "conclusion." The *Haftarah* is a reading from the Prophets that concludes the biblical reading for the day. In antiquity, it may have been the conclusion of the entire service.

Today, the reading of the *Haftarah* is the high point of a bar mitzvah or bat mitzvah. However, the bar mitzvah is a relatively recent institution. It was unknown before the fourteenth century.[520] The bat mitzvah is still more recent, having originated in the early twentieth century.[521] In talmudic times, solemn occasions were marked by the calling up of congregants to read the Torah, accompanied by special poetic introductions called r'shut (literally, "permission," because they were, in essence, a request for the congregation's permission to interrupt the service to mark the special occasion), which were often quite lengthy.[522] This was the custom for bridegrooms, for the inauguration of an Exilarch or *Gaon* in Babylonia, and for other happy occasions, such as a boy's reaching adulthood.[523]

As the Torah reading became significantly longer owing to the adoption of the one-year cycle, and the population became less literate in Hebrew and less able to read lengthy Torah portions, this custom was modified so that happy occasions were marked by the honoree's being called to the Torah merely to recite the blessings rather than to read the Torah portion itself. After the advent of printing, the *Haftarah* became easier to read, since unlike the Torah it could be read with the vowels and *trope* (cantillation) marks intact,[524] and congregants celebrating a wedding or other festive event, such as the passage of a boy into adulthood, were allowed to read the *Haftarah*.

Out of concern that the *Haftarah* would overshadow the Torah reading and cast doubt on the relative importance of the Torah and the Prophets—a doubt raised in the early Middle Ages by the Karaites, a dissident movement in Judaism that held that all of God's words were of equal importance, but denied the authority of rabbinic interpretations of those words—the *maftir aliya* was created for the *Haftarah* reader, a repetition of the last few sentences of the seventh *aliya* to be recited in addition to the *Haftarah*. Reading an easy three or four sentences of the Torah at least preserved the principle that the Torah reading was of primary, and the *Haftarah* of secondary, importance. Thus developed the custom of the bar mitzvah, in which thirteen-year-old boys were, and today still are, required to read the *maftir aliya* and the *Haftarah* as a rite of passage.

Medieval scholars hypothesized that the *Haftarah* was introduced when the Greek-Syrians prohibited Torah reading and burned the Torah scrolls at the time of the Maccabean revolt in the second century B.C.E.[525] This is a possible explanation, but it is more plausible that the custom of reading from the Prophets originated at the time of Ezra the Scribe with the *d'rasha*, in which relationships between passages from the Prophets and from the Torah were explored, and then was expanded in reaction to the Samaritans' denial of the sanctity of the prophetic writings.[526] Reading excerpts from the Torah and the Prophets and then sermonizing on their common message became the standard formula for a *d'rasha*.

In any event, the *Haftarah* became an established custom long before the Common Era.[527] Like the Torah reading, it began with Festival and special Sabbath readings and later became a feature of every Sabbath morning service.[528]

The selections of *Haftarah* readings changed over time. Originally they were much shorter; in fact, one *Haftarah* even consisted of just a single verse, Isaiah 52:3.[529] The *Haftarot* in use today did not become fixed until the Middle Ages.

Why read the *Haftarah*? The key may lie not in the reading from the Prophets itself, but in the blessings after the reading. Those blessings, believed to be as old as the *Haftarah* itself, parallel the structure of the *Amida*, leading modern scholars to believe that at one time what are now the blessings after the *Haftarah* may have been the main prayer of the day, or perhaps were an alternative to the *Amida* for latecomers (before the destruction of the Temple led to the institution of the *Musaf* service in the synagogue on Shabbat and holidays, which then assumed that function), or were a substitute for the *Amida* at a time when the recital of the *Amida* was forbidden.[530] They begin with a hymn praising God for the fulfillment of His promises for the future. In the middle is a petition for national redemption, referring to the restoration of Zion and the coming of the Messiah. The final blessing expresses gratitude to God for granting the Holy Day.

In their earliest known form, the middle blessings after the *Haftarah* referred specifically to the fall of the Second Temple. They included "Console us, O Lord our God, for Zion," and "And take vengeance on behalf of the sorrowful one soon in our days." These requests for consolation and revenge later were softened to petitions for mercy and salvation.[531]

The striking parallels between the blessings after the *Haftarah* and the *Amida* reinforce the idea that the Torah service must be considered a separate entity from *Shacharit*, with its own complete structure. Although today they occur in sequence, the Torah service and *Shacharit* developed independently and served distinct functions. One can speculate that the blessings after the *Haftarah* were included before the *Musaf Amida* became part of the service (i.e., before the destruction of the Second Temple led the rabbis to substitute the *Amida* for the Temple sacrifices) to enable attendees at the Torah service who had arrived too late for *Shacharit* to accomplish the same function of addressing their collective petitions to God.

Ironically, the persistence of the *Haftarah* as part of the liturgy owes a great deal to the efforts of the talmudic rabbis to downplay the Prophets relative to the Torah. Because the *Haftarah* was regarded as subordinate to the Torah reading, minors were allowed to recite the *Haftarah*—indeed, some communities allowed no one else to recite it—but not to read the Torah.[532] The *Haftarah* made the service "child-friendly."

The *Haftarah* also has helped make the service "woman-friendly." According to the Talmud, Jewish law does not prohibit women from having *aliyot* and reading the Torah; however, the Talmud went on to say that women should not be allowed these privileges because of the "honor of the congregation."[533] This cryptic phrase may mean that because some men were unable to read the Torah, it would embarrass them to permit women to do so.[534] In the early twentieth century in the Reform and Conservative movements, however, the custom of having girls become bat mitzvah developed. Even in congregations where women were not permitted to read the Torah, because of greater leniency concerning the reading of the *Haftarah*, women were allowed to read the *Haftarah* to become bat mitzvah.

Reform Judaism has long maintained gender equality, and it recently issued gender-neutral versions of its *Gates of Prayer* prayerbook for *Shabbat* and Festivals and its *Gates of Repentance Machzor* for the High Holidays. Within the past fifteen years, the Conservative movement has begun permitting, though not requiring, congregations to accord equal privileges to women in reading the Torah and having *aliyot*, as well as in other matters of ritual, and has begun to ordain women as rabbis. Orthodox Judaism continues to adhere to the separation of men and women in the synagogue and to the traditional separation of male and female roles in religious life.

The blessing before the *Haftarah* also reflects the rabbinic effort to downplay the Prophets. We bless God "Who chose good prophets," which parallels the wording of the blessing before the Torah reading, taken from the *Midrash Deuteronomy Rabba*, where we bless God "Who chose us [to receive] His Torah." The blessing then refers to the Torah and Moses. Peculiarly, this is one of the few places in the Sabbath liturgy where Moses is explicitly mentioned.

THE CANTILLATION OF THE TORAH AND *HAFTARAH* READINGS

The Torah and the *Haftarah* are chanted. Marks above and below the Hebrew words of the Torah and *Haftarah* readings are the musical notation. Each mark signifies a musical phrase. These cantillation marks are called, in Yiddish, *trope*.

The *trope* date from about the sixth century C.E.[535] They appear to have been written to memorialize hand and finger movements that had been used at least since the second century C.E. to signify musical phrases. For example, the *trope kadma* and *azla* resemble outstretched fingers in curved positions, and this is not coincidental. The Jews were not alone among ancient peoples in employing body movements as a primitive form of musical notation.[536] Musicologists refer to this practice as "chironomy."

Musiologists have attempted to reconstruct the ancient Torah chants, drawing analogies to other ancient musical forms as well as to chants apparently of great antiquity still used by isolated Jewish communities such as the Jews of Bukhara, in Central Asia.[537] These attempts have indicated that the cantillation was a form of psalmody not unlike the Gregorian chants of the early Christian church, and also bore a similarity to the music of the ancient Greeks, who, under Alexander the Great, had conquered the Middle East and left their mark on its culture.

In contrast, the music of the First and Second Temples appears to have been overwhelming, employing choirs of Levites and orchestras that sang and played while the sacrifices burned on *Shabbat*, the Festivals, and *Rosh Chodesh* (the New Moon).[538]

RETURNING THE TORAH TO THE ARK: RENEWING OUR SPIRITUAL COMMUNITY

Returning the Torah to the Ark, like removing it from the Ark, entails reading a patchwork of verses from different sources. Like the liturgy for taking out the Torah, the liturgy for putting it back is of relatively recent vintage.

In returning the Torah to the Ark, as when we removed it, we reinforce our sense of community. On *Shabbat* and Festivals, we are about to begin another reading of the *Amida*, the *Musaf Amida*, which requires our renewed *kavana* and a renewed sense of spiritual community if it is to be effective. On weekdays, we are about to recite the *Kedusha D'Sidra*, *U'Va L'Tzion Goel*, a prayer that was originally a substitute for the *Amida*, for which our spiritual community is required, and we are about to return to our daily activities. We are collectively trying to keep our spiritual transformation alive, to convert it from *kavana* (focused concentration) to *devekut* (oneness with God) so that we can carry a transformed mind into our daily lives and reap the benefits of prayer.

The *chazan* begins by reciting the first part of a verse from Psalm 148, *Y'hal'lu et shem Adonai ki nisgav sh'mo l'vado* (Let them praise the name of the Lord, for only His name is exalted). The congregation continues with the next line of the verse, beginning *Hodu al eretz*. These verses are the earliest known prayer for returning the Torah, and apparently accompanied the procession of the Torah in early medieval times.[539] The Torah is then carried through the synagogue a second time as the congregation sings Psalm 29 (on *Shabbat* and Festivals) or Psalm 24 (on weekdays).[540]

When the *chazan* returns the Torah to the Ark, he recites the continuation of the verse from Numbers that was recited when the Torah was taken out, beginning with *Uv'nucho yomar* (And when it [the Ark] halted, he would say, 'Return, O Lord, to the ten thousands of the families of Israel'" (Num. 10:36). By reciting the words of Moses at the end of the day's journey, we signify that this halt in our own journey through the Torah, by virtue of replacing it in the Ark, is only temporary.

Verses from Proverbs follow, admonishing the congregation not to forsake the ways of the Torah. These include *Eitz chayim hi* (It is a tree of life to those who grasp it, and whoever holds on to it is happy) (Prov. 3:18). We are trying to reinforce the changes in our state of mind that we have achieved through prayer as we prepare to conclude the service.

Finally, because returning the Torah to the Ark is a sad occasion, the liturgy for returning it concludes with the final verse of Lamentations, *Hashiveinu Adonai eilecha v'nashuva chadesh yameinu k'kedem* (Take us back, O Lord, to Yourself, and let us come back; renew our days as of old) (Lam. 5:21). This sentence, from a book that calls to mind the sadness of the destruction of the First Temple, also sounds a hopeful note, as if the person who included it in the liturgy thought, "If this verse could give hope to the Jews exiled after the destruction of the First Temple, it can lift our spirits now."

The Musaf (Additional) Service for Shabbat, Rosh Chodesh, and Festivals

ORIGIN AND PURPOSE OF THE *MUSAF* SERVICE

The *Musaf* service probably originated as an additional set of daily prayers said by the *ma'amadot*, the group of laypeople who came to Jerusalem in shifts, starting in the sixth century B.C.E., to observe the Temple sacrifices and monitor the work of the priests.[541] The *ma'amadot* held four services per day. In the Temple, an additional sacrifice was offered on Sabbath and Festivals only, but the fourth daily service of the *ma'amadot* was not initially related to that Sabbath and Festival sacrifice. Instead, the poem found in Deuteronomy 32 was recited, in six-week cycles.[542]

When the Second Temple was destroyed in 70 C.E., the additional service of the *ma'amadot* was adopted by the *Tannaim* (the rabbis who compiled the *Mishna*) as a replacement for the additional Temple sacrifice on *Shabbat* and Festivals, which could no longer be offered. This had the added practical advantage of offering another recitation of the *Amida* for those who arrived late for the service.

The *Musaf* service consists primarily of the *Musaf Amida*. Thus far in the *Shabbat* and Festival morning service we have prepared our minds in *P'sukei D'Zimra*, listened to God in the *Shema*, spoken directly to God and visualized the path to redemption in the *Shacharit Amida*, and pulled our community together to study the Torah as a first step on that path. On days when we have extra time, on *Shabbat* and Festivals, we reinforce our minds further with *Musaf* before we go back out into the world, the better to

131

ensure that our transformed sate of mind, our *devekut*, lasts until the next time we pray.

What is the point of reciting the *Musaf Amida* today? The *Musaf Amida* remains in the Orthodox and Conservative liturgies; the Reform movement sees no point in it, and has eliminated it as a vestige of the sacrificial rite that it feels has no place in modern religion. If the function of the *Musaf Amida* is to articulate theology, then this view is accurate. We already articulated what is in the *Amida* when we said it before the Torah service during *Shacharit*, and repeating the same statements only serves as a memento of the extra sacrifice on *Shabbat* and Festivals in the Second Temple. For Reform Jews, who reject on theological grounds the longing for restoration of the Temple in Jerusalem that most traditional Jews espouse (or, at least, pay lip service to), a memento of the sacrificial ritual has no place in liturgy. For Orthodox Jews and many Conservative Jews, such a memento has been seen as a means of keeping alive through two thousand years of Exile the hope of a return to the land of Israel; but Israel is once more a Jewish nation, and many question the need for mementos of two thousand years ago to preserve a hope that they feel has already been realized.

If the function of the *Musaf Amida* is neither to make a theological statement nor to preserve hope for a restoration of sacrificial worship, but rather is to transform our minds through a sequence of visualizations to enable us to perform *mitzvot* and resist the temptation to do evil, then the *Musaf Amida* still makes sense in modern life. At least once a week, we give ourselves an extra mental reinforcement in the *Musaf Amida*. Almost two thousand years after the destruction of the Second Temple in Jerusalem, our lives are sufficiently complex that we need mental reinforcement more than ever.

ASHREI AND CHATZI KADDISH: RESTORING OUR CONCENTRATION FOR THE MUSAF AMIDA

The *Musaf* service lacks any equivalent to the long period of mental preparation leading up to the *Shacharit Amida*. We are to achieve through that period of preparation an intensity of mental state sufficient to carry us not only through the petitions of the *Shacharit Amida*, but all the way through the Torah Service to the middle blessings of the *Musaf Amida*. In a sense, the *Musaf Amida* is a test of whether our spiritual transformation earlier in the morning has been successful.

This implies that our mental focus on the Torah reading and the associated *d'rasha* or sermon is not supposed to be less than our focus on the

Shacharit Amida. The sermon is not merely an emulation of the practice in Christian churches on Sundays; we are required to maintain our state of *kavana* long enough to focus on the sermon to the same degree as the *Shacharit Amida*.

Now, if our spiritual transformation has been successful, all we need to return to the requisite state of mind for the *Amida* is a brief "refresher," *Ashrei*. *Ashrei*, which is Psalm 145 preceded by two verses from other psalms that begin with the word *ashrei* (happy), was the core prayer of *P'sukei D'Zimra*, before *Shacharit*, and was discussed in detail earlier in this book.[543] It is repeated after the Torah and *Haftarah* have been read, before returning the Torah to the Ark and beginning *Musaf*.

The reason for this repetition is twofold. First, *Ashrei* is said as a symbolic repetition of the *P'Sukei D'Zimra* to prepare our minds for saying the *Musaf Amida*.[544] Second, a part of the Talmud written in the third century C.E. stated that whoever recited Psalm 145 each day was "sure to inherit the World-to-Come" (*B. Ber.* 4b), and so it became customary to recite it at each service. In antiquity, the second recitation of *Ashrei* normally followed the *Tachanun* prayer on weekdays and, with the full *Kaddish*, preceded a daily Torah lesson and the *Kedusha D'Sidra* prayer (*U'Va L'Tzion Goel*) that came after the lesson, so that *Ashrei* was, at least before 1300 C.E., the penultimate prayer of the morning service. Since neither *Tachanun* nor *Kedusha D'Sidra* is said on *Shabbat* and Festivals, the second recitation of *Ashrei* comes before *Musaf* instead.

To mark the transition from community activity and intellectual discourse back into our own minds, we recite a *Chatzi* (Half) *Kaddish*.

As there is no *Musaf* service in the Reform liturgy, there also is no recital of Psalm 145, and no *Chatzi Kaddish*.

THE *MUSAF* (ADDITIONAL) *AMIDA*

The Middle Blessings of the *Musaf Amida*

At first, the *Amida* of the Additional service was identical to the *Shacharit Amida*. Rav, the leader of the early Amoraim (the Babylonian scholars who wrote the *Gemara*, the second part of the Talmud) in the third century C.E., however, wanted it changed:

Rav said, "One must say something new in it," and Samuel says, "There is no need to say something new in it." R. Zeera asked in the presence of R. Yose, "Must one say something new in it?" He said to him, "Even if he said, 'And we shall perform before You our obligatory sacrifices, the daily sacrifice, and the additional sacrifice,' he has done his duty" (*Y. Ber.* 4:6, 8c).

Accordingly, the middle blessing of the *Amida* was changed for *Musaf* to include the two biblical verses, Numbers 28:9 and 28:10, that describe the additional sacrificial offering.[545]

Early on, various introductions for these verses were composed. Two of them are included in the present *Musaf Amida*—one, a reverse alphabetical acrostic beginning *Tikkanta Shabbat*,[546] and the other "Y'Hi Ratzon Mil'Fanecha.[547] These were probably originally rival introductions, but at some point it was decided to include both.[548] *Tikkanta Shabbat* is a historical recounting of the establishment of the Sabbath and its sacrifices, while *Y'Hi Ratzon Mil'Fanecha* is a petition for the restoration of Israel and the renewal of the Temple service.

The sentence after the biblical quotation in the *Musaf Amida*, beginning *Yis'm'chu b'malchut'cha*, is an alternative version, apparently of Sephardic origin, of the first part of the paragraph of the *Shacharit* version of the *Amida* that begins, *V'lo n'tato*. The contrast between the two is interesting. The *Shacharit* version recites that God did not grant the Sabbath to heathens, idolators, or the unrighteous, He granted it just to the Jewish people. The *Musaf* version, however, is a petition: "May those who observe the Sabbath and call it a delight rejoice in Your kingdom." Where the *Shacharit Amida* voices the idea of the Jews as the Chosen People, the *Musaf* version asks that God favor all who joyfully observe *Shabbat*.

In the Middle Ages, anti-Semites often used Jewish prayers referring to the Jews as the Chosen People as a pretext for persecuting them. The discrepancy between the two *Amidot* may derive from liturgical changes made in response to these events.

The *Musaf Kedusha*

The only other change from the *Shacharit Amida* to the *Musaf Amida* in the *Shabbat* service is in *Kedusha*. As in the *Shacharit Amida*, the silent reading of the *Musaf Amida* includes only the most ancient form of *Kedusha, Ata Kadosh*. However, the *Kedusha* for the repetition of the *Amida* is different.

The *Musaf Kedusha*, in the Ashkenazic tradition, begins with the most ancient form of introduction to *Kedusha, Na'aritz'cha v'nak'dish'cha* (We will declare Your awesomeness and holiness), a quotation from the Talmud (*Sof.* 16:12). This is to be recited "as though we are inviting ourselves to say *Kedusha*."[549] This was the version recited in ancient Israel, but adopted by Saadya Gaon, a Babylonian scholar of the tenth century, in his prayer code, which became the model for the Ashkenazic siddur.[550] A similar form is reflected in fragments found in the Cairo Geniza.[551]

The connecting verses in the *Musaf Kedusha* are also different than those said in *Shacharit.* The connecting sentence between *Kadosh, kadosh, kadosh* and *Baruch k'vod Adonai mim'komo* in the *Musaf Amida, K'vodo malei olam,* is a payyetanic addition (i.e., a poetic addition by one of the authors of *piyyutim* in the early Middle Ages).[552]

Beginning with *Mim'komo hu yifen,* between *Baruch k'vod Adonai mim'komo* and the *Shema* in the *Musaf Kedusha* is a reference to saying the *Shema* twice daily, as an introduction to the *Shema.* The *Shema* is included in the *Musaf Kedusha,* unlike the other *Kedushas.* In the fifth century C.E. in Persia, persecution of the Jews resulted in the government's prohibiting the reading of the *Shema* in public. A government agent would stand in the synagogue during services to enforce this law; after the time for the saying of the *Shema* had passed, he would leave. To thwart the authorities, the rabbis slipped the *Shema* into the *Musaf Kedusha,* by which time the government agent had left.[553] As a remembrance of these events, the reading of the *Shema* during the *Musaf Kedusha* was retained.

Between the *Shema* and *Ani Adonai Eloheichem* lie the remains of an ancient *piyyut, Echad Hu Eloheinu* (One is our God). Like many other parts of *Kedusha,* this appears to date from the late Amoraic period in Babylonia.[554]

Ani Adonai Eloheichem is quoted from Numbers 15:41 as a response of God to the quoted lines from the Prophets in which the angels addressed God. After a connecting line, the congregation responds, "*Yimloch Adonai l'olam, Elohayich tziyon, l'dor va'dor halleluya,* the last line of Psalm 146.

The final paragraph of *Kedusha* is the same in both *Shacharit* and *Musaf,* beginning, *L'dor va'dor* (May God reign). This paragraph, from Exodus 15:18, originated as a proof-text for the *Yimloch* line, but was substituted for *Yimloch,* probably in Babylonia, because an Aramaic translation was needed for the *Kedusha D'Sidra* (*Kedusha* of the Lesson, another version of the *Kedusha*) in keeping with the practice of having the *meturgeman* (interpreter) translate biblical quotations into the vernacular, and there was no authorized Aramaic translation for the Hagiographa at the time.

KEDUSHA D'SIDRA (KEDUSHA OF THE LESSON): U'VA L'TZION GOEL (AND A REDEEMER SHALL COME TO ZION)

On weekdays, instead of the *Musaf Amida,* we recite at this point on Aramaic prayer called the *Kedusha D'Sidra* (*Kedusha* of the Lesson), which begins *U'va l'tzion goel* (And a redeemer shall come to Zion) (Isa. 59:20). This originated in antiquity, and is mentioned in the Talmud[555] as a prayer recited after a public Torah lesson. It was originally attached to *Tachanun*,[556] the personal private prayer, and its presence may indicate that study sessions were followed by private prayer, meditation, and contemplation, in the same manner as the *Amida*. According to Natronai Gaon, a medieval Babylonian leader, at the end of the lesson, verses of the Prophets were recited, beginning with Isaiah 59:20 and culminating with the two verses that Isaiah and Ezekiel heard the angels say to God, which form the core of the *Kedusha*.[557] The verses were translated into the vernacular of the time, Aramaic. As survival became harder and there was no longer time during the week for study, the daily lesson eventually disappeared, but the verses that form the *Kedusha D'Sidra* remained.[558]

This is another example of mystical influence on the service, and it is therefore omitted in the Reform liturgy. The *Merkava* mystics, the earliest practitioners of Jewish mysticism, believed that *Kedusha* had special powers to aid the worshipper in ascending to the heavenly realm, and so inserted *Kedusha* at several points in the service to ensure that the worshipper would say it at least once.

Consistent with its origin as a vernacular form of the *Amida* to assist those unable to read Hebrew and to culminate a study session, the *Kedusha D'Sidra* is a time to go back through the sequence of mind-states of the *Amida* with greater comprehension, to gain understanding of what one is doing. One should go slowly through it and take time after it for personal meditation, as after the *Amida*.

Concluding Prayers

KADDISH SHALEM (COMPLETE KADDISH)

As discussed earlier, *Kaddish*, in various forms, punctuates the traditional service. Now we pass again from deep focus to a sense of spiritual community. The full *Kaddish* is said after *Musaf* or the *Kedusha D'Sidra* because the service is ending. See p. 47 for a discussion of *Kaddish*. *Kaddish Shalem* is omitted in the Reform service, as is the entire *Musaf* service. The Reform service includes only *Aleinu* and the Mourner's *Kaddish* after the Torah and *Haftarah*.

EIN K'ELOHEINU

This popular hymn was inspired by a sentence in the prayer of Hannah. "There is no holy one like the Lord, there is none beside Thee; There is no rock like our God" (1 Sam. 2:2). It originated in ancient Israel and was included in the first written prayer code, the *Seder Rav Amram* (ninth century).

Ein K'Eloheinu entered the Sabbath and holiday liturgy due to a mishnaic tradition that every man is supposed to recite one hundred blessings each day. On Sabbath and holidays, the *Amida* is reduced from nineteen to seven blessings, so *Ein K'Eloheinu* is added to make up part of the difference.[559] It can be regarded as a "*beracha* machine," designed to yield as many *berachot* (blessings) as possible. It is also a joyous hymn intended to rekindle community feeling in preparation for *Aleinu*, the "Jewish Pledge of Allegiance," which concludes public prayer.

The prayer is acrostic. Originally the stanzas were arranged so that the

137

prayer began, *Mi K'Eloheinu?* (Who is like our God?) This question was then answered: *Ata Hu Eloheinu* (You are our God). Rashi or his students rearranged the stanzas so that the first letters of the first three stanzas form the word *amen* a total of four times. Together with the words *baruch* and *ata* appearing four times each in the last two stanzas, this makes four acrostic blessings, making up the bulk of the "blessing deficit" left by the *Shabbat* and holiday *Amida*..

At the end of *Ein K'Eloheinu* it is customary to recite a line from the Talmud,[560] "You are He to Whom our forefathers burnt the fragrant incense" (*Ata hu she'hiktiru avoteinu l'fanecha et k'toret ha'samim*).[561] In the Ashkenazic ritual, a paragraph from the Talmud (*Ber.* 64-end) follows, which recapitulates the matching in the last part of the *Aleinu* of the past (there the Creation, here the Temple sacrifices) and hopes for the future. "When all your children shall be taught of the Lord," it says, "great shall be the peace of your children." The Orthodox liturgy adds other talmudic excerpts, including one from the *Mishna* describing the Levites' songs for the days of the week that accompanied the daily *tamid* offerings, and excerpts extolling the virtues of religious scholarship.

Reading talmudic excerpts here has a subtle purpose. In antiquity, *Kaddish* could only be said immediately after a session of studying the Bible or the Talmud, consistent with its ancient function of closing a study session. *Ein K'Eloheinu* does not contain any excerpts from the Bible or the Talmud. Therefore, to make it possible to say *Kaddish* after *Ein K'Eloheinu*, a talmudic excerpt had to be tacked onto the end of that prayer.

In the prayerbooks used in Conservative congregations, *Ein K'Eloheinu* appears after *Kaddish Shalem* and before *Aleinu*, which is followed in turn by the Mourner's *Kaddish*. Many congregations reverse the order of these prayers so that the Mourner's *Kaddish* can be said after a talmudic excerpt is read at the end of *Ein K'Eloheinu*.

In the Orthodox liturgy, no fewer than three types of *Kaddish* are recited during the concluding prayers. *Kaddish Shalem* follows the *Amida*, marking the end of that segment of the service. *Ein K'Eloheinu* follows, and after the "study" of the ensuing talmudic excerpts, the mourners present recite the Scholar's *Kaddish*, *Kaddish D'Rabbanan*, which traditionally follows a study session. *Aleinu* is then recited in the Orthodox liturgy, concluding the formal prayer service, followed by recital of the Mourners' *Kaddish* as the non-mourners present perform their first *mitzvah* in their newly altered mind-state by responding as a congregation.

Ein K'Eloheinu is offered in the Reform prayerbook as one of many optional songs and hymns.

TALMUD STUDY AND *KADDISH D'RABBANAN*

In the Orthodox liturgy, a brief talmudic study session follows *Ein K'Eloheinu*. The passages studied parallel the *Aleinu* which we are about to recite.

In Orthodox congregations, the Scholar's *Kaddish, Kaddish D'Rabbanan*, is then recited by mourners. See page 47.

ALEINU (IT IS OUR DUTY): THE "JEWISH PLEDGE OF ALLEGIANCE"

Aleinu is a symbol of loyalty to Judaism in the face of persecution, a "Jewish Pledge of Allegiance." Through prayer and study we have tried to achieve *devekut*, a mental state of cleaving to God in daily life. We have fortified our minds to observe the *mitzvot*, the commandments, and to resist evil. Now we contemplate the example of our medieval ancestors, who used prayer to fortify their minds so powerfully that they resisted evil even on pain of death.

In 1171 in Blois, France, thirty-four Jewish men and seventeen Jewish women, falsely accused of ritual murder, chanted *Aleinu* as a sanctification of God's name, a *kiddush Hashem*, as they were burned at the stake.[562] The heroism of these martyrs was honored by Simcha ben Samuel, (a student of Rashi who wrote the *Machzor Vitry*, one of the early written prayer codes, during the eleventh century), by making *Aleinu* a regular part of the service.[563]

Aleinu thus became a symbol of loyalty to Judaism in the face of persecution. It is, for us, a pledge of allegiance to God and the Jewish people. Rather than merely pledging loyalty, however, we acknowledge in *Aleinu* the obligations that loyalty imposes upon us. Being Jewish is not easy.

Since the thirteenth century, *Aleinu* has ended the official service. The recitation of hymns like *Adon Olam* and *Ein K'Eloheinu* at the end of the service is optional, a relatively recent addition to the Ashkenazic service out of consideration for mourners present to say the Mourner's *Kaddish*.[564]

According to rabbinic authorities, *Aleinu* was written by Rav, one of the founders of the Babylonian academies, in the third century c.e.[565] It was originally part of the intermediate blessings of the *Amida* on the High Holidays, the introduction to the *Malchuyot*, and included the ancient Temple ritual of prostrating oneself on the floor, still practiced on the High Holidays in Ashkenazic congregations. Instead of prostrating ourselves, on other occasions when *Aleinu* is said, we bow on the words *Va'anachnu kor'im u'mistachavim u'modim* (And we bend our knees, prostrate ourselves, and give thanks).

Although *Aleinu* did not originate as a mystical prayer, the early *Merkava* mystics had a legend that Rabbi Akiva was able to ascend to heaven through its recital. They put *Aleinu* into the first-person singular so that it could be used by individuals as a meditative device.[566]

Its theme of the duties of being a Jew may explain why *Aleinu*, along with the *Shema*, came to be one of the prayers sung by Jewish martyrs before and during the Crusades as *kiddush Hashem*, the sanctification of God's name at the time of death. We accept those duties even at the time when they are most difficult to perform.

The first paragraph of *Aleinu* focuses on Jews as the Chosen People. For what are we chosen? For duties, not for privileges. It begins: *Aleinu l'shabeach la'Adon ha'col, la'tet g'dula l'yotzer b'reishit*—We have "the duty to praise the Lord of all things, and to give [better, accord or proclaim] greatness to the Creator of the Genesis." This duty to praise God is an allusion to the duty of Jews to pray. As the structure of the *Amida* reflects (as discussed above), we have to achieve the necessary mental state to praise God before we can make our collective requests, before God will consider us worthy to be heard.[567] These collective requests are for the benefit of all humankind, not just the Jewish people. Thus, *Aleinu* articulates our duty to the outside world. It is an acknowledgment of our societal obligations, and of prayer as an instrument in achieving them.

Why do we, and not other people, have these duties? Because, says *Aleinu*, God made us different: *Shelo asanu k'goyei ha'aratzot v'lo samanu k'mishpa'chot ha'adama* (For He did not make us like the pagans of the world, nor did He place us like the heathen tribes of the earth). We have this responsibility because that is what God has willed. We cannot be sure why a Jew—Moses—was selected to be given the Torah, and not an Edomite or Philistine or Babylonian—or, indeed, someone from China, Africa, or some other part of the world. By being and remaining Jews, we accept this responsibility.

Having accepted the duty to praise and glorify God through prayer, we proceed to ritually perform this duty in *Aleinu* itself. We continue with the verse, perhaps from the ancient Temple ritual, in which we bow or, on the High Holidays, prostrate ourselves before God.

What comes next, beginning with *She'hu noteh shamayim v'yosed aretz*, is a description of God's kingship—appropriate in view of the prayer's origin as an introduction to the Kingship verses of the High Holidays—that paraphrases the biblical description of the Creation of the universe. This description of God's kingship ends with a quotation from Moses: *V'yadata ha'yom va'hashevota el l'vavecha, ki Adonai hu ha'Elohim ba'shamayim mi'ma'al v'al ha'aretz mi'tachat, ein od* (Know therefore today and keep in mind that the Lord alone is God in heaven above and on earth below; there is no other) (Deut. 4:39).

The final paragraph of *Aleinu*, beginning, *Al kein n'kaveh l'cha* (We therefore hope in You), is of later origin, and is read only in the Ashkenazic service. Perhaps because it is not part of the original prayer, it is customary to read it silently up to the final quotations from the Torah and the Prophets.

Having alluded to the beginning of time in the first part of the prayer, we now express our hopes for the end of time, when "the world will be perfected under God's kingship." The prayer ends with quotes from the Torah (Exod. 15:18) and the Prophets (Zech. 14:9) that contain such predictions: "The Lord will reign forever and ever," and "The Lord shall be king over all the earth; in that day the Lord shall be One and His name One."

Aleinu historically has attracted criticism from anti-Semites. The prayer today reads, in part, *She'lo sam chelkeinu ka'heim v'goraleinu k'chol ha'monam, va'anachnu kor'im* (Who has not made our portion like theirs, nor our lot like that of their masses; and we bow . . .). Originally, however, it read, *She'hem mishtachavim l'hevel va'rik umit'pal'lim el El lo yoshia* (Nor our lot like that of their masses, for they bow to emptiness and vanity, and pray to a god who cannot save; but we bow . . .).[568]

Though the words "emptiness and vanity" were taken from Isaiah 30:7, reputedly by a rabbi who lived in a non-Christian country four centuries before the founding of Islam, both the Christians and the Muslims claimed that this language was intended as an insult to them. Beginning in the 1370s, the Inquisition in France and Germany (then the Holy Roman Empire) attempted to forbid the recital of *Aleinu*. It was bolstered by the coincidence, pointed out by an apostate, that the numerical value of the Hebrew letters in the word "vanity" was the same as that of the Hebrew letters in the name of Jesus. This charge was temporarily overcome in 1399. However, starting in the 1440s, when Gutenberg invented printing, the Church began a campaign of censorship of books. Various parts of the *siddur*, including *Aleinu*, were attacked as heresy, and Hebrew books were burned in many places in Europe.

In an attempt to quell this continuing form of persecution, in 1554 the Jewish community, at a meeting of congregational representatives in Ferrara, Italy,[569] adopted a system of self-censorship in which a panel of local rabbis, called the *haskama*, had to give prior approval before any Hebrew book could be published. Under this system, *Aleinu* was altered throughout Europe by the end of the sixteenth century to excise the reference to the masses bowing to "emptiness and vanity" and substitute the less controversial text we use today.

Another thing the *Haskama* did was to prohibit spitting[570] during

Aleinu. The Hebrew word for vanity, *rik,* also means "spittle." It became customary in Europe during the Middle Ages to spit when this word was said.[571] This custom reinforced the impression of Gentiles, unaware of the synonym, that these words were intended as a slight against their religion, and that is why the *Haskama* forbade the practice.[572]

In the Reform prayerbook, four different versions of *Aleinu* are included, in keeping with the Reform view that congregations should be offered a variety of liturgical options. All omit part or all of *Al kein n'kaveh l'cha,* and three omit the sentences that begin *Shelo assanu k'goyei ha'aratzot* (Who has not made us like other nations of the earth) and *Shelo sam chelkeinu ka'heim* (Who has not assigned us a portion like theirs). This conforms to the theological position of the many Reform Jews who oppose the concept of the Jews being considered the Chosen People.

MOURNER'S *KADDISH*

For information on the Mourner's *Kaddish,* see page 56. Its recital after the service has been formally ended with *Aleinu* is at once the conclusion of the service and the performance of the first *mitzvah* after finishing the service. The mourner is performing a *mitzvah* by remembering a loved one, and the other worshippers present are performing the *mitzvah* of comforting the mourners.

ADON OLAM, PSALM OF THE DAY, AND *AN'IM Z'MIROT*

Spiritually transformed, with joy and a feeling of fulfillment at having performed a good deed in comforting the mourners in our spiritual community, we prepare to depart. We retain a sense of unity with the community until we meet again for prayer.

We signify this sense of unity, and comfort mourners, with final hymns. On the Sabbath and Festivals, *Adon Olam* is recited. On weekdays, a Psalm of the Day, the psalm recited on that day of the week by the Levites in the Second Temple, is recited. In mystically inclined congregations, the mystical prayer *An'im Z'mirot,* also known as *Shir Ha'Kavod,* the Song of Glory, may be said. *An'im Z'mirot* is discussed on page 48. It was believed by the Lurianic kabbalists to aid in the ascent of the worshipper's soul to a higher spiritual realm and to hasten *tikkun olam,* the restoration of the original harmony of the universe.

The poetic hymn *Adon Olam* has been attributed to the poet Solomon ibn Gabirol, who lived in eleventh-century Spain, but scholars think that it may be much older, perhaps originating in the Babylonian academies. Its recital has been customary in the service since fourteenth-century Germany. It originally may have been used as a prayer to be recited at the end of the *Ma'ariv* (evening) service, before going to sleep. That would explain why it ends: "My soul I give to His care asleep, awake, for He is near, and with my soul, my body, too, God is with me, I have no fear."[573]

Adon Olam is not really part of the service. It probably was added to make mourners feel more comfortable after having said the Mourner's *Kaddish*, and it should be recited with that idea. For that reason, the melodies to which it is sung in the Ashkenazic service tend to be boisterous and upbeat, in contrast to *Kaddish*. One melody reputedly was taken from a nineteenth-century German drinking song.

YIZKOR

The custom of memorializing deceased members of one's family during the *Yom Kippur* services dates from the Gaonic period in Babylonia, and is first mentioned in *Midrash Tanhuma, Ha'azinu,* dating from the fifth century C.E.[574] It was extended in the Ashkenazic ritual to the three pilgrimage Festivals, *Sukkot*, Passover, and *Shavuot*, in the wake of the massacre of the Jewish communities of Mainz and Speyer in the Rhineland during the First Crusade.[575] The custom of the *yahrzeit*, lighting a candle and reciting the Mourner's *Kaddish* on the anniversary of the death of a parent, arose in Germany at the same time.[576]

First comes the *Yizkor* prayer itself, a short paragraph. This prayer originally was the introduction to the reading of a list of a community's victims of the Crusades.[577] The names of those in the original lists were lost, but were replaced by the custom of inserting the names of one's own loved ones.[578]

The next prayer is *El Malei Rachamim* (God, Full of Mercy). This was written by rabbis in Poland following the Chmielnicki Pogroms of 1648, in which an estimated 100,000 Jews were murdered.[579] Reflecting kabbalistic influence, the prayer is an attempt to ease the condition of loved ones in the afterlife.[580] Mentally, we reach into the afterlife and commune with the deceased.

The custom is for people whose parents are still living to leave the room during *Yizkor*. This custom may have its origin in medieval superstition, as one commentator put it, "so as not to tempt Satan, or on account of the evil eye,"[581] and it has been eliminated by the Reform movement and in many Conservative synagogues.

Immediately following *Yizkor* on the pilgrimage Festivals, *Av Ha'Rachamim* is recited. It also is recited on *Shabbat* during the Torah service. This prayer originated after the Rhineland Jews were massacred in the First Crusade in 1096, as a plea for divine retribution against the soldiers who had killed them.[582] The purpose of seeking retribution is to bring peace to the souls of the departed, viewed as appropriate on a day of rest.[583] It is omitted in the Reform liturgy, except during the Martyrology on *Yom Kippur*.[584]

The Afternoon and Evening Services

MINCHA: THE AFTERNOON SERVICE

The traditional weekday afternoon service came to be recited in lieu of the afternoon sacrifice after the destruction of the Second Temple. It consists of *Ashrei*, Half *Kaddish*, the *Amida*, *Tachanun*, *Kaddish Titkabal*, *Aleinu*, and the Mourner's *Kaddish*.

This order possesses a logic that is apparent from the functions and origins of the component prayers, as follows:

Ashrei: Psalm 145; it is recited as a representative of all the psalms, to prepare the mind for the *Amida*.

Half *Kaddish*: The ancient prayer for ending a study session punctuates the service, marking the boundaries between its major components. Here, it marks the boundary between preparing the mind and addressing God with our requests.

Amida: We speak to God, progressing through a series of visualizations from personal enlightenment to community revival to world peace. Because the Priestly Blessing was not recited in the Second Temple at the afternoon sacrifice, it is omitted, and *Shalom Rav* is said instead of *Sim Shalom* for the final Peace Blessing.[585]

Tachanun: This originated as a time to address God through silent meditation regarding our personal needs and feelings, after having addressed our collective requests to God in the *Amida*.

Kaddish Titkabal: Again *Kaddish* punctuates the service, marking the

145

boundary between the *Amida* and *Aleinu*, between addressing
God in an altered mind-state and pledging allegiance to the
Jewish people.

Aleinu: The service formally ends with the assembled worshippers,
having collectively achieved a new state of mind, solidifying the
spiritual community that has been formed between them by
reciting a prayer that has been a symbol of Jewish steadfastness
since it was recited by the martyrs who were burned at the stake
in Blois, France, by the Crusaders in 1171.

Mourners' *Kaddish*: The spiritual community in its new state of mind
performs its first *mitzvah* together—that of comforting mourners
by responding to their recital of the Mourner's *Kaddish*.

Note that the *Shema* is not recited as part of *Mincha*. This is because the
Mishna prescribed the recital of the *Shema* three times a day—once in the
morning, once in the evening service, and once when going to bed.[586]
Saying the *Shema* a fourth time would be to say a prayer for no purpose, an
act forbidden by talmudic law.

On *Shabbat*, it was customary in antiquity for the afternoon service to
be recited around noon following a lengthy sermon.[587] In later centuries,
the sermon and the afternoon service were moved back to accommodate a
siesta following the *Musaf* service. Because of this linkage with the sermon,
on *Shabbat* afternoons, *U'va L'Tzion Goel* (A Redeemer Will Come to Zion),
called the *Kedusha D'Sidra* (*Kedusha* of the Lesson), a prayer that always
served to conclude the study of the Torah, came to be recited immediately
after *Ashrei* in the afternoon service.[588] This prayer may have originated as
a short form of the *Amida*, judging from its internal structure.

The Half *Kaddish* then is recited, followed by Psalms 69:14. This verse,
beginning, "May my prayer to You, God, be at a propitious time," was
probably inserted by Rashi, who may have regarded its reference to a
"propitious time" as including the afternoon.[589] The same verse was also
inserted into *Ma Tovu,* the introductory prayer of the preliminary service in
the morning. We cannot be certain what time is propitious for prayer, the
verse implies; therefore we should pray at a variety of different times.

The Torah service follows on *Shabbat* and Festivals, and is followed in
turn by the *Amida*. A special paragraph is inserted in the *Amida* after the
silent *Kedusha*. This paragraph is the afternoon introduction to *Kedushat
Ha'Yom*, Sanctification of the Day. The Priestly Blessing is generally omitted
at *Mincha* on *Shabbat* and Festivals, except on fast days, out of fear that the
priests may have drunk wine and be unfit to recite it.[590] In the Ashkenazic
liturgy, *Shalom Rav* is recited at *Mincha* instead of *Sim Shalom* as the final
Peace Blessing of the *Amida*. The rest of *Mincha*, through *Aleinu* and the

Mourner's *Kaddish*, is essentially the same as on weekdays. At the end, however, a series of psalms beginning with Psalm 104, *Barchi Nafshi*, is appended during the winter, while, at other times in the Orthodox liturgy, *Pirkei Avot* (Ethics of the Fathers) from the *Mishna* is read. Medieval legend has it that Moses died on a *Shabbat* afternoon, and that, therefore, God's justice must be praised through these readings as it must be praised in any case of mourning.[591]

KABBALAT SHABBAT: WELCOMING THE SABBATH

Introduction

When we welcome the Sabbath on Friday night, we do so first in the synagogue, in a special service that is tacked onto the beginning of the evening service. We then go home and perform the rituals of lighting candles and saying blessings on the wine and *challa* (Sabbath bread).

Although the customs of lighting candles on Friday night and saying the home blessings on the wine and *challa* are ancient, the synagogue prayers with which Jews today usher in the Sabbath on Friday night developed, for the most part, among the sixteenth century kabbalists of Safed under the leadership of Moses Cordovero and Isaac Luria and their followers.[592] It was the custom of the kabbalists in Safed to celebrate the beginning of the Sabbath outdoors, in an open field or garden,[593] and then to return to their homes singing songs such as *Shalom Aleichem, Mal'achei Ha'Shareit* (Hello to You, Ministering Angels), which was written for that purpose. The song, written as a greeting to angels, was based on a mystical legend that each person was accompanied home from services on Friday night by a good angel and a bad angel. If the angels found the *Shabbat* candles lit, the good angel gained ascendancy over the bad angel.

Prior to the late sixteenth century, only Psalms 92 and 93 were recited on *Shabbat* evening before the official beginning of *Shabbat*, with *Barchu*.[594] They were chosen because, according to the *Midrash*, they were composed by Adam—Psalm 93 (Friday's psalm) on the day he was created, before his sin, and Psalm 92 after he repented.[595] They thus symbolize the link between *Shabbat* and the primeval purity of man before the fall of Adam. This link took on special meaning in the Lurianic Kabbalah, which holds that Adam's sin caused the sparks of divinity to be scattered and mixed with the profane throughout the world.[596] Man's essential state of exile from the divine can be ended only through *tikkun olam*, the "mending of the world."[597] *Shabbat* foreshadows the day when *tikkun olam* will be complete.

The Six Psalms

In the mid-1500s, Rabbi Moses Cordovero, *dayan* (judge) of Safed, introduced the practice, still customary in the Ashkenazic ritual, of welcoming the arrival of the Sabbath with the recitation of six psalms, symbolic of the six weekdays, followed by the singing of a hymn, *Lecha Dodi* (Come, my beloved, to meet the bride; let us welcome the Sabbath day).[598] These are preceded by an initial poetic hymn, or *piyyut*, of kabbalistic origin called *Yedid Nefesh*, or, in the Orthodox liturgy, by the Song of Songs. The Song of Songs, like *Lecha Dodi*, carries out the theme of greeting the Sabbath with the same emotions as a groom greeting his bride.

The kabbalistic innovation of reciting six psalms was actually a revival of a much older custom. In ninth-century Babylonia, six psalms (not those later selected by the kabbalists) were recited, possibly to commemorate the long-discontinued Second Temple practice of sounding the *shofar* six times at regular intervals on Friday afternoon.[599]

When the kabbalists selected additional psalms for the other days of the week, they skipped Psalm 94, which had no reference to God's kinship, and selected Psalms 95, 96, 97, 98, and 99, all of which do. They added, for Friday, Psalm 29, which was given special significance in the Talmud since it contains the word *kol* (voice) seven times, the same number of times the word is found in the biblical account of the giving of the Torah at Mount Sinai (Exod. 19:1–20:8) and, therefore, was associated with the revelation at Sinai.[600] This also accounts for the custom of reciting Psalm 29 during the return of the Torah to the Ark on *Shabbat* morning and standing during its recitation.[601]

Today, the six Kingship psalms, 95 to 99 and 29, are recited in the Ashkenazic liturgy as an acknowledgment that God is in charge of us the entire week, not only on *Shabbat*. Then we sing *Lecha Dodi*. In the Sephardic liturgy, however, the service begins with Psalm 92.

Lecha Dodi (Come My Beloved)

Lecha Dodi is a hymn that is normally attributed to Solomon Halevi Alkabez, a Jew of Safed during the mid-sixteenth century. Alkabez was the brother-in-law of Moses Cordovero, judge of the rabbinical court of Safed and a student of Joseph Karo, author of the *Shulchan Aruch*, still the most authoritative code of Jewish law for Sephardic Jews.

Alkabez borrowed from an earlier composition by Moses ben Machir, a poet who had lived in Safed in his youth, which contained the identical *Lecha Dodi* refrain and seven stanzas. Alkabez's principal contribution to the poem recited in the liturgy today appears to have been to rewrite most of the stanzas and add an eighth one so that they formed an acrostic of his Hebrew name, *Shlomo Ha'Levi.*

The first stanza of *Lecha Dodi* begins, *Shamor v'zachor b'shir echad* (Observe and remember with a single song [simultaneously]). The Fourth Commandment, on observance of the Sabbath, begins in Deuteronomy 5:12 with *shamor* (observe) and in Exodus 20:8 with *zachor* (remember). The rabbis explained this discrepancy by saying that God spoke both words simultaneously.[602]

Lecha Dodi contains an allusion to the midrashic idea that the Sabbath was the purpose of Creation. "Last in Creation, first in conception," it says. The same theme is found in the excerpt from the Torah that is recited as part of the *Kiddush* on Friday night.

At the end of *Lecha Dodi*, the congregation rises and turns to face the doorway,[603] to "greet the Sabbath bride." This is both a dramatization of the kabbalistic personification of the Sabbath as a bride and a reminiscence of the kabbalists' custom of greeting the Sabbath outdoors.

Psalms 92 and 93

As discussed above, Psalms 92 and 93 originally began the *Shabbat* evening liturgy, and they remain the beginning of the Sephardic service. Psalm 92 was the psalm recited by the Levites during the *tamid* offering on *Shabbat*, so it can be assumed that its recital on *Shabbat* in the synagogue is ancient. Similarly, Psalm 93 was recited by the Levites during the *tamid* offering on the sixth day of the week.[604]

Chatzi Kaddish

The *Shabbat* psalms and *Lecha Dodi* having been said, we now pass from *Kabbalat Shabbat* to the *Ma'Ariv* service. To make this transition, a Half-*Kaddish* is said. For a detailed discussion of *Kaddish*, see page 47.

Shabbat Home Observance

LIGHTING THE SABBATH CANDLES

The Talmud required only one Sabbath candle to be lit, as an *oneg Shabbat* (Sabbath delight) and a symbol of domestic harmony.[605] The candle was a Sabbath "delight" because, in antiquity, having light in the evening was a luxury. As the Diaspora moved north to Germany, however, the late summer sunset gave rise to new eating habits. It became impractical to delay dinner until sunset. Lighting only one candle at dinner would not be a Sabbath delight, because it was still light outside; it would serve an exclusively religious purpose. Consequently, the rationale for the Sabbath candle-lighting changed in medieval Germany. One candle was to perform the *mitzvah* of candle-lighting at the start of the Sabbath, but that candle's light could not be used for a practical purpose. Therefore, a second candle was required to be lit at sunset, so that one could say, when using the light of the candles, that it was the second candle's light that was used.[606]

The custom of candle-lighting originated as a home and family observance, and it remains so among Orthodox and Conservative Jews. Reform congregations, however, may elect to light the candles in the synagogue.[607] The ten alternative Friday night services contained in the Reform prayerbook *Gates of Prayer* all indicate that the candles are to be lighted before the *Kabbalat Shabbat* prayers are said.

The blessing associated with lighting the candles originated in the eighth century in response to the Karaite sect, which asserted that only biblical, and not rabbinical, law was binding. The Karaites, quoting the verse "You shall kindle no fire throughout your settlement on the Sabbath day" (Exod. 35:3), insisted that one must sit in darkness on Friday night. The rabbis interpreted this verse as meaning that the lights could be kindled

150

if it was done before the Sabbath began. To strengthen their position and assert their authority, the rabbis proclaimed that lighting the candles not only was permitted, but was a religious obligation, citing the prophetic designation of the Sabbath as a "delight" (Isa. 58:13) as meaning that the Sabbath was intended to be spent pleasantly, not sitting in darkness. As with all other religious obligations, once the obligation was established, a blessing was required to be said on performing it. This principle was extended to lighting candles on Festivals as well.[608]

Contrary to common understanding, the obligation to light the *Shabbat* candles falls equally on men and women. However, medieval rabbis assigned the obligation primarily to the woman of the house, on the theory that "[b]ecause she is normally found at home and involved in the work of the house, it is easier for her to meet this obligation."[609] More specifically, women were exempt under Orthodox Jewish law from the requirement of attending prayer services at the synagogue, and could not form part of a *minyan*, the ten adults required for public prayer, so it became customary for women to light the candles before the men returned from the synagogue. There is no injunction in Jewish law against men lighting the candles, and the rule seems really to be that the primary duty falls on whichever adult member of a family has the easiest time meeting the obligation. Since women now count toward a *minyan* in many American synagogues, the rationale for reserving the candle-lighting to women has lost much of its vitality.

It is customary for the person lighting the candles to cover her eyes while lighting them. This custom arose to reconcile three conflicting principles of Jewish law. A blessing is to be recited before the experience for which it is pronounced, but this is not possible in lighting the Sabbath candles, because the Sabbath begins when the blessing on lighting the candles is made, and once the Sabbath begins, it is not permitted to light a fire. Therefore, the person lights the candles before making the blessing, but shields her eyes from the light while saying the entire blessing.[610] There is no reason for anyone else present to shield their eyes as well, but it has become common for the person lighting the candles to use the occasion for personal meditation, and, accordingly, for others present to use the time for the same purpose. A meditational prayer beginning *Y'hi ratzon l'fanecha* based on *B. Shabbat* 23b is included in the Orthodox liturgy, but any method of personal meditation is appropriate.

THE BLESSING ON THE CHILDREN,
SHALOM ALEICHEM, AND *EISHET CHAYIL*

After lighting the candles and before the Friday evening home *Kiddush*, it is customary, though not mandatory, among traditional Jews, to bless their children, to sing a song—*Shalom Aleichem*—and to recite an excerpt from Proverbs, *Eishet Chayil* (A Woman of Valor). These are omitted in the Reform liturgy, except that *Shalom Aleichem* may be sung at the table.

Traditionally, the mother would light the candles while the father was in synagogue. When the father returned from synagogue, he would bless the children, and then the family would sing *Shalom Aleichem* together.[611]

When we bless the children, we are emulating the ancient priests. We recite the Priestly Blessing, beginning, *Y'varech'cha Adonai v'yish'm'recha*, the most ancient of our prayers and one that may have originated in First-Temple times, or even earlier as a faith-healing incantation. We place our hands on the children's heads, in a manner reminiscent of the lifting of the hands by the priests while reciting the Priestly Blessing in the Temple in Jerusalem. We become as holy as priests, as capable of transmitting divine power and light to our children as any priest could be. In Judaism, unlike Roman Catholicism and Eastern Orthodox Christianity, each person has a direct relationship with God. As parents, we invoke our relationship with God for the protection of our children, who are not yet old enough to understand their own relationship with the Divinity.

As a preface to the Priestly Blessing, with our hands on our children's heads, we recite one blessing for our sons and another for our daughters. The blessing for sons is biblically commanded; it is the blessing Jacob gave on his deathbed to his grandsons Ephraim and Menashe, the sons of Joseph (Gen. 48:20). The significance of this is that Ephraim and Menashe were the first Jews born in the Diaspora. Though born and raised in Egypt, in an alien land and culture, they turned out to be the progenitors of a great people (as Jacob prophesied), and remained loyal to their parents and their faith. Jacob's blessing worked.[612] We hope that the same blessing will be equally effective for our own children.

The blessing for daughters is not of biblical origin, but invokes the examples of the Matriarchs: Sarah, Rebecca, Rachel, and Leah. Dr. Ron Wolfson writes, "Sarah was a woman of courage whose response to adversity was laughter. Rebecca, even more than Abraham, is the biblical model of hospitality and human concern. And Rachel and Leah are the two biblical characters who fully model being 'their sibling's keeper,' showing real sisterhood. These are the values we wish on any child."[613]

After blessing the children, we sing *Shalom Aleichem*. This is a song sung to angels. It originated among the Lurianic kabbalists in Safed, Israel in the 1500s. The followers of the Ari, Rabbi Isaac Luria, would go out to the fields to welcome the Sabbath; then they would walk back to their homes, bless their children, and sing this song.

According to a legend of Rabbi Jose ben Rabbi Yehuda recorded in the

Talmud (*B. Shab.* 119a), on every *Shabbat* eve, two angels visit every home—the Angel of Good and the Angel of Evil. If the house is messy, the parents are unhappy, the children are fighting, and the table is not set for *Shabbat*, then the Angel of Evil rejoices and says, "May all of your *Shabbatot* be just like this one," and the Angel of Good is forced to agree. But if the angels see the house clean, the candles lit, and the family seated happily at the table, then the Angel of Good rejoices and says, "May all of your *Shabbatot* be just like this one," and the Angel of Evil is forced to agree.

By singing *Shalom Aleichem* to these angels, we demonstrate our happiness, our *shalom bayit* (household peace), for them and, it is hoped, inspire the Angel of Good to prevail.[614] The importance of *shalom bayit* has long been emphasized. For example, the twelfth-century German mystic Judah He'Chasid wrote:

> A simple vegetable meal on the *Shabbat* in a home where there is love between husband, wife, and children is better than a fatted ox in a home where there is hatred. A man should not plan to honor the *Shabbat* with delicacies while he knows that he will quarrel with his wife, or father, or mother. Whether it be *Shabbat* or Festival—"better a dry morsel and quietness there, than a house full of feasting with conflict" (Prov. 17:1). One should honor the *Shabbat* by having no conflict on it.

The Reform movement has reversed the order of *Shalom Aleichem* and the candle-lighting, so that *Shalom Aleichem* precedes the lighting of the candles.[615] Presumably, this reflects the Reform movement's rejection of kabbalistic practices such as the notion of singing to angels, and of the sexist (to some) notion that women would stay at home and light the candles while their husbands were at the synagogue. However, if *Shalom Aleichem* is viewed as a celebration of domestic peace once *Shabbat* has commenced with the candle-lighting, it makes sense to preserve the traditional order.

After singing *Shalom Aleichem*, the Orthodox liturgy includes a lengthy meditation of kabbalistic origin to get into the right frame of mind for *Kiddush*. This meditation is omitted in the Conservative liturgy, but meditation to get into the proper frame of mind for prayer is a valuable and traditionally Jewish method of worship; there is no apparent reason for omitting meditation from the Friday evening home ritual.

It is traditional after this meditation, and immediately before Kiddush, to recite Proverbs 31:10–31 (*Eishet Chayil*), which begins, "What a rare find is a capable wife!" Some families today add Psalm 112, "Happy Is the Man," so that the wife and husband bless each other. Ironically, the recital of *Eishet Chayil* on Friday night was not originally intended as a husband's blessing for his wife, but as an allegory, variously understood as a kabbalistic greeting for the *Shechina*, the feminine personification of the Divine Presence, or for the Sabbath Bride, a personification of *Shabbat*.[616]

KIDDUSH: THE BLESSING ON THE WINE

Unlike many other religions, such as Buddhism, Hinduism, and Catholicism, Judaism does not consider asceticism a virtue. When we begin and end the Sabbath, we use material luxuries to sanctify the occasion. We begin the Sabbath on Friday night with wine, and end it on Saturday night with wine and with spices, which were precious and hard to obtain in antiquity. The concept of the blessing on the wine, or *Kiddush* (sanctification), is to infuse the material with the spiritual, the sacred with the secular.[617]

Kiddush originated with the wine-offering in the Second Temple. Pouring wine on the altar was part of the sacrificial ritual, specifically the part during which the Levites sang psalms.[618] It is logical, in view of this origin, that *Kiddush* still coincides with the singing of psalms.

This origin of *Kiddush* also demonstrates another key concept: *Kiddush* is a sanctification—not of the wine, but of ourselves and of time. Pouring wine on the altar made it holy for the time of the sacrifice; pouring wine into our bodies makes them holy for the time of the Sabbath. The philosopher Abraham Joshua Heschel wrote, "Judaism teaches us to be attached to holiness in time, to be attached to sacred events, to learn how to consecrate sanctuaries that emerge from the magnificent streams of a year. The Sabbaths are our great cathedrals; and our Holy of Holies is a shrine that neither the Romans nor the Greeks were able to burn."[619]

While the Second Temple was still standing, the use of wine in the home came to mark the beginning and the end of *Shabbat*. The Christian Eucharist, the use of wine and a wafer to symbolize the blood and body of Jesus, may be derived, in part, from this use of wine in Jewish home ritual.[620]

After the Temple was destroyed, it was disputed whether *Kiddush* should be recited in synagogue or at home. The decision of the third-century Babylonian Rabbi Samuel was that it should be said where and when one was going to eat the Sabbath meal, so it became primarily a home observance.[621]

Kiddush was reincorporated into the synagogue liturgy in Babylonia during the Gaonic period of the first millennium C.E. Synagogues there offered lodging and meals to travelers, and *Kiddush* was said for their benefit.[622] Wine was unavailable, so "the reader would go to the lectern and recite a summary of the seven blessings of the *Shabbat Amida*, called *Magen Avot* (Shield of the Fathers), concluding with "Blessed be the Lord Who sanctified Israel and the Sabbath."[623] *Magen Avot*, originally a Sabbath evening substitute for or predecessor of the *Amida*, remains part of the Sabbath evening service even though the evening *Amida* was restored. *Kiddush*, too, continues to be said in the synagogue as well as in the home on Friday night, to sanctify the occasion for those unable to do so with their families at home.

Kiddush on Friday night begins with a quotation from Genesis 1:31–2:3, commonly called *Va'y'chulu* (And He finished), the end of the biblical description of the Creation and the description of how God rested on the seventh day. The quotation begins with the words *yom ha'shishi*, (the sixth day), which are the end of the preceding sentence in Genesis. The reason is that these two words together with the first two words of the next sentence, *Va'y'chulu ha'shamayim*, form an acrostic for the tetragrammaton, the four-letter name of God.[624] Because the words *yom ha'shishi* had no intelligible meaning in themselves, the medieval rabbis added the preceding words, *Va'y'hi erev va'y'hi boker*, forming the sentence, "And there was evening and there was morning, the sixth day."[625]

Va'y'chulu (Gen. 2:1–3) is also found in the Friday evening *Amida* in the synagogue service, as an introduction to the Middle Blessing and a commemoration of the event. It was probably added to the home *Kiddush* to allow those who did not attend services to hear this passage, thereby bringing to mind why we are celebrating. The message of these biblical verses is that the Sabbath was not merely a moment of rest after the work of Creation; rather, it was the reason for the Creation.

The corresponding introductory verse for the Saturday noon *Kiddush* is *V'shamru b'Nai Yisrael* (Exod. 31:16–17), which sets forth the biblical commandment to the Jewish people to observe the Sabbath day. Again, this introductory verse is taken from the introduction to the Middle Blessing of the *Amida*, this time the *Shacharit Amida* for *Shabbat*. As on Friday night, the purpose probably was to allow people who could not attend services to hear the biblical passage explaining the basis for the occasion.

After the benediction *borei p'ri ha'gafen* (Who created the fruit of the vine), we do not drink, but recite a paragraph that calls the Sabbath both a "reminder of Creation" (*zikaron l'ma'aseh v'reishit*) and "the first among our days of sacred assembly recalling the Exodus from Egypt" (*yom t'chila l'mikra'ei kodesh zeicher l'tziyat mitzrayim*). We are celebrating not only the creation of the world, but also the creation of the Jewish people.

We refrain from drinking until we have recited another benediction, *m'kadesh ha'shabbat* (Who made the Sabbath holy). This is because the wine is merely a device for sanctifying the moment.[626] We have to say *borei p'ri ha'gafen* because this is the talmudically prescribed blessing upon the act of drinking wine, but we are supposed to say that blessing every time we drink wine, not just on *Shabbat*. The drinking of wine to sanctify the Sabbath is special; therefore we must say a special blessing.

By drinking the wine, we sanctify the time and ourselves. "Sanctification" is a state of mind in time. The wine is a vehicle by which we help ourselves undergo a change in our state of consciousness, a change that has been characterized as "a foretaste of heaven." This change is not mere intoxication, but a heightened state of mind achieved through the device of association with the candles, the wine, the *challa*, and the other stimuli provided by Jewish tradition. This altered state of consciousness lasts until *Havdala* the next evening, but a bit of it carries through to enhance our *devekut*, the quiet state of mind that prayer assists us in maintaining in our daily lives. The Sabbath is our occasion to take some extra time to give our *devekut* a weekly reinforcement.

It is customary for the prayer leader to preface the *Kiddush*, after the biblical introduction, with *Sav'ri maranan*. This is a *re'shut*, a request for permission, in Aramaic and of Babylonian origin. The leader is presuming to lead those present in achieving a holy condition even though he or she has no special merit or rank that entitles him or her to do so; hence he or she may do so only with the permission of the others.

CHALLA: THE SABBATH BREAD

The basis for eating *challa* on *Shabbat* is found in the biblical story of the double portion of manna that God had the Jews wandering in the desert gather on the sixth day of the week so that they would not have to gather the manna on the seventh day in violation of the Sabbath.[627] The *challa* is supposed to be two loaves, not one. The two loaves are said to symbolize the two forms of the Fourth Commandment: "*Remember* the Sabbath day" (Exod. 20:8) and "*Observe* the Sabbath day" (Deut. 5:12).[628]

The loaves are covered until *Kiddush* has been said. Two reasons were suggested by the Tosafists, followers of the eleventh-century scholar Rashi, who apparently originated the custom: (1) to distinguish the *Shabbat* meal from ordinary meals, for which bread would be put on the table at the outset; and (2) to symbolize the two layers of dew between which the Talmud said the manna had fallen, protecting it from the sand below and the heat of the sun above.[629]

It is traditional to sprinkle salt on the first piece of *challa* immediately after the *Ha'motzi* is recited. This is an ancient Second-Temple custom: Salt was sprinkled on the sacrificial offering in the Second Temple. By doing this, we transform the meal into a sacred ritual.[630]

Ma'ariv: The Evening Service

INTRODUCTION

In Orthodox and Conservative congregations, the weekday evening (*Ma'ariv*) service is built around *Barchu*, the *Shema*, the *Amida*, and *Aleinu*. The blessings before, and the first blessing after, the *Shema* are different than, though parallel to, the ones used in the morning service, and a second blessing, *Hashkiveinu*, is added after the *Shema* in the evening. On Friday evening, *Kiddush* is added before *Aleinu* as a sanctification of the occasion, and a series of prayers called *Kabbalat Shabbat* (Receiving the Sabbath), already discussed, is recited before *Ma'ariv*. On Saturday evening, *Havdala* is added before *Aleinu* for the same purpose.

The Reform prayerbook *Gates of Prayer* offers four weekday alternatives titled "Evening or Morning Service" and numbered I, II, III, and IV. These are built around *Barchu*, an abbreviated *Shema*, an abbreviated *Amida*, and a choice of concluding prayers, one of which is *Aleinu*. No fewer than ten alternative Sabbath evening services are found in *Gates of Prayer*. In the new *Gates of Prayer for Shabbat and Weekdays* (1994), the evening *Amida* is eliminated on weekdays, but is preserved on *Shabbat*, and only three alternative *Shabbat* evening services are included, in an apparent effort to restore greater uniformity as well as a recognition that some of the alternative services did not gain widespread popularity.

Of the *Ma'ariv* prayers, only the *Shema* is mandatory, because the recitation of the *Shema* morning and night is a biblical commandment.[631] The *Ma'ariv Amida* is not mandatory, because there was no evening sacrifice in the Second Temple. It is permitted because, in the Temple, those parts of animals proper for sacrifice that had not been burned on the altar during the day were burned at night.

158

V'HU RACHUM

Since at least the ninth century, the weekday *Ma'ariv* service has begun with Psalms 78:38 and Psalms 20:10, *V'Hu Rachum.*[632] This is not a formal part of the service since it precedes *Barchu*, the call to public prayer, so it is in the nature of a personal meditation.

In the Middle Ages, as today, there was danger in the night. It was not uncommon for Jews to be attacked after dark. The first sentence in *V'Hu Rachum* has thirteen words. These were viewed, in medieval times, as corresponding to the thirteen attributes of God.[633] By reciting *V'Hu Rachum* in the evening, medieval Jews invoked all of the attributes of God for their protection. We, too, can meditate on the danger in the night, and on our ultimate dependence on God's protection.

BARCHU

With the call to formal public worship, we form a spiritual community for the purpose of reciting the *Shema* and the *Amida* together. See p. 98.

MA'ARIV ARAVIM (WHO MAKES THE EVENING FALL): THE FIRST BLESSING BEFORE THE EVENING *SHEMA*

The first blessing before the evening *Shema* is similar to the *Yotzer* blessing before the morning *Shema*, except that it praises God as Creator of the night rather than as Creator of light. In antiquity, these blessings may have been the same, as they were both derived from a polemic in Isaiah against religious dualism such as that which prevailed among the ancient Persians.[634]

AHAVAT OLAM (ETERNAL LOVE): THE SECOND BLESSING BEFORE THE *SHEMA*

The second blessing before the evening *Shema*, like the first, parallels its morning equivalent, which is a prayer of thanks to God for giving us the Torah. Where in the morning we refer to God's "great" love (*Ahava Rabba*), in the evening we refer to God's "eternal" love (*Ahavat Olam*). Not only are God, and His gift of the Torah, "great;" God, and the gift of the Torah, are eternal, and—unlike God's human worshippers—will last through this night and all other nights.

THE *SHEMA*

The evening *Shema* is the same as the one recited in the morning, consistent with the commandment to recite it "when you lie down and when you rise up." As in the morning *Shema*, we visualize ourselves at Mount Sinai receiving the Torah and listen to God, so that we may merit being heard later when we recite the *Amida*. In ancient Israel, however, the final Torah excerpt of the *Shema, Va'Yomer*, was not said in the evening. Other texts were substituted for it that commemorated the Exodus and began with *Modim anachnu lach*.[635] This difference in the evening liturgy was eliminated by the Jews who migrated to Babylonia during the third century c.e. and, as in many liturgical matters, it was the Babylonian Jewish custom that prevailed.

EMET VE'EMUNA (TRUE AND FAITHFUL): THE FIRST BLESSING AFTER THE EVENING *SHEMA*

This version of the first blessing after the *Shema* became the version recited in the evening at the urging of Rav, an early leader of the Babylonian Jewish community, during the third century c.e.[636] Like its morning equivalent *Emet V'Yatziv*, its focus is on redemption, and particularly the Exodus from Egypt, continuing the theme of the final Torah excerpt of the *Shema*. As in the morning version, the Song at the Sea, *Mi Chamocha*, is recited, and we try to achieve a state of mind in which we feel as if we, too, had together witnessed a miracle at the Red Sea.

HASHKIVEINU (LET US LIE DOWN IN PEACE): THE SECOND BLESSING AFTER THE EVENING *SHEMA*

Unique to the *Ma'ariv* service, the *Hashkiveinu*, the second blessing after the evening *Shema* in the liturgies of all denominations, is really a petition to God to protect us from harm during the night. What is a petition doing in the blessings after the *Shema* rather than the *Amida*, which ordinarily is the time when we address our requests to God?

The answer is that the *Shema* and its blessings predated the *Amida*. At one time there was no *Amida*, and even after the *Amida* developed during the first century c.e., it was not recited at night until centuries later. The need for protection at night was felt so strongly that, lacking another evening prayer appropriate for making requests of God, Jews added a special request for protection to the evening *Shema*.[637]

The implication of this origin of *Hashkiveinu* is that our *kavana*, our intensely focused state of mind, should already be at a peak by the time we reach this point of the *Ma'ariv* service. The special request for protection at night is no less important than requests we make in the middle blessings of the *Amida*. Our mind-state needs to reflect the importance of the *Hashkiveinu* blessing.

BARUCH ADONAI L'OLAM AMEN V'AMEN

There is danger in the night today, and there was danger in the night in Babylonia during the Amoraic period, from about 200 to 1000 c.e. At sunset, Jews in Babylonia would still be in the fields, at risk of attack by bandits. They would gather on their way home to say *Ma'ariv* prayers outdoors. Because of the risk this posed, and the fact that recital of the full *Amida* in the evening was not obligatory, a shorter prayer beginning *Baruch Adonai L'Olam Amen V'Amen*, consisting of a collection of eighteen biblical verses, was devised. This prayer was either a predecessor of or a substitute for the eighteen blessings of the evening *Amida*, so the service could be completed more quickly, and the subjects of the selected verses therefore correspond to the themes of the blessings of the *Amida*.[638] By placing special emphasis on God's not "abandoning His people" and on the worshipper's "entrusting [his] spirit" to God, this prayer continues the evening theme of protection from the dangers of night. We meditate on God's watching over us, and we try to achieve a frame of mind in which we are able to entrust our spirit to Him to keep safe until morning.

However, it is conjectured that the full *Amida* continued to be recited in Israel.[639] Probably for this reason, the earliest written prayerbooks included both the shorter Babylonian prayer and the full *Amida*, and it came to be customary to recite both. It is not obligatory to do so, and the Reform prayerbook omits this prayer entirely, in all ten alternate weekday evening services.

Because it contains requests of God similar to those in the middle blessings of the weekday *Amida*, most of this prayer is omitted from the traditional service on Friday night, in keeping with the principle that we should not make requests of God on *Shabbat* other than the fundamental plea that God "purify our hearts" so that our prayers will be heard and our rest will be accepted.

Interestingly, *Hashkiveinu*, the final blessing after the evening *Shema*, is not omitted on *Shabbat* even though it, too, contains a request of God. Since the request is, in essence, to preserve our lives against the dangers of the night, this may be viewed as a life-and-death matter, and all other rules may be broken to save lives.

The last paragraph of this prayer, beginning, *Yir'u eineinu* (May Our Eyes See), is another collection of biblical verses, also of Babylonian origin, that make up a petition for the coming of the Messiah.[640] In some traditional liturgies, it is recited even on *Shabbat*.

CHATZI KADDISH

In view of the origin of *Baruch Adonai L'Olam Amen V'Amen*, one might think that it belongs in the same major segment of the *Ma'ariv* service as the *Amida*. Indeed, one might think the same of *Hashkiveinu*, which also contains requests of God. However, it is not treated as such. The Half-*Kaddish*, recited to mark major divisions of the service, is placed between *Baruch Adonai L'Olam Amen V'Amen* and the *Amida*. As always, the Half-*Kaddish* is optional in the Reform liturgy.

THE EVENING AMIDA

The *Amida* follows, in the Orthodox and Conservative liturgies, but it may be omitted in the Reform service. It differs in two ways from the morning *Amida*: (1) Only the silent prayer is recited, without repetition; and (2) an alternate version of the final blessing is recited in the Ashkenazic ritual, beginning, *Shalom Rav*. That the *Ma'ariv Amida* is not repeated reflects the non-obligatory nature of the *Amida* at this time of day. *Shalom Rav* was introduced in Germany in the eleventh century, though not specifically for the evening service, and became a staple of the liturgy at the time of Rabbi Meir of Rothenburg, a follower of Rashi and a prolific liturgist who died in 1293 at the hands of the Crusaders.[641] Since two versions of the final blessing of the *Amida* now coexisted, it was decided, with admirable tact, to assign one version, *Sim Shalom*, to the morning service, and the other, *Shalom Rav*, to the evening.[642]

KADDISH SHALEM (COMPLETE KADDISH)

Again *Kaddish* is recited to mark a major division, this time *Kaddish Shalem*, or Complete *Kaddish*.

ALEINU

Aleinu is then recited to conclude the evening service, for reasons already discussed on p. xxx. In reciting it, we pledge our allegiance to our faith and cement our ties to the spiritual community we have formed.

MOURNER'S *KADDISH*

In our renewed state of *devekut*, we now are able to perform our first *mitzvah* after prayer: responding to the Mourner's *Kaddish* to comfort mourners.

Nighttime Home Observance: Kri'at Shema Al-Ha'Mittah (Recital of the *Shema* upon Retiring)

While the morning home prayers, the *Birchot Ha'Shachar*, were incorporated into the synagogue service owing to the inability of medieval worshippers to say them on their own, this did not happen to the nighttime home prayers. By biblical injunction, the Shema had to be recited "when you lie down and when you get up."[643] When people began, in early Amoraic times, to slough off the recital of the afternoon and evening prayers, as they did the morning home blessings, the rabbis decreed that afternoon prayers were mandatory and made the evening prayers into a public service.[644] When the evening prayers became public, it was necessary to fulfill separately the biblical *mitzvah* to recite the *Shema* at bedtime, so the Talmud required its recitation again at home.[645] There was a debate between Hillel and Shammai in the *Mishna* about whether the evening *Shema* needed to be recited while reclining, or whether "when you lie down" referred to a time when God would accept it. Hillel's position—that only a time, not a posture, was meant—became the accepted view.[646]

Apart from its being a biblical commandment, reciting the *Shema* at bedtime was perceived as a protection against the dangers of the night.[647] Rabbi Abraham Millgram has called it "a sort of spiritual insurance policy against the frightful possibility of 'sleeping the sleep of death.' Should he not awaken from his sleep, God forbid, the Jew had the comforting assurance of having finished his mortal existence with the traditional affirmation of God's unity."[648]

More than the performance of a *mitzvah* and a ritual incantation to gain physical protection, however, the bedtime prayers are a method of achieving peace and protection of mind. We must prepare for the worst when we go to sleep; we must retire as if it will be our last conscious act. We therefore use prayer and meditation at bedtime to prepare our minds for death. The person's mental condition was considered by the talmudic rabbis to have a causal relationship to the fate of his or her soul in the afterlife;[649] by setting our minds at peace and asking forgiveness for our sins, we prepare ourselves in case we never wake up.

Rav Abaye said, in the Talmud, that even for scholars (who presumably could assume the necessary state of mind more quickly than the average person), the bedtime *Shema* should be accompanied by at least one verse of supplication, a personal prayer to set one's mind at peace. He suggested, but did not mandate, reciting Psalms 31:6: "Into Your hand I entrust my spirit, You redeem me, O Lord, faithful God."[650] Presumably Abaye thought of this verse because of the reference to entrusting one's spirit to God, as we do when going to sleep, coupled with the reference to personal redemption. Often used today in the Orthodox liturgy instead is a longer medieval supplication beginning with the formula *Ribono Shel Olam*, which prays more specifically for forgiveness for sins committed during the day.[651] The supplication is omitted in the Conservative liturgy.

For the average person, the Talmud prescribes a much longer sequence of night prayers. These include a blessing prescribed in *Berachot* 60b, called *Ha'Mapil*, which reads: "Praised are You, Lord, our God, King of the universe, who causes the bands of sleep to fall upon my eyes and slumber on my eyelids." The Talmud indicates that *Ha'Mapil* should follow the *Shema*, but Maimonides reversed the order, so that in most prayerbooks *Ha'Mapil* comes first.[652]

Ha'Mapil parallels the last of the fifteen morning home blessings, "Who removes sleep from my eyes and slumber from my eyelids." It is followed by a segment prescribed in the Talmud that begins with the ancient meditation formula, *Y'hi ratzon mil'fanecha* (May It Be Your Will), and asks God to "make me lie down in peace." Apart from the first line of *Ha'Mapil*, this prayer is intended as a personal meditation, and the words prescribed should be understood as a suggestion for the content of that meditation rather than as a ritualistic incantation to ward off physical danger. By altering our state of mind, we can achieve God's protection.

Achieving a new mind-state alone does not suffice, however. After *Ha'Mapil* comes the recitation of the first paragraph of the *Shema*, the biblical statement of our obligation to show love for God through our conduct. We recite only the first paragraph at bedtime in accordance with a view of Maimonides. There are a number of possible reasons for this: (1) The first paragraph is God speaking to individuals in the second-person singular, while the second paragraph is in the second-person plural, God speaking to Jews as a group, and at bedtime we pray alone; (2) the Talmud questioned reciting the third paragraph at night because its subject, the commandment of *tzitzit*, was inapplicable at night; (3) the custom of reciting the *Shema* to sanctify God's name at the time of one's death originated with the account of Rabbi Akiva's reciting it while being executed by the Romans, and Rabbi Akiva said only the first verse.

In the Orthodox, but not the Conservative, liturgy, after the *Shema* follows a sequence of psalms, to further prepare the mind so that we will die in peace if that is our fate during the night. Psalms 90:17, beginning, *Vi'y'hi no'am* (May the Pleasantness), leads into the recitation of Psalm 91, beginning, *Yoshev b'seter elyon* (Whoever Sits in the Refuge of the Most High). The Talmud called Psalm 91 the Song of Plagues, because one who recites it with faith in God will be helped by God in time of danger.[653]

Psalms 3:2–9, beginning *Adonai ma rabu tzaray* (Lord, My Foes Are So Many), follows in the Orthodox liturgy. This psalm was written by David when he awoke from slumber to perceive, by divine inspiration, that his salvation was forthcoming.

Both the Orthodox and Conservative liturgies include *Hashkiveinu*, the evening blessing after the *Shema* designed to ward off danger, but *Emet Ve'Emuna*, which does not deal with this subject, is omitted. In the Conservative liturgy, *Hashkiveinu* immediately follows the *Shema* and the intervening psalms are omitted. Another prayer from the *Ma'ariv* service, *Baruch Adonai L'Olam Amen V'Amen*, follows *Hashkiveinu*.

Next comes a sequence of biblical verses having to do with God's rescuing the Jews from danger, beginning *Ha'Malach* (The Angel). The last, from Song of Songs 3:7–8, describes the "couch of Solomon, encircled by sixty warriors of the warriors of Israel, all of them trained in warfare, skilled in battle, each with sword on thigh because of terror by night." The kabbalists, observing that the Priestly Blessing from Numbers 6:24–26, found in the *Amida*, contains sixty letters, and therefore must have had a mystical connection to the preceding verse; they inserted it here, and then added Psalms 121:4: "Behold, the Guardian of Israel neither slumbers nor sleeps."

The Conservative liturgy, for some reason, kept the Priestly Blessing, which is out of place here, but excised another passage of kabbalistic origin from the Orthodox service, which reads, "In the name of the Lord, God of Israel, may [the angel] Michael be at my right, Gabriel at my left, Uriel before me, and Raphael behind me, and above my head the *Shechina*

[Presence of God]." This omission presumably was for theological reasons, a rejection of the literal notion of invoking the personal protection of angels, but the omission of one of the most graphic passages in the liturgy is less defensible if the passage is viewed as an aid to visualizing God's presence and thereby achieving *devekut*.

Psalm 128 and another passage from the Song of Songs follow in the Orthodox, but not the Conservative, liturgy. Finally, the bedtime prayers conclude in both liturgies with *Adon Olam*, which probably was originally written for bedtime use.

Kol Nidrei: A Yom Kippur Addition to the Ma'ariv Service

On *Yom Kippur* we preface the usual *Ma'ariv* service with the *Kol Nidrei* prayer, and add to the *Ma'ariv Amida* the *Selichot* (penitential prayers) and the *Vidui* (confessional prayers). In addition, numerous *piyyutim*, poetic hymns of medieval origin, are added.

The gist of the *Kol Nidrei* prayer, which is written in Aramaic, is the annulment of vows made by the worshipper to God. Several types of vows are enumerated:

1. *Nidrei:* "Religious obligations," such as a vow to make a sacrifice or to become a Nazirite.
2. *Esarei:* "Restrictions" assumed by the worshipper.
3. *Charamei:* "Pledges," such as the pledge of an object for a sacred purpose.
4. *Konamei:* "Promises" using the formula *konam* (consecrated).
5. *Kinnuyei:* "Substitute terms," an allusion to the mishnaic rule that "any terms used by people as substitutes for the official formulae for making vows are as binding as the officially accepted terms."
6. *Kinnusei:* "Variant terms," an allusion to a corollary of the foregoing mishnaic rule; inaccurate variants of required terms for making vows would also be binding.
7. *Shevuot:* "Oaths," a vow to deny oneself any benefit from a particular object.[654]

There are various theories regarding the historical origin of *Kol Nidrei*.[655] The prayer is known to have been in use in Babylonia prior to about 750 C.E. when the Gaon Y'hudai referred to it as an already-established custom,[656] and its Aramaic wording closely resembles magical formulas in use in Babylonia at the time.[657] It has been plausibly suggested that the references to annulling different types of vows were a way of annulling curses consistent with Babylonian magical practices; Babylonian magicians typically used code words for different types of curses, and the suggestion has been made that the enumeration of vows originated as a series of these code words.[658]

Whatever its origin, in most of the extant theories, the original, or at least very early, purpose of the *Kol Nidrei* prayer was to give special dispensation to people who had been excommunicated from the Jewish community so that they could pray with the Jewish community on *Yom Kippur*.[659] *Kol Nidrei* is a legal formula releasing the reciter from vows. In its original Orthodox form, it releases the worshipper from vows he or she has made during the past year. In the Conservative and Reform *Kol Nidrei* prayers, as well as in many Orthodox versions that follow a revisionist interpretation of the prayer by the medieval commentator Rabbeinu Tam, it releases the worshipper from vows that he or she will make during the coming year. The vows might be vows to follow another religion, or vows excommunicating a fellow Jew from the community for his or her transgressions. Through this legal device, converts to Christianity, such as German Jews during the Crusades and the Spanish Marranos, were given permission to return and pray with the community on this occasion.[660] This device assisted not only the excommunicated Jews and the converts, but the entire Jewish community, because, according to the Babylonian Talmud, the prayers of fast days are invalid unless all members of the community participate in them, even those who had left or had been expelled from it.

Throughout its history, the *Kol Nidrei* prayer has been cited by anti-Semites as evidence that Jews could not be trusted to keep their promises. Even the Karaites, a dissident group of Jews in Babylonia in the ninth century, scorned the rabbis "who break vows even on the eve of the Day of Atonement."[661] In reaction to such criticism and embarrassed by its effect on public opinion of the Jews, the early Reform rabbis in nineteenth-century Germany eliminated the *Kol Nidrei* prayer from their liturgy.[662] It was restored relatively recently to the Reform *machzor Gates of Repentance*, but with a loose English translation that stresses, rather apologetically, that only vows made between man and God, and not vows made between men, are being annulled, and, even then, only "should we, after honest effort, find ourselves unable to fulfill them."[663]

The real message of *Kol Nidrei*—a message already lost on many even in the ninth century—is not the annulment of vows, but the need to set aside differences and unite the Jewish community to respond to a public emergency. We speak of annulling vows because vows of excommunication and vows made to observe other religions were major points of division among Jews when the prayer was in its formative period. Even apostates and transgressors must be permitted back into the fold for this grave occasion. Taking the point a step further, by reciting *Kol Nidrei* as a spiritual community, we acknowledge that we are all transgressors; each year on the High Holidays we all make pledges to reform our lives which, in some sense, we fail fully to keep. Moreover, since *Yom Kippur* is a day of community atonement and not just atonement of the individual, by reciting *Kol Nidrei* collectively we acknowledge our collective responsibility for the transgressions and broken vows of others in our community.

Home Observances and Festival Customs

Some home observances have already been discussed: *Shabbat* evening home observances, including *Kiddush*, candle-lighting, and *challa* (p. 150 ff.); the Sunrise Blessings (p. 36); and the bedtime prayers (p. 164). Other observances include the following.

DAILY BLESSINGS BEFORE MEALS: *KIDDUSH* AND *HA'MOTZI*

Kiddush has already been discussed on p. 154. *Ha'Motzi* (blessing on bread) also is ancient, and was already widespread in rabbinic times.[664] Addressed to God "Who brings forth bread out of the earth," it is derived from Psalms 104:14–15: "You make the grass grow for the cattle, and herbage for man's labor that he may get food out of the earth—wine that cheers the hearts of men, oil that makes the face shine, and bread that sustains man's life."

Ha'Motzi is only nominally a blessing on bread. Bread and water are used in the Bible to symbolize all food, or man's basic nutritional needs.[665] Saying this blessing acts as a dispensation from reciting individual blessings on all the other foods one eats in a meal, except for wine and fruit.[666]

These blessings are among the *Birchot Ha'Nehenin* (Blessings of Enjoyment). The Talmud says that whoever enjoys the earth's pleasures without reciting a blessing is tantamount to one who steals from God.[667] Weaving blessings into the fabric of daily life is a means of constantly reminding us of our connection to God and perpetuating our *devekut*, the state of mind achieved through prayer.

BIRKAT HA'MAZON (GRACE AFTER MEALS)

Birkat Ha'Mazon, the Grace After Meals, is much longer than the blessings made before meals. Its core consists of four lengthy benedictions. The first three are so ancient that their origin was unknown even in rabbinic times. The Talmud emphasizes their antiquity by attributing them to Moses, Joshua, and King Solomon, respectively.[668] The scholar Louis Finkelstein dates the third benediction to the second century B.C.E., when, he theorizes, it was composed as a prayer for the Temple and Jerusalem under siege by the Seleucid Greeks.[669] The Talmud indicates that the fourth benediction was written by the rabbis at Yavneh after the destruction of the Second Temple.[670] The other benedictions of *Birkat Ha'Mazon* may have originated in the *chavurot*, prayer groups of men and women that met over dinner in ancient Israel, or in sects such as the one at Qumran, where a prayer resembling *Birkat Ha'Mazon* for a Grace After Meals at the house of a mourner was found in one of the Dead Sea Scrolls.[671] Women were specifically not exempted by the Talmud from reciting *Birkat Ha'Mazon*.

Birkat Ha'Mazon is really a mental journey not unlike the *Amida*. We begin with a vision of food and sustenance as a divine gift; travel in spirit to the land of Israel and visualize it as the source of that gift; then visualize the reunification of our community as a nation sovereign over that land, with its national institutions (such as the Temple) restored. It is another method of maintaining and reinforcing our *devekut*, our consciousness in daily living of the divine connection to all things, which can fortify us in doing good and resisting evil.

Since the time of the sixteenth-century kabbalists, *Birkat Ha'Mazon* has been prefaced on *Shabbat* and Festivals in all liturgies with Psalm 126, *Shir Ha'Ma'alot* (A Pilgrim Song). In the Orthodox liturgy, however, there is also a weekday preface, Psalm 137, *Al Naharot Bavel* (By the Rivers of Babylon), as a memorial to the destruction of the First Temple. Psalm 126, which speaks of the joy we will experience when God returns the Jews to Zion, originally was a substitute preface on *Shabbat* and Festivals, and at other joyous occasions such as *b'rit milah* (circumcision of a baby boy), to avoid intruding on the occasion with memories of tragedy. The Conservative and Reform liturgies have no preface on weekdays.

What comes next, when three or more participate in a meal, is a call to formal prayer analogous to the *Barchu* recited in the synagogue, the formation of a miniature spiritual community around the table. This is, in fact, how the recital of *Birkat Ha'Mazon* at group meals began: with ancient *chavurot*, groups among the Pharisees and sects like the Essenes who met for community feasts, especially on *Shabbat*.[672] In the traditional liturgy, the prayer leader says, *Rabotai n'varech* (literally, "My masters, let us praise

[God]"). This call to prayer originated in Babylonia in talmudic times, and in the Orthodox liturgy may be recited only if three or more men are present. The Conservative movement permits it to be recited regardless of gender. The Reform movement has changed this call to prayer to, *Chaverim v'chaverot n'varech* ("Friends [male and female], let us praise [God]").

The participants respond to the call to prayer with the ancient response, similar to the congregation's response to the *Barchu* in the synagogue: *Y'hi shem Adonai m'vorach mei'ata v'ad olam* (Praised be the name of God now and forever). The leader repeats the response, since he or she also is a participant, not an intermediary between the participants and God. Then the leader asks permission (*r'shut*) of those *maranan, rabbanan,* and *rabotai* (various distinguished titles in antiquity)[673] present to praise God, "of whose bounty we have partaken." Through their response, the participants grant that permission.

Asking permission is a show of humility on the part of the leader for assuming the role of leading the others present, just as referring to the attendees by various respectful titles shows humility.

The participants then recite the first blessing of *Birkat Ha'Mazon,* called *Birkat Hazan* (literally, Blessing of the Feeding). Said to be composed by Moses to thank God for the manna sent to the Jews wandering in the desert, *Birkat Hazan* praises God for providing food for all God's creatures.

The second benediction begins with *Nodeh l'cha.* It is called *Birkat Ha'Aretz* (Blessing of the Land). Believed to be composed by Joshua in gratitude for the Land of Israel, it thanks God for the "good land" given to the Jews.

The third benediction of *Birkat Ha'Mazon* begins with *Racheim.* Called *Birkat Yerushalayim* (Blessing of Jerusalem) and, according to talmudic legend,[674] composed by King David and King Solomon, it praises God for rebuilding Jerusalem. Rabbinic lore explains the inconsistency of attributing to King David a prayer that refers to a Temple not yet built in his time by asserting that the reference to the Temple was added by his son Solomon. The further inconsistency, that the conclusion of the benediction prays for Jerusalem to be rebuilt, a condition irrelevant at the time of David and Solomon, is explained by assuming the conclusion to be an insertion added after the destruction of the Temple.[675]

It is more likely that the third benediction (and perhaps even the first two) was composed during the Maccabean era in the second century B.C.E., when Israel was in great danger from the Seleucid Greeks.[676] Praying for Jerusalem did not begin with the fall of the Second Temple; it went on while Jerusalem was standing, suggesting that we pray not just for the physical integrity of Jerusalem, but for Jerusalem to reach its full potential as a beacon for the nations.[677]

However, it is also clear that some portions of the third benediction are later additions. One later addition is the part beginning, *Eloheinu, avinu, r'einu, zuneinu*, which was added in the Middle Ages, and pleads with God not to let us fall into poverty and thereby be shamed and embarrassed.[678]

On *Shabbat, R'tzei* from the *Avoda* blessing of the *Amida* is inserted in the third benediction of *Birkat Ha'Mazon* as a remembrance of the Temple service. On festivals, *Ya'Aleh V'Yavo*, also from the *Amida* and also an account of the Temple ritual, is inserted.

A fourth benediction called *Ha'Tov V'Ha'Meitiv* (Who is good and does good) was added to *Birkat Ha'Mazon* early in the second century. It praises God's goodness and articulates specific wishes for grace, kindness, mercy, relief, salvation, success, blessing, help, consolation, sustenance, support, mercy, life, and peace. Again, this "wish list" is reminiscent of, though more abbreviated than, the middle blessings of the *Amida*. The fact that God granted these wishes in the past is evidence that we can count on God's doing so again in the future.

The Talmud ascribes the fourth benediction to the period immediately after the Bar Kochba revolt was crushed by the Romans in 135 c.e., and says it was inserted by the rabbis of Rabban Gamaliel's court at Yavneh (the religious center of Israel after the fall of the Second Temple in 70 c.e.) because the bodies of the Jews slain at Bethar, the worst of all Jewish defeats in the revolt, did not rot and were able to be given a proper burial.[679] By this interpretation, the fourth benediction was inserted to acknowledge a kind of silver lining in the storm cloud of the revolt's defeat, and thereby to fight the widespread sense that God had forsaken the Jews. The scholar Louis Finkelstein, however, has pointed out that the fourth benediction was known to Eliezer ben Hyrcanus, who died before the revolt began, and therefore probably originated early in the reign of Hadrian prior to the revolt, sometime between 117 and 132 c.e.[680]

With the end of the fourth benediction at *L'olam al y'chasreinu, Birkat Ha'Mazon* is officially over. However, the prayer continues with a number of informal later additions beginning with *Ha'Rachaman*, (The Merciful One). Although a standard text appears in the prayerbooks, *Ha'Rachaman* is supposed to be a time for private, personal prayers. Just as the *Amida* is followed by private, personal prayers, so is *Birkat Ha'Mazon*. Just as the private, personal prayers following the *Amida* have been supplanted by prescribed "meditations" of others, so have those following *Birkat Ha'Mazon*.

Highlighting this parallel to the *Amida*, the *Ha'Rachaman* prayers end with the same line that ends the meditation following the *Amida*: *Oseh shalom bi'm'romav, hu ya'aseh shalom, aleinu v'al kol yisrael, v'imru, Amen* (He who makes peace in His heights, He will make peace, for us and for all Israel, and let us say, Amen).

After *Ha'Rachaman*, the Grace After Meals concludes with a collection of verses from the Prophets and Psalms on the theme of righteousness and peace, beginning with *Yir'u et Adonai k'doshav*. This collection includes the troubling verse from Psalms 37:25: "I have been young and am now old, but I have never seen a righteous man abandoned, or his children seeking bread." Commentators have interpreted this verse as suggesting that righteous people never feel abandoned, and that, in the long run, across the generations, righteousness is rewarded.[681]

The Reform version of *Birkat Ha'Mazon* includes the call to prayer and the first benediction. It then includes the second paragraph of the second benediction and the final two sentences of the third benediction. The first half of the second benediction, most of the third benediction, the entire fourth benediction, and the informal additions are omitted, except for one line of *Ha'Rachaman* on *Shabbat*, the final line of *Ha'Rachaman* beginning with *Oseh shalom*, and the final line of the collection of biblical verses.[682]

HAVDALA: THE "SEPARATION"

Havdala marks the separation between sacred time and secular time. Like *Kiddush*, it dates from the early Second-Temple period, and is attributed to the Great Assembly.[683] It consists of four blessings—over wine, over sweet-smelling spices, and over light, plus the *Havdala* blessing itself, a blessing to God as the One who distinguishes between sacred time and secular time. The blessings over spices and light are of talmudic origin.[684] The *Havdala* blessing begins *Ha'mavdil* (The one who separates), the core of which is the prayer recorded in the Talmud that was recited by the Babylonian scholar Rava at the end of *Shabbat*.[685]

The end of *Shabbat* was observed in ancient times by *chavura* meals, at which wine was drunk and the *Havdala* blessing was recited. At nightfall, candles or lamps were lit. It was customary to place sweet-smelling incense on hot coals at the end of every meal, and this was done at the end of the meal at *Havdala* as well.[686] Blessings for these activities—drinking wine, candle-lighting, and placing incense on the coals—became part of the *Havdala* ritual in commemoration of these ancient meals.[687]

The spices are often kept in spiceboxes shaped like castles. Legend has it that this is because spices were so valuable in the Middle Ages that they were kept in castles. The real explanation is more poignant. In medieval Europe, Jews were not permitted to be silversmiths. Christian silversmiths were experienced in making relicries for the church in the shape of castles, and, when asked to make spiceboxes for the Jews, they made them in the same shape.[688]

A braided candle with a minimum of two wicks is used for *Havdala*. This is to form a "torch" that sheds a greater light.[689] Since lighting a fire is forbidden on *Shabbat*, the *Havdala* light is "as though fire were renewed for us."[690] Moreover, the Talmud says that God enabled Adam to discover fire on the first *Shabbat* night.[691]

It is customary to hold one's hands to the flame and examine them while saying the blessing for the light at *Havdala*. This is to derive some use from the light.[692] The talmudic rule is that when reciting *Birchot Ha'Nehenin* (blessings of enjoyment), one ought to derive the benefit of the object of the blessing. However, the blessing for light or fire, unlike the blessing for spices that precedes it, is not classified as a blessing of enjoyment,[693] so this custom is not obligatory, and may have originated from uncertainty as to the classification of the blessing. It is also a custom to use the wine left in the *Kiddush* cup to put out the fire of the *Havdala* candle; again, this originally may have been to put the wine to use if one was not going to drink it (e.g., where a small child recited the *Kiddush*), so that the wine, over which the blessing on the wine—a blessing of enjoyment—had been recited, could be put to use.

The talmudic rabbis regarded the *Havdala* ceremony, whatever its origin, as a needed lift to offset the sadness occasioned by the departure of the Sabbath. It is the time when the additional soul, the *neshama yeteira*, the spiritual serenity,[694] which arrived on Friday evening like a bride with the recital of *Lecha Dodi*, leaves us. It was said that "three things restore a man's good spirits: sounds, sights, and smells."[695] All three are used in the *Havdala* ritual.

LIGHTING THE *CHANUKA* LIGHTS

Chanuka was a holiday so minor in mishnaic times (the first two centuries C.E.) that it is barely mentioned in the *Mishna*, and was not widely observed.[696] It originated as a celebration of Jerusalem's liberation from the Syrian-Greeks by the Hasmoneans, but the Pharisaic rabbis and the Hasmonean rulers were at odds, so the celebration was downplayed.[697] The only significant discussion of *Chanuka* in the *Mishna* is a debate between the aristocratic Shammai and the plebeian Hillel about whether to light eight candles the first night and reduce the number each night thereafter— Shammai's view—or to light one the first night and increase the number nightly, the view of Hillel. Hillel's view prevailed.[698]

Lighting the candles may have originated as a celebration, but its popularity may well have come as an act of defiance. In third-century Persia, the Magian rulers, who fanatically persecuted the Jews, banned the kindling of the *Chanuka* lights, among many other rites. In response, kindling the *Chanuka* lights became an act of defiance. The rabbis in nearby Babylonia composed special blessings for it (and similar ones for Purim), *L'hadlik ner shel Chanuka* (Who . . . commanded us to kindle the *Chanuka* lights) and *She'asa nissim l'avoteinu ba'yamim ha'heim ba'z'man ha'zeh* (Who performed miracles for our ancestors in the days of old, at this season).[699]

The explanation normally given for celebrating eight days of *Chanuka* is the legend recounted in the *Mishna*—that, by a miracle, one day's worth of undefiled oil found in the reconquered Temple kept the *ner tamid*, the eternal light, burning for eight days until new oil could be prepared by the priests.[700] Some scholars believe that the holiday originated as an ancient Semitic winter solstice festival, and that its eight-day length either was an attempt to equate it to the harvest festival of *Sukkot* (which, with *Shemini Atzeret*, is eight days long), or shows that originally *Sukkot* and *Chanuka* were derived from the same holiday.[701] The Talmud, 2 *Maccabees* 10:5–8, explains that the holiday was patterned after *Sukkot* because it was remembered how "a little while before, during *Sukkot*, they had been wandering in the mountains and caverns like wild animals" and had been unable to celebrate the Festival properly.[702]

The use of the *shamash* (literally "guard"), an extra candle, to light the others has a religious significance that is not commonly known. The Talmud says that the light of the *Chanuka* candles is not supposed to be used for ordinary illumination.[703] The *shamash* is lit first, and remains lit, to maintain the idea that the light of the *chanukiah*, the special *menorah* used on *Chanuka*,[704] is being used only for ritual purposes. If one happens to use its light to perform a household task, for example, it is said the light of the *shamash*, and not the light of the ritually required candles, illuminates the task.

It is also required by the Talmud that the *chanukiah* be positioned outside the entrance of the house, on the side opposite the *mezuzah*, to affirm publicly the *Chanuka* miracle.[705] In other words, *Chanuka* is a time when we are supposed to publicly express our pride in being Jewish. The *chanukiah* may be kept inside the house in a place not visible to the public only if displaying it would endanger the occupants.

A prayer called *Ha'Nerot Hallalu* (These Lights We Kindle) was added to the *Chanuka* blessings during the Gaonic period in Babylonia to explain the significance of the occasion. It should be read in a way that makes the explanation clear, so if those present do not understand Hebrew, it should be translated for them.

The popular *Chanuka* hymn *Ma'Oz Tzur* (Rock of Ages) was written in the thirteenth century by a poet named Mordecai whose name is spelled out in acrostic in the first five stanzas. The tune to which it is normally sung is actually an old German folk melody. Its recitation is not obligatory, but the festive mood it can help us enter is essential.

SUKKOT: HOSHANOT, THE FOUR SPECIES, AND THE SUKKAH

After the *Musaf Amida* on *Sukkot*, the congregation in the synagogue forms a procession around the *bima* and recites *piyyutim* (poetic hymns) called *Hoshanot*, so called because of the refrain *Hosha Na* (Deliver Us). This ritual was performed around the altar in the Second Temple and was transferred to the synagogues. The custom of circling the synagogue seven times on the seventh day of *Sukkot, Hoshana Rabba*, is based on the account in the *Mishna* of the Second-Temple ritual.[706]

Why are we pleading with God to save us on *Sukkot*? Wasn't our fate sealed on *Yom Kippur*? At the time of the Second Temple, *Sukkot* was a celebration of the end of the harvest and a water Festival. With the harvest finished, it was now time for the rains to come and for new crops to be planted. To bring rain, water was ritually poured each day.[707] A special prayer for rain is still added to the *Musaf Amida* on *Shemini Atzeret*, the day of solemn assembly that immediately follows *Sukkot*. A good harvest and abundant rain were the source of life in ancient Israel. People had to plead with God to send these necessities, and they did so in the *Hoshanot*.

Today, we have much more to plead for than a good harvest and abundant rain, but in pleading with God in the *Hoshanot*, like our ancestors and like Jews throughout the world, we focus our minds on the still-basic connection between God and our personal well-being.

During the *Hoshanot*, we carry four species: a palm branch (*lulav*) bound with willow twigs and myrtle branches, and an *etrog*, or citron. Various explanations are given in the Talmud and the *Midrash* for the four species, but their association with water is evident. The *etrog* was the only citrus fruit known to have been cultivated in ancient Israel, and it was unique among the fruits in cultivation there in requiring extensive irrigation.[708] The palm and the willow are both trees that flourish in hot, wet areas, such as the valleys and coastal lowlands of Israel. The myrtle is distinguished by its sweet aroma and by leaves that are always green. It is plausible, perhaps even likely, that the four species originally were carried and shaken on *Sukkot* as a plea for rain, enough rain to allow plants requiring sufficient moisture, such as the *etrog*, palm, and willow, to flourish, and to keep the myrtle aromatic and green.

As we carry the four species around the synagogue, we can visualize an oasis in ancient Israel, with tall palm trees, broad willows, and aromatic myrtles and *etrogim*. We visualize the connection between God and the lives of our ancestors, who depended on God to send rain so that they could flourish like the plants that were an intimate part of their experience. We open our hearts unabashedly to pray for the natural elements of our existence and to revel in our primordial connection with them—water, food, the warmth of the sun, the shelter of a tree, the scent of a flower.

We also construct our own ancient oasis at home by building a *sukkah*. The biblical commandment regarding the four species, read in context in the book of Nehemiah, is a description of the building materials from which a *sukkah* was to be fashioned, though it was later interpreted in the Talmud as a separate obligation.[709]

It is also customary to build a *sukkah* at the synagogue, a custom that both Philo and Maimonides suggested was to show misfortune at a time of good fortune and thereby to remind the rich of the poor.[710]

The kabbalists, based on a passage of the *Zohar*, established the tradition of the Ushpizin, the mystical seven "guests"—Abraham, Isaac, Jacob, Joseph, Moses, Aaron, and David—who visit the *sukkah* during the seven days of *Sukkot*. An invitation to them to enter is found in the Orthodox liturgy.[711] The invitation to the Ushpizin consists of a statement of readiness to perform the commandments regarding the *sukkah*, followed by a sequence of meditations beginning with the rabbinic meditational formula, *Y'hi ratzon mil'fanecha*. This is an occasion to visualize the *sukkah* as if it were "the aura of God, holy and pure, spread over our heads from above like an eagle arousing its brood."[712] We visualize our being purified from sin, that the hungry and thirsty are granted food and "an unfailing supply of water," and—an allusion to the fiery winged vision of Ezekiel—God's protecting us with His wings at the time of our death "from the stream of fire and the fiery rain, when You rain coals upon the wicked."[713]

SIMCHAT TORAH: HAKAFOT (PROCESSIONS)

Simchat Torah (Joy of the Torah) originated as the second day of *Shemini Atzeret*, generally regarded as the eighth day of *Sukkot* but called a separate holiday in the Talmud. *Shemini Atzeret* required a second day in the Diaspora owing to uncertainty about the date of observance in Israel.

Simchat Torah became a holiday in its own right when the annual cycle of Torah reading was instituted in the Babylonian academies. It is the day when the reading of the Torah is both concluded and begun anew.

A joyous holiday, Simchat Torah is celebrated by often raucous processions called *Hakafot* in which the Torah is carried seven times around the *bima*. Most Jews, engaged in revelry, do not pause to think about the prayers recited during the *Hakafot*. While dancing around the synagogue carrying the Torah, we are, in fact, pleading with God to save us, to "answer us when we call."[714]

Why do we plead with God on a joyous occasion in a manner seemingly more appropriate for *Yom Kippur*, the Day of Atonement? There are a number of reasons:

1. *Shemini Atzeret*, of which *Simchat Torah* is the second-day extension, is a day of solemn assembly on which a special prayer unit for rain, called *Geshem*, is included in the repetition of the second blessing of the *Musaf Amida*. Traditionally, the reader dons a white robe as on *Yom Kippur* and recites the introductory *Kaddish* in the *Yom Kippur* mode.[715] Thus, at its root, *Simchat Torah* is not joyous; it is a time of pleading with God for rain which, in ancient Israel, was the source of all life. The "joy of the Torah" was superimposed on this solemn occasion, and the prayers recited during the *Hakafot* reflect this fact.

2. The *Hakafot* begin with an excerpt from Psalm 118, the last psalm of *Hallel*, which, in antiquity, was recited by the Levites on the pilgrimage Festivals as a form of rejoicing during the sacrifices, which, though offered to expiate sins, were considered a joyous occasion when Jews from throughout Israel assembled in the Temple. In effect, we take the rejoicing of *Hallel* and embellish it in the liturgy for the *Hakafot*, on an occasion when Jews from throughout the community gather in the synagogue.

3. The *Simchat Torah Hakafot* themselves appear to have originated in the fourteenth or fifteenth century as a form of magic to ward off evil spirits.[716] Walking around the *bima* (which, in traditional synagogues, is in the middle of the sanctuary) with the Torah was a means of protecting it and, by implication, the community of Jews whose representative prayed from it. The custom of beginning to read Genesis on the same day we complete Deuteronomy originated out of the fear, expressed in the *Midrash*, that evil spirits would intrude if the Jews showed disdain for the Torah by not immediately reviewing it after completing it.[717] The pleading with God to "save us" to "answer us when we cry out," at one time was a plea to be saved from the evil spirits that, it was thought, would attack if we did not remain constantly in a cycle of reading the Torah.

The *Hakafot* are preceded by opening the Ark and taking out the Torah. A collection of biblical quotations, beginning, *Ata Har'eitah*, is added to the usual liturgy for removing the Torah from the Ark. The quotations generally laud God's power and attempt to invoke that power through the remembrance of the virtues of our ancestors, leading up to the pleas to God that ensue during the *Hakafot*.

PASSOVER: THE SEDER AND THE *HAGGADA*

The Purpose of the Seder: A Ritualized Talk-Feast in Which We Visualize Ourselves Being Freed from Slavery

The Passover seder (order), the Passover night family ceremony, began as a meal, not as a ritual.[718] The meal of roasted paschal lamb evolved, under Hellenistic influence, to follow the same pattern as a Greek symposium, or "talk-feast."[719] Our seders today are, in reality, ritualized symposia like those of the ancient Greeks.

A symposium had a predetermined theme. The theme of the seder is the Exodus from Egypt and the founding of the Jewish nation. The reason for this theme is that we are using the ancient Greek symposium as a pedagogical device, to teach children about the Exodus of the Jews from Egypt, in fulfillment of the biblical commandment to "explain" to our children the ancient story.[720]

Calling the seder a "pedagogical" device is to understate its purpose. We fulfill the biblical commandment by causing everyone present at the seder to visualize himself or herself as if he or she were a participant in the Exodus. The Talmud says, "In each and every generation each person is obligated to see himself as if he left Egypt."[721] Maimonides added to this, "In each and every generation each person is obligated to show [demonstrate] himself as if he, himself, had presently left the bondage of Egypt."

Rabbi Yitzchak Handel has written:

The Rambam [Maimonides] intensifies the experiential aspect of this goal. Not only was each of us a slave and then freed, but that enslavement must be seen as having taken place now, not fifty years ago, and not 3500 years ago. We were not visitors in Egypt, but slaves in bondage. The Rambam adds the expression, "he, himself" to eliminate the possibility of the statement being interpreted in a general and non-personal manner. We must see the Jews—we ourselves who now sit at the seder—each one of us, as having been slaves.

. . . [T]he Rambam also changes his text from "to see" to "to demonstrate." This introduction of activity constitutes a behavioral component. One should not leave the experience in the realm of internal thought and feeling, but must express the experience in one's actions. . . .

Why are such experiences necessary? The answer is straightforward; only when one has experienced slavery can the full meaning of freedom be appreciated.[722]

Much of the seder is designed to provoke the curiosity of those present, or, at least, was designed to do so given the usual customs of the period when the seder developed. There is an abundance of tactile and visual aids at the table. The display and use of the items on the seder plate, the lifting of the *matza*, and the spilling of drops of wine as the plagues are recited are all intended for this purpose.[723]

Origins of the Seder: The Democratic Sacrifice, and the Post-Sacrificial Meal

During the late Second-Temple period, in the first century B.C.E. and the first century C.E., Passover was the most popular festival, because it was the most democratic. It was the one time of the year when the Jewish common people were permitted to make their own sacrifices in the Temple. The rest of the year, a person wishing to offer a sacrifice had to give the animal to the Levites, who then would prepare the animal for sacrifice, slaughter it, place it on the altar, and chant psalms while the *Kohen*, or priest, ritually sprinkled the animal's blood on the altar and burned all or part of its flesh. On Passover, the person bringing the paschal lamb was permitted to slaughter it in the Temple himself or herself, although the priest still performed the ritual functions at the altar. After the priest had sprinkled the lamb's blood on the altar, it was roasted in ovens specially constructed for this purpose, after which the person who brought it could take it to his or her temporary shelter in the outer parts of the Temple and have the Festival meal.

Hundreds of thousands of people would make the Passover pilgrimage to the Temple from all over Israel, to the point where the crowds posed a serious risk of revolt to the Roman authorities.[724] During Passover, Jerusalem was a mob scene, with people camped out in the streets and in the courtyards of the Temple. Passover was a time for mass partygoing and also for nationalistic ferment.

These family feasts at which the paschal lamb was eaten were shared occasions; one can imagine that it was not easy to prepare for a Festival meal in the streets of Jerusalem, with many thousands of other families trying to do the same thing at the same time, so families pooled their resources and ate together. Josephus gave this account: "A little fraternity, as it were, gathers round each sacrifice, of not fewer than ten persons (feasting alone not being permitted), while the companies often include as many as twenty."[725]

The observance of Passover in the Second-Temple period was, in effect, a revival of a revival. After the time of Moses and Joshua, the Festival was little observed until the reforms of King Josiah late in the First-Temple period. After Josiah, it again lapsed until the Jews, led by Ezra, returned from Exile and the Second Temple was built.[726]

At first, the sacrifice of the paschal lamb had been reserved for adult men.[727] Later in the Second-Temple period, however, during the first century B.C.E. and the first century C.E., Passover became a family occasion, and wives and children joined the men in bringing the paschal lamb to the Temple and then celebrating by roasting the lamb and eating it.

As part of the ritual of sacrificing the paschal lamb, a declaration was recited by the farmer while making the sacrifice. We know that there was such a declaration at the time of the offering of the first fruits on *Shavuot*, and that the first fruits declaration included the verses in Deuteronomy 26:5–8, which read:

> My father was a fugitive Aramean. He went down to Egypt with meager numbers and sojourned there; but there he became a great and very populous nation. The Egyptians dealt harshly with us and oppressed us; they imposed heavy labor upon us. We cried to the Lord, the God of our fathers, and the Lord heard our plea and saw our plight, our misery, and our oppression. The Lord freed us from Egypt by a mighty hand, by an outstretched arm and awesome power, and by signs and portents.[728]

When the Second Temple was destroyed, the Jews were no longer able to commemorate the Exodus through the sacrifice and declaration in the Temple. Therefore, the post-sacrificial meal and the account of the Exodus were combined.

The Origins and Meaning of the Seder Plate

The seder plate, which is placed on the table in preparation for the seder and is the focal point of the ritual, originally was food for the post-sacrificial meal. The meal originally began at the outset along with the liturgy, the telling of the story of the Exodus.[729] The meal was already served when the story was told at ancient seders. However, once the food was served, the children were easily distracted or became sleepy, so to hold their attention it became customary to delay the meal until the account of the Exodus had been completed.[730] By placing the seder plate with several foods required by the *Mishna* on the table at the outset, we enable the meal to begin symbolically even though the eating is delayed.

The origin of the seder plate as the post-sacrificial meal explains its contents, which include the following:

Karpas *(Leafy Vegetable)*

In Greco-Roman festive meals, a leafy green vegetable such as celery was a common hors d'oeuvre.[731] The *karpas*, the leafy vegetable that is part of the Seder plate, derives from this Hellenistic hors d'oeuvre.

However, in ancient Israel, while lettuce was dipped first at the Passover meal (when it could be obtained), the lettuce was called *chazeret*.[732] It had to be dipped in hot water to get rid of worms.[733] Because ancient Israeli lettuce was rather bitter, it was considered one of the "bitter herbs" (the phrase is plural—*merorim*—in Numbers 9:11) required to be eaten.[734] The word *karpas* was an ancient term whose meaning had almost been forgotten by talmudic times, but it was identified by one third-century rabbi as rock-parsley,[735] and did not come into common usage again until the eleventh century c.e., about the time of Rashi.[736]

Beitza *(Roasted Egg)*

In Rome, one way to begin the meal proper was with eggs.[737] The roasted egg on the seder plate may derive from a Roman first course. Alternatively, it may have been added after the fall of the Second Temple, because the egg is an ancient symbol of mourning and is the ritual food eaten after a funeral.[738] One can speculate that eggs may have been a common first course of the post-sacrificial meal, and that after the Temple was destroyed it became the custom to roast the egg to symbolize the various Temple sacrifices (other than the paschal lamb, which has its own symbol on the seder plate in the roasted shankbone) instead of eating it. The custom of serving hard-boiled eggs with salt water at the beginning of the meal proper probably has a similar derivation.

Z'ro'a *(Roasted Shankbone)*

After the fall of the Second Temple in 70 c.e. made it impossible to sacrifice the paschal lamb and eat its roasted meat at the post-sacrificial meal, a roasted shankbone was included in the seder plate as a reminder of this main course of the post-sacrificial meal.

Maror (Bitter Herb)

The Torah commanded the children of Israel to eat *merorim*, "bitter herbs," with unleavened bread and the paschal offering both in Egypt on the night before the Exodus[739] and "throughout their generations."[740] The second commandment (from Numbers 9:11), taken in context, actually applies only to those who are ritually unclean owing to contact with a corpse or who, like the ancient Passover pilgrims, are on a long journey.

While the *maror*, or "bitter herb," was vested by the Talmud with the symbolism of the bitterness of slavery in Egypt, it also symbolizes the extent to which impoverished Jews were prepared to forage in Second-Temple times to make the Passover pilgrimage to Jerusalem.

While the *Mishna* permitted five different types of vegetables to be used as bitter herbs, including lettuce,[741] the one most frequently used was probably the plant *sonchus oleraceus*, called *murar* in Arabic. This is a common roadside weed in Israel. Its leaves and roots, which were eaten by the poor, have a bitter taste. It was said, in antiquity, to possess curative properties for various ailments.[742]

One can imagine that the thousands of pilgrims camping out in the Temple courtyards and streets of Jerusalem during Passover must have had to forage for whatever they could from the streets for the seder unless they had enough money to pay what probably were inflated prices charged by the local merchants for food. It is a fair speculation that those who scrounged for food may have eaten bitter weeds—*maror*—at the post-sacrificial meal not only to fulfill a commandment, but because they could not afford sweeter-tasting vegetables.

The seder plate also contains a second place for bitter herbs, here specified as lettuce, *chazeret*. These are eaten as part of the "Hillel sandwich," the sandwich of *matza*, *maror*, and *charoset*.

Charoset (A Mixture of Nuts, Fruit, Cinnamon, and Wine)

Eating *charoset* is commanded in the *Mishna*.[743] It is supposed to symbolize the clay used as mortar in Egypt. The word *charoset* is thought to come from the word *cheres*, meaning "clay."[744]

However, the symbolism of the *charoset* was probably an afterthought. *Charoset* probably originated as a special treat for the post-sacrificial meal. It is still served as one course of the Passover meal in many households, and that custom is consistent with its origins.

Matza (*Unleavened Bread*)

Three pieces of *matza* are placed on the table. Two represent the double portion of manna God sent to the Jews wandering in the desert immediately before a day of rest.[745] The third *matza* is the Bread of Affliction, the bread the Jews made immediately before leaving Egypt when they lacked sufficient time for it to rise.[746] In other words, two *matzot* would put Passover on the same footing as any *Shabbat* or Festival; it is the third *matza* that is special.

We break off a piece of the *matza* on the seder plate and wrap it in a napkin. This custom is derived from the biblical account that the freed slaves "carried their dough before it was leavened, their kneading-troughs bound up in their clothes."[747] It also is justified as a showing of sensitivity for the poor, who, not knowing where the next day's food will come from, will not consume all their provisions at one time, but will save some for the next day.[748]

The Four Questions (or, the "Three Exclamations")

The Four Questions, which today come long before the meal, at one time were said with the food already served. The child would be stimulated to exclaim, "How different this night is from all other nights" (the correct translation of the first "question," *Ma nishtana ha'layla ha'zeh mi'kol ha'leilot*) upon seeing how different the food being served was than the usual fare, and how differently it was eaten.[749]

The Four Questions should more properly be called the "Three Exclamations." The original text was: "How different this night is from all other nights! On other nights we eat seasoned food once, but on this night twice. On other nights we eat leavened or unleavened bread, but this night all is unleavened. On other nights we eat meat either roasted, stewed, or cooked, but on this night all is roasted."[750] The *Mishna* makes it clear that these were only suggestions, and that others could be added or substituted.[751] In response to the child's exclamations, the father was to give an explanation of the meaning of the Exodus. The original idea, in other words, was that the child's questions should be spontaneous, evoked by the unusual nature of the food being served.

The reference to roasted meat in the "Three Exclamations" was deleted after the destruction of the Second Temple made sacrificing the paschal lamb, and dining on its roasted meat, impossible.[752]

The father's answer is described in the *Mishna*: "He begins with the shame and ends with the glory." Today we begin with the shame of having been slaves in Egypt, reciting, "We were slaves in Egypt" (*Avadim hayinu l'pharoah b'mitzra'im*), but, in antiquity, some rabbis argued that the real shame to start with should be that we once worshipped idols.

The Four (or Five, or Six) Cups of Wine

It was customary at ancient Greek "talk-feasts" to drink wine throughout the meal. Many courses would be served, and wine would be served with each.[753]

The Talmud says that one should drink four cups of wine at the seder. The number four is rationalized in the Jerusalem Talmud as based on the four promises God made to Israel: "I will free you from the labors of the Egyptians," "I will deliver you from their bondage," "I will redeem you with an outstretched arm and through extraordinary chastisements," and "I will take you to be My people and I will be your God."[754] Two of the cups of wine have other functions: the cup over which *Kiddush* is recited, and the cup used for *Birkat Ha'Mazon*. The other two, coming after the story of the Exodus has been told, are unique to the seder.

However, there was a dispute among the rabbis as to whether a fifth cup of wine should be drunk. If each divine promise of freedom was to be celebrated with a cup of wine, some asserted, then a fifth cup should be drunk in celebration of a fifth promise that immediately followed the other four in Exodus 6:8: "I will bring you [into the land]."[755] Whenever the rabbis couldn't agree on the solution to a problem, it was said that the prophet Elijah would solve it when he came to herald the coming of the Messiah.

There is even authority for a sixth cup of wine. It was the custom of the ancient Romans and Greeks to dilute wine to reduce the strong flavor of the pitch or resin that was smeared inside the earthenware amphorae or wine jars as a sealant.[756] Wine in ancient Israel similarly needed to be mixed with water to be enjoyed. If one drank four cups of wine straight, it was said that one had fulfilled the duty of celebrating Passover, but not the duty of symbolizing his freedom. For that, one had to *enjoy* the wine.[757] To drink the equivalent of four cups of wine and enjoy them, one would have to drink more than four cups of watered-down wine. If one accepted the view that a fifth cup of wine was obligatory, then to enjoy the equivalent of five cups of pure wine, an additional cup was required.

Pouring Elijah's Cup and Opening the Door for Elijah:
Sh'foch Chamat'cha

The origin of "Elijah's Cup," the extra cup of wine left for Elijah at the seder, has already been suggested in the preceding section. It is the fifth cup which, when the prophet Elijah arrives to announce the redemption of Israel from its Exile, and to resolve all disputes, he may determine we should drink at the seder.[758] We pour it and leave it out as a symbol of faith that redemption will come, perhaps even tonight while we sit at the seder table.[759]

We pour the cup for Elijah after the meal, after *Birkat Ha'Mazon* has been recited and before *Hallel*. As we do so, we also open the front door for Elijah to enter, and recite a prayer, beginning, *Sh'foch chamat'cha*: "Pour out Your wrath on the nations that do not know You." This prayer was written in the eleventh century,[760] and incorporates quotes from Psalms 79:6–7 and 69:25 and from Lamentations 3:66.

The sad reason for this prayer is that, in the Middle Ages, it was dangerous for Jews to open their doors, because anti-Semites were afoot. The prayer was probably written around the time when the Gentiles began to accuse the Jews of mixing gentile blood in the *matzot*.[761] It reflects the fear that was mixed with the joy of Elijah's cup. Opening the door and saying (or shouting) that God should "pour out [His] wrath" on the Gentiles was an act of defiance, in stark contrast to the Jews of Egypt, who were forced to remain in their homes while God put to death the first-born of the Egyptians.[762]

Rather than take *Sh'foch chamat'cha* literally as an anti-gentile prayer, we should say it in the spirit in which it was composed, the spirit of defiance against demagoguery, brutality, and ignorance.

The *Afikoman*

We know the *afikoman* today as the piece of the broken middle *matza* that is designated as the "bread of affliction" and is hidden by the children during the seder, then sought by the parents, ransomed, and eaten as dessert.

However, the word *afikoman* originated as a transliteration of the Greek word *epikomion*, meaning "revelry."[763] Greek banquets customarily ended with *epikomion* in the form of licentious entertainment. The rabbis of the *Mishna* distinguished the seder from the Greek symposium, or "talk-feast," on which it was based by banning the licentious entertainment. Thus, the *Mishna* says, "We do not end the Passover meal *afikoman*."[764] Most translators, thinking that *afikoman* refers to the *matza* eaten as dessert, have rendered this as, "We do not eat anything after the *afikoman*," but its correct meaning is apparent once one knows that it is a transliteration of a Greek word.

Eating a piece of *matza* for dessert at a seder was a let-down compared to the sweets and entertainment that ended a Greco-Roman banquet. The custom developed to make the *matza* dessert more palatable to children by allowing them to hide it, and then offering the children a reward for returning it. The original meaning, however, lies in its *not* being fun, in its being a reflection of the spartan lives of the Israelites in Egypt, who had no sweets and entertainment to end their meals. By eating the *afikoman* at the end of the meal, we are destroying the final symbol of slavery in the room and completing our liberation.

The Fifteen Steps: The Order of the Seder

Since the time of Rashi[765] the seder traditionally has been divided into fifteen steps:

Kadesh (sanctification—recitation of *Kiddush* over wine)
    [The first cup of wine is drunk]
Rachatz (washing the hands)
Karpas (eating the leafy green vegetable dipped in salt water)
Yachatz (breaking the middle *matza*)
Maggid ("telling the story")
    [The second cup of wine is drunk]
Rachtza (washing the hands again)
Motzi (recitation of *Ha'Motzi* over the *matza*)
Matza (recitation of special blessing for *matza*, eating *matza*)
Maror (blessing and eating bitter herbs dipped in *charoset*)
Korech (eating a combination of *matza* and *maror*)
Shulchan Orech (eating the festive meal)
Tzafun (eating the *afikoman*)
Barech (the recitation of *Birkat Ha'Mazon*)
    [The third cup of wine is drunk]
Hallel (recitation of *Hallel*, Psalms 113 to 118)
    [The fourth cup of wine is drunk]
Nirtza (concluding prayers and songs)

The number fifteen stands for the number of steps the Levites ascended in the Second Temple from the Women's Court (a courtyard in which women and men prayed together) in their procession toward the altar, and which individuals ascended on Passover to sacrifice the paschal lamb.[766] The seder "talk-feast" was divided this way in order to yield fifteen steps for symbolic purposes, not because it logically falls into fifteen parts.

A look at *Maggid*, the telling of the story of the Exodus, reveals the semi-arbitrary nature of this fifteen-part division of the seder. *Maggid* is the longest segment of the seder. It is easily divisible into several parts, but it is lumped into a single step of the seder. If this were done, however, we would have twenty or twenty-five steps, and there were only fifteen in the Second Temple, thus *Maggid* is one long step of the seder.

The order of the seder service proceeds to a climax with *Hallel*. Passover is the only time *Hallel* is said at night. *Hallel*, as discussed elsewhere (pp. 111–112), consists of the six psalms that were sung repeatedly by the Levites while the sacrifices took place on the altar of the Second Temple. One can visualize the crowds of farmers climbing up the fifteen steps to the altar and sacrificing their paschal lambs as a choir of Levites chanted the six psalms (Psalms 113 to 118) that make up *Hallel*.

The six psalms of *Hallel* actually are interspersed throughout the meal. Psalms 113 and 114, beginning *Halleluya Hallelu Avdei Adonai* and *B'Tzeit Yisrael*, are recited before the second cup of wine, before dinner, at the end of the telling of the story of the Exodus.

Here is the functional order of the seder. We:

Prepare for dinner by sanctifying the occasion and purifying our bodies (*Kadesh, Rachatz*).

Eat an appetizer of the kind eaten by the ancient Greeks (*Karpas*).

Create the Bread of Affliction by breaking the middle *matza* (*Yachatz*), setting the stage for our "time travel" back to Egypt and the Exodus.

Tell the story of the Exodus using a variety of traditional gimmicks and aids to pique curiosity and stimulate discussion (*Maggid*).

Begin to sing *Hallel*, the psalms that formerly were sung during the sacrifice of the paschal lamb (end of *Maggid*).

Wash our hands for dinner (*Rachtza*).

Bless and eat the foods that were featured in the post-sacrificial meal in ancient times (*Motzi, Matza, Maror, Korech*).

Eat the festive meal (*Shulchan Orech*).

Have "dessert" by eating the Bread of Affliction, the *afikoman* (*Tzafun*).

Recite the Grace After Meals (*Barech*).

Finish the psalms that were sung during the sacrifice of the paschal lamb (*Hallel*).

Celebrate with holiday songs (*Nirtza*).

Structure of the *Maggid*, the Telling of the Passover Story

The scope of this book does not permit a page-by-page analysis of the *Haggada*, the Passover seder prayerbook. However, there is enough room to outline the basic structure of *Maggid*, the recounting of the story of the Exodus.

Maggid comes from the same root as *Haggada*, the name of the seder prayerbook. *Haggada* means "the telling" of a story; *Maggid* means "the teller" of a story.

Ha Lachma Anya: *Arousing Interest in the Story of the Exodus and the Experience of Slavery and Freedom*

Maggid begins with the prayer *Ha Lachma Anya* (This Is the Bread of Poverty). This prayer is in Aramaic, the vernacular of the time when it was written after the destruction of the Second Temple,[767] because its purpose was to arouse interest in the story that is about to be told, and it could only do so if understood by the listener.[768]

The Four Questions and the Parent's Response: *Why We Tell the Story*

The Four Questions (or Three Exclamations, see p. 186) follow, expressing the curiosity that (presumably) has been aroused in even the youngest child in the room. The parent replies by giving a short explanation, beginning, *Avadim hayinu l'pharoah b'mitzrayim* (We were slaves of Pharoah in Egypt). The gist of the explanation is that we were enslaved, God freed us, and we are obligated to recount the story, even if everyone already knows it. The explanation includes a brief telling of the story, a taste of it to whet the curiosity of the children. This also ensures that even very young children who cannot sit through the rest of *Maggid* hear at least a cursory version of the story.

The Rabbis at B'nai Brak: *We Don't Just Tell the Story, We Discuss It*

Maggid expounds upon the obligation to recount the story of the Exodus with another story, beginning, *Ma'aseh b'Rabbi Eliezer*. The wisest men of their time, Rabbis Eliezer, Yehoshua, Elazar ben Azariah, Akiva, and Tarfon, sat up all night in B'nai Brak (near present-day Tel Aviv) discussing the Exodus. What specifically were they discussing? They were debating whether the source of the obligation to tell the story of the Exodus at night was biblical or rabbinic. Elazar ben Azariah contended the former, and his colleagues the latter.

The point of this story is not which rabbi was right; rather, it is to give an example of the kind of discussion of the Exodus that is expected of those already familiar with the story itself. The message is that one is never too knowledgeable or too wise to glean something new from this discussion.

We are not just to tell the story, but to develop an understanding of it through discussion.

The Four Types of Children: How to Tell the Story

Having aroused interest in the story, and having established the need to tell it, discuss it, and understand it, *Maggid* then explains how to tell it. This is the discussion of how to tell the story to four types of children: one wise, one wicked, one simple, and one who does not know how to ask a question.

The discussion of the four types of children is taken from the *Midrash* (Mechilta, Par. Bo:18) and, in a variant form, the Jerusalem Talmud (*Pes.* 10:4).[769] It is based on a collection of biblical verses on the Exodus, expressed in question form. The obligation to explain to our children the significance of the Exodus is set forth four times in the Bible.

> "When it shall come to pass that your children shall say to you, what does this service mean to you. . . ."[770] This the *Midrash* understands as the question of the wicked child.
>
> "And you shall tell your son on that day saying, this is done because of what God did for me. . . ."[771] This is understood as the explanation to be given to a child "who does not know how to ask," i.e., a child who is very young.[772]
>
> "And it shall be when your son asks you in time to come saying, what is this. . . ."[773] This is the question of the simple child.
>
> "When your son will ask you in time to come saying, what is the meaning of the testimonies and the statutes and the judgments which the Lord our God has commanded you. . . ."[774] This is the question of the wise child.

The four verses are phrased slightly differently. It is assumed in biblical exegesis that God does not use words unnecessarily, so the rabbis inferred that there must be a reason for the apparent redundancy. The midrashic explanation is that each verse is directed at a different type of questioner, and so it gives a different method of answering each.

V'Higad'ta L'Vincha: When to Tell the Story

After the discussion of the four types of children comes a short discussion of when the story is to be told, beginning, *V'higad'ta l'vincha yachol mei'rosh chodesh* giving a justification for reciting the story at night. We have discussed the "why," "who," and "how" of the telling of the story; now we discuss "when." This discussion appears after the Four questions because it is taken from the *Midrash* on the same phrase of the Torah quoted in the answer to the child who does not know how to ask a question.[775]

The Complete Story: The Roots of the Jewish People

Finally, we begin the telling of the complete story, beginning with *Mi't'chilah ov'dei avoda zarah hayu avoteinu* (From the beginning our ancestors were idol-worshippers). However, it is not just the story of the Exodus, but the story of the roots of the Jewish people, that we tell.

We begin the story again, having told it already once briefly in the parent's response to the Four Questions, because of a controversy recorded in the *Mishna* between Rav and Rabbi Sh'muel. Rabbi Sh'muel's opinion was that we are obliged to talk about our physical bondage in Egypt and liberation from that bondage, an obligation already fulfilled with *Avadim Hayinu*, the parent's response to the Four Questions. Rav, however, asserted that we should start much earlier, with *Mi't'chilah*, the pagan origins of our ancestors.[776]

One commentator suggested that *Avadim Hayinu* is an adequate response to the wise child, but not to the wicked child. The wicked child, who does not identify with the Jewish people and addresses his fellow Jews as "you" rather than "we," needs to be educated in the history of the Jewish people in order to become infused with a Jewish identity. The wise child already possesses that identity.[777]

The *Mishna* says that the story should be told in the form of an exposition of the First Fruits Declaration (Deut. 26:5–8), beginning, "My father was a fugitive Aramean" and ending, "The Lord freed us from Egypt by a mighty hand, by an outstretched arm and awesome power, and by signs and portents."[778] The exposition of the First Fruits Declaration, which originally was recited by farmers at the Temple on *Shavuot*, occupies several pages of the *Haggada*.

The First Fruits Declaration is one of the three fixed prayers prescribed by the Torah, the others being the declaration on tithing (Deut. 26:13–15) and the *Birkat Kohanim*, the Priestly Blessing (Num. 6:24–26). These are the oldest fixed prayers recorded in Judaism.[779]

Why Is There No Mention of Moses?

Nowhere in the story of the Exodus contained in the *Haggada* is there any mention of the role of Moses. This omission was deliberate. When the *Haggada* evolved during the first and second centuries, the issue of God's use of intermediaries was critical. The early Christians asserted that humankind could be redeemed only through Jesus. The Pharisaic view was that humankind would be redeemed through God alone.

To discuss the role of Moses at the seder would have invited misinterpretation.[780] Instead, the *Maggid* stresses that the Jew had no hand in their own liberation. On the crucial night they were forced to remain in their homes, and were not even allowed to prepare food for the journey.

Another explanation for the omission of Moses from the *Haggada* is given by the scholar Louis Finkelstein. Finkelstein argues that much of the *Haggada* is preserved from pre-Maccabean times, and was written by priests of the Second Temple. The priests, he says, constantly played down the role of Moses, who was a mere Levite.[781]

The Reform liturgist Lawrence Hoffman points out that the farmer's declaration recited while offering the first fruits in the Temple, on which the account of history in the *Haggada* appears to have been based, omitted any mention of the reception of the Torah. He says:

> Reading the farmers' story, one would never have an indication that Israel had once traveled through Sinai and received the Ten Commandments. Of course, the farmers believed in those commandments, just as they believed in the entire written Torah whence they drew the obligation to give their first fruits in the first place. But Torah *per se* was as yet unimportant in Jewish consciousness. Only after the destruction of the Temple in the first century would a new leadership class, known generally to us as the rabbis, convert the concept of Torah into the essence of Judaism, claiming even that it was a blueprint, equivalent to Plato's Ideas, on which creation depends. It was the rabbis who would consider Mount Sinai the pinnacle of a modified sacred myth.[782]

The Ten Plagues

Now we make a transition from telling the story to discussing it. The last sentence of the Torah discussed in the midrashic account of the roots of the Jewish people and the Exodus is interpreted as a reference to the plagues. This leads into a quote from the prophet Joel cited as a proof-text, "Blood, fire, and pillars of smoke," during which it is customary to spill a drop of wine as each is mentioned.[783] The Ten Plagues are then recited, and again a drop of wine is spilled with each plague. This custom of spilling drops of wine is to honor the biblical principle, "When your enemy falls, do not rejoice."[784] We symbolically dampen our enjoyment out of respect for the Egyptians who died.

A memory aid suggested by Rabbi Yehuda follows—an acronym for the Ten Plagues in the order given in the Torah. Rabbi Yehuda sought to teach the Plagues in a concise form so that children would remember them in the correct order.[785] This is necessary because Psalms 78 and 105 also contain lists of the Plagues, but in different numbers and different orders than given in the Torah's account.[786]

The Rabbinic Debate About the Number of Plagues

There follows a debate, taken from the *Midrash*,[787] among Rabbis Yose, Eliezer, and Akiva about the number of plagues. This debate, which begins, *Rabbi Yose Ha'Galili omer*, (Rabbi Yose the Galilean said), was incorporated into the *Haggada* in the Middle Ages and was not considered a mandatory part of *Maggid* by Maimonides. In the debate, Rabbi Yose "proves" that there were not ten, but sixty plagues. Rabbi Eliezer expands the number to 240, and Rabbi Akiva, in a kind of augmentio ad absurdum, "proves" the number of plagues to have been three hundred.

Why try to increase the number of plagues that befell the Egyptians? According to the Vilna Gaon in the eighteenth century, the reason is that Deuteronomy 7:15 says: "All the afflictions of Egypt with which you are familiar, these I will not bring upon you." The greater the number of plagues that could be proven to have been visited upon the Egyptians, the fewer the Jewish people could expect to endure, if they listened to God's word.[788]

Dayyenu: *Ascending the Fifteen Steps to Communicate with God*

Next comes the most popular song of the seder, the poetic hymn *Dayyenu*. Again, this is a part of the *Haggada* that Maimonides considered optional, since it discusses miracles other than the Exodus.

Dayyenu is structured as a sequence of fifteen ascending steps, fifteen favors from God culminating in the building of the Temple. This coincides with the fifteen steps that people had to climb to reach the altar in the Temple. *Dayyenu* conceivably originated as a song sung while climbing the steps to sacrifice the paschal lamb, or, if of later origin, it was structured so as to simulate climbing the steps. The sacrifice of the paschal lamb was a primitive means of communicating with God, and we are replacing it with prayer in the seder, just as synagogue prayer replaced the daily Temple ritual. One can see *Dayyenu* as a way of getting into the proper mind-set for this communication.

Nowhere in *Dayyenu* is there any mention of the rebuilding of the Temple in Jerusalem, nor of Jerusalem as the capital of the Jewish nation. Louis Finkelstein has argued that these omissions indicate that *Dayyenu* was written while the Temple was still standing, during the period before the Maccabean War in 168 B.C.E.[789] At that time the importance of Jerusalem as a capital was downplayed by the priests, who emphasized instead the importance of the Temple.[790] Finkelstein argues that the author of *Dayyenu* was the High Priest Jason, and that various portions of the *Haggada* were compiled by the priests, who were strongly anti-Egyptian and pro-Syrian before the Temple was invaded by Antiochus.[791]

Pesach, Matza, *and* Maror: *The Explanation*

The discussion continues. Citing the opinion of Rabban Gamaliel,[792] leader of the surviving Pharisees after the destruction of the Second Temple and designer of the *Amida*, the *Haggada* now explains the *pesach* (paschal lamb), the *matza*, and the bitter herbs. We are instructed not to point at the shankbone on the seder plate while explaining about the paschal lamb, because pointing would imply that the shankbone is an adequate substitute. The middle *matza* then is raised for all to see, and is explained as symbolic of the fact that the Israelites were not given time to allow the dough to rise on the night they left Egypt. Finally, the bitter herb is displayed, and is explained as a symbol of the bitterness of slavery.

This section, like the section on the Plagues, is worded in question-and-answer format. This format was established in the Middle Ages to comply with the mishnaic instruction that the discussion of the evening must be in dialogic form.[793]

The Objective: *"In Every Generation, It Is a Person's Duty to Regard Himself as if He Personally Had Come Out of Egypt"*

Beginning with *B'chol dor va'dor*, the *Haggada* now sets forth the purpose for which the story has been told: so that we can see ourselves as if we had personally experienced slavery and redemption. The story of the Exodus is not to be told as if it were a bedtime tale; it must be told with enough drama to enable us to feel the experience of slavery, and the experience of being released from slavery.

This statement of purpose is taken from *Mishna Pesachim* 10:5. A proof-text, Deuteronomy 6:23, is added, according to the opinion of Rav (*Pes.* 116b). The Jews were freed, it says, for the purpose of being given the land of Israel which God promised to our ancestors.

Introduction to Hallel

What follows, beginning with *L'Fichach*, is an introduction to *Hallel* taken from *Mishna Pesachim* 10:5. Foreshadowing the words of *Hallel*, it ends: "Let us sing before Him a new song, *Halleluya!*"

The Beginning of Hallel

We next begin *Hallel* by reciting Psalm 113 (*Halleluya Hallelu Avdei Adonai*) and Psalm 114 (*B'Tzeit Yisrael Mi-Mitzrayim*). We do not, however, finish *Hallel* immediately; rather, *Hallel* which consists of Psalms 113 to 118, is split.

Why split the *Hallel*? Historically, it probably has something to do with the fact that Psalms 113 and 114 were the ones originally recited, with the remainder of *Hallel* being a later addition.[794] However, if *Hallel* were merely symbolic of the sacrifice, it should all come at the beginning, since the sacrifice preceded the post-sacrificial meal and the eating of the paschal lamb, which are symbolically represented in the earlier steps of the seder. *Hallel* is completed only after we have eaten the meal and completed the Grace After Meals (*Birkat Ha'Mazon*), and have then opened the door for Elijah and recited *Sh'foch chamat'cha*.

The reason is that we are doing two things at the same time with *Hallel*: harkening back to the Second Temple, when we were a nation, and celebrating freedom after we are symbolically released from slavery by eating the Bread of Affliction, the *afikoman*. When we finish telling the story (*Maggid*), we are intellectually ready to celebrate freedom. To be emotionally ready, however, we must *experience* freedom by recreating the most democratic and nationalistic of our ancient rituals, and then eating a feast, reclined to one side all the while like ancient Roman aristocrats. Having worked ourselves into this liberated and exuberant mind-state, we are ready to symbolically do away with the one remaining symbol of slavery in the room: We destroy the Bread of Affliction by eating it for dessert. After saying *Birkat Ha'Mazon*, itself a mental journey to Jerusalem and the source of our blessings, we are now completely free, and we celebrate the completion of our liberation by completing *Hallel* and singing holiday songs.

For more on *Hallel*, see pp. 111–112.

The Blessing on Redemption: Praying for Freedom of the Spirit, We Make Our Requests of God

After beginning *Hallel*, we pause. We recite a lengthy blessing prescribed by Rabbi Akiva that is found in *Mishna Pesachim* 10:6. This is not only a blessing but a moment of supplication, the only place in the seder where we affirmatively ask God for something.

For what do we ask? We ask God to "enable us to celebrate many other Festivals and holy days which will come peacefully upon us; joyful in the rebuilding of Your city, and exulting in Your service: and may we eat there of the festive sacrifices, and of the *Pesach* sacrifices, whose blood, touched to the wall of Your altar, has been favorably accepted. And may we thank You with a new song for our redemption and for our spiritual freedom."

This blessing packs into one sentence several of the communal requests we make daily in the *Amida*: peace, the rebuilding of Jerusalem and the Jewish nation, the acceptance of prayer, and the redemption of the community. There is one request that is unique to Passover, however: *p'dut nafsheinu* (spiritual freedom; literally, "freedom of the soul"). In *Hallel*, in which we have paused in the middle, we are thanking God with a "new song for . . . spiritual freedom."

Where the direct communication of our requests to God in the daily *Amida* is preceded by a lengthy process of preparing the mind through prayer, at the seder our minds have been specially prepared through the telling of the story of the Exodus and discussion of freedom, and through the recital of *Hallel*. Tonight we have personally gone through the invigorating experience of redemption from slavery. We do not need the mental preparation to make requests of God that we require in other contexts. Moreover, we are now free, and we are permitted to exercise the rights of free people by making requests, even of the highest ruler.

We end the requests with a one-line blessing of God, "Redeemer of Israel," which is the same one that immediately precedes the *Amida* in the synagogue service. Then comes the second glass of wine, and *Maggid* is over.

We then eat a symbolic meal, sampling the various items on the seder plate symbolic of the ancient foods, followed by an actual meal and *Birkat Ha'Mazon* (Grace After Meals). We finish *Hallel*, reading Psalm 115 to 118, and, in the process, drink two more cups of wine to reach the required number of cups for the evening. Finally, the seder is concluded with joyous songs—some of them, such as *Chad Gadya*, quite old.

SHAVUOT: COUNTING THE OMER, TIKKUN LEIL SHAVUOT, AKDAMUT

For the forty-nine days between Passover and *Shavuot*, we count the *omer*. Counting the *omer* is a vestige of the ancient grain harvest, which began on the second day of Passover with the waving of a measure (*omer*) of barley in the Second Temple and ended with the wheat harvest on *Shavuot*.[795] The counting of the *omer* was a festive occasion in the Second Temple, but became a tragic one after its destruction. About 24,000 of Rabbi Akiva's students and followers were killed by a plague during the first thirty-three days of the *omer*. The thirty-third day, when the plague ended, is celebrated as *Lag Ba'Omer*, the *lamed* and *gimel* of *Lag* being the Hebrew letters that have the numerical equivalent of 33. Kabbalists also celebrate the thirty-third day of the *omer* as the anniversary of the death of Shimon bar Yochai, the mishnaic rabbi to whom the *Zohar*, the most prominent kabbalistic text, was attributed.[796]

Kabbalistic interest in the *omer* grows from the linkage between the counting of the *omer* and the ten *sefirot*, the mystical attributes of God.[797] The counting of the *omer* is an occasion to meditate on the *sefirot*. For this purpose, the kabbalists assign to each day a different pair of *sefirot* as a subject for meditation. For example, on the second day of the *omer* we meditate on the *sefirot gevurah* (power or valor) and *chesed* (righteousness or love), focusing on *d*, "the power that is in righteousness;" while on the forty-second day, we meditate on the *malchut* (kingship, also represented as the *Shechina* or mystical presence of God) that is in *yesod* (the basis or foundation of all active forces in God).[798]

The liturgy for counting the *omer* reflects the mystical and meditative nature of the occasion. After an opening kabbalistic prayer about unifying the first two and last two letters of the tetragrammaton (the four-letter name of God), and an initial blessing, the day of the *omer* is recited. The occasion to meditate on the *sefirot* was obscured, as in *Birkat Ha'Mazon*, by a line beginning, *Ha'Rachaman*. Psalm 67 is then inserted, featuring the words *Ya'er panav itanu* (May He illuminate His face upon us), for obvious mystical reasons. A mystical poem follows, beginning, *Ana B'Cho'Ach*: "We beg You! With the strength of Your right hand's greatness, untie the bundled sins." Ascribed by legend to the first-century rabbi Nechuniah ben Ha'Kanah, *Ana B'Cho'ach* was probably written by a medieval reader at an ancient Israeli synagogue. It is in the ligrugy because the kabbalists discovered that the prayer consisted of forty-two words. The early and medieval kabbalists constructed a mystical name of God that consisted of forty-letters.[799] The number 42 also corresponds to the number of days between the last day of Passover and the beginning of *Shavuot*.

The kabbalists found mystical references in *Ana B'Cho'ach*. For example, the reference to "bundled sins" may have been seen as an allusion to the *kelipot*, or "encrustations [literally, bark of a tree] of evil," with which the later kabbalists, led by sixteenth-century Rabbi Isaac Luria, believed the sparks of the divine light of the *Shechina* were mixed through the universe by the "breaking of the vessels" when Adam and Eve were expelled from Eden. The theory of Lurianic Kabbalah is that goodness was thus mixed with evil in the world, and that the mission of humankind is *tikkun olam*, the "repairing [or rearranging] of the world" by acts of righteousness, through which the divine light is separated from the *kelipot* and lifted up to its proper place.[800]

The final prayer in the liturgy of counting the *omer* is a kabbalistic meditation, beginning with the mystic (and, later, Chasidic) meditational formula *Ribono Shel Olam*, which makes specific reference to the *kelipot* and to forgiving "whatever blemish I have caused in the *sefirah*."[801]

Another innovation of the Lurianic kabbalists was the *tikkun leil Shavuot*, the all-night study session on the first night of *Shavuot*, a practice recommended in the *Zohar*.[802] On *Shavuot* one is not merely observing the anniversary of the reception of the Torah at Mount Sinai; one is supposed to experience its reception. This visualization of being at Mount Sinai and receiving the Torah is experienced every day during the *Shema*, but on *Shavuot* we undergo special preparation to enhance the visualization. This preparation consists of a night of Torah study. In the Orthodox tradition, excerpts are read from each weekly portion of the Torah, each of the Prophets, each book of the Writings, and each talmudic tractate. The excerpts consist of several verses from the beginning and end of each, plus certain particularly significant passages such as the Creation, the *Shema*, and the Ten Commandments.

The theory is that reading the beginning and end is a method of abbreviation equivalent to reading the whole,[803] because, at least to one already somewhat familiar with the material, it brings the entire work to mind. To draw an analogy to a computer, it is as if we were trying in one night to copy from storage into memory all of the data we possess about the Bible and its interpretation, so that we can use that data the next morning to enhance our vision of ourselves receiving the Torah from God. We use abbreviation as a rapid method of bringing up the "data" into "memory" — through association.

This method will not work for the novice who is not familiar with the Torah. For that person, an abbreviation will not bring anything to mind. Instead, any method that serves as a "crash course" or overview will suffice.

On *Shavuot* morning, a poetic hymn, or *piyyut*, called *Akdamut* is added to the traditional liturgy in both Orthodox and conservative synagogues. The first forty–four lines of this Aramaic hymn form a double alphabetical acrostic (two lines begin with *aleph*, two with *bet*, etc.), followed by an acrostic of the name of the author, Rabbi Meir ben Yitzchak of Worms (Germany) who lived in the eleventh century, and followed finally by an acrostic of a blessing on the author: "Meir, the son of Rabbi Yitzchak, may he grow in Torah and in good deeds. Amen. Be strong and of good courage." The first four lines are a request for permission (*r'shut*), because the person reciting the hymn is about to presume to explain the Torah to the others present, and failure to ask permission would be an act of arrogance. In Judaism, the prayer leader stands on no higher footing than the congregation.

Each verse of *Akdamut* ends in the Aramaic suffix *taf* (*tar* and *aleph*), the last and first letters of the alphabet, as a symbol that the cycle of Torah study is endless.

Akdamut, one of the most stunning poems in the Jewish liturgy, is a lesson in Jewish mysticism, full of concepts of the early kabbalists. It begins by saying that God cannot be adequately described, even if all the earth's inhabitants were "recorders of initials," i.e., scribes writing only the initials of entire chapters describing God's greatness.[804] It then attempts to describe God in the manner in which He was visualized by the Prophet Ezekiel. It initially alludes to the talmudic account of God's Creation of the earth through the expansion of a single rock:[805] "In isolation He established the earth and controlled [its expansion] with constraint." Then follows a vivid description of the heavenly hosts based on Ezekiel's account as elaborated by early Kabbalah:

> Flaming Seraphim, each one six winged,
> Until permission is granted them, they must be still, in total silence.
> Upon receiving [permission] from one another, in unison with no delay [they chant]:
> 'All the world is filled with His glory'—after three times chanting 'Holy.'
> Like the sound emanating from the Almighty, like the sound of torrential waters.
> Cherubim responding to galgalim, exalting in a crescendo. . . .[806]

In essence, *Akadamut* sets forth as full a description as ever appears in the liturgy of what the mystics attempted to visualize while they prayed on *Shavuot*. It describes the prayers of Israel being woven into a crowning wreath for God, which God keeps next to His *tefillin*, which in turn bear an inscription—reciprocal to that contained in earthly *tefillin*—praising Israel, "the reciters of the *Shema*."

Reflecting the hatred with which Jews were surrounded in eleventh-century Germany, the poem goes on to vividly describe the insults directed at them by the Christian population:

> The wicked come and gather, appearing like sea waves,
> With wonderment they inquire of Israel regarding proofs:
> 'Whence and Who is your Beloved, O nation of beautiful appearance,
> That for His sake you perish in a lions' den?
> Honored and comely would you be, if you would blend into our dominion;
> We would grant your wish in every place.'[807]

The "proofs" are proofs demanded by the Christians that God protects Israel and that the Messiah will come. Without such "proofs," the Christians would throw the Jews into "the lions' den." The sarcastic reference to Israel as the "nation of beautiful appearance" echoes gentile mockery of the way Jews dressed.

Rabbi Meir then hurls back a response:

'If your wise men could but know Him with full awareness!
What value has your greatness compared to His praise?
Of the great things He will do for me when redemption shall arrive;
When He will bring me light, and you will be covered with shame. . . .[808]

The final thirty-four verses of *Akdamut* set forth a mystical vision of the end of time, when God will bring "pure vessels [the vessel containing the divine light] to the City of Jerusalem as He gathers in the Exile." The *Shechina*, the mystical Presence of God, will construct a bridal canopy, adorned with clouds, to shelter Jerusalem. Separate shelters upon gold armchairs will be built for each of the righteous, classified into seven categories according to their merit. They will shine with a beauty not seen even in prophetic visions. Inside the Garden of Eden they will dance in a circle before the *Shechina*. God will slay the Leviathan and the Behemoth, the giant fish and the giant bull created on the fifth and sixth days of Creation according to talmudic legend, and the righteous will dine on them around tables made of precious stones, drinking sweet wine that has been preserved in tanks since the Creation, seated under canopies made of the skin of the Leviathan. The poem ends with a wish for the righteous ones in the congregation, that they may be "appointed among that company, being privileged to be seated in the foremost row—if you listen to His words. . . ."[809]

PURIM: LITURGY FOR READING *MEGILLAT ESTHER*

On *Purim*, as on *Chanuka*, a special prayer, *Al Ha'Nissim* (For the Miracles), is added to the thanksgiving blessing of the *Amida*, as a commemoration of God's rescue of the Jews from the plot of Haman.

The reading of the *Megilla* (the Scroll)[810] is prefaced by three blessings ascribed by the Talmud to the men of the Great Assembly, who lived in the fifth century B.C.E.[811] One is for the commandment to read the *Megilla*; one, also recited on *Chanuka*, is for the miracles performed "for our ancestors in days of old, at this season;" and the third is *Shehecheyanu*, for

God's having "preserved us and enabled us to reach this season." A separate benediction is prescribed by the Talmud to be recited after the reading of the *Megilla*.[812] An ancient hymn in alphabetical acrostic form, beginning, *Asher Heini*, is sung after the benediction, which concludes by cursing Haman and his wife and blessing Mordecai and Esther.[813]

Some Implications for the Synagogue Liturgy

The Jewish service has a subtle but logical structure. It begins with prayers, often lengthy, designed to assist the congregation in achieving a state of intense concentration, or *kavana*. This concentration is needed to enable the congregation to listen to God in reciting the *Shema* with sufficient intensity, and to visualize itself receiving God's word with such immanence as if standing ourselves at Mount Sinai, so as to become worthy of God's attention when it reaches the middle blessings of the silent *Amida*. At that point, our collective requests are communicated to God, and, through a sequence of visualizations, we undergo a collective spiritual transformation. To undergo this collective transformation, the congregation first must unite as a spiritual community. The objective of this collective transformation is to achieve *devekut*, a frame of mind in which the worshipper will be fortified in performing *mitzvot* and resisting evil in his or her daily life.

What is now called the Torah service might be better termed the "*D'rasha* (Sermon) service," because the Torah and *Haftarah* readings developed as insertions and focal points in sermons designed to explain their teachings. These sermons developed from study sessions that followed the synagogue service in ancient times. The Torah service is really a form of study rather than part of the liturgy per se, and the sermon is actually a more central part of the service than the Torah reading, appearances to the contrary in most modern synagogues notwithstanding.

Musaf is, in reality, a separate religious service developed from the additional sacrifice on *Shabbat* and Festivals customary in the Second

Temple. It is preceded by a repetition of *Ashrei* to renew our state of *kavana* for the reading of the *Amida*.

The service is concluded with *Aleinu*, a pledge of allegiance to God and a declaration of the duties we owe to all people, not just to our own, as Jews.

This structure has implications for synagogue practices, as suggested in the following sections.

BIRCHOT HA'SHACHAR: WAKING UP OUR SPIRITUAL CONSCIOUSNESS

The *Birchot Ha'Shachar* are not really part of the synagogue liturgy. They are intended for the home, to convert mundane acts like waking and dressing into reminders of our duty to behave in a manner that makes us worthy of God's attention, and they should be said while those acts are being performed. They are recited in synagogue only for the benefit of those unable to say them on their own, and as an optional part of the synagogue service, they may be shortened, or even omitted, if desired. Where the choice is made to recite them in the synagogue, they should be used as a spiritual wake-up call that gently brings our senses, our bodies, our minds, and, finally, our spiritual consciousness into a state of readiness for worship. Speeding through *Birchot Ha'Shachar* in a matter of minutes, as if they were merely a collection of words we are duty-bound to mouth, is worse than not saying them in the synagogue at all.

P'SUKEI D'ZIMRA: DEEPENING OUR CONCENTRATION ON PRAYER

The *P'sukei D'Zimra*, as well as everything else in the synagogue service that precedes *Shacharit* on the Sabbath and Festivals, are a means of collective preparation of the mind for reciting the *Amida*. They are not the only way of preparing the mind. What makes them a preferable way is their collective nature: Reciting the same liturgy tends to bind together a congregation, and this collective spirit is crucial to the *Amida's* success. However, silent meditation and personal prayer may also be used for this purpose. Indeed, many personal prayers of various rabbis have become part of the service. It is imperative that the collective prayers preparatory to the *Amida* are to be used not as an excuse for chatting or as a forum for operatic showmanship, but as a way of preparing the mind in the manner intended. The common practice of whipping through this portion of the service with blinding speed is improper; it promotes the exact opposite of the contemplative, focused atmosphere that fulfills the function of P'sukei D'Zimra.

SYNAGOGUE DESIGN AND PROTOCOL: PROMOTING SPIRITUAL COMMUNITY

Synagogue protocol such as seating arrangements ought to encourage the concentration of the worshippers and the feeling that they form a warm and cohesive group. The *bima* should be situated in the middle of the room; it is not a stage. Rather than separating men and women, the correct distinction should be between quiet areas for adults who wish to focus their attention, and areas for people with small children, persons unacquainted with the manner of worship, and others who may not be able to achieve the requisite concentration. Group participation in rituals should be promoted, and seats arranged in a circle in another manner that promotes the feeling of being part of a spiritual collectivity.

Another method of promoting a sense of spiritual community is to divide the community into smaller prayer groups, or *chavurot*. The *chavura* is an institution of ancient origin that was revived in the 1960s in the United States. Members of a *chavura* typically meet for regular *Shabbat* dinners and other celebrations, as did *chavurot* in ancient Israel. Members can help each other to learn about Judaism and to experience joy in performing home rituals. Some *chavurot* have even formed collective households built around the observance of Judaism.

What sometimes seems to be missing in the *chavura* movement is a connection between the *chavura* and the larger community. The ultimate objective—that the spiritual community we form should serve as a nucleus for the repentance and redemption of our people, the restoration of the Jewish nation as a world force for peace, and, in the end, peace on earth—should not be forgotten. To forge this social cohesion, *chavurot* should join the larger community for prayer, perhaps sitting as groups in the synagogue. The individual can experience more of a "spiritual" feeling within the larger community and less alienation from it if that community is built as a network of smaller, close-knit groups.

BARCHU: FORMATION OF A SPIRITUAL COMMUNITY

Barchu, the ancient call to worship, signifies the formation of a spiritual community. By the time *Barchu* begins, worshippers should be in the synagogue to form this community. Unfortunately, the Torah service has been overemphasized in the liturgy, and the importance of forming this spiritual community is lost on congregants who mistakenly believe that if they arrive in time to catch part of the Torah service, they have prayed. This problem can be solved either by deemphasizing the Torah service or by emphasizing more strongly a sense of community among the worshippers. Congregants should be encouraged to sit close together, perhaps even to form a circle around the *bima*, during *Barchu* to symbolize the formation of a community.

THE *SHEMA* AND ITS BLESSINGS

The *Shema* is always to be said as if it were being recited for the first time. It is a means of visualizing ourselves receiving the Ten Commandments at Mount Sinai, and of being on a pinnacle in time from which we can experience the distant past and future and put the present in perspective. It should not become formulaic. Different melodies should be used, and different parts should be read aloud each time. It should be recited slowly and meditatively, not raced through. There is no reason to give the first paragraph greater prominence than the other two paragraphs. It should be a dramatic and profound spiritual experience. We must listen to God first if we expect God to listen to us.

The blessing after the *Shema* and the *Ge'ula* originally culminated in personal prayer. They still can be an occasion for personal prayer to God, or they can act as a final concentrator of the mind in preparation for the *Amida*.

THE *AMIDA*: THE HIGH POINT OF THE SERVICE

The silent reading of the *Amida*, and particularly the reading of the middle blessings, should be treated as what it is: the high point of the service. Ample quiet time should be allotted to it, at the expense, if necessary, of shortening other portions of the service. It should not be assumed that the average worshipper is capable of reciting the *Amida* lickety-split with the required *kavana*. For most people, even knowledgeable Jews, reciting the *Amida* in a meaningful fashion means doing so slowly and thoughtfully, and with an understanding of what one is saying and why one is saying it.

Spiritual transformation is hard work, but in view of the small number of Jews who participate in daily services, it is suggested that the custom of leaving out the thirteen middle blessings of the *Amida* on *Shabbat* and Festivals be reconsidered, or that a substitute be found in communal visualization at *Shabbat* and Festival services. Greater emphasis should be placed on the middle blessings of the *Amida* than is currently the case.

TACHANUN

Tachanun is an ideal occasion for adding depth and spirituality to the traditional service. It is an underemphasized part of the service. On weekdays, time must be allotted for individuals to offer their personal meditations silently after finishing the *Amida*. On *Shabbat* and Festivals, there should be silent, collective meditation for this purpose after the silent reading of the *Amida* (for which extra time should be given), and during the repetition of the *Amida* following the middle blessing and before beginning *R'tzei*, at both *Shacharit* and *Musaf*. This meditation is a key point in the service and should not be glossed over or rushed through.

    Tachanun also is a part of the service highly amenable to increasing women's participation in and appreciation of prayer. Use of *techinnot*, the informal personal prayers usually composed by women, during *Tachanun* should be encouraged, and booklets of *techinnot* should be made available along with the prayerbooks, though no fixed text should be imposed on the congregation.

EDUCATION IN THE *SHEMA*, THE *AMIDA*, AND *TACHANUN*: KNOWING PRAYERS SO WELL THAT WE CAN TRANSCEND THEM

The middle blessings of the weekday *Amida* essentially make up two visualizations: a visualization of spiritual transformation of the community, and a visualization of national unity of the Jews that results in restoration of our homeland and, ultimately, world peace. The *Shema* also is a visualization—of being at Mount Sinai with Moses and receiving the Ten Commandments. The prayers are vehicles to facilitate these visualizations.

    The immediate goal, attainable through *kavana*, is to be able to transcend the words of the prayers, to know the words so well that they come to mind effortlessly as we become immersed in the visions that go with them. The broader goal is for the worshippers to be mentally transformed, as a group, by constant repetition of this experience, in a way that carries over into our daily behavior. This objective should not be kept a secret, but should be explained by prayer leaders, and appropriate training and practice should be offered by synagogues to enable congregants to reach this level of knowledge of the liturgy.

    One may ask, Why bother to learn the Hebrew words of these prayers?

Why not recite them in the vernacular, or replace them with meditations using techniques borrowed from other religions, such as Zen Buddhist breathing exercises?

The answer lies in the objective of Jewish prayer. The objective of Jewish prayer is the formation of a spiritual community through which *devekut* can be achieved on a mass basis, with the desired result, ultimately, being the attainment of world peace. Virtually the only things Jews throughout the world have in common, through which this objective can collectively be pursued, are the Hebrew language and the basic prayers of the liturgy. Perfect or not, they are the best tools given to us by our culture. Reform Judaism today is returning to the use of Hebrew and is restoring many of the basic prayers to the synagogue service, because it was realized by many in the Reform movement that these common denominators among Jews are the glue that holds us together as a people. Rather than try to replace the glue, we need to strengthen it.

One way to strengthen this "glue," paradoxically, is to recognize that the words of the prayers are merely aids to a sequence of mind-states. This sequence is also a common denominator among Jews, but one that has been lost through ignorance—by Jews not knowing what was supposed to be happening when they prayed. If, realistically, many Jews cannot learn the Hebrew words well enough to transcend them, at least we should know what we are supposed to be visualizing or meditating upon at the various points in the service. Shared visions and thoughts can compensate for our inability to share the words of the prayers.

THE TORAH SERVICE

The Torah service is not really a prayer service, and it currently is overemphasized. This overemphasis historically developed when what originally was a study session after prayer became the focal point of community celebrations; it became so because, after prayer had been completed, one could let go of the required concentration. As Jews in the Diaspora became less fluent in the Hebrew and Aramaic of the prayers and as they lost the concept of prayer as a means of spiritual transformation, the misconception developed that the Torah service was the pinnacle of Jewish prayer.

The Torah reading is not the pinnacle of Jewish prayer, but a time for study and an occasion for community feeling to be expressed and community events to be celebrated. It should be treated as ancillary to the sermon or *d'rasha*, which should include group discussion rather than just lectures, with the purpose of increasing the congregation's collective understanding.

The pomp and circumstance commonly accorded to the taking out and returning of the Torah to the Ark should be reduced significantly; we are there to learn from the Torah's words, not to glorify the Torah scroll as an object.

Most important, however, congregants should be made to understand that by the time the Torah is removed from the Ark, the most important and most spiritual part of the prayer service is already over. Most Jews arrive late for Sabbath and holiday services for at least two common reasons: (1) the mistaken and often-articulated belief that the prayers prior to the Torah service are less important—a belief reinforced by the elaborateness of the ceremonies associated with taking out and returning the Torah—and (2) the less often admitted, but equally widespread, feeling of boredom at sitting through lengthy and little-understood prayers whose significance is never explained.

Instead of encouraging people to come late on *Shabbat* to be "seen" at a bar mitzvah or bat mitzvah and stay for *Musaf,* people should be encouraged to come early so that they are present for the most important parts of the service, the *Shema* and the *Amida.* For example, nothing in Jewish law necessarily precludes holding the Torah study session and *D'rasha*—or even reading the weekly *Haftarah*—before *Shacharit.* The bar mitzvah or bat mitvah should be given a role in the beginning of the service, which would attract people to arrive earlier. In the conventional order of things, this role might be to act as prayer leader for *Birchot Ha'Shachar* or *P'sukei D'Zimra.* Those whose time is limited should be encouraged to come early and leave early, rather than to arrive after *Shacharit* is over.

THE TORAH AND *HAFTARAH* READINGS

The three-year cycle of Torah reading should be encouraged, as it fosters greater group participation and less reliance on a professional reader (*ba'al koreh*), and makes it easier to spend more time on building *kavana* and communicating with God in the *Amida.* The *Haftarah* reading should be made more flexible, as there is no rule against shortening the *Haftarot* or changing the verses that accompany a given *sidra.*

Restoration of the *meturgeman* (Torah interpreter), or appropriate substitutes, should be considered, in the spirit of promoting mass comprehension of what is read. Having one of the *gabbaim* perform this function would be consistent with precedent.

B'NAI MITZVAH

B'nai mitzvah should give a sermon, and it should take on primary rather than secondary importance. The honoree is showing that he or she is old enough to understand a Torah and Haftarah reading, not just to read it. Less stress should be placed on how well the boy or girl chanted the Haftarah, and more on how well he or she demonstrated an understanding of it and increased the understanding of the congregation.

Families of b'nai mitzvah should be made to understand that the celebration of the event is really an interruption in the service, albeit a happy one. The interruption can be lessened by having b'nai mitzvah perform functions—giving a d'rasha, reading the Haftarah—that are part of the service, rather than give speeches of a secular nature.

MUSAF

On Shabbat and Festivals, either the Musaf service should be preceded by more than a token effort (such as reading Ashrei) to restore kavana in time for the Musaf Amida, or kavana should be maintained throughout the Torah service by allotting quiet time for silent reflection during that service. One option is to have a meditation after the Torah has been returned to the Ark. Another is to treat the blessings following the Haftarah reading as a "mini-Amida," consistent with their origin, use them as an occasion for visualization, and follow this "mini-Amida" with a "mini-Tachanun."

ALEINU, MOURNER'S KADDISH, AND THE CONCLUDING HYMNS: THE SPIRITUAL COMMUNITY SHARES THE FEELINGS ENGENDERED BY PRAYER

Aleinu ought to be treated as the "Jewish Pledge of Allegiance" it is. Worshippers should be encouraged to put their hands on their hearts, hold hands, or otherwise express their unity during Aleinu in a concrete fashion.

In medieval times, the Mourner's Kaddish followed a sermon or study session in honor of the deceased. It was originally intended to follow a tribute to deceased scholars, and, for the mystically inclined, was meant to be participation in an act of creation that could aid the soul of the deceased in the world-to-come. The Mourner's Kaddish today should follow a visualization of the merits of the departed loved one, and also might be preceded by an act of creation or the visualization of such an act. For example, mourners could plant a seed, sing a song, recite a verse, or recount to the other congregants, as a tribute, one of their fond memories of the deceased.

The concluding hymns, like *Adon Olam*, are not mandatory, and were intended to console mourners. Mourners can be consoled in other, perhaps more effective, ways, like hugging and talking.

These functions of the concluding prayers suggest that congregants should not remain in their seats, but should gather together, perhaps in a circle, for the concluding part of the service. Each congregant should experience feelings of unity and intimacy with his or her peers in the closing moments. It is a time for the community of worshippers to share the feelings engendered by prayer.

Conclusion

If the purpose of prayer is to transform the human mind, why petition God for anything? Do we change God's actions through prayer? If prayer makes us think differently, why does that affect God in any way? Do we pray "for the sake of the *Shechina*," as the Chasidim believe,[814] or for our own sake?

The answer, I submit, is that:

Through prayer, we become able to perceive the divine spark within ourselves, and we make it possible to transform our minds.

By transforming our minds, we change our behavior to do good and resist evil, and to engage in *tikkun olam*.

By changing our own behavior to do good and resist evil, to engage in *tikkun olam*, we alter the course of the world.

By altering the course of the world, we carry out God's plan.

By carrying out God's plan, our petitions, our personal and communal requests, ultimately are answered, though often in ways hidden from us.

Prayer in Judaism is not merely a human instrument; it is a divine instrument. By transforming a community of individuals, prayer can alter human events. The sequence of mind-states in the traditional Jewish prayer service is an ancient system designed ultimately to achieve this outcome.

Viewed as an instrument of spiritual transformation, traditional forms of Jewish worship cease to be inconsistent with the need for an infusion of spirituality perceived by writers and leaders of the Jewish Renewal movement such as Roger Kamenetz, author of *The Jew in the Lotus*. The traditional liturgy originated with spirituality in mind. History drained that spirituality. This early spirituality was lost because the contemplative and ecstatic spots in Jewish prayer were scribbled over with unnecessary extra words and rituals.

These moments of contemplation and ecstasy can be restored without compromising the essential elements of the traditional liturgy. By reemphasizing ancient customs that fell into disuse, by revamping the structure of the liturgy to conform to its original function and intent, traditional Judaism can make the synagogue service a deeper spiritual experience and attract a large segment of the Jewish community that otherwise would desert its faith.

However, Jewish spirituality must stay within the framework of the peculiarly Jewish system for spiritual transformation, or it will no longer be Jewish. Jewish spirituality is not just a cornucopia of Hebrew mantras, *Shema* breathing exercises, and other imitations of Oriental religions with a *Yiddishe* twist. It is not just throwing around kabbalistic terminology or waxing mystical about counting the *omer*. Jewish spirituality is a complex system that takes a great deal of learning, a lot of time, and much dedication to master. Being a spiritual Jew is not easier than or separate from being an observant Jew or a good person, but it is a powerful technique for becoming both.

Notes

1 See *The Jew in the Lotus*, (New York: Harper-Collins, 1994), 98, where both the Dalai Lama and Orthodox rabbi Irving "Yitz" Greenberg are quoted as likening the recitation of psalms on *Shabbat*, in which we visualize ourselves as being back in Israel, to the visualizations practiced by Tibetan Buddhists during meditation. The same may be said for the *Shema*, in which we visualize ourselves as being at Mount Sinai receiving the Ten Commandments, and the *Amida*, in which we visualize ourselves approaching God and then becoming spiritually transformed and restored to our ancient unity in a nation that becomes the focal point of world peace. As we shall see, much of the Jewish liturgy is in the nature of an aid to visualization.

2 Rabbi Jeffrey M. Cohen, *Horizons of Jewish Prayer* (London: United Synagogue, 1986), 135, quoting *Mishna Ber.* 5:1.

3 *Ber.* 5:1.

4 Ibid., 134, citing *Ber.* 34b and *Hilchot T'filla* 4:5.

5 Ibid., 137.

6 Ibid., 136, quoting *Shulchan Aruch, Orach Chayyim* 98:1.

7 David Blumenthal, *Understanding Jewish Mysticism*, vol. II (New York: Ktav Publishing House, 1982), 129.

8 Ibid., 132, quoting A. Green, *Your Word Is Fire*, 51, 55–59.

9 Barry W. Holtz, *Finding Our Way: Jewish Texts and the Lives We Lead Today* (New York: Schocken Books, 1990), 40.

10 Ibid., quoting *Tzava'at Rivash* 3b.

11 Moshe Idel, *Kabbalah* (New Haven: Yale University Press, 1988), 38, citing *Sanh.* 64a.

12 Gershom Scholem, *The Messianic Idea in Judaism and Other Essays on*

Jewish Spirituality (New York: Schocken Books, 1971), 205, citing *Guide for the Perplexed* III, 51.

13 Ibid., 205.

14 Blumenthal, *Understanding Jewish Mysticism*, vol. II, op. cit., 127.

15 Louis Jacobs, *Hasidic Prayer* (New York: Schocken Books, 1973), 70ff and 93ff.

16 Ezekiel, Chap. 1. This was a technique used particularly by the *Merkava* mystics, the "mystics of the Chariot," who were the earliest Jewish adherents to mysticism.

17 Idel, *Kabbalah*, op. cit., 74–111.

18 *B. Chag.* 14b.

19 Gershom Scholem, "Merkabah Mysticism and Jewish Gnosticism," in Gersham Scholem, *Major Trends in Jewish Mysticism* (New York: Schocken Books, 1995), 47–48.

20 Florentino Garcia Martinez, *The Dead Sea Scrolls Translated* (Leiden: E.J. Brill, and Grand Rapids, MI: William B. Eerdmans, 1996), 423, 429, 430. It is revealing that the most mystical of the Dead Sea documents, the most consistent with the mysticism of the *Heichalot* literature, consists of liturgical material that indicates it was intended for the Sabbath sacrifice in the Temple. This suggests that the sacrificial ritual itself was deeply associated with altered states of mind of the donors of the offerings, and that an offering would not be effective unless it was made with the proper state of mind. A similar thesis was put forth by Yohanan Muffs of the Jewish Theological Seminary in a pair of articles, "Joy and Love as Metaphorical Expressions of Willingness and Spontaneity in Cuneiform, Ancient Hebrew, and Related Literatures," in Jacob Neusner, ed., *Christianity, Judaism, and Other Greco-Roman Cults* (Leiden: E.J. Brill, 1975), and "Love and Joy as Metaphors of Volition in Hebrew and Related Literatures, Part II: The Joy of Giving," *Journal of the Ancient Near Eastern Society*, vol. 11, 91 (1979), in which he points out that the ancient Babylonians had the same idea.

21 Idel, *Kabbalah*, op. cit., 103.

22 Ibid., 112.

23 Ibid., 120.

24 Ibid., 126.

25 Ibid., 131.

26 Moshe Idel, "Mystical Union in Jewish Mysticism," in Moshe Idel and Bernard McGinn (eds.), *Mystical Union in Judaism, Christianity and Islam* (New York: Continuum Publishing Co., 1996), 43.

27 Moshe Greenberg, *Biblical Prose Prayer as a Window to the Popular Religion of Ancient Israel*, (Berkeley, CA: University of California Press, 1983), 38. The only fixed prayers found in the Torah are the Priestly Blessing (Num. 6:24–26), the First Fruits Declaration (Deut. 26:5–8), and the Declaration on Tithing (Deut. 26:13–15). Though preserved in group prayer today in the *Amida*, the Priestly Blessing is worded in the second-person singular, suggesting that it originally was used by priests in "one-on-one" situations, perhaps when an individual brought a sacrificial offering or sought healing.

28 Moshe Idel, *Studies in Ecstatic Kabbalah* (Albany: State University of New York Press, 1988), 109–110. One of the earliest references to *hitbodedut* in Jewish literature is a comment by Hai Gaon, a Babylonian Jewish leader who lived in the tenth and early eleventh centuries in a part of the world where Sufism was influential:

> God arranged the order of creation so that all things are bound to each other. The direction of events in the lower world depends on entities above them. . . . Human souls are also bound to higher levels, and therefore, when a perfect individual becomes involved in meditation [*hitbodedut*] upon wisdom, it is possible for him to predict future events. As a result of his deep meditation, his consciousness and mind fall into a trance, and through his deep probing of the mysteries of existence, he reaches the First Cause. The faculties of his heart then become like the Urim and Thumim, mystically bound to the angels in heaven and he becomes attached to the Ultimate Good.

(Quoted in Rabbi Aryeh Kaplan. *Meditation and the Bible* [Northvale, NJ: Jason Aronson Inc., 1995], 11.)

29 Kaplan, *Meditation and the Bible*, 5, citing Rabbi Abraham Maimonides, son of the medieval philosopher Moses Maimonides.

30 Ibid., 5–6.

31 Ibid., 7–8.

32 *B. Ber.* 2lb; *Meg.* 23b. The Talmud observes that the word *eda* (assembly) also is applied to the ten spies (Num. 14:27); thus the rabbis inferred that ten are sufficient to constitute an "assembly."

33 Idel, *Studies in Ecstatic Kabbalah*, op. cit., 120.

34 Ibid.

35 Cited in Kaplan, *Meditation and the Bible*, op. cit., 88.

36 Joseph Heinemann, *Prayer in the Talmud* (revised English version of *Ha'T'Filla Bi't'kufat Ha'Tanna'im V'Ha'Amora'im*) (New York: Walter de Gruyter, 1977), 280–281. Heinemann theorizes that prayers like *Kaddish*, which refer to God in the third person, must have originated in a context in which people were talking about God rather than talking to Him. He locates this context in the ancient *Bet Midrash*.

Heinemann's approach recently has come under attack by a talented Israeli scholar, Ezra Fleischer. Fleischer argues that obligatory communal worship outside the Temple in Jerusalem was found only among dissident sects like the Essenes prior to the destruction of the Temple by the Romans in 70 c.e., and that the synagogue as a place of organized communal worship did not yet exist. See Ezra Fleischer, *On the Beginnings of Obligatory Jewish Prayer* (Hebrew), *Tarbiz*, vol. 59, 397 (1990), and the English summary of the article, III. For a useful synopsis of the debate about the origins of Jewish liturgy, see Stefan C. Reif, *Judaism and Hebrew Prayer: New Perspectives on Jewish Liturgical History* (Cambridge, England: Cambridge University Press, 1993).

37 See, for example, Moshe Greenberg, *Biblical Prose Prayer as a Window to the Popular Religion of Ancient Israel*, op. cit.

38 Lawrence A. Hoffman, *Beyond the Text: A Holistic Approach to Liturgy* (Bloomington, IN: Indiana University Press, 1987); see also Tzvee Zahavy, "The Politics of Piety: Social Conflict and the Emergence of Rabbinic Liturgy," in Paul F. Bradshaw and Lawrence A. Hoffman (eds.), *The Making of Jewish and Christian Worship* (Notre Dame: University of Notre Dame Press, 1991).

39 Lawrence A. Hoffman, "Reconstructing Ritual as Identity and Culture," in Bradshaw and Hoffman, 38.

40 Tzvee Zahavy, loc. cit., in Bradshaw and Hoffman, 47.

41 Tzvee Zahavy, *Studies in Jewish Prayer* (Lanham, MD: University Press of America, 1990), 87, following Elias Bickermann, "The Civic Prayer for Jerusalem," *Harvard Theological Review*, vol. 55, 163 (1962). There are problems with this theory, in that both the *Mishna* and Josephus say that the *Shema*, and not the *Amida*, was recited by the priests in morning prayers at the Second Temple. See Solomon Zeitlin, "The Temple and Worship," *J.Q.R.*, vol 57, 209 (1960); Mishna *Tamid* 5:1; Josephus, *Antiquities*, IV, vii, 13. There is also evidence linking rules and practices for reciting the *Shema* with the houses of Hillel and Shammai (*M. Ber.* 1:3), and the *Shema* appears on phylacteries found at Qumran. This evidence suggests that the practice of reciting the *Shema* was ancient and, by the late Second-Temple period, universal, and that it predated the rivalry between the scribes and the priests.

42 See Kamenetz, *The Jew in the Lotus*, 69, for a discussion of early Jewish contacts with the Orient. It is startling to realize that the name of at least one Hindu deity, Krishna, appears in the Book of Esther. *Esther* 1:14 ("Krishna" is identified as one of King Ahasuerus's close advisors); Ari L. Goldman, *The Search for God at Harvard* (New York: Ballantine Books, 1991), 84.

43 Franz Cumont, *The Oriental Religions in Roman Paganism* (New York: Dover, 1956) (reprint of 1911 original edition), 96. The conventional view has been that "[i]n the realm of ideas the Egyptian civilization exercised no influence whatever upon Israel. . . . The Egyptian religion with its devotion to the worship of beasts and reptiles and with its deification of the Pharaohs must have aroused in the breast of the Israelite feelings of profound repugnance and contempt." See M.H. Segal, "The Religion of Israel Before Sinai," *J.Q.R.*, vol. 52, 41 (1961), 65.

44 Serge Sauneron, *The Priests of Ancient Egypt* (New York: Grove Books, Inc., 1960), 84.

45 S.H. Hooke, *The Origins of Early Semitic Ritual* (London: The British Academy, 1938), 10.

46 Morris Jastrow, Jr., *Aspects of Religious Belief and Practice in Babylonia and Assyria* (New York: Benjamin Blum, Inc., 1971) (reprint of 1911 original edition), 303–305.

47 Jastrow, ibid., 307; Hooke, op. cit., 9.

48 H.W.F. Saggs, *The Encounter with the Divine in Mesopotamia and Israel* (London: The Athlone Press, 1978), 125ff.

49 Lowell K. Handy, *Among the Host of Heaven: the Syro-Palestinian Pantheon as Bureaucracy* (Winona Lake, IN: Eisenbrauns, 1994).

50 Richard N. Frye, "Qumran and Iran: the State of Studies," in Jacob Neusner, ed., *Christianity, Judaism and Other Greco-Roman Cults* (Leiden: E.J. Brill, 1975), 172.

51 Mary Boyce, *Zoroastrians: Their Religious Beliefs and Practices* (London: Routledge & Kegan Paul, Ltd., 1979), 31.

52 Ibid., 37. The Zoroastrian liturgy includes the "worship of the seven chapters," a collection of ancient mantras bracketed by the sayings of Zoroaster.

53 H.D. Saffrey, "The Piety and Prayers of Ordinary Men and Women in Late Antiquity," in A.H. Armstrong, *Classical Mediterranean Spirituality* (New York: Crossroad Publishing Co., 1986), 202–203. The Anatolian and Mesopotamian religions even included human sacrifice—often of foreign prisoners.

54 James D. Newsome, *Greeks, Romans, Jews: Currents of Culture and Belief in the New Testament World* (Philadelphia: Trinity Press International, 1992), 27.

55 Ibid., 28.

56 Ibid., 29.

57 Ibid., 30.

58 See the English summary of Fleischer, "On the Beginnings of Obligatory Jewish Prayer" (Hebrew), *Tarbiz*, vol. 59, 397 (1990), III.

59 Namely, the debate between Fleischer and the Cambridge University scholar Stefan Reif on the earliest development of Jewish prayer in *Tarbiz*, vol. 60, 677, 683 (1991).

60 See Lawrence Hoffman, "Jewish Liturgy and Jewish Scholarship," in Jacob Neusner, ed., *Judaism in Late Antiquity* (Leiden: E.J. Brill, 1995), Part I, 239, 246; J.B. Segal, "Popular Religion in Ancient Israel," *Journal of Jewish Studies*, vol. 27, 1 (1976); Dan Urman, "The House of Assembly and the House of Study: Are They One and the Same?" *Journal of Jewish Studies*, vol. 44, 236 (1993).

61 Moshe Idel, "Secrecy, Binah and Derishah," in H.G. Kipperberg and G.G. Strousma, eds., *Secrecy and Concealment: Studies in the History of Mediterranean and Near Eastern Religions* (Leiden: E.J. Brill, 1995), 311, 334–335. See also Louis Finkelstein, "The Origin of the Synagogue," *Proceedings of the American Academy of Jewish Research*, vol. 1, 49 (1928); compare Solomon Zeitlin, "The Origin of the Synagogue," *Proceedings of the American Academy of Jewish Research*, vol. 2, 69 (1930).

62 Ibid., 318 ("the verb *hevin* is commonly used to denote the prophetic enlightenment of the community by its priestly leaders and by God," quoting Steven Fraade, *From Tradition to Commentary: Tradition and Its Interpretation in the Midrash to Deuteronomy* [Albany: SUNY Press, 1991], 249 n. 140), 322 ("inner understanding" connected with *bina* is, "together with other acts, a prerequisite for mystical experience").

63 Yohanan Muffs, "Love and Joy as Metaphors of Volition in Hebrew and Related Literatures, Part II: The Joy of Giving," *Journal of the Ancient Near Eastern Society*, vol. 11, 91 (1979) and op. cit., "Joy and Love as Metaphorical Expressions of Willingness and Spontaneity in Cuneiform, Ancient Hebrew, and Related Literatures," in Jacob Neusner, ed., *Christianity, Judaism, and Other Greco-Roman Cults* (Leiden: E.J. Brill, 1975), 172.

64 Nehama Leibowitz, *New Studies in Shemot (Exodus)* (Jerusalem: Haomanim Press, 1993), 671.

65 Ibid.

66 See p. 182.

67 Menahem Haran, *Temples and Temple-Service in Ancient Israel* (Winona Lake, IN: Eisenbrauns, 1985), 221. Haran observes, among other things, that the Ark and the Ark-cover of the Temple had originally derived from a throne and a footstool on which God figuratively sat, but they were no longer thought of in this fashion even in biblical times. Ibid., 220.

68 Ibid., 224.

69 Moshe Idel, "Secrecy, Binah and Derishah," op. cit., 342.

70 Chayim Cohen, "Was the P Document Secret?" *Journal of the Ancient Near Eastern Society*, vol. 1, 39 (1969).

71 Solomon Gandz, "The Robeh or the Official Memorizer of the Palestinian Schools," *Proceedings of the American Academy for Jewish Research*, vol. 7, 5 (1935); Jacob Neusner, "The Rabbinic Traditions About the Pharisees Before A.D. 70: The Problem of Oral Transmission," *Journal of Jewish Studies*, vol. 22, 1 (1971).

72 Neusner, loc. cit., 17.

73 B. *Temura* 14b.

74 Dov Zlotnick, "Memory and the Integrity of the Oral Tradition," *Journal of the Ancient Near Eastern Society*, vol. 17, 229 (1985), 231–232.

75 Canaanite worship is known chiefly from Ugaritic tablets found at Ras Shamra that lay out in detail the offerings, the gods who benefited from them, and the types of sacrifice made, as well as the precise time they were required. They indicate that the king was made holy through bathing, and was central to the sacrificial rite. We know that the Canaanites, like the Babylonians, practiced soothsaying. "Men of the gods" were recognized in addition to the priests, perhaps in the nature of prophets, and birds were sacrificed in their honor.

Sacrifice was for the purpose of collective expiation of sins, particularly anger, impatience, and neglect of ritual duties. Men and women had to undergo this expiation separately using different liturgies. Special rituals existed for community emergencies. See A. Caquot and M. Sznycer, *Ugaritic Religion* (Leiden: E.J. Brill, 1980), 16–18.

76 Menahem Haran, "Priest, Temple, and Worship," *Tarbiz*, vol. 48, 175 (1978).

77 Ibid.

78 Solomon Zeitlin, *The Temple and Worship*," *J.Q.R.* vol. 51, 209 (1960), 218–220.

79 Ibid.

80 Ibid., 220–221; M. *Midot* 2:5.

81 The prevailing view has been that the synagogues and their liturgies began to develop during the Second-Temple period. However, Fleischer has argued that the synagogues did not exist until after the fall of the Second Temple. He contends that what existed in the towns and villages of Israel prior to that time were merely houses of study dedicated to preaching and the study of the holy works, and that these

houses of study were converted to houses of worship when it became impossible to worship in the Temple. Fleischer bases this view on the strong tendency of the rabbis to avoid "stepping on the toes" of the priests.

It seems implausible, however, that the large numbers of people, unable to worship at the Temple and brought together at a house of study for a religious purpose, would avoid prayer altogether. Doubtless the rabbis felt it was necessary to discourage it. However, one can easily envision people in distress entrusting to the delegates of the *ma'amadot* (the delegations sent to Jerusalem to monitor the work of the priest) their pleas to God for relief. One can also envision those people in the houses of study in their towns and villages reciting the same prayers said by their delegates to Jerusalem at the same appointed times, as a way to improve their effectiveness or to guard against a delegate's forgetfulness. Thus communal prayer may have arisen in Judaism.

82 Compare Abraham Millgram, *Jewish Worship* (Philadelphia: Jewish Publication Society of America, 1971), 78, with Lawrence Hoffman, "Jewish Liturgy and Jewish Scholarship," op. cit., 246–247.

83 Lawrence Hoffman, *The Canonization of the Synagogue Service* (Notre Dame: University of Notre Dame Press, 1979), 60.

84 Ibid. Hoffman seems to assume that the Merkava mystics were doing this merely for the sake of viewing God, a kind of drugless "trip," and that the sole function of prayer for them was to keep on praising God until they rose up and had their "trip." This is inconsistent with the evidence available to us, which Hoffman acknowledges (ibid., 61), that such luminaries as Rabbis Akiva and Yochanan ben Zakkai had strong mystical tendencies. Surely they had a more serious purpose.

85 The "canonization" of the synagogue service in Babylonia in the ninth century c.e. is amply detailed in Lawerence Hoffman, *The Canonization of the Synagogue Service,* op. cit.

86 Literally, "concentration of the heart." The heart was regarded, in antiquity, as the center of thought and emotion.

87 Ehud Ben-Or, *Worship of the Heart* (Albany: State University of New York, 1995), 1.

88 Lawrence Fine, *Safed Spirituality* (New York: Paulist Press, 1984), 17.

89 Ibid., 16–23.

90 Moshe Idel, *Hasidism: Between Ecstasy and Magic* (Albany: State University of New York Press, 1995), 33ff.

91 Jacobs, op. cit., 21–23.

92 Ibid., 21.

93 Ibid., 26.

94 Ibid., 24.

95 Ibid.

96 See *Encyclopedia Judaica*, vol. 7, "Hasidism," 1397–1398.

97 Norman Lamm, "Some Comments on Centrist Orthodoxy" (New York: Rabbinical Council of America, 1986), reprinted in Ronald H. Isaacs and Kerry M. Olitzky, *Critical Documents of Jewish History: A Sourcebook* (Northvale, NJ: Jason Aronson Inc., 1995).

98 *M. Ber.* 20a–20b; Rachel Biale, *Women and Jewish Law* (New York: Schocken Books, 1984), 18.

99 Biale, op. cit., 20.

100 *B. Megilla* 23a; Biale, op. cit., 27.

101 Solomon Freehof, "Devotional Literature in the Vernacular," *Central Conference of American Rabbis*, vol. 33 (1923), 375. See also Norman Tarnor, *A Book of Jewish Women's Prayers: Translations from the Yiddish* (Northvale, NJ: Jason Aronson Inc., 1995).

102 Jakob Petuchowski, *Prayerbook Reform in Europe* (New York: World Union for Progressive Judaism, 1968), 49, 51–52, 54, 90, 93, 209.

103 Calling it the Standing Prayer would not make sense in the Reform movement, which does not regard standing during it as obligatory. Nor would it make sense to call it the Eighteen Blessings, since the Reform movement does not regard the number of blessings as significant.

104 Jules Harlow, "Revising the Liturgy for Conservative Jews," in Paul F. Bradshaw and Lawrence A. Hoffman, eds., *The Changing Face of Jewish and Christian Worship in North America* (Notre Dame: University of Notre Dame Press, 1991), 125–126.

105 The editors of *Siddur Sim Shalom* rejected this change because the "Hebrew formula reflects biblical usage and we felt there was insufficient reason to introduce a change that would break that connection with our past." Ibid., 135. However, the English translation of the word *Avot* was made gender-neutral.

106 A. Stanley Dreyfus, "The *Gates* Liturgies: Reform Judaism Reforms Its Worship," in Paul F. Bradshaw and Lawrence Hoffman, eds., *The Changing Face of Jewish and Christian Worship in North America*, op. cit., 145–146.

107 Ibid., 145.

108 Ibid., 146.

109 For more on the attitude of the Jewish Renewal movement toward prayer, see Michael Lerner, *Jewish Renewal: A Path to Healing and Transformation* (New York: HarperCollins Publishers, Inc., 1994), 394ff.

110 The progenitor of this group was Leopold Zunz, the nineteenth-century founder of the Wissenschaft des Judentums (Science of Judaism) movement in Germany that promoted the scientific study of the Jewish people and Jewish history and religion. Others included Ismar Elbogen, who was trained at the Breslau rabbinical seminary that had been founded by Zachariah Frankel (who also helped found the Conservative Jewish movement) and was a leader of Liberal Judaism in Germany until 1938, when he became a professor at both the Jewish Theological Seminary and the Hebrew Union College in the United States; and A.Z. Idelsohn, a professor at Hebrew Union College.

111 Another example is addition of the *Imahot*, a reference to Sarah, Rebecca, Leah, and Rachel, to the first blessing of the *Amida*. The eulogy "God of Abraham, God of Isaac, and God of Jacob" in that blessing is not a sexist statement, but originated (as far as scholars can tell) in the context of a rabbinic effort to restrain the Jews from humbling themselves before God as abjectly as Gentiles of that time humbled themselves before worldly rulers. A gentile commoner addressing a ruler,

in antiquity, would be required to go through paragraph upon paragraph of titles, extolling him or her as "conqueror of this," "ravager of that," and so on, before being allowed to speak freely. The establishment of a few standard ways of addressing God (such as "God of Abraham, God of Isaac, and God of Jacob"), instead of institutionalized groveling, to us today a subtle distinction, was at the time not a sexist manifesto, but an eloquent statement about the essential dignity of all people.

112 Ismar Elbogen, *Jewish Liturgy: A Comprehensive History* (1913; trans. by Raymond Scheindlin, Jewish Publication Society, New York, 1993), 76. Rav Amram ben Sheshna (d. 875), who compiled the earliest-known written prayer code upon the request of a congregation in Spain, referred to this custom, but Maimonides (1135–1204) knew it only as a practice of individuals.

113 Elbogen, ibid., 72–73.

114 There are five manuscripts of the *Seder Rav Amram* extant. At least two, printed by Coronel in 1865 and by Frumkin in 1912, include *Ma Tovu*. Goldschmidt, however, in his 1971 printed and edited version of another of the manuscripts, does not. Coronel has been criticized as frequently inaccurate. It must be recognized that the "original" manuscripts in existence are all late medieval renditions of what may have been multiple, and variant, originals, and relying on them is fraught with difficulty.

115 A.Z. Idelsohn, *Jewish Liturgy and Its Development* (1932; reprinted by Schocken Books, New York, 1960), 73. The custom of saying *Ma Tovu* probably derived from two traditions: the tradition of using its ten-word second sentence to count the *minyan*, and the view of Rav Amram that the same sentence should be said upon entering a synagogue. See A. Hilvitz, "Amirat P'sukei 'Ma Tovu' Lifnei Ha 'T'Filla," *Sinai*, vol. 78, 263 (1976) (Hebrew).

116 Psalms 15, 24:3–6; Isaiah 33:14–16; Moshe Weinfeld, "Instructions for Temple Visitors in Ancient Israel and in Ancient Egypt," *Tarbiz*, vol 62, 5 (1992).

117 Rabbi Reuven Hammer, *Entering Jewish Prayer* New York: (Schocken Books, 1993), 253. The Talmud records that Rabbi Judah put *tzizit* on the garments of all the women in his household. Rabbi Shimon disagrees, asserting that "since they are worn only during the day, they fall into the category of commandments that are time-connected, and women are exempt from such commandments," Ibid; *Men* 43a. Even Rabbi Shimon, however, argues only that women are not required to wear *tzizit*, not that they are prohibited from wearing them.

118 *Sab.* 10a.

119 *Moed Katon* 24a.

120 *R.H.* 17b.

121 *Y. Ber.* VII–end.

122 *Sab.* 43b.

123 Elbogen, op. cit., 379–380.

124 Israel Abrahams, *A Companion to the Authorized Daily Prayerbook* (London, 1922; reprinted in New York: Hermon Press, 1966), 26–27.

125 Abraham Millgram, *Jewish Worship* (Philadelphia: Jewish Publication Society of America, 1971), 245.

126 The Talmud quotes Rabbi Meir as saying that the *tzitzit* are blue because

"blue resembles the sea; the sea resembles the sky; and the sky resembles the 'Seat of Glory'" (B. Men. 43b).

127 Hammer, op. cit., 252, citing research by the biblical scholar Rabbi Jacob Milgrom of the University of California at Berkeley.

128 Encyclopedia Judaica, vol. 15, "Tekhelet," 913; Ben Zion Bokser, "The Thread of Blue," Proceedings of the American Academy for Jewish Research, vol. 31, 1 (1963).

129 Bokser, op. cit., 30.

130 Samuel Krauss, "The Jewish Rite of Covering the Head," Hebrew Union College Annual, vol. 19, 121, 130 (1945–1946).

131 Rabbi Jeffrey M. Cohen, Blessed Are You: A Comprehensive Guide to Jewish Prayer (Northvale, NJ: Jason Aronson Inc., 1993), 276, citing B. Shab. 118b, Kid. 31a, Chag. 14b, R.H. 17b, Taanit 20a. See also Eric Zimmer, "Men's Headcovering: The Metamorphosis of This Practice," in Jacob Schacter, ed., Reverence, Righteousness, and Rahmanut—Essays in Memory of Rabbi Dr. Leo Jung (Northvale, NJ: Jason Aronson Inc., 1992), 325.

132 Krauss, op. cit., 126, 134.

133 Ibid., 126–127. It is noteworthy that the Persian followers of Zoroaster wore (and today still wear) sacred cords wound around the waist, and that the Vedas describe ancient Hindus as wearing sacred cords over their shoulders. Also, ancient Romans wore their togas over their heads on solemn occasions.

134 Ber. 60b.

135 Abrahams, op. cit., 28.

136 Hayim Halevy Donin, To Pray as a Jew (Basic Books, 1980), 200–201.

137 Elbogen, op. cit., 294.

138 Donin, op. cit., 201.

139 Donin, ibid., 185.

140 Martin L. Gordon, "Netilat Yadayim Shel Shaharit: Ritual of Crisis or Dedication?" Gesher, vol. 8, 36 (1981).

141 Donin, op. cit., 186.

142 As Gordon, op. cit., points out, the medieval kabbalists viewed the ritual of washing differently—as a retrospective relief from the crisis of the soul's having left our body for the night.

143 Hammer, op. cit., 109.

144 Idelsohn, op. cit., 74.

145 Elbogen, op. cit., 79. A similar compromise explains why mezuzot are to be affixed to one's doorpost on a diagonal slant. One group of rabbis argued that they should be hung vertically; another argued for the horizontal position. Attempts to reconcile these views having failed, the halachic outcome was that they were to be hung diagonally.

146 Idelsohn, op. cit., 108.

147 Idelsohn, ibid., 76. It is first found in the Machzor Vitry, which was compiled by Simcha ben Shemuel of Vitry, a student of Rashi, around 1100 C.E., ibid, 60.

148 Hammer, op. cit., 109; private communication from Professor Joseph Tabory of Bar-Ilan University, June 13, 1996.

149 Raphael Posner et. al., *Jewish Liturgy* (Jerusalem: Keter, 1975), 121.

150 Hammer, op. cit., 109.

151 For theological reasons, the Reform liturgy also omits two other blessings: "Who creates the heavens and the earth" and "Who provides for all my needs." The Reform version also divides the final blessing, which, in other liturgies, includes a lengthy sequence beginning, *vi'y'hi ratzon mi'l'fanecha*, that really is a personal meditation of rabbinic origin, inaccurately calling these verses of meditation "blessings for conscience." They are proper meditations, given as examples rather than as mandates, and may be replaced with one's own thoughts and feelings.

152 Elbogen, op. cit., 78.

153 Ibid.

154 Private communication from Professor Joseph Tabory of Bar-Ilan University, June 13, 1996.

155 Elbogen, op. cit., 78.

156 Public morning blessings bearing some resemblance to the private morning blessings in the Talmud have been found in one of the Qumran scrolls. See Robert Brody, "Morning Benedictions at Qumran?" *Tarbiz*, vol. 81, 493 (1982).

157 Perhaps the Orthodox version relates to the awareness a man has of his genitalia—its presence, and the fact it is circumcised—as he gains consciousness.

158 Ibid. One can conjecture that in Babylonia, where this sequence of blessings developed, there perhaps was confusion between the two passages. In the Babylonian academies at Sura and Pumbedita, the worshippers undoubtedly knew both passages by heart, and no *siddurim* had been written yet.

159 B. *Yoma* 87b.

160 Artscroll *Siddur, Siddur Ahavat Shalom* 34 fn., quoting the *Zohar*.

161 Idelsohn, op. cit., 85, 86–87.

162 The earliest recorded use of *Kaddish* in the liturgy was in Israel in around 600 C.E. (Elbogen, op. cit., 81). By the time of Rav Amram's prayer code in the ninth century, the liturgical *Kaddish* had received its present form (ibid.).

163 I am grateful to Professor Joseph Tabory for these observations.

164 Millgram, op. cit., 155.

165 Hammer, op. cit., 209.

166 Millgram, op. cit., 482.

167 Elbogen, op. cit., 292.

168 Millgram, op. cit., 490–494.

169 Psalm 30 originally was used in the Sephardic ritual on *Chanuka*. It was inserted into the *Shabbat* service, possibly by mistake, but its content is well-suited to the transition to *P'sukei D'Zimra* (Elbogen, op. cit., 73).

170 Rabbi Yitzchak Sender, *The Commentator's Siddur* (Chicago: Sender, 1995), 126.

171 Artscroll, op. cit., 55 fn., citing Rabbi Raphael Hirsch.

172 Elbogen, op. cit., 82.

173 Israel Ta-Shema, "Some Notes on the Origins of the 'Kaddish Yathoni' (Orphan's Kaddish)," *Tarbiz*, vol. 53, 559 (1984).

174 Ibid.

175 Gerald J. Blidstein, "Kaddish and Other Accidents," *Tradition*, vol. 14, 80 (1974).

176 Hammer, op. cit., 284; *Ber.* 57a.

177 Millgram, op. cit., 155.

178 Marvin Lowenthal, *The Jews of Germany* (New York: Longman, Green & Co., 1936), 109.

179 Millgram, op. cit., 483.

180 Idelsohn, op. cit., 80.

181 Posner, op. cit., 122, says that the psalms are recited prior to formal prayer "to help the individual worshipper to achieve the required state of mind, and at the same time to overcome the difficulties posed by inarticulate meditation."

182 Elbogen, op. cit., 73.

183 Zeitlin, "The Temple and Worship," op. cit., 221: *M. Midot* 2:5.

184 Hammer, op. cit., 111 ("Rabbi Yose ben Halafta prayed that his portion might be with those who complete the Book of Psalms every day"); Leon J. Liebreich, "The Compilation of the Pesuke De-Zimra," *Proceedings of the American Academy for Jewish Research*, vol. 18, 255 (1949), 265.

185 Interestingly, the word *baraka* in Islam, obviously from the same root as the Hebrew word *beracha*, refers to a mystical quality of blessing that can be bestowed on a person or thing by a holy man. *Rak'ah*, in Islam, means bending the knee.

186 Liebreich, op. cit., 259.

187 Zahavy, "The Psychology of Early Rabbinic Prayer," in Tzvee Zahary, *Studies in Jewish Prayer*, op. cit., 112.

188 Thus the name *P'sukei* (Verses) rather than *Pirkei* (Chapters) *D'Zimra*. See Liebreich, op. cit., 265; Posner, op. cit., 122.

189 Hammer, op. cit., 111–112.

190 Posner, op. cit., 123.

191 Ibid., 122.

192 Ibid., 123; Elbogen, op. cit., 74.

193 Elbogen, ibid.

194 Ibid.

195 Donin, op. cit., 176.

196 Artscroll *Siddur*, op. cit., 63 fn.

197 Elbogen, op. cit., 74.

198 Hammer, op. cit., 115.

199 Donin, op. cit., 175.

200 *Sof.* 17:11, 18:2; Elbogen, op. cit., 75.

201 Gershom Scholem, *Major Trends in Jewish Mysticism* (New York: Schocken Books, 1941, reprinted 1995), 56, 133.

202 Artscroll *Siddur*, op. cit., 65 fn.; *Chul.* 60a.

203 Ibid.

204 Artscroll *Siddur*, op. cit., 374 fn.

205 Ibid. In Kabbalah, the four parts of the morning prayers are equated to four worlds: the material world (*Olam Ha'Asiya*), the heavens and firmaments (*Olam Ha'Yetzira*), the world of the angels (*Olam Ha'B'riya*), and the world of the divine, which is beyond human comprehension (*Olam Ha'Atzilut*). As we progress through the morning prayers, in the kabbalistic view, we elevate the sparks of holiness to higher worlds, thus liberating them from the *kelipot* (shells) that entrap them, with the ultimate goal of *tikkun olam* (repairing the world) by reuniting the sparks of holiness that were dispersed when Adam and Eve were expelled from the Garden of Eden. See Rabbi Yitzchak Sender, *The Commentator's Siddur*, op. cit., 126.

206 Psalm 92 is discussed on p. 147.

207 Liturgical reforms in the nineteenth and early twentieth centuries included some Reform prayerbooks that eliminated *P'Sukei D'Zimra* altogether, except for *Baruch She'Amar* in the vernacular; some that retained them in Hebrew; and some that distributed them among different days of the week. See Jakob Petuchowski, *Prayerbook Reform in Europe*, op. cit., 49, 51–52, 54, 90, 93, 209.

208 Artscroll *Siddur*, op. cit., 378 fn.; *Ned.* 39b.

209 Ibid., 380 fn.; *Shav.* 15b.

210 It is also possible that Psalm 135 entered the liturgy because it preceded Psalm 136, the Great *Hallel*, which was attributed with mystical powers by the kabbalists. Perhaps the mystics thought that the Great *Hallel* could not fully serve its purpose if it was recited completely out of context. Pairs of psalms are recited elsewhere in the liturgy, e.g., Psalms 90 and 91 in *P'sukei D'Zimra*, and Psalms 92 and 93 on Friday evening.

211 Hammer, op. cit., 116–117.

212 Ibid., 116.

213 Ibid.

214 Ibid., 112–113.

215 Elbogen, op. cit., 75; Hammer, op. cit., 113.

216 Elbogen, op. cit., 87–89.

217 1 Chron. 29:10–13.

218 Neh. 9:6–11.

219 Exod. 14:30–15:19.

220 Artscroll *Siddur*, op. cit., 75 fn., citing Abudraham.

221 Donin, op. cit., 180.

222 Ibid., *Ber.* 59b; *Taanit* 6b.

223 Elbogen, op. cit., 96.

224 Ibid.

225 *Yishtabach* actually contains a total of fifteen praises of God—one for each step to the ancient Temple altar—taken from the praises delivered in the Torah by David, Nehemiah, and Moses.

226 Posner, op. cit., 123.

227 Ibid.

228 Elbogen, op. cit., 81.

229 Idel, "Secrecy, Binah and Derishah," op. cit.

230 Elbogen, op. cit., 80.

231 Ibid., 190.

232 Ibid.

233 The Torah is read only on *Shabbat*, on Festivals, and on Mondays and Thursdays, the ancient market days when farmers unable to be present on *Shabbat* could attend.

234 Posner, op. cit., 106.

235 Hammer, op. cit., 136, 326. Since the *Shema* is not said in the afternoon (*Mincha*) service, Barchu—the invitation to the *Shema*—is not said, either.

236 Elbogen, op. cit., 17.

237 Posner, op. cit., 106.

238 The proper procedure is for the *chazan* to bow on the first line of *Barchu*, and the congregation to bow on the second line. The *chazan* bows when he praises God in calling people to prayer; the congregation bows when it acknowledges and joins in his call.

239 Posner, op. cit., 15.

240 Elbogen, op. cit., 17.

241 Posner, op. cit., 106.

242 Ismar Elbogen, *Studies in Jewish Liturgy*, in Jakob Petuchowski, ed., *Contributions to the Scientific Study of Jewish Liturgy* (New York: Ktav Publishing House, 1970), 20, citing *Ber.* 7:3 and *J. Ber.* 7:3, 11c.

243 Ancient Persian religion taught that the god of light and the god of darkness were in constant battle with each other.

244 This change may have been to avoid accusations that the Jewish God was responsible for the woes of the world, or it may have been to avoid violating a rabbinic tenet that a blessing could not consist exclusively of a biblical quotation. Hammer, op. cit., 138 and fn. 32.

245 Ibid., 135.

246 Ibid.

247 Elbogen, op. cit., 15; *Midrash Tehillim* 65b, 17.

248 The *Merkava* movement, similar to the Chasidic movement almost a thousand years later, was a reaction—in this case, to the sterile preoccupation with religious law in the Babylonian academies. Elbogen describes the *Merkava* mystics as people "who observed fasts on consecutive days and hung their faces to the ground as they murmured all sorts of hymns in order to become filled with the divine. They called this 'descending to the *Merkava* [chariot].'" Elbogen, op. cit., 287.

249 Hammer, op. cit., 139.

250 Isa. 6:3; Ezek. 3:12.

251 Hammer, op. cit., 139–140.

252 Elbogen, op. cit., 59–62.

253 Ibid., 287.

254 Ibid., 59.

255 *B. Ber.* 12a, *Y. Ber.* 1:8, 3b; Millgram, op. cit., 99.

256 Hammer, op. cit., 141.

257 Elbogen, op. cit., 17; "In the morning two benedictions are said before [the *Shema*] and one after it" (*M. Ber.* 1:4).

258 Elbogen, op. cit., 19.

259 Zahavy, "Psychology of Rabbinic Prayer," op. cit., 112.

260 Hammer, op. cit., 81.

261 Ibid.

262 *Men.* 99b.

263 Zahavy, op. cit., 114.

264 *M. Ber.* 2:5.

265 *M. Ber.* 3:1.

266 Hammer, op. cit., 128.

267 Ibid., 129.

268 Ibid., quoting *Sifre* Deut. 33.

269 Ibid. It was the custom, in antiquity, for one person to proclaim the *Shema* in prayer services, so that the congregation could hear it being proclaimed; it was uncomfortable for all present to proclaim it and to have no Jew to listen to it being proclaimed. See n. 268.

270 *Ber.* 61b.

271 Donin, op. cit., 148.

272 *Ber.* 61b; Elbogen, *Studies in Jewish Liturgy*, in Petuchowski, op. cit., 8.

273 Hammer, op. cit., 124, quoting *Sifre* Deut. 33.

274 Elbogen, *Studies in Jewish Liturgy*, in Petuchowski, op. cit., 2ff. The Israeli scholar Ezra Fleischer argues that the phrase *poreis al Shema* meant that one person would proclaim the first line of the *Shema* and the congregation would quietly respond, followed by reading the three Torah passages *V'Ahavta, V'Haya Im Hamoa,* and *Va'Yomer* together as a group. See Ezra Fleischer. "Towards a Clarification of the Expression 'Poreis' Al Shema," *Tarbiz,* 41, 133 (1972). Fleischer argues that the word *poreis* (divide) refers to the fact that the congregation would designate one person to proclaim the first line because it was uncomfortable for the worshippers to have everyone proclaim it with no other Israelite around to hear the proclamation. Given the difficulty of remembering the entire *Shema* by heart, Elbogen's and Fleischer's ideas are not necessarily mutually exclusive; what was intended as a group reading may well have taken the form of a prompted reading.

275 Ibid., 10.

276 Hammer, op. cit., 128.

277 *Y. Ber.* 1:9; Elbogen, op. cit., 21.

278 Elbogen, op. cit., 23.

279 Another such place is in *Kaddish*, when the congregation says *yitbarach* at the end of *Y'hei shmei rabba m'vorach.* . . .

280 Hammer, op. cit., 148–149.

281 Elbogen, *Studies in Jewish Liturgy*, in Petuchowski, op. cit., 31, citing *Tosefta Ber.* 2:1 and *J. Ber.* 1:9, 3d.

282 Elbogen, op. cit., 22, citing *B. Pes.* 117b.

283 The weekday service has preserved this tradition of private supplications

and petitions to God after the *Shema* in the *Tachanun* prayer. See Elbogen, op. cit., 66–67.

284 Abraham Katsh, *Judaism in Islam* (New York: New York University Press, 1954), xxi, citing Louis A. Ginzberg, *A Commentary on the Palestinian Talmud*, vol. I (New York: Jewish Theological Seminary, 1941), p. 73. Interestingly, the Zoroastrians of ancient Persia also were required to pray five times a day. See Boyce, *The Zoroastrians*, op. cit., 32.

285 Elbogen, *Studies in Jewish Liturgy*, in Petuchowski, op. cit., 43–45.

286 Tzvee Zahavy, "The Politics of Piety," in Bradshaw and Hoffman, *The Making of Jewish and Christian Worship*, op. cit., 50.

287 Ibid., 62.

288 Hammer, op. cit., 176–177.

289 *Sefer Chasidim*, Ch. 553.

290 This mode of analysis is roughly consistent with the observations of Reuven Kimelman in "The Daily *Amidah* and the Rhetoric of Redemption," *J.Q.R.*, vol. 79, 165 (1989). Kimelman, however, characterizes the sequence of the *Amida* as a "drama of redemption" (ibid., 189), and misses the point that the *Amida* is a visualization, not a work that we view from a distance like a play.

291 *M. Ber.* 2:4.

292 Compare Elbogen, op. cit., 26–27, with Ezra Fleischer, "The *Shemone Esre*—Its Character, Internal Order, Content and Goals," *Tarbiz*, vol. 62, 179 (1993). But see Hoffman, *The Canonization of the Synagogue Service*, op. cit., 50, in which he argues for a date after the *Mishna* had been compiled.

293 Ibid., 25, citing *B. Meg.* 17b; Elbogen, op. cit., 31–32, 201–202. See Naomi G. Cohen, "The Nature of Shim'on HaPekuli's Act," *Tarbiz*, vol. 52, 547 (1983) (Hebrew).

294 Elbogen, op. cit., 25. Fleischer has argued that the *Amida* was not initiated until after the destruction of the Second Temple. See n. 52. This, however, does not rule out the possibility that elements of the *Amida* already existed as informal prayers, offered in the house of study or in the Temple courts, that were edited at the request of Rabban Gamaliel.

295 Rabbi Aryeh Kaplan, *Jewish Meditation* (New York: Schocken Books, 1985), 105. It is interesting that the reading of the Koran in Islamic prayers today is similarly very slow, pensive, and full of long pauses, as the recitation of the *Amida* must have been in ancient times.

296 Elbogen, op. cit., 66.

297 Ibid., 31–32, 201–202.

298 Ibid.

299 Ezra Fleischer, "The *Shemone Esre*—Its Character, Internal Order, Content and Goals," op. cit.; Leon J. Liebreich, "The Intermediate Benedictions of the *Amidah*," *J.Q.R.*, vol. 42, 423 (1952). Contrast M. Liber, "Structure and History of the *Tefilah*," *J.Q.R.*, vol. 40, 347 (1950), who contended that the middle blessings of the *Amida* included prayers for private needs; and George Foote Moore, *Judaism in the First Centuries of the Christian Era*, vol. I, 294.

300 For a discussion of this format, see Heinemann, *Prayer in the Talmud*, op. cit., 77.

301 Fleischer, op. cit.

302 Reuven Kimelman, in "The Daily *Amidah* and the Rhetoric of Redemption," *J.Q.R.*, vol. 79, 165 (1989), argues that the standard tripartite categorization of the *Amida* blessings is flawed. He generally is correct; thus the term "roughly in the text."

303 *B. Ber.* 26b. Psalms 106:30 says: "Then Phineas stood up and wrought judgment." "The rabbis understood judgment to mean 'prayer.'" (Idelsohn, op. cit., 92).

304 *B. Ber.* 10b; Joel L. Grishaver, *19 Out of 18* (Los Angeles: Torah Aura Productions, 1991), 9.

305 Grishaver, op. cit., 9.

306 Both Abraham, when he petitioned God to spare Sodom and Gomorrah, and Elijah, in petitioning God for help in proving himself to the priests of Baal, "approached" God before petitioning Him. Grishaver (ibid.), citing Genesis 18:23 and 1 Kings 18:36. The Talmud compares this practice to the way in which a disciple would take leave of his teacher; it says that, without this showing of respect, "it would have been better for him not to have prayed at all." *Yoma* 53b; Hammer, op. cit., 316 n. 3.

307 Earl Klein, *Jewish Prayer: Concepts and Customs* (Columbus, OH: Alpha Publishing Company, 1986), 85.

308 Elbogen, op. cit., 200–202. Despite the formalization of the prayers, even a century after Rabban Gamaliel it was still being demanded that the text of the *Amida* not be frozen (ibid., 202). Various versions of the *Amida* were still in common use as late as the fourth century (ibid., 37).

309 Ibid.

310 "Hannah spoke in her heart. Only her lips moved. Her voice could not be heard" (1 Sam. 1:13).

311 Elbogen speculates that the reference to God as Redeemer in the first blessing may have been made to counter the Christian belief that the redemption, and the redeemer, had already come (Elbogen, op. cit., 38).

312 Ibid., citing *B. Ber.* 32b; *B. Meg.* 25a; *Y. Ber.* 9:1, 12d; *Midrash Tehillim*, 82b to Ps. 19; Hammer, op. cit., 163.

313 Ibid., 38–39.

314 Ibid. The focus on natural phenomena is preserved in the words, "Who makes the wind blow and the rain fall," which Rabbi Eliezer instructed to be added between *Sukkot* and Passover, which is the rainy season in Israel. In ancient Israel there were other similar inserts connected with natural phenomena, but the talmudic rabbis did not accept them into the liturgy (ibid.).

315 Hammer, op. cit., 165.

316 Some in the Reform movement have also tried to do so. See R. Gradwohl, "Eine Ueberfluessige Textanderung," *Tradition und Erneuerung*, vol. 40 (1976), 36–38.

317 Hammer, op. cit., 167.

318 Isa. 6:3; Ezek. 3:12.

319 Hammer, op. cit., 139–140. The angels in Isaiah did not have articulated feet; they moved by jumping, as if on a pogo stick. We imitate that jumping. Private communication from J. Tabory of Bar-Ilan University to the author, June 25, 1996.

320 Elbogen, op. cit., 59–62.

321 Thus the custom of rising to one's toes while saying *Kadosh, kadosh, kadosh* (Hammer, op. cit., 172).

322 Ibid., 171–172.

323 Ibid.

324 Elbogen, op. cit., 287.

325 Note the inference: If *Kedusha* is not recited during the silent reading of the *Amida* because of its public nature, then the silent reading must be a private act and, therefore, somewhat malleable in its content to reflect the uniqueness of each reader. Yet we pray for the public good, for our collective welfare; the wording is in the first-person plural. The message is that through our private but concerted spiritual transformation, we can change the world while preserving what is unique about each of us.

326 Idelsohn, op. cit., 98.

327 Ibid., 97; Posner, op. cit., 85. This was discovered in an eighth-century fragment from the Cairo Geniza that went on to say, "Since the Ishmaelites [Muslims] conquered the kingdom of Edom, and it is again permitted to recite *Shema* and to pray, everything must be said in its proper place."

328 Abrahams, op. cit., 130.

329 Hammer, op. cit., 191. There is no concrete evidence that the Ten Commandments were ever part of the *Amida*. However, the fact that the *Amida* may have been pieced together from earlier materials leaves open the possibility that *Yismach Moshe* originated as a preface to their recitation, that subsequent parts of the middle blessing originated as a postscript to their recitation, and that the deletion of the Ten Commandments predated the inclusion of these materials in the *Amida*.

330 The Ten Commandments also were deleted from the *Shema*. See the discussion of the *minim* on page 66.

331 Hammer, op. cit., 192.

332 Notice that the first letters of the words of *Tikkanta Shabbat* are the Hebrew alphabet in reverse order. Many prayers from the early post-Second-Temple period are alphabetical acrostics, probably used as a memory aid before the existence of prayerbooks.

333 Hammer, op. cit., 192.

334 The Second Temple had more than just a ceremonial function. The Temple was the center of legal, religious, and judicial authority. The Sanhedrin (the legislative body) and the law courts sat in the Chamber of Hewn Stone and in the outer courts of the Temple, and the Sanhedrin had its full powers only when the sacrificial ritual was in operation (*Encyclopedia Judaica* 15, "Temple," 983). The treasury of the Temple served as the central bank of the Jewish people; it collected taxes and stored valuables deposited there by individuals (ibid., 979).

335 They also may have been inserted as a reaction to the Judeo-Christians, who asserted that the Second Temple's destruction was proof that God no longer

wanted the people to follow the Mosaic laws. Synagogue worship became, in part, a vicarious observance of the sacrificial rite, showing that the Mosaic law was not dead.

336 Grishaver, op. cit., 87–88.

337 Hammer, op. cit., 189.

338 Ibid.

339 Abrahams, op. cit., 190.

340 Donin, op. cit., 130–132.

341 In his book *To Pray as a Jew* (p. 131), Rabbi Donin includes a diagram of this ascent to the sacrificial altar.

342 "The intermediate blessings have no order" (*B. Ber.* 34a).

343 In 2 Chron. 1:10, Solomon, asked by God what He should grant him, answered, "Grant me then the wisdom and the knowledge to lead this people." The *Amida* employs the same verb. In the version of this story in 2 Kings 3:9–12, Solomon asks God to "grant . . . an understanding mind to judge Your people, to distinguish between good and bad," and recounts God's pleasure at this request.

344 Hammer, op. cit., 175.

345 Jacobson, op. cit., 228, quoting a medieval commentator, the Tur (*Orach Chaim*, 115).

346 At least one commentator has drawn the distinction that in Hebrew, *cheit* refers to unintentional sin, while *pesha* refers to intentional sin. Both are mentioned in the sixth blessing of the weekday *Amida*.

347 *Y. Ber.* 2:4, 4d and 4:3, 8a.

348 Three verses later in Psalm 86, one finds the opening verse of the Torah service, *Ein Camocha.*

349 A service called *Selichot* is recited during the period prior to and during the High Holidays. The service derives its name from the penitential *Selichot* poems. The *Selichot* service is discussed on p. 104.

350 Jacobson, op. cit., 230.

351 Based on medieval commentators' views, most works on the subject refer to the first six petitions in the *Amida* as "personal," and to the next six as "collective." In reality they are all collective. They are all worded in the plural, even at the cost of altering biblical quotations, as shown in the seventh blessing. Personal petitions are found in the service in *Tachanun* (Supplications), discussed later.

352 Compare *Y. Ber.* and *B. Shab.* 12a.

353 Elbogen, op. cit., 44.

354 Ironically, the Ten Lost Tribes never did return from Assyria.

355 "I will restore your magistrates as of old, and your counselors as of yore."

356 This phrase, *V'haser mi'meinu yagon va'anacha*, first appeared in the *Machzor Vitry*. See Jacobson, op. cit., 193–194.

357 *B. Meg.* 17b; Elbogen, op. cit., 45.

358 So argues David Flusser based on new evidence from Qumran. See David Flusser, "Some of the Precepts of the Torah From Qumran (4QMMT) and the Benediction Against the Heretics," *Tarbiz*, 61, 333 (1992).

359 Cairo Geniza manuscripts show that the reference to Christians was

retained in Egypt after the rise of Islam (Jacobson, op. cit., 194). Islamic rulers were presumably more sensitive about the condemnation of apostates, who might be Muslims, than the condemnation of Christians.

360 That is why there is a *vav* ("and") at the beginning of the first sentence; "and the slanderers" replaced "and the sectarians," which had the "and" because of the word "Christians" before it.

361 Jacobson, op. cit., 239.

362 Elbogen, op. cit., 47.

363 One of the last Jewish rulers of ancient Israel, known for his cruelty and tyranny.

364 Abrahams, op. cit., 65.

365 Elbogen, op. cit., 48.

366 Abrahams, op. cit., 66.

367 Private communication from Professor Joseph Tabory of Bar-Ilan University, June 25, 1996.

368 Jacobson, op. cit., 247, citing the medieval Spanish scholar Abudraham. The closing benediction, "Who hears prayer," is taken from Psalms 65:3.

369 Elbogen, op. cit., 49. "A person may ask for his own needs in the benediction, 'Who hears prayer'" (*B. Ber.* 31a; *B. A.Z.* 8a). Elbogen says, "By the beginning of the third century Rav relies upon this rule as authoritative, and it apparently was what led to the creation of the new petition, . . . "and from before us, our King. . . ." The petition alluded to, better translated, reads, "Do not, therefore, let us leave Your presence devoid of any result."

370 *M. Ber.* 34 a.

371 Elbogen, op. cit., 50. Thus, while the blessing first asks for the restoration of the *Avoda*—obviously an addition after the Temple was destroyed—it goes on to ask that God accept the fire-offerings of Israel and that the *Avoda* "always be acceptable to You," a remnant of the original version.

372 Idelsohn, op. cit., 106.

373 This was how King David addressed God in the quoted passage.

374 Idelsohn, op. cit., 106.

375 Elbogen, op. cit., 53, citing *B. Sota* and *Y. Ber.* 1:5, 3d.

376 Ibid., 52.

377 Ibid.

378 *U'ch'tov l'chayim tovim kol b'nei b'ritecha* (Inscribe all the people of Your covenant for a good life). The preceding paragraph, *Avinu malkeinu, z'chor rachamecha* (Our Father, our King, let Your compassion overwhelm Your wrath), also a High Holiday, apparently originated among the Jews of Greece and was included in the *Machzor Vitry*, a medieval prayer code written in France, from which it came to be adopted in the Ashkenazic service. See Elbogen, op. cit., 52.

379 Elbogen, op. cit., 52.

380 Dr. J.H. Hertz, ed., *Pentateuch and Haftorahs*, 2nd ed. (London: Soncino Press, 1980) 594; Elbogen, op. cit., 62.

381 Elbogen, op. cit., 63.

382 Hertz, op. cit., 596, n. 27.

383 It is a plausible speculation that synagogue prayer may have originated in faith healing. The *ma'amadot*, the delegations sent on annual tours of duty to monitor the performance of the priests in the Second Temple, developed prayers and rituals that formed the basis for much of the synagogue service. Why did people in the towns and villages from which the delegations were sent, far from Jerusalem, begin to form local prayer groups and recite these prayers of the *ma'amadot* while the Second Temple was still standing? One can speculate that there was a perceived benefit to reciting the prayers locally at the same time that the *ma'amad* was reciting them at the Temple. Perhaps people in need of help would ask the *ma'amad* to pray for them at the Temple, and, to enhance the potency of the prayers, would also recite them at the appointed time of day.

384 Elbogen, op. cit., 63.

385 Ibid.

386 Ibid.

387 Ibid.

388 Ibid.

389 Ibid.

390 This may have been due to superstitious beliefs about magical activity inherent in the blessing, as Elbogen suggests (ibid., 63), or perhaps to the ambiguity of the verse in Leviticus that refers to Aaron "lifting his hands." The Torah doesn't say he lifted his arms. One can speculate that extending the fingers as well as lifting the arms was a way to make sure the required act of "lifting the hands" was being performed.

391 Ibid., 63. Rabbi Akiva was the source of the rule against looking at the priests during the blessing. This may have had to do with the notion that God was "standing by" the priests (Hertz, op. cit., 596, n. 27, citing a talmudic source) and "lifting up His countenance" upon the congregation; the congregation was required to rise in His presence, but not to look at Him.

392 Elbogen, ibid., 63.

393 Elbogen, ibid., 64.

394 Ibid.

395 Ibid.

396 Ibid., 53.

397 Ibid., 53–54. The Amoraim in Babylonia "strived to achieve two things to bring everything into fixed forms, and to imitate the exemplary behavior of famous men" (ibid., 211). Disciples would ask their masters (like Mar ben Ravina) for their private prayers and then imitate them, even to the tiniest detail. Eventually these prayers became part of the fixed liturgy. This tendency contributed mightily to the lengthening of the synagogue service, which, in mishnaic times, was much shorter than it is today (ibid.).

398 Ibid., 53.

399 Ibid., 170.

400 Ibid., 54. *Oseh shalom* first appeared in the *Machzor Vitry*, which originated in France in about 1100 C.E.

401 Idelsohn, op. cit., 205. Since arks did not exist yet in synagogues when

the early *piyyutim* were written, Elbogen's explanation of the derivation of the word *kerova* may be in error. Perhaps the leader of the *Amida* was called a *kerova* because, in the *Amida*, we approach God. The community's leader is at the forefront of the approach to God, like a general leading his troops.

402 For a more comprehensive explanation of the High-Holiday prayers in the Orthodox tradition, see Rabbi Jeffrey M. Cohen, *Prayer and Penitence* (Northvale, NJ: Jason Aronson Inc., 1994).

403 Encyclopedia Judaica, 8, "*Hineni He'Ani Mi-Ma'as.*"

404 Elbogen, op. cit., 38–39.

405 Ibid.

406 Posner, op. cit., 171.

407 Ibid.

408 Elbogen, op. cit., 118.

409 Ibid.

410 Ibid. For a contrary view, see Joseph Tabory, *Jewish Festivals in the Time of the Mishna and Talmud* (Hebrew) (Jerusalem: Magnes Press, 1995).

411 Idelsohn, op. cit., 213–214. The verses are as follows: *Malchuyot*; Exod. 15:18; Num. 23:21; Deut. 33:5; Psalms 22:29, 93:1, and 24:7; Isa. 44:6; Obad. 1:21; Zech. 14:9; and Deut. 6:4. *Zichronot*: Gen. 8:1; Exod. 2:24; Lev. 26:42; Psalms 111:4, 111:5, and 106:45; Jer. 2:2; Ezek. 16:60; Jer. 31:19; and Lev. 26:45. *Shofarot*: Exod. 19:16, 19:19, and 20:18; Psalms 47:6, 98:6, and 81:4; Isa. 18:3 and 27:13; Zech. 9:14; and Num. 10:10. Psalm 150 is inserted in *Shofarot* because *Halleluya* appears ten times.

412 Posner, op. cit., 170.

413 See Joseph Tabory, "The Place of the Malkhiyyot Benediction in the Rosh Ha-Shana Additional Service." *Tarbiz*, 48, 30 (1979).

414 Elbogen, op. cit., 119.

415 Ibid., 118.

416 Idelsohn, op. cit., 213–214.

417 Elbogen, op. cit., 118.

418 *Encyclopedia Judaica*, 2, "*Aleinu Le'Shabbe'ah*," 555, 557. Because *Aleinu* contains no mention of the restoration of the Temple, but refers to prostration, a Temple practice, *Aleinu* may actually date from an earlier period. See ibid., 557.

419 Posner, op. cit., 170.

420 Idelsohn, op. cit., 232–233.

421 Elbogen, op. cit., 174.

422 Ibid.

423 Ibid.

424 But not on *Rosh HaShana* itself, according to the *Midrash*. Cf. Mordechai, *Yoma*, beginning. The custom at one time was to fast for the entire forty days from the first day of *Ellul*, when God gave Moses the Ten Commandments for the second and final time, until *Yom Kippur*, when Moses descended Mount Sinai with them. This is strikingly similar to the Islamic custom practiced during the month of Ramadan.

425 *Encyclopedia Judaica*, 14, "Selihot," 1134.

426 The content categories of *Selichot* include the following: *Tochacha* (self-rebuke), *Bakasha* (petition), *Gezerot* (descriptions of persecutions), *Akeida* (commemoration of the binding of Isaac), *Tachana* (prayer about relations between God and the Jewish people, always connected with *Tachanun* [Supplications], the conclusion of the fast-day liturgy), *Mukdamot* (*Rosh HaShana Selichot* that relate to the special High-Holiday blessings of the *Amida*), and *Vidui* (confessions of sins). Of the form categories, the most noteworthy is *Pizmon*, a *selicha* with a refrain. Elbogen, op. cit., 182–183.

427 Ibid.

428 Ibid., 178.

429 Ibid., 179.

430 Ibid.

431 *Encyclopedia Judaica*, 14, "Selihot," 1134.

432 Elbogen, op. cit., 180.

433 *Encyclopedia Judaica*, 14, "Selihot," 1134, citing *Tanna d'Vei Eliyahu Zuta* (23–end).

434 Hertz, op. cit., 364, n. 1.

435 Rabbi Morris Silverman, ed., *High Holiday Prayer Book* (New York: United Synagogue, 1951), 381. Idelsohn attributes *Eileh Ezkera* to the late sixth century Israeli poet Eliezer Kallir. See Idelsohn, op. cit., 320.

436 *Gezerot* were used only in the Ashkenazic ritual. Sephardic Jews recite *Eileh Ezkera* on the ninth of Av as one of the *kinot* (poems of lamentation). See ibid., 349.

437 Posner, op. cit., 182.

438 Ibid.

439 Idelsohn, op. cit., 237.

440 *Encyclopedia Judaica*, 5, "Confession of Sins."

441 Posner, op. cit., 176.

442 Other parts of *Vidui* include *Tavo L'fanecha*, which dates from the third century C.E.; *Ata Yodea*, attributed to the Babylonian talmudic rabbi Rav; *V'al Hataim*, which appears in the ninth-century *Seder Rav Amram*, the earliest Jewish prayer code, and describes the offerings that people sacrificed in antiquity to atone for their sins; and *Elohai Ad Shelo Notzarti*, written by Rav Hamnuna, another Babylonian talmudic rabbi, and which was said to have been the daily meditation of Rava. See Idelsohn, op. cit., 228–229.

443 Posner, op. cit., 174; Elbogen, op. cit., 124.

444 The alphabetical organization of a prayer generally indicates that it originated in the talmudic or medieval period. Such organization was for the purpose of helping Jews to remember the prayers during the difficult centuries that followed the fall of the Second Temple, despite the Jews' tradition of not having written liturgical materials, and despite the severe restrictions placed on their religious observance by a series of foreign rulers.

445 *Encyclopedia Judaica*, 5, "Confession of Sins."

446 Posner, op. cit., 176. Elbogen believes, based on its structure, that *Al Cheit* dates from the fifth century C.E. Elbogen, op. cit., 125.

447 Idelsolm, op. cit., 229, points out that the Yemenite ritual still refers only to the six sins originally listed in *Al Cheit*.

448 The inclusion of bribery on the list seems to us an exception to the rule; by contemporary standards, bribery is hardly universal. Remember, however, that *Al Cheit* was written in the medieval Middle East.

449 Elbogen, op. cit., 125.

450 Ibid., citing the opinion of the Babylonian scholar Mar Samuel.

451 Cohen, op. cit., 50; *Taanit* 25b.

452 Ibid., 50.

453 Elbogen, op. cit., 66. See Solomon B. Freehof, "The Origin of the Tahanun," *Hebrew Union College Annual*, 2, 339 (1925); *M. Tamid* VII, 3 Sirach 50, 16–21.

454 Ibid., citing *T. Ber.*, 3:6.

455 Ibid., 341.

456 Ibid.

457 Ibid.

458 Ibid., 67, citing *B. Meg.* 23a, *Y. A.Z.* 4:1ff, 43d top.

459 Freehof, op. cit.

460 Ibid., 343.

461 Millgram, 462.

462 *Encyclopedia Judaica*, 7, "Hallel," 1198.

463 Solomon Zeitlin, "The Hallel," *Jewish Quarterly Review*, 53, 22 (1962); Louis Finkelstein, "The Origin of the Hallel," *Hebrew Union College Annual*, 23, 319 (1950).

464 *Encyclopedia Judaica*, 7, "Hallel," 1198, citing the view of Rabbi Judah, who attributed the origins of recitation of *Hallel* to the prophets.

465 Millgram, op. cit., 210–211.

466 Ibid., 211.

467 Harry Orlinsky, et al., eds., *Tanakh: A New Testament of the Holy Scriptures* (Philadelphia: Jewish Publication Society, 1985), 1250.

468 Elbogen, op. cit., 138 ("The reading . . . was not originally an end in itself, but preparation for the explanatory homily. . . .").

469 Ibid., 137. On *Simchat Torah,* it was still the custom, as recently as the early twentieth century, of the Jews of Rome to recite the first five verses of Genesis by heart, as in ancient times, rather than to read them from the scroll.

470 Millgram, op. cit., 118.

471 Elbogen, op. cit., 131.

472 Ibid., 130.

473 Ibid., 131.

474 Ibid., 131. But see D.J. Silver, "The Shrine and the Scroll," *Journal of Reform Judaism*, 31/2 (1984), 31 (arguing that the High Priest's reading was adopted from the early synagogue).

475 Ibid.

476 *Shabbat Shekalim, Shabbat Zachor, Shabbat Parah,* and *Shabbat Ha'Chodesh.*

477 Elbogen, op. cit., 131.

478 Ibid., 131, n. 13.

479 This ancient custom is preserved today in the rule that the minimum length of an *aliya* is three lines.

480 Op. cit., 134.

481 Fleischer has theorized that the annual cycle of Torah-reading predated the triennial cycle, and that the Babylonian academies were more reluctant to break with precedent than the rabbis in Israel. Ezra Fleischer, "Annual and Triennial Reading of the Bible in the Old Synagogue," *Tarbiz* 61, 25 (1991).

482 The Jews in ancient Israel apparently did celebrate *Simchat Torah*, but not on a fixed date in the year.

483 Elbogen, op. cit., 140.

484 Millgram, op. cit., 187.

485 Elbogen, op. cit., 138.

486 Millgram, op. cit., 113.

487 One result was that the *meturgemanim*, no doubt anxious to encourage congregants to pray more often, depicted the biblical heroes as resorting to prayer perhaps more frequently than the actual text would suggest. Michael Maher, "The Meturgemanim and Prayer," *Journal of Jewish Studies*, 44, 220 (1993).

488 Millgram, op. cit., 113, citing commentary in the *siddur* compiled by the Babylonian scholar Saadya Gaon in the tenth century.

489 M. *Meg.* 4:1 ("The first and last reader of the Torah recites a blessing before and after").

490 Elbogen, op. cit., 141.

491 Donin, op. cit., 239.

492 Posner, op. cit., 94.

493 Neh. 8:4–5; Millgram, op. cit., 70.

494 The *bima* actually originated during the Second-Temple period. The word *bima* is a transliteration of a Greek word meaning "tower" (in Hebrew, *migdal*), from which, according to Nehemiah, Ezra read the Torah. See Elbogen, op. cit., 360–361.

495 Posner, op. cit., 94.

496 Ibid., 96.

497 Elbogen, op. cit., 159.

498 Hammer, op. cit., 202–203.

499 Private communication from Professor Joseph Tabory, Bar-Ilan University, June 25, 1996. But see Elbogen, op. cit., 159, asserting that they first became customary in thirteenth-century Germany.

500 Idelsohn, op. cit., 114.

501 The *Zohar* actually was written in the thirteenth century c.e. by a Spanish Jewish mystic who apparently attributed its authorship to Shimon bar Yochai to give it more credence. See n. 796.

502 Elbogen, op. cit., 160.

503 Idelsohn, op. cit., 51.

504 Ibid.

505 Elbogen, op. cit., 161.

506 Millgram, op. cit., 187.

507 Ibid.

508 Ibid.

509 Ibid., 188. Elbogen, op. cit., 162, points out that Rabbi Judah of Barcelona objected to this custom, to no avail.

510 Ibid., 189, citing Jer. 29:7 and *Yoma* 69a. The Talmud says that when Alexander the Great came to Israel, he was met by Simon the Just, who greeted him and asked if he would "destroy the House wherein prayers are said for you and your kingdom that it be never destroyed."

511 *Avot* 3:2.

512 Jer. 29:7.

513 Millgram, op. cit., 190.

514 Elbogen, op. cit., 103; Donin, op. cit., 272.

515 Elbogen, op. cit., 103; *So.* 19:9.

516 Ibid., 103.

517 Ibid.

518 Ibid., 104.

519 Ibid.

520 Millgram, op. cit., 466; Posner, op. cit., 235.

521 Posner, op. cit., 235. The Reform movement, in the nineteenth century, discarded the bar mitzvah entirely and adopted the practice of "confirming" boys and girls at age sixteen, based on the notion that thirteen was too early to consider a person an adult in the modern world. Eventually, however, the Reform movement restored the bar mitzvah and also instituted the bat mitzvah. The Conservative movement approved the practice of bat mitzvah in about 1920, but originally bat mitzvot were conducted on Friday nights and did not include reading the Torah, so as to keep them ceremonial and to avoid a change in *halacha* (Jewish law).

522 Elbogen, op. cit., 160.

523 Even the age of thirteen as the year of a boy's majority is not as ancient as is popularly assumed. It was derived by the talmudic rabbis from Roman law, under which boys achieved adulthood at puberty. Millgram, op. cit., 466, quoting Solomon Schechter on the point. See *Avot* 5:21.

524 The *Haftarah* originally was read from a parchment scroll without vowels, like the Torah, but this changed with the advent of printing. In contrast, the Torah continued to be read from a scroll without vowels or *trope* marks.

525 Elbogen, op. cit., 143, citing the writings of Elijah Levita (1469–1549).

526 Donin, op. cit., 246.

527 This can be inferred from the lack of an equivalent reading from the Hagiographa, indicating a date before the Hagiographa was canonized. Also, references in the New Testament to Jesus' reading from Isaiah in a synagogue service—and the fact that he was given Isaiah to read—indicate that the *Haftarah* reading was already established by that time. See Elbogen, op. cit., 143–144.

528 Ibid., 144.

529 Ibid., 145.

530 Ibid., 147, citing Joseph Heinemann, *Hatefilah Bitequfat Hatana'Im Veha'Amora'Im* (Jerusalem: Magnes Press, 1964), 143ff. Although the Roman rulers of

Israel forbade Jewish prayers at various times, once the Roman Empire became a Christian domain, it was impossible to forbid reading the Bible. The parallels between the blessings after the *Haftarah* and the *Amida* conceivably stem from the use of the former as a substitute for the *Amida* under the guise of blessing the weekly Bible reading.

531 Elbogen, op. cit., 147.

532 Ibid., 146.

533 Posner, op. cit., 92–93.

534 Ibid.

535 This was a time when scholars in the Babylonian academies, led by Ashi, were writing down the Oral Law in what became the *Gemara*. Creating a form of written notation for the *trope* may have been another contribution of these scholars.

536 *Encyclopedia Judaica*, 12, "Music," 578.

537 Studies of the music of Jewish communities that have existed in semi-isolation since before the Common Era (like Yemen, Bukhara, Iran, and India) have disclosed similarities from which scholars have been able to deduce what the ancestral musical forms must have been like. See, for example, the example from Bukhara given in *Encyclopedia Judaica*, 12, "Music," 578, example 3.

538 Cohen, *Horizons of Jewish Prayer*, op. cit., 23.

539 Elbogen, op. cit., 160, citing *Seder Rav Amram* (ninth century).

540 Psalm 148 evidently was too short for the procession. Psalm 29, and Psalm 24 from verse 7 to the end, were added in approximately 1100 c.e. These apparently made the liturgy too long for the procession, so after 1600 c.e. it became customary to say Psalm 29 on *Shabbat* and Psalm 24 on weekdays. See ibid., 160.

541 Ibid., 97–98.

542 Ibid., 98.

543 Ibid., 62–63.

544 Millgram, op. cit., 158. Millgram points out that, on weekdays, *Ashrei* is said the second time toward the end of the service after saying *Tachanun* (Supplications), a group of prayers descended from the personal meditations congregants used to recite after finishing the *Amida*, and before saying the *Kedusha D'Sidra*, a prayer that begins, *U'va l'tzion goel*. The *Kedusha D'Sidra* is so called because, in antiquity, a public Torah lesson concerning the *sidra* of the week followed the daily morning service. It became customary to say a prayer as a *Kedusha* following the Torah lesson. See Elbogen, op. cit., 70. Thus, *Ashrei* was actually the conclusion of the service. *Tachanun* is supposedly a sad prayer, and, for that reason, is not said on *Shabbat* and Festivals. However, *Ashrei* is said the second time anyway.

The concept that *Tachanun* is necessarily sad is questionable; as discussed elsewhere in this book, it originally was a time to spontaneously address God regarding our personal needs and desires. See p. 109.

545 Silverman, op. cit., 141.

546 Ibid., 140.

547 Ibid., 141.

548 Elbogen, op. cit., 98. Fragments found in the Cairo Geniza reveal a third, and longer, introduction that was added to the other two, but later fell into disuse.

549 Donin, op. cit., 127, quoting the *Aruch Ha'Shulchan*, a nineteenth-century compendium of Jewish law by Rabbi Yehiel Epstein.

550 Ibid., 128.

551 Elbogen, op. cit., 57.

552 Ibid., 58.

553 Donin, op. cit., 124.

554 Elbogen, op. cit., 58–59.

555 Ibid., 70; B. *Sota* 49a.

556 Ibid.

557 Ibid.

558 Ibid.

559 Idelsohn, op. cit., 117.

560 *Baraita, Kritut* 6.

561 It appears that, over time, the Temple rite changed. Although originally animal sacrifice had been the First Temple's central aspect, by the time the Second Temple was destroyed, offerings of incense were more common.

562 Millgram, op. cit., 455.

563 Idelsohn, op. cit., 116. Recent work by I. Ta-Shma indicates that *Aleinu* may have been part of the daily service at an earlier date in some locations, but the Blois incident appears to have caused it to be incorporated into the daily service throughout the Jewish world.

564 Elbogen, op. cit., 90.

565 It may be much older, however. Posner notes that *Aleinu* makes no mention of restoring the destroyed Temple, suggesting that it was written before the destruction of the Second Temple in 70 c.e. Also, when recited on the High Holidays, it is the only prayer to retain the ancient Temple rite of prostration, again suggesting an earlier origin. The description of God as the "King of the king of kings" (*Melech malchei ham'lachim*) indicates Persian influence, since the Persians referred to their king in this fashion. The Persians controlled the land of Israel when the Temple was rebuilt in 444 b.c.e., so this evidences an early Second-Temple date for the writing of *Aleinu*. See Posner, op. cit., 109.

566 Michael D. Swartz, "Alay Le-Shabbeah: A Liturgical Prayer in Ma'aseh Merkabah," *Jewish Quarterly Review*, 77, 179 (1987).

567 It is interesting that *Aleinu* first mentions praising God, as in the first three blessings of the *Amida*, and then refers to God as the *Yotzer B'reishit*, perhaps an allusion to the *Yotzer* blessing that precedes the *Shema*. These references appear to be allusions to the duty of all Jews to say the two principal prayers of the daily service.

568 Elbogen, op. cit., 71.

569 This meeting occurred in Italy because that was the center of Jewish publishing at the time, being the situs of the Soncino publishing house. [The author thanks Rabbi Henry Schreibman for this observation.]

570 The *Aleinu* controversy did not end with the Haskama. It broke out again

in Prussia in 1703. A governmental edict then forbade not only spitting, but "hopping" during *Aleinu*, perhaps a reference to hopping back up after bowing. (It was [and, in some places, still is] customary to keep the feet close together, as when reciting the *Amida*, so hopping may have been necessary at times to avoid falling over.) Why hopping would have been offensive to Gentiles is difficult to understand; then again, the secular authorities understood nothing about the Hebrew prayers and relied on unreliable hearsay from informers.

571 Posner, op. cit., 110.

572 Ibid.

573 Ibid., 111.

574 Millgram, op. cit., 449; Artscroll, op. cit., 810.

575 Ibid. The earliest text of a *Yizkor* service, and the first reference to its being conducted on the pilgrimage festivals, is found in the *Machzor Vitry* (1208).

576 Ibid., 448.

577 Lawrence A. Hoffman, *Gates of Understanding 2: Appreciating the Days of Awe* (New York: Central Conference of American Rabbis, 1984), 147.

578 Ibid.

579 Ibid., 148.

580 Artscroll, op. cit., 815.

581 Hoffman, op. cit., 148, quoting J.D. Eisenstein (1917).

582 Ibid., 148.

583 Artscroll, op. cit., 454, citing *Levush* (Ch. 284).

584 Hoffman, op. cit., 148.

585 Elbogen, op. cit., 85.

586 B. *Ber.* 4b–5a.

587 Elbogen, op. cit., 99.

588 Ibid.

589 Ibid., 100.

590 Private communication from Professor Joseph Tabory, Bar-Ilan University, June 25, 1996.

591 Elbogen, op. cit., 100.

592 Luria himself served as spiritual leader of the Jews of Safed only from 1570 to his death in 1572. His innovations in mystical philosophy and liturgy left such an impression, however, that his followers, such as Chayim Vital and, most importantly, Israel Sarug, were able to spread them throughout the Middle East, North Africa, and Europe. Gershom Scholem, the leading scholar on Lurianic Kabbalah, points out that the ascendancy of Lurianic Kabbalah in the late sixteenth and early- to mid-seventeenth centuries was the last time a spiritual movement in Judaism gained a uniform degree of acceptance among Jews throughout the world. See Scholem, *Major Trends in Jewish Mysticism* op.cit., 285–286. Subsequent movements, such as the messianism of Sabbatai Zevi, Chasidism, and Reform Judaism, have been better accepted in some places than others.

593 Max Arzt, *Joy and Remembrance* (Bridgeport, CT: Hartmore House, 1979), 20.

594 Arzt, 26. The kabbalistic innovation of reciting six psalms was actually a revival of a much older custom. In ninth-century Babylonia, six psalms (not those later selected by the kabbalists) were recited, to commemorate the long-discontinued Temple practice of sounding the *shofar* six times at regular intervals on Friday afternoon. See Donin, op. cit., 258; B. *Shabbat* 35b.

595 Ibid.

596 See Scholem, *Major Trends in Jewish Mysticism*, op. cit., 265–268.

597 Ibid.

598 Arzt, op. cit., 17.

599 Donin, op. cit., 258; B. *Shabbat* 35b.

600 Arzt, op. cit., 27, citing *Yalkut, Teh.* 709, and *Zev.* 116a.

601 Ibid.

602 Ibid., 53, citing Horowitz-Rabin, ed., *Mekhilta*, 229.

603 Normally synagogues in this hemisphere are built so that the Ark in front is toward the east, and the congregation is facing Jerusalem during worship. Typically the entrance is opposite, at the back, although this is not mandatory.

604 Arzt, op. cit., 66, citing *Mishna Tamid* 7:4.

605 See Isaac Ta-Shma, "Two Sabbath Lights," *Tarbiz* 45, 128 (1975).

606 Ibid.

607 See *Gates of Prayer*, 117.

608 Millgram, op. cit., 296–297.

609 Donin, op. cit., 336, citing Maim. *Hil. Shabbat* 5:3.

610 Millgram, op. cit., 296.

611 Wolfson, op. cit., 117.

612 Ibid., 129, describing the *Midrash* on this passage.

613 Ibid.

614 Ibid., 116; Hammer, op. cit., 222.

615 Rabbi Chaim Stern, ed., *Gates of Prayer for Shabbat and Weekdays* (New York: Central Conference of American Rabbis, 1994), 165.

616 Artscroll, op. cit., 358.

617 Donin, op. cit., 321. Donin attributes this idea to Rabbi Hayim David Halevy.

618 Ibid., 320.

619 Abraham Joshua Heschel, *The Sabbath: Its Meaning for Modern Man* (New York: Farrar, Straus & Young, 1951); see the excellent discussion of this concept in Dr. Ron Wolfson, *The Art of Jewish Living—The Shabbat Seder* (New York: Federation of Jewish Men's Clubs, 1985), 147.

620 On the origin of Christian Sunday morning services and Jewish Saturday-night meals that marked the end of the Sabbath, which included recitation of the blessing on the wine, see n. 687.

621 *Pes.* 101a; B. *Bat.* 97a.

622 Donin, op. cit., 320; *Pes.* 101a, *Tos. s.v. d'achlu.*

623 Arzt, op. cit., 143; Y. *Ber.* 11d.

624 Rabbi Nosson Scherman and Rabbi Meir Zlotowitz, eds., Artscroll *Siddur*, op. cit., commentary, 360–361.

625 Ibid.
626 Wolfson, op. cit., 149.
627 Donin, op. cit., 322 fn., citing Exod. 16:22.
628 Ibid.
629 Ibid., citing *Yoma* 75b and *Pes.* 100b, *Tos. s.v. she'ein.*
630 Wolfson, op. cit., 170.
631 Donin, op. cit., 10; Deut. 6:6–7, 11:19.
632 Elbogen, op. cit., 85.
633 Artscroll, op. cit., 257 fn.
634 Elbogen, op. cit., 86; see 68.
635 Ibid.; *Y. Ber.* 1:9, 3d; *B. Ber.* 14b.
636 Elbogen, op. cit., 86.
637 Hammer, op. cit., 153.
638 Artscroll, op. cit., 264 fn.; Elbogen, op. cit., 87–88. Elbogen points out that none of the versions of this prayer now extant actually have eighteen verses; most have only fifteen or sixteen.
639 Elbogen, op. cit., 88.
640 The verses include Isa. 52:7, Psalms 10:36, Psalms 93:1, and Exod. 15:18.
641 Elbogen, op. cit., 53.
642 Millgram, op. cit., 138–139.
643 Deut. 6:7.
644 Elbogen, op. cit., 206.
645 *Ber.* 4b: "Rav Yehoshua ben Levi says: 'Though a man has recited the *Shema* in the synagogue, it is a *mitzvah* to recite it again at bedtime.'"
646 *Encyclopedia Judaica*, 14, *Shema*, 1370; *Ber.* 1:3.
647 Artscroll, op. cit., 288 fn.; *Ber.* 5a.
648 Millgram, op. cit., 292.
649 *Encyclopedia Judaica*, 5 "Death," 1423. "The way in which a person dies, and the day on which he dies, were thought to be significant as good or bad omens for the deceased. Thus, for example, should he die amid laughter, or on the Sabbath eve, it is a good sign, whereas to die amid weeping, or at the close of the Sabbath, is a bad omen" (*Ket.* 103b).
650 *Ber.* 4b–5a.
651 Artscroll, op. cit., 288.
652 Ibid., 288 fn.
653 Ibid., 380 fn.
654 Rabbi Jeffrey Cohen, *Prayer and Penitence: A Commentary on the High Holiday Machzor*, op. cit., 142.
655 See ibid., 139–141; Hoffman, *Gates of Understanding 2: Appreciating the Days of Awe*, op. cit., 114–115.
656 Cohen, op. cit., 141.
657 Hoffman, op. cit., 115.
658 Cohen, op. cit., 140.
659 Ibid., 139.
660 It has been argued that vows made to convert are invalid, and need not be

annulled. That was the case if the vows were coerced; but not all converts were coerced.

661 Daniel al-Qumisi, a ninth-century Karaite writer, quoted by Cohen, op. cit., 141.

662 Hoffman, op. cit., 117.

663 Ibid., 118.

664 Millgram, op. cit., 293; Num. *Rabba* 20:21.

665 *Encyclopedia Judaica*, 4, "Bread," 1334, citing Gen. 21:14 and 1 Kings 19:6.

666 Ibid., citing *Shulchan Aruch, Orach Chayim* 167.

667 *Ber* 35a. The Talmud infers the power of *berachot* by harmonizing two verses of psalms: "To God belongs the earth and the fulness thereof" (Psalms 24:1), and "The heavens are God's heavens, but the earth He has given to the children of men" (Psalms 115:16). The Talmud says that the first verse reflects the situation before one has uttered a *beracha*, while the second reflects the situation after a *beracha* has been said.

668 Millgram, op. cit., 293; *Ber.* 48b.

669 Louis Finkelstein, "The Birkat Ha-Mazon," *Jewish Quarterly Review*, 19, 211 (1929).

670 *Ber.* 48b.

671 Moshe Weinfeld, "Grace After Meals at the Mourner's House in a Text from Qumran," *Tarbiz*, 16, 15 (1991).

672 *Encyclopedia Judaica*, 7, "Grace After Meals," 840.

673 *Mar*, of which *maranan* is the Aramaic plural, was a title given to great scholars in Babylonia. *Rabbi*, of which *rabanan* is the Aramaic plural, was a title given to scholars ordained in Israel, but could not be given in the Diaspora. *Rav*, of which *rabotai* is first-person possessive plural in Aramaic (literally, "our *ravs*"), was a respectful but more common title, similar to "sir" or "mister," in Babylonia. See *Encyclopedia Judaica*, 11, 939 and 13, 1446. The purpose of these titles, rather than excluding women, was to show respect for all present and to accord particular respect to people of great learning. While it is true that in the sexist (compared to today) society of early medieval Babylonia women did not hold those titles, there is nothing to prevent women today in Reform and Conservative Judaism from being ordained as rabbis, or from calling themselves, or each other, *Rav*, or, in the Ashkenazic dialect, *Reb*, as a respectful form of address. Changing the form of address to "friends," as in the Reform liturgy, does not have the same connotation of respect.

674 *Ber.* 48b; Artscroll, op. cit., 188 fn.

675 Ibid.

676 Hammer, op. cit., 269, points out that the Book of Ben Sira, written in the second century B.C.E., contained a similar prayer, citing *Ben Sira* 36:17–19.

677 Ibid.

678 Ibid., 268–269.

679 Ibid., 270; *Ber.* 48b.

680 *Encyclopedia Judaica*, 7, "Grace After Meals," 838.

681 Artscroll, op. cit., 195–196 fn., citing Rabbi Samson Raphael Hirsch and others.

682 *New Gates of Prayer*, 168–171.

683 Elbogen, op. cit., 101.

684 Millgram, op. cit., 299–300; *Pes.* 103a.

685 Ibid., *Pes.* 103a–b.

686 Elbogen, op. cit., 101.

687 There is evidence that the Christian custom of observing the Sabbath on Sunday morning is derived from these ancient *Havdala* meals. The talmudic rule is that *Havdala* may be observed at any time after sundown Saturday, even as late as Tuesday morning if circumstances preclude observance earlier. For the first few decades after Jesus' death, while the early Christians still attended synagogue services and considered themselves Jews, they emulated the "Last Supper" each week on Saturday night at *Havdala* dinner, holding community meals in the manner of the *chavurot* common at the time among the Pharisees, and adopted the custom of the Eucharist at those meals. Basing his account on Paul's Epistle to the Corinthians, the Anglican scholar Hugh Wybrew describes what these meals were like: "The congregation gathered in the dining-room of one of its members on Saturday evening, the beginning of the first day of the week. It was probably crowded: not everyone could recline at table. Some might have been obligated to sit on the window-sill, like the unfortunate young man at Troas who, having fallen asleep during Paul's lengthy sermon, fell to the ground from the third storey (*Acts* 20:9). There were many lights to make the room bright. Everyone had brought their contribution to the common meal. It was not always a seemly performance, as Paul's rebuke to the Corinthians makes clear. Some ate and drank only too well, 'failing to discern the Lord's Body. . . .'" Hugh Wybrew, The Orthodox Liturgy (Crestwood, NY: St. Vladimir's Seminary Press, 1990), 13–14. Apparently, performing the Eucharist at *Havdala* dinners became impractical, either because the congregations outgrew people's homes or because of the kinds of disorderly behavior described by Paul, so the Eucharist ritual became detached from the Saturday-night dinners. After the expulsion of the Christians from the synagogues, the Eucharist that had begun as part of a *Havdala* dinner was combined with the synagogue liturgy and became the Sunday morning Christian service.

688 Private communication of the author with the Israel Museum, July 1991.

689 Donin, op. cit., 332; *Pes.* 103b.

690 Ibid.

691 *Pes.* 54a.

692 Donin, op. cit., 333.

693 Ibid., 332; *Pes.* 53b.

694 Ibid., 331; Rashi, *Beitza* 16a.

695 *Ber.* 57b.

696 Millgram, op. cit., 317.

697 Ibid.

698 Ibid.

699 Ibid.

700 *Shab.* 21b.

701 Shammai's reasoning for beginning with eight *Chanuka* lights and working down to one was that the *Chanuka* lights should follow the same rule as the sacrifice of bullocks on *Sukkot,* when thirteen bullocks were sacrificed the first night, twelve the second, and so on. See Millgram, op. cit., 270 n. 5.

702 Hammer, op. cit., 240.

703 *Encyclopedia Judaica,* 7, "*Chanuka,*" 1288.

704 The *menorah* actually is an ancient symbol of Jewish nationhood dating back to the First-Temple period. See Gershom Scholem, *The Messianic Idea in Judaism and Other Essays on Jewish Spirituality* (New York: Schocken Books, 1971), 261; *Encyclopedia Judaica,* 11, "Menorah." The *menorah* was, in antiquity, a seven-headed candelabrum, and was given an extra candle on *Chanuka;* thus *chanukiah* is a more accurate name for the *Chanuka menorah.* Interestingly, the Star of David is not nearly as ancient, having probably become a Jewish symbol when the hexagram, which had taken on an association with the Shield of David (which supposedly had afforded King David magical protection) in early Jewish mysticism, was used on the flag of the Jewish community of Prague in 1527. Ibid., 264–266, 274–276. The Star of David did not come to be used in synagogues until the early nineteenth century, probably in an attempt to develop a Jewish religious symbol that would fulfill the same function as the cross in the Christian church. Ibid., 279.

705 *Encyclopedia Judaica,* 7, "*Chanuka* Lamp," 1289.

706 Millgram, op. cit., 219; *Suk.* 4:5.

707 *Encyclopedia Judaica,* 15, "*Sukkot,*" 498.

708 *Encyclopedia Judaica,* 6, "Etrog," 949.

709 In Neh. 8:14–15, it is recounted that the heads of the clans, the priests and the Levites, assembled with Ezra the Scribe, found it written in the Torah scroll that "the Israelites must dwell in booths during the Festival of the seventh month, and that they must announce and proclaim throughout all their towns and Jerusalem as follows: 'Go out to the mountains and bring leafy branches of olive trees, pine trees, myrtles, palms, and [other] leafy trees to make booths, as it is written.'" The Torah, however, in Lev. 23:39–43, commands us to "take the product of *hadar* [traditionally understood to mean citron] trees, branches of palm trees, boughs of leafy trees, and willows of the brook," and does not say they are to be used as the building materials for the *sukkah.* Did the dignitaries assembled by Ezra misread Leviticus? The Talmud, in Tractate *Sukkot,* Ch. 3, wrestles with this question. Nehemiah makes it clear that the commandment to build *sukkot* had not been followed during the time of the First Temple, having been abandoned after Moses and Joshua, so it is at least fair to say that the earliest custom was to use the four species as the building materials.

710 *Encyclopedia Judaica,* 15, "Sukkah," 494, citing Philo, *Spec. Leg.* 2:208–9 and Maimonides, *Guide to the Perplexed,* 3, 43.

711 Artscroll, op. cit., 720.

712 Ibid.

713 Ibid.

714 The actual words of the refrain recited during the procession are, *Aneinu b'yom kar'einu,* taken from Psalms 20:10.

715 Millgram, op. cit., 221.

716 *Encyclopedia Judaica,* 7, "Hakkafot," 1154.

717 Artscroll, op. cit., 758 fn.

718 Chaim Raphael, *A Feast of History: Passover Through the Ages as a Key to Jewish Experience* (New York: Simon & Schuster, 1972), 68.

719 Ibid., 87–88.

720 Ibid., 86. The commandment actually is found in multiple places: Exod. 12:26, 13:8, 13:14, and Deut. 6:20–21.

721 Rabbi Yitzchak Handel, "Educational Principles of the Haggada," in Cohen and Brander, eds., *The Yeshiva University Haggada* (New York: Yeshiva University, 1985), 21.

722 Ibid., 21.

723 Ibid., 22.

724 Josephus asserts that a census taken under Cestius, the Roman proconsul of Israel from 64 to 66 C.E., counted 255,600 sacrifices offered at Passover. The number of people present was much larger, since groups of at least ten gathered around each sacrifice. See Raphael, op. cit., 81.

725 Ibid., 81.

726 Idelsohn, op. cit., 175.

727 Raphael, op. cit., 68.

728 This declaration has been called a "sacred myth" of the Jewish people by one of the leading liturgists of the Reform movement. See Lawrence Hoffman, *Beyond the Text: A Holistic Approach to Liturgy* (Bloomington: Indiana University Press, 1987), 79–80.

729 Ibid.

730 Ibid.

731 Raphael, op. cit., 69.

732 M. *Pes.* 10:3; Rabbi George Wolf, *Lexical and Historical Contributions on the Biblical and Rabbinic Passover* (New York: George Wolf, 1991), 167.

733 Wolf, op. cit., 168.

734 Ibid., 169.

735 Ibid., 186.

736 Private communication from Professor Joseph Tabory of Bar-Ilan University, June 25, 1996.

737 Ibid.

738 Ibid., 243.

739 Exod. 12:8.

740 Num. 9:11.

741 M. *Pes.* 2:6; Arthur Schaffer, "The History of Horseradish as the Bitter Herb of Passover," *Gesher,* 8, 217 (1981).

742 Pliny, *Historia Naturalis* 22:88–90; 26:163; *Encyclopedia Judaica,* 11, "Maror," 1014–1015.

743 M. *Pes. X,* 3; B. *Pes.* 115–116.

744 *Encyclopedia Judaica*, 7, "Haroset," 1346.

745 Idelsohn, op. cit., 177; Exod. 16:22. This is the same origin as the *Shabbat challa*. See ibid., 181.

746 Ibid., 177; Deut. 16:3.

747 Exod. 12:34; Cohen and Brander, op. cit., 2 fn., citing the Rashbam.

748 Ibid., 2 fn.

749 Raphael, op. cit., 69.

750 Ibid.

751 Ibid.

752 Ibid., 76.

753 Ibid., 89. This custom is reflected in the *Midrash* on Lamentations, which records that at a banquet before *Yom Kippur* a visiting rabbi was offered eighty courses, and wine was served with each.

754 *Jer. Pes. X*, 1. The promises that are quoted are contained in Exod. 6:6–7.

755 Millgram, op. cit., 304.

756 Wolf, *Lexical and Historical Contributions on the Biblical and Rabbinic Passover*, op. cit., 156.

757 Ibid., 135.

758 Raphael, op. cit., 132.

759 Millgram, op. cit., 304.

760 Cohen and Brander, op. cit., 36 fn.

761 Ibid; Raphael, op. cit., 136, 141–142.

762 See Rabbi Nosson Scherman and Rabbi Meir Zlotowitz, eds., Artscroll *Haggada* (New York: Mesorah Publications, 1977), 177, citing *Sfat Emet*.

763 Raphael, op. cit., 79.

764 Ibid.

765 The fifteen steps are ascribed either to Rashi or to Rabbi Sh'muel of Falaise, one of his students. See Artscroll *Haggada*, liii.

766 Ibid.

767 Artscroll *Haggada*, 66 fn.

768 *Ha Lachma Anya* begins with a reference to *matza* only, although the Bible requires the story of the Exodus to be told "at the time when *Pesach, Matza*, and *Maror* lie before you." *Pesach* and *Maror* are excluded because *Ha Lachma Anya* was not incorporated into the seder until the Exile. In Exile, the *Pesach* (paschal lamb) is not available to us, and the biblical commandment of *Maror* cannot be fulfilled in its absence; the *maror* we use in the seder is a talmudically adopted substitute. See Artscroll *Haggada*, 66 fn.

769 Cohen and Brander, op. cit., 7 fn.

770 Exod. 12:26.

771 Exod. 13:8.

772 The section of the traditional *Haggada* about the child who does not know how to ask is the only one phrased in the second-person-feminine gender. It is addressed to the mother, who is assumed to be giving the explanation to children who are too young to ask questions about the seder. The sections pertaining to the

other three types of children are worded in the masculine gender—in other words, these children are old enough to have a dialogue with their father.

773 Exod. 13.14.

774 Deut. 6:20.

775 Cohen and Brander, op. cit., 9 fn.

776 Artscroll *Haggada*, 90 fn.; *Pes.* 116a.

777 Artscroll *Haggada*, 91 fn., citing *Yalkut Tov.*

778 *Mishna Pes.* 10:4.

779 The Priestly Blessing probably is older than the two fixed prayers in Deuteronomy. Deuteronomy probably was unknown before the High Priest Hilkiah "found" a scroll containing it in the late seventh century B.C.E. If some of the psalms actually were written by King David, they would be older, or at least known to the people of Israel earlier, than Deuteronomy.

780 Artscroll *Haggada*, 74 fn.

781 Raphael, op. cit., 133.

782 Hoffman, *Beyond the Text: A Holistic Approach to Liturgy*, op. cit., 81.

783 Joel 3:3.

784 Prov. 24:17. Note the confluence of quotations from the Torah (the account of the Plagues), a quotation from the Prophets (Joel 3:3) and a custom based on the Writings (Prov. 24:17). The early rabbinic homilies constantly tied together verses from the three parts of the Bible to demonstrate the divinity of each. Perhaps the proverb was used together with the quotations at one time in rabbinic homilies, but was replaced in the *Haggada* by the custom of spilling wine.

785 Artscroll *Haggada*, 132 fn.

786 Psalm 78 omits lice, boils, and darkness, and Psalm 105 omits pestilence and boils.

787 *Mechilta*, Parashat B'Shalach 6.

788 Cohen and Brander, op. cit., 20 fn.; Artscroll *Haggada*, 136 fn.

789 The Yeshiva University *Haggada*, however, indicates that *Dayyenu* is not found in talmudic or midrashic literature, and was not universally accepted until the Middle Ages. Ibid., 22 fn.

790 Raphael, op. cit., 132–133.

791 See Louis Finkelstein, "The Oldest Midrash: Pre-Rabbinic Ideals and Teachings in the Passover Haggada," *Harvard Theological Review*, xxxi 1938, 291 ff., and "Pre-Maccabean Documents in the Passover Haggada," *Harvard Theological Review*, xxxv 1942, 291 ff., xxxvi 1943, 1 ff.

792 *Mishna Pes.* 10:5.

793 Cohen and Brander, op. cit., 24 fn.

794 Louis Finkelstein, "The Origin of the Hallel," *Hebrew Union College Annual*, 23, 319 (1950). This evidence of a "proto-*Hallel*" for Passover in psalms 113 and 114 corroborates the great antiquity of both *Hallel*, which scholars date roughly to the first two centuries of the Second Temple period, and the seder.

795 Millgram, op. cit., 218.

796 In fact, the *Zohar* was almost certainly written by Moses ben Shemtov de Leon, a late thirteenth-century Spanish mystic. De Leon falsely claimed that he had

"found" the text and that it had been authored by the second-century rabbi Shimon bar Yochai. After his death, his wife acknowledged that de Leon had written it himself, and that he had attributed it to Shimon bar Yochai so that it would be taken seriously. See Gershom Scholem, *Major Trends in Jewish Mysticism*, op. cit., 156–204. De Leon's false attribution of the book does not diminish the significant merits of his work.

797 These are *keter elyon* (supreme crown), *chochmah* (wisdom), *binah* (understanding), *chesed* (righteousness, love), *gevurah* or *din* (power or valor, chiefly manifested as the power of God to judge and punish wrongdoing), *rachamim* or *tiferet* (compassion or beauty), *netzach* (lasting endurance), *hod* (majesty), *yesod* (basis or foundation of all active forces in God), and *malchut* (the kingship of God, described in the *Zohar* as the *keneset Yisrael*, the mystical archetype of Israel's community, or as the *Shechinah*, the mystical presence of God). See Scholem, op. cit., 213.

798 A chart of the combinations of the *sefirot* for the different days of the *omer* is found in the Artscroll *siddur*, 286.

799 Millgram, op. cit., 498.

800 Scholem, op. cit., 267, 280.

801 Artscroll *siddur*, op. cit., 285.

802 Millgram, op. cit., 505; *The Zohar, Emor*, trans. Harry Sperling and Maurice Simon (London, 1949), 5:123 (97b–98a).

803 Ibid., 505.

804 This allusion to the use of abbreviated references for their associational value is particularly a propos after *Tikkun Leil Shavuot*, which is based on such associations. See 200.

805 *Chag.* 12a.

806 Artscroll *siddur*, op. cit., 715.

807 Ibid., 717.

808 Ibid.

809 Ibid., 719.

810 The book of Esther is called in the Talmud the Scroll, (in Hebrew, the *Megillah*), because in the days of the *Mishna* it was the only scroll read in the synagogue. There are actually four other *megillot* in the Bible: the Song of Songs, read on Passover; Ruth, read on *Shavuot*; Lamentations, read on Tisha B'Av; and Ecclesiastes, read on *Sukkot*. Millgram, op. cit., 616, n. 8.

811 Ibid., 273; *Meg.* 2a. The men of the Great Assembly probably did not exist, but the phrase was a shorthand way for the Talmud to say that the origin of something was so ancient that it was no longer known even in talmudic times.

812 *Meg.* 21b.

813 Millgram, op. cit., 274.

814 Jacobs, *Chasidic Prayer*, op. cit., 24.

The Morning Service[1]

Key to Prayerbooks Referenced

- Sil = Rabbi Morris Silverman, ed., *Sabbath and Festival Prayer Book* (New York: Rabbinical Assembly of America, 1946): Conservative
- Art = Rabbi Nosson Scherman, ed., *The Complete Artscroll Siddur* (*Siddur Kol Ya'akov and Siddur Ahavat Shalom*) (Brooklyn: Mesorah Publications, Ltd., 1984): Orthodox
- AS = *Artscroll Siddur*, page number for Sabbath and Festivals.
- Sim = Rabbi Jules Harlow, ed., *Siddur Sim Shalom* (New York: Rabbinical Assembly, United Synagogue of Conservative Judaism, 1989): Conservative
- SmS = *Siddur Sim Shalom*, page number for Sabbath and Festivals.
- GP = Rabbi Chaim Stern, ed., *Gates of Prayer* (*The New Union Prayer Book*) (New York: Central Conference of American Rabbis, 1975: Reform
- GPS = *Gates of Prayer* (1975 ed.), page number for Sabbath.
- NGP = Rabbi Chaim Stern, ed., *Gates of Prayer for Shabbat and Weekdays: A Gender Sensitive Prayerbook* (New York: Central Conference of American Rabbis, 1994): Reform
- NGS = *New Gates of Prayer* (1994 ed.), page number for Sabbath.
- KH = *Kol HaNeshamah: Shabbat VeHagim* (Wyncote, PA: Reconstructionist Press, 1994): Reconstructionist
- SS = *Siddur Shilo* (Shilo Prayer Book) (New York: Shilo Publishing House, Inc., 1960) Orthodox
- SSS = *Siddur Shilo*, page number for Sabbath and Festivals.

Page	Prayer	Function	State of Mind	Comments
42 Sil 12 Art 2 Sim 283 GP 11 NGP 104 NGS 141 KH 7 SS	*Ma Tovu* Prayer of Transition	Making the transition to prayer as we enter the synagogue. Not said at home. First sentence was said by Balaam, who was sent to curse the Jews, but God changed Balaam's mind and he praised them instead. It reminds us that God can change our minds, too.	We undergo a mental transformation, putting the daily routine out of our minds.	The second verse has ten words and is traditionally used to count the *minyan*. Note the progression in references from *ohel* (tent) to *mishkan* (sanctuary) to *bayit* (home) to *heichal* (palace) — even modest surroundings are transformed into palaces if we are in the right frame of mind.
42 Sil 4 Art 2 Sim	Blessing on Donning the *Tallit*	We are putting on our prayer uniform to focus our minds on the divine.	In our still-torpid state, we are being reminded of something important (the 613 commandments symbolized by the knots	

[1] This outline accurately charts the weekday, Sabbath, and Festival services. High-Holiday additions and additions for specific Festivals (e.g., *Akdamut* for *Shavuot*, *Hoshanot* for *Sukkot*) are not included.

Reference	Blessing	The mitzvah	Spiritual meaning	Halachic note
—GP 9 NGP 143 KH 1 SS		The uniform, which originated as a form of tribal identification, is the same for everyone, including the rabbi, establishing the equality of all members of the prayer community before God.	on the *tzizit*) and forming a spiritual community. We visualize ourselves as our ancient ancestors, the Hebrews, who wore the fringes on the corners of their clothing.	
42 Sil 6 Art 4 Sim —GP 10 NGP —KH 3 SS	Blessing on *tefillin* (weekdays only)	Wearing God's commandments prominently, just as a bride wears flowers at her wedding. A spiritual "coming out" as a Jew and a part of a spiritual community.	Pride. We begin prayer with pride in being a Jew. We are not afraid or embarrassed to be in public wearing the *tefillin* as an emblem of our Jewishness and as a symbol of our *devekut*, our bond with God.	We say two blessings—one on the act of putting on the *tefillin*, and the other on the precept of putting them on. Then we say the prayer recited by a couple at their wedding, *V'Airastich Li* ("And I Will Betroth You Forever").
43 Sil 14 Art 2 Sim —GP —NGP —KH 1 SS	Blessing on Lifting up the Hands After Washing	Purifying our physical selves for prayer, in the same manner as the priests of the ancient Temple in Jerusalem.	We've put on the uniform; now we emphasize the solemn nature of the occasion by carrying out the ancient purification ritual.	The blessing is on lifting the hands, not washing them. We lift our hands "so that water below the joint would not flow back and render [them] unclean" (*Sot.* 4b).
44 Sil 14 Art 6 Sim 284 GP 12 NGP 162 KH 11 SS	Blessing of Gratitude for the Gift of Our Body (*Baruch ata Adonai Eloheinu melech ha'olam asher yatzar et ha'adam b'chochma . . .*)	A home ritual to be said after going to the bathroom in the morning.	Awareness of the *Shechina*, the Presence of God, in even the most mundane physical act.	The order of the morning blessings in the *siddur* is mixed up. Each should be recited as the act to which it corresponds is performed.
44 Sil 16 Art 6 Sim 284 GP 12 NGP 104 NGS 169 KH 11 SS	Blessings of Gratitude for the Torah (*Baruch ata Adonai Eloheinu melech ha'olam asher kidshanu b'mitzvotav v'tzivanu la'asok b'divrei Torah*)	We fulfill the *mitzvah* of studying Torah and Talmud daily. Even if we die before completing the morning blessings, we have fulfilled this commandment.	As we awaken, our awareness moves from the physical to the intellectual.	Three blessings reflect a split of rabbinic opinion. The excerpt of Torah we read is the Priestly Blessing (Num. 6:24–26), which is the oldest prayer in Judaism.

45 Sil 18 Art 8 Sim 285 GP 13 NGP 105 NGS 165 KH 12 SS	*Elohai N'Shama* Blessing of Gratitude for the Gift of the Soul	Thanksgiving for the return of the soul to the body upon awakening.	As we rise beyond the intellectual to become aware of the spirit within ourselves, we experience a rebirth of the soul.	The Reconstructionist service changes the order of the *Birchot Ha'Shachar*. *Elohai N'Shama* becomes a meditation on the connection between breathing and the soul.
45 Sil 18 Art 10 Sim —GP 286 GPS 14 NGP 106 NGS 153 KH 13 SS	Sunrise Blessings of Thanksgiving	A series of blessings that follows the following sequence: becoming conscious of the cock's crow; becoming aware of who we are; opening our eyes; putting on clothing; throwing off our covers; standing up; looking out the window; "meeting our needs" (going to the bathroom, eating breakfast); walking; feeling strong; and feeling the "splendor" that "crowns Israel."	As we perform the routine of getting up, we arouse our sense of *devekut*, of being close to the divine.	The Orthodox service includes blessings on not being made a Gentile, a slave, or a woman. These originated not as chauvinism, but in an ancient Persian prayer adopted by the Jews as a rejection of the divinity of Jesus, in response to the preaching of Paul that the death of Jesus meant that all distinction between Jew and Gentile, slave and free man, and man and woman had become void. The Reconstructionist service puts these immediately after the donning of the *tallit*.
46 Sil 20 Art 12 Sim 287 GP 15 NGP 107 NGS —KH 15 SS	Personal meditations, and (Orthodox only) Torah and Talmud study	We prepare for public prayer with meditation and study.	We are trying to achieve an intense state of concentration, called *kavana*.	Meditations include personal confessions of talmudic rabbis Yochanan ben Zakkai and Mar Samuel, but may include any personal means of focusing the mind, such as breathing exercises. Torah, *Mishna*, and *Gemara* study in Orthodox liturgy includes the *Akeida* (the binding of Isaac) and other readings describing the preparations for the daily sacrifice in the Second Temple. These preparations—washing hands and feet, taking ashes from previous day's sacrifices, etc.—were a means of purifying the body and preparing the mind. We do the same through meditation and prayer.

Reference	Prayer	Description	Transition	Notes
49 Sil 52 Art 20 Sim —GP —NGP 172 KH 30 SS	*Kaddish D'Rabbanan* Kaddish After Study	*Kaddish*, the ancient prayer recited after a study session, punctuates the service. Here, *Kaddish* in its original form marks the end of the study session that follows the Sunrise Blessings.	We are making a transition from personal prayer to communal prayer. We depart the mundane.	*Kaddish D'Rabbanan* evolved into a mourner's prayer because it became customary to hold memorial study sessions in honor of deceased scholars.
50 Sil 54 Art 22 Sim —GP —NGP 175 KH 32 SS 43 SSS	Psalm of the Day (in Orthodox liturgy, Psalm 30) and the Song of Glory	We recite the psalms that, in the Second Temple, meant that the altar had been cleaned and the Temple was open for business. We enter communal prayer.	Using raw materials from the ancient Temple, we build our sense of spiritual community as we embark on public worship. We ascend to a higher realm.	The Song of Glory, beginning *"An'im Z'Mirot*, is the ending of the mystical Song of Unity written by kabbalists in twelfth- century Germany. Its purpose was to unify the words *Adonai* and *Yahweh* (the tetragrammaton, the four-letter name of God) into a single divine name and thereby unify the divine Essence damaged upon the expulsion of Adam and Eve from Eden. We seek not only to unify ourselves, but to achieve *Tikkun Olam*, the "repair of the world," through communal prayer.
61 Sil 56 Art 368 AS 52 Sim —GP 16 NGP 108 NGS —KH 33 SS 44 SSS	*Kaddish Yatom* (in Orthodox and Conservative liturgy, Mourner's *Kaddish*; in Reform liturgy, Half-*Kaddish*)	We complete our transition to public prayer. As we enter public prayer, we perform the *mitzvah* of comforting mourners by responding *Y'hei sh'mei rabba m'vorach* as they recite *Kaddish*.	We arrive in the higher realm, just as death is an arrival in a higher realm. Mourners recite *Kaddish*, the prayer on finishing a study session, because life is a constant learning process, that ends only upon death.	Mourner's *Kaddish* originated in the practice of permitting orphans to call the public to prayer by reciting *Barchu*. It originally served as a mourner's introduction to *Barchu*, the call to public prayer. Because mourners were anxious to aid the deceased by having the congregation respond *Y'hei shmei rabba m'vorach*, in accordance with an ancient legend about Rabbi Akiva, they could be relied on to call people to prayer.
62 Sil 58 Art 370 AS 54 Sim 290 GP —NGP 177 KH 34 SS 44 SSS	*Baruch She'Amar* Blessing Before Reading Psalms	We begin public prayer. This is the blessing on reciting psalms that prefaces the *P'Sukei D'Zimra*, Verses of Song, a series of psalms intended to focus the mind in preparation for listening to God in the *Shema* and addressing God in the *Amida*, which make up the heart of the service.	Deep concentration, *kavana*. We should avoid chatting with others from here through the *Amida*.	*Baruch She'Amar* fuses two prayers. The first part is a kabbalistic hymn interpreted as an exposition of different meanings of God's name. The second part, beginning with *Ha'm'hulal b'fi amo*, is the blessing before and after any biblical reading. The Reform service omits *P'sukei D'Zimra* entirely.

Excerpts from Psalms and Chronicles
- *Hodu* (1 Chron. 16:8 ff.)
- *Rom'mu* (excerpts of several psalms)
- *Psalm 100 (weekdays)*
- *Y'hi ch'vod (weekdays)*
- *Psalm 19*
  (Shabbat/Festivals)
- *Psalm 34*
  (Shabbat/Festivals)
- *Psalm 90*
  (Shabbat/Festivals)
- *Psalm 91*
  (Shabbat/Festivals)
- *Psalm 135*
  (Shabbat/Festivals)
- *Psalm 136*
  (Shabbat/Festivals)
- *Psalm 33*
  (Sabbat/Festivals)
- *Psalm 92*
  (Shabbat/Festivals)
- *Psalm 93*
  (Shabbat/Festivals)

Scholars used to sing all 150 psalms each day as a device to achieve an altered mind-state. We sing the last six, so we can be said to have "completed" the Psalms each day. In lieu of the first 144 psalms, we preface the recital of Psalms 145 to 150 with two collections of excerpts from Psalms and Chronicles, and a smattering of Psalms ascribed with special importance. The excerpts are arranged subtly to mirror the structure of the *beracha*; they are in a sense, a grand composite blessing.

Hodu: We visualize ourselves in Jerusalem with King David, singing as the Ark is returned by the Philistines. This is a practice visualization, to work up the necessary intensity before the *Shema*, in which we must visualize ourselves receiving the Torah at Mount Sinai with sufficient intensity to experience a spiritual transformation.

Rom'mu and Psalm 100: We meditate on the many dangers we encounter in our daily lives of which we never even become aware, and on our dependence upon God to avert these dangers.

Y'hi Ch'vod, Psalm 100, Psalm 34: We meditate on the idea that every being exists as part of God's plan and is dedicated to God's service, and that this can be seen both by contemplating the beauty and perfection of nature (*Y'hi Ch'vod*, Psalm 100) and by meditating on the divine purpose of those of God's creations that we perceive as dangerous and destructive (Psalm 34).

Psalms 90, 91, and 135: Having contemplated the purpose of the negative forces in the world, we concentrate on repentance and redemption as a means—demonstrated in the Exodus—for us to be saved from those negative forces.

Psalms 136, 33, 92, 93: Through visualization, we briefly transport ourselves to the world-to-come, to experience the rewards we can achieve. With Psalms 92 and 93, we put ourselves in the position opposite of Adam: returning to the Garden of Eden through repentance and redemption.

The Reform service may include excerpts from Psalms 19, 33, and 92; all others are omitted.

Psalm 136 is called, misleadingly, the Great Hallel. German kabbalists in the twelfth century ascribed it great importance because the number of repetitions of the refrain *Ki L'Olam Chasdo*—26—equaled the numerical value of the letters in the tetragrammaton. The Reconstructionist service adds Psalms 121 and 122 from the Sephardic rite. These are selections from the Psalms of Ascents, which were recited in antiquity while ascending the steps of the Temple.

Sources	Prayer			
76 Sil 66 Art 390 AS 80 Sim 294 GP —NGP 219 KH 41 SS 60 SSS	Psalms 145 to 150: the Daily Hallel • *Ashrei* (Psalm 145) • *Halleluyah, Halleli Nafshi* (Psalm 146) • *Halleluya, Ki Tov Zamra Eloheinu* (Psalm 147) • *Halleluya, Hallelu Et Adonai Min Ha'Shamayim* (Psalm 148) • *Halleluya, Shiru L'Adonai Shir Chadash* (Psalm 149) • *Halleluya, Hallelu El B'Kodsho* (Psalm 150)	Beginning with the final two verses of Psalm 144, we read the last six psalms to symbolically complete the psalms each day, as scholars did in antiquity. The purpose is to achieve the requisite spiritual frame of mind to be transformed by God's words in the *Shema* and, thereby, to merit God's attention to our requests in the *Amida*.	These psalms are supposed to lead us into increasingly deeper concentration, *kavana*. We have awakened; met our physical needs; ascended to the higher realm; practiced visualization; and meditated on God's wonders, both beautiful and deadly. Now we assume the same holy frame of mind as the ancient *Chasidim* (righteous ones). The six psalms lead us through the theme of redemption of the Jewish people, and culminate in an explosion of fervor in Psalm 150.	We begin with the last two verses of Psalm 144 because the first of those verses, *Ashrei Yoshvei Veitecha* (Happy are those who sit in Your House), was interpreted as a reference to those who sit in meditation and prayer. *Ashrei* is omitted in the Reconstructionist service.
80 Sil 74 Art 396 AS 90 Sim —GP —NGP —KH 47 SS 65 SSS	*Baruch Adonai L'Olam Amen V'Amen* Blessing After the Reading of Psalms	We recite a blessing after reading biblical verses. This blessing includes praises of God uttered by David, Nehemiah, and Moses (the Song at the Sea).	We visualize the events at which David, Nehemiah, and Moses uttered their praises: gathering materials for the First Temple; the end of the first Festival season after the return of the Exiles to Jerusalem; and the saving of the Israelites at the Red Sea.	
84 Sil 400 AS 334 SmS 297 GP —NGP 233 KH 70 SSS	*Nishmat* The Blessing of the Song (*Shabbat* and festivals)	Having just completed Moses' song at the Sea, his expression of thanks to God at the Red Sea, we read part of what the Talmud called the Blessing of the Song, an addition to the blessings recited after the Song at the Sea.	We feel the relief one experiences when an emergency has ended. We visualize situations in which we may have personally experienced relief after an emergency.	Parts of *Nishmat* are derived from an ancient prayer of thanksgiving for rainfall that ends a drought, one of the most common and pressing emergencies Jews faced in the arid land of Israel in antiquity.

Shochen Ad (Shabbat and festivals) and Yishtabach

86 Sil
82 Art
404 AS
336 SmS
299 GP
—NGP
241 KH
53 SS
73 SSS

This marks the end of P'sukei D'Zimra. The kabbalists thought that Yishtabach's thirteen praises of God would activate the thirteen mystical attributes of God that were inferred from the Torah passage (central to the Selichot [penitential] service) that begins, Adonai, Adonai, El Rachum V'Chanun. This Torah passage was used in antiquity as part of a prayer of public emergency.

A sense of urgency. We call on God in time of need. We have visualized relief from an emergency; now, with Yishtabach, we become conscious of our need—that we as a community require the relief God gave to Moses.

Shochen Ad is the end of the ancient Blessing of the Song. It leads into Yishtabach, which actually is a separate prayer that concludes P'sukei D'Zimra.

Chatzi (Half) Kaddish

86 Sil
82 Art
406 AS
338 SmS
300 GP
—NGP
245 KH
54 SS
75 SSS

Again, we punctuate the service with Kaddish, the ancient prayer after study. Here it marks the transition from P'sukei D'Zimra, the communal preparation for public prayer, to the convocation of formal public prayer.

We experience a transition. Our minds are prepared. Thus far we have awakened; met our physical needs; ascended to the higher realm; practiced visualization; meditated on God's wonders, both beautiful and deadly; assumed a holy frame of mind; experienced relief from an emergency; and realized our own collective need for that relief. Now we bond with our spiritual community to listen to God and plead with Him to grant us the relief we need.

The Reform service does not use Kaddish as a separation of segments of the service, and generally omits it at this point.

Barchu
The Ancient Call to Worship

87 Sil
84 Art
406 AS
96 Sim
340 SmS
55 GP
301 GPS
17 NGP
109 NGS
247 KH
54 SS
75 SSS

The ancient call to public worship. In antiquity, Barchu was called out in the middle of the village so that the public would know it was time to gather for prayer. Today, it marks the convocation of the formal prayer community.

We establish our prayer community. Prayer is reaching its culmination. We have a sense of anticipation as we symbolically enter God's Presence.

The custom of bending the knees and bowing is extremely ancient. The words Barchu and baruch come from the Hebrew word berech, meaning "knee." When the prayer leader says, Barchu et Adonai ha'm'vorach, he or she is saying, literally, "Let us bend the knee to the Lord, the One to whom knees must bend."

87 Sil 84 Art 406 AS 96 Sim 340 SmS 55 GP 301 GPS 17 NGP 109 NGS 249 KH 54 SS 75 SSS	*Yotzer* (Former of Light) First Blessing Before the *Shema*	We are about to listen to God in the *Shema*, which consists of three Torah excerpts. Before and after any Torah reading, we must recite a blessing.	We focus on the unity of God and the span of history since Creation. Light and darkness have the same source; well-being and woe are manifestations of the same Presence. We visualize ourselves ascending Mount Sinai, approaching that Presence, reaching a pinnacle in time from which all of history is revealed to us.	This blessing, adapted from Isa. 45:7, is a denial of religious dualism, such as that which prevailed in ancient Persia. The passage in Isaiah is addressed to Cyrus, King of Persia, who had defeated the Babylonian conquerors of Jerusalem. Deutero-Isaiah[2] saw this defeat as fulfilling God's "first promises," and as proof that God would also fulfill the "new promises"—the redemption of the Jews and their return to Jerusalem.[3]
88 Sil 410 AS 342 SmS —GP —NGP 253 KH 57 SS 77 SSS	Mystical Shabbat inserts in the *Yotzer* • *El Adon* • *Kedusha* of *Yotzer*	*El Adon:* An alphabetical acrostic hymn inserted by early mystics. Each word of an alphabetical prayer said on weekdays becomes the first word of an entire verse on *Shabbat*. The idea is that we are to take extra time on *Shabbat* to prepare our minds for the *Shema*. *Kedusha:* Another early mystical insert.	*El Adon:* We fight the desire to rush through the service. We allow ourselves the luxury of time, the freedom to linger as we approach the *Shema*, as we ascend the mountain on the day of rest. *Kedusha:* We visualize ourselves as angels. We praise God with the same words Isaiah and Ezekiel heard the angels use in God's Presence. We rise to our toes as we say *Kadosh, kadosh, kadosh,* to imitate angels with winged feet.	Both prayers were inserted by the *Yordei Ha'Merkava,* literally, the Descenders of the Chariot, Jewish mystics who lived before 600 C.E. They tried to ascend to heaven through prayer. Believing that *Kedusha* had special powers to aid in the ascent, they inserted *Kedusha* at three strategic spots in the service.

2 The book of Isaiah is generally considered to have been the work of two people who lived at different times: Isaiah son of Amoz, who lived in the eighth century B.C.E., and "Deutero-Isaiah," who lived in the sixth century B.C.E. during the Babylonian Exile. *Encyclopedia Judaica,* 9, "Isaiah," 46, 64.

3 Ibid., 64.

91 Sil
88 Art
412 AS
98 Sim
346 SmS
52 GP
302 GPS
18 NGP
110 NGS
273 KH
58 SS
81 SSS

Ahava Rabbah
Second Blessing Before the *Shema*

To preface the *Shema*, we have pronounced a blessing on God's unity. The other distinctive feature of the *Shema* is that it is a reading from the Torah. We now say a blessing in gratitude for the revelation of the Torah.

We visualize ourselves atop Mount Sinai about to receive the revelation of the Torah from God. We have ascended the mountain; now we bless what we are about to receive.

---

92 Sil
90 Art
414 AS
100 Sim
346 SmS
57 GP
303 GPS
18 NGP
111 NGS
276 KH
58 SS
82 SSS

The *Shema*
· The Proclamation of Faith:
Shema Yisrael, Adonai Eloheinu, Adonai Echad
(Hear, Israel, the Lord is our God, the Lord is One)
· *V'Ahavta*
(And you will love your God)
· *V'Haya Im Shamoa Tish'm'U*
(And it will come to pass, if you earnestly heed My commandments)
· *Va'Yomer*
(And God said to Moses)

Before we can ask anything of God, we must listen—with extreme concentration, so as to be spiritually transformed— to God's most important message to us.

· The *Shema*; the proclamation of faith: We always say this as if we were saying it for the first time, to catch our own attention in case our own minds are not yet sufficiently focused.

· *V'Ahavta*: We show our love for God by our conduct, by "clinging to God's ways."[4]

· *V'Haya Im Shamoa*: Why show our love for God? Because God notices and judges our actions.

· *Va'Yomer*: What conduct shows our love for God? Observance of the *mitzvot* (commandments).

We visualize ourselves receiving the Torah from God on Mount Sinai. We are not just listening to the Torah being read; we are allowing it to transform us, as if we were transfixed by the brilliance of God's Presence before us. The span of history, from the distant past to the end of time, is visible from our temporal height. The *Shema* is a "cathedral in time," according to Abraham Joshua Heschel, is a "pinnacle in time;" the *Shema* is a "pinnacle in time."

The Torah excerpts that make up the *Shema* are taken from Deut. 6:4–9 (The *Shema* and *V'Ahavta*), Deut. 11:13–21 (*V'Haya Im Shamoa*), and Num. 15:37–41 (*Va'Yomer*). The response *Baruch shem k'vod malchuto l'olam va'ed* is not from the Bible, but is the ancient response worshippers made whenever the name of God was pronounced.

In the Reform liturgy, *V'Haya Im Shamoa* and the first part of *Va'Yomer* are omitted; the first because it articulates a concept of divine reward and punishment rejected by the Reform movement, and the second because it expresses the commandment of wearing *tzitzit*, the ritual fringe, which the Reform movement does not consider obligatory. The Reconstructionist liturgy offers an alternate biblical selection for *V'Haya Im Shamoa* taken from Deut. 28:1–6 and 30:15–19.

[4] *Sifre* Deut. 33.

94 Sil
94 Art
416 AS
102 Sim
350 SmS
58 GP
304 GPS
20 NGP
112 NGS
287 KH
67 SS
84 SSS

Blessing After the *Shema* and Prayers of Redemption
• *Emet V'Yatziv* (True and Enduring)
The Blessing After the *Shema*
• *Mi Chamocha*
The Song at the Sea
• *Tzur Yisrael*
Rock of Israel

We must follow the Torah readings that make up the *Shema* by saying a blessing. The rabbis had different ideas about which subjects the blessing should concern; as a compromise, *Emet V'Yatziv* and its evening equivalent, *Emet VeEmuna*, include all of their proposals—the Exodus, God's kingship, the parting of the Red Sea, and the smiting of the first-born.

The Song at the Sea follows the blessing, because the saving of the Jews at the Red Sea was the only time in history that all the Jews witnessed a miracle. It was the time in our history in which there was the greatest unity of belief in God. In *Tzur Yisrael* we pray that, having redeemed us once, God will redeem us again.

At Mount Sinai there were doubters among the Jews; that is why the Golden Calf was fashioned while Moses was atop the mountain. At the Red Sea, there were no doubters; everyone saw the miraculous parting of the sea. We now attempt to achieve the kind of unity of mind that the Jews have achieved only once before, as a means to the redemption through which our communal requests, which we are about to address to God in the *Amida*, may be granted.

Imagine how different our history might have been if the Jews had been as united at Mount Sinai in accepting God's commandments as they had been at the Red Sea in accepting God's assistance!

With *Tzur Yisrael* we visualize the end of time, and we make the transition from listening to God to petitioning God. Therefore, we stand, as a showing of respect to a ruler whom we are trying to persuade, through our state of mind—our *devekut*—to grant our communal requests.

96 Sil
98 Art
420 AS
354 SmS
60 GP
306 GPS
22 NGP
114 NGS
292 KH
64 SS
87 SSS

The *Amida*, the Standing Prayer, also called the *T'fillah* (The Prayer) and the *Sh'moneh Esrei* (The "Eighteen [Blessings])
The weekday *Amida* consists of:
• 1. *Avot* (Ancestors)
• 2. *Gevurot* (Wonders)
• 3. *Kedusha* (Holiness)
• 4. *Da'at* and *Bina* (Knowledge and Understanding)
• 5. *Teshuva* (Repentance)

Having listened to God, and having allowed ourselves to be spiritually transformed, we are now in the proper frame of mind to address our requests to God and to merit God's attention to them.
• All *Amidot*, weekday, *Shabbat*, and Festivals, begin with an approach to God in *Avot*, *Gevurot*, and *Kedusha*. We visualize God bowing, as if entering the presence of a ruler.

The *Amida* is a spiritual journey in itself, a visualization of personal, communal, and national redemption and world peace as a sort of "virtual reality."
• Before starting, we take three steps backward, leaving our earthly realm, and three steps forward, entering the Presence of God. We begin by visualizing our ancestors and gaining self-confidence from their example (*Avot*). We visualize the natural cycle of birth and creation, death and renewal, that links our ancestors to us; we transcend time (*Gevurot*). Then we visualize the supernatural,

This prayer was substituted for daily-Temple sacrifice after the destruction of the Temple in 70 C.E. The spiritual intensity of the *Amida* probably had its counterpart in the ancient sacrificial ritual. The names of the sacrifices suggest this: *korban*, from the Hebrew root meaning "to get close to," suggests giving a part of oneself to get closer to God;[5] *olah*, meaning that which "goes up" [to heaven] implies transcending space; *tamid*, meaning "eternal," implies transcending time.

[5] I am indebted to Rabbi Alan Lew for pointing out that, in Genesis, Jacob, when describing himself, included his livestock as if it were part of himself. The animals sacrificed to God in ancient Israel were perceived as being part of the person who offered them.

- 6. Selichah (Forgiveness)
- 7. Redemption
- 8. Health
- 9. Sustenance
- 10. Return of the Exiled Communities
- 11. Restoration of Justice
- 12. Protection from Those Who Sow Disunity
- 13. Assistance for Those Who Unite Us
- 14. Rebuilding of Jerusalem as an Eternal Structure of the World
- 15. Flourishing of the Jewish Nation
- 16. Acceptance of Our Requests
- 17. Avoda [the Ancient Sacrificial Service]
- 18. Hoda'ah (Thanksgiving)
- 19. Peace [including the Priestly Blessing]

- The weekday Amida then takes us on a spiritual journey through thirteen "middle blessings" described in the Talmud as petitions.
- On Shabbat, we do not ask God for things, except for what is special about Shabbat: We ask God to "accept our rest."
- On Festivals, we visualize the event commemorated (V'Hasieinu) and read a synopsis of the manner in which that event was commemorated in the Second Temple (Ya'Aleh V'Yavo).
- Finally, on all occasions we take leave of God's Presence by offering prayers of thanksgiving (Avoda, Hoda'ah) and a prayer for world peace (Sim Shalom).

and become for a moment angels in heaven; we transcend space (Kedusha).

On weekdays, we then move through a sequence of requests and visions of what may be.

- We pray for the knowledge and understanding to tell good from evil (Da'at and Binah). We pray to achieve a repentant mental state (Teshuva). We pray for forgiveness for those sins we have committed inadvertently, despite our knowledge, understanding, and repentant state of mind (Selicha). We pray that, by knowing enough to avoid evil, repenting from the evil we already have done, and being forgiven for inadvertent wrongs of which we are unaware, we will receive a practical benefit from peril, relief from peril and suffering (Redemption). Relieved from imminent peril, we then pray for Health, and then for our community's material well-being (Sustenance).

- Our immediate community having achieved well-being in our vision, we then pray for the return of exiled Jewish communities around the world (Return of the Exiled Communities). Restored to their homeland, the exiled communities require a just government (Restoration of Justice). But they need more than justice; to become a force for world peace, they also need unity, both through God's Protection from Those Who Sow Disunity, and through God's Assistance for Those (whether Jews by birth or Jews by choice) Who Unite Us.

The Reform siddur calls this prayer by its ancient name, the Tefillah, while it is usually referred to in the Conservative and Orthodox liturgies as the Amida or the Shemoneh Esrei (Eighteen), referring to the eighteen original blessings of the weekday Amida. Since the early Middle Ages, a nineteenth blessing has been included.

In reciting the Amida we stand erect, feet together, the position assumed by the angels in the presence of God as described in Ezek. 1:7. We face Jerusalem, because King Solomon asked God to accept the prayers of worshippers facing in the direction of the Temple "when they sin against You . . . and they repent . . . and then later they turn back to You with all their heart and soul" (1 Kings 8:44–48).

We read the Amida silently first. It should be read slowly, with deep concentration. In antiquity, the sages were said to have taken an hour to complete it. The repetition by the prayer leader is primarily for the benefit of those unable to read it themselves.

The Reform and Reconstructionist liturgies excise references to God's making the dead live and add references to the Foremothers. Some Conservative congregations add references to the Foremothers, but preserve references to God's making the dead live.

- Our vision propels us further. A united Jewish nation would be able to rebuild Jerusalem—not as an ordinary city, but as an eternal Structure of the World (*Rebuilding Jerusalem*). The Jewish nation, sovereign, just, unified in spirit, would multiply and become powerful, regaining the eminence it enjoyed briefly during the reign of King David (*Flourishing of the Jewish Nation*).

On Festivals, instead of this sequence of visions, we visualize the ancient celebration of the event commemorated by the Festival, to recreate it in our minds (*Ya'Aleh V'Yavo* on Passover, *Sukkot*, and Shavuot, *Al Ha'Nissim* on Chanukah and Purim).

We draw back for a moment. None of this will matter if God does not heed our requests.

- We pray to God to accept our prayers (*Acceptance of Our Requests*). On *Shabbat*, we pray to God to "accept our rest"—i.e., to find us worthy enough, by virtue of observing *Shabbat*, for Him to grant the requests we made in our daily prayers during the week—and to "purify our hearts to serve [God] in truth."

- On all occasions, weekdays, *Shabbat*, and Festivals, we then thank God in advance for the favors granted by reciting modified excerpts from the ancient Temple service (*Avodah*, *Hoda'ah*, the Priestly Blessing).

Finally, having laid the groundwork through our requests, through acceptance of our prayers, and through our expressions of thanks, on all occasions we reach the crown of our vision:

• We pray for world peace and prosperity (*the Peace Blessing. Sim Shalom*).

This is, in many ways, the most profound moment of the service; yet it is too often ignored. This is our time to communicate with God, privately and spiritually, about our personal situation. We close our eyes, assume the traditional position by resting our head on our forearm, and meditate.

The traditional liturgy supplies us with suggested meditations, including the beautiful *Elohai n'tzor l'shoni mei'ra* written by Mar ben Ravina, a fifth-century Babylonian scholar. However, our meditations should be spontaneous, not confined to a script. It is incongruous that the most important part of the liturgy for women's prayer has been scribbled over with fixed texts written by medieval rabbis and has been virtually deleted from the liturgy in many synagogues.

Reform liturgy abbreviates *Hallel*, using only Psalms 117 and 118.

We have been praying as a spiritual community in order to meet the needs of that community. Now it is time for our own personal, spontaneous prayers. This was especially important in women's prayer, and a time for which personal meditations called *techinnot* were written by women in Eastern Europe.

Private Supplications
• *Elohai n'tzor l'shoni mei'ra* (My God, keep my tongue from evil)
• *Tachanun*

101 Sil
118 Art
430 AS
120 Sim
364 SmS
70 GP
—GPS
36 NGP
123 NGS
323 KH
77 SS
96 SSS

In the *Amida* and *Tachanun* we made our requests, both communal and personal. Now our state of mind is one of confidence and resolve—to do what God requires to have these requests fulfilled. In antiquity, while the Temple stood, this involved sacrifices. Today, we are judged by our conduct. On Festivals, just as special acts (the Festival sacrifices) were required in antiquity, special acts appropriate for the Festival are still required today, such as abstaining from work, residing in the *sukkah* on *Sukkot*, and eating unleavened bread on *Pesach*. *Hallel* is an extra bit of mental fortification to strengthen us for the extra things we must do on Festivals.

A substitute for the ancient Festival sacrifices. These are the psalms sung by the Levites while the sacrifices were being performed. The sacrifices were performed in a festive mood; *Hallel* marks a festive occasion.

Hallel
Psalms 113 to 118 (Festivals only)

110 Sil
632 Art
378 Sim
176 NGP
356 KH
175 SSS

116 Sil
138 Art
430 AS
136 Sim
392 SmS
—GP
300 GPS
—NGP
—NGS
380 KH
90 SS

Kaddish
On weekdays: *Chatzi* (Half)
Kaddish
On the Sabbath and Festivals,
Kaddish Shalem (Long
Kaddish)

Again, we punctuate the service with *Kaddish*, the ancient prayer after study. Here a short *Kaddish* on weekdays and an expanded *Kaddish* on the Sabbath and Festivals mark the transition from the Sunrise (*Shacharit*) service to the Torah service. The Torah service originated as a *D'rasha* (Seeking) service, an occasion for preaching and group study, not really a prayer service as we know it.

We experience a transition. Our minds have been fortified. We have awakened; met our physical needs; ascended to the higher realm; practiced visualization; meditated on God's wonders, both beautiful and deadly; assumed a holy frame of mind; experienced relief from an emergency; realized our own collective need for that relief; bonded with our spiritual community to listen to God; and pleaded with God to grant us the relief we need. Now, through sermons, discussion, Bible study, and community celebrations, we seek the means and the group spirit to enable us, as a community, to pursue our common goals. Relief depends not only on God, but on ourselves.

The Reform service does not use *Kaddish* as a separation of segments of the service, and generally omits it at this point.

117 Sil
138 Art
432 AS
139 Sim
395 SmS
415 Gp
415 GPS
141 NGP
141 NGS
383 KH
91 SS
97 SSS

Removing the Torah from the Ark
• *Ein Camocha* (*Shabbat* and Festivals)
• *Va'y'hi binsoa ha'aron*
• *Brich Sh'mei*
• *Shema*
• *Gadlu*
• *L'cha Adonai Hag'dula*

Going through the progression followed in the ancient *drasha*, from Torah to Prophets to Writings, biblical passages extolling God and the Torah are linked. We carry the Torah around the synagogue as the Israelites carried the Ark forty years through the desert. We manifest our willingness to put in that same magnitude of effort to make our requests, expressed minutes ago in the *Amida* and in personal meditation, come true.

We move from a state of concentration, *kavana*, to a sense of group celebration and intellectual awareness. In its origin, the Torah service is a public discussion and a community meeting, not really a prayer service. At the moment when the Ark is opened, according to the *Zohar*, "the gates of heaven are opened and the divine love is aroused," so we recite a blessing in Aramaic from the *Zohar*, *Brich Sh'mei*.

The Reform service omits the references to the Israelites carrying the Torah in the desert (*Va'y'hi binsoa ha'aron*) and the kabbalistic insert, *B'Rich Sh'Mei*.

Prayers During the Torah and Haftarah Readings

- Aliyot
- Mi'She'berach
- Y'Kum Purkan
- Prayer for the Government
- Rosh Chodesh blessings
- Chatzi (Half) Kaddish
- Blessings before and after the Haftarah
- Bar mitzvah/bat mitzvah

Aliyot. The blessing recited before the Torah reading begins with words of the *Barchu.* We are convoking a new spiritual community with each *aliyah. Chatzi* (Half) *Kaddish* separates the Torah reading from the prayers that follow it.

Mi-She'berach, Y'kum Purkan, Prayer for the Government: Prayers for community well-being. These replaced what probably originated as a time of private meditation after the Torah reading and before the *drasha* (sermon), but became a time of fundraisng for community purposes and celebrating community events.

Rosh Chodesh: Prayers for the New Moon, originally an important day of public gathering before there was a fixed calendar, are accompanied by a meditation that resumes where we left off at the end of the *Amida.*

Haftarah and its blessings: Haftarah means "dismissal." We read an excerpt from the Prophets related to the same theme as that of the week's Torah portion. Blessings after it parallel the structure of the *Amida.*

Bar mitzvah/bat mitzvah: A child's "coming of age" marked by reading the *Haftarah* and the Torah and having an *aliya.* Originally the bar mitzvah was called up by the *darshan,* who was to give the sermon, to

Aliyah means "going up." The person called to the Torah is the symbolic representative of the Jewish people who assembled to receive the Torah. Each time we have an *aliyah,* we figuratively ascend Mount Sinai to receive the Torah from God. The *gabbai,* who at one time functioned as an interpreter of the reading into the vernacular, plays the role of Moses overseeing the process.

The Torah reading is intended as public instruction. We should be in a receptive mood, having prepared our minds through prayer.

Between the Torah reading and the concluding prayers (or *Musaf,* on Sabbath and Festivals) is the time for celebration for community events such as bar and bat mitzvot. We recognize the personal accomplishments and joyous occasions of members of our spiritual community, and also wish well members of our spiritual community who are experiencing personal difficulties. In our quiet and focused mind-state, having made our requests of God and having received instruction in the Torah, we reap some of the benefits of prayer; now we can experience the joys and heal the sorrows of the others in our spiritual community.

With the blessings after the *Haftarah,* which originally ended the community gathering and which parallel the *Amida,* we renew our *devekut* and prepare our minds to deal with the outside world. We try to reinforce our sense of spiritual transformation, our quiet state of mind, so that we can carry it out of the synagogue and into the daily life of the community.

The custom of reading the Torah from a raised platform, the *bima,* is based on the example of Ezra, who read the Torah in public for the first time from atop a wooden tower. Public simultaneous translation of the Torah reading is another ancient custom that is consistent with its purpose of public instruction.

Cantillation of the Torah and *Haftarah* readings follows the sixth-century musical notation that memorializes hand and finger movements used in antiquity to signify musical phrases.

The *Haftarah* originated as part of the ancient *drasha* (sermon), which in formulaic fashion related Torah passages to Prophets and Writings and then discussed their meaning. Historically, the function of the Torah reading as ancillary to public instruction was replaced, mistakenly, by an exaggerated glorification of the Torah as a holy object. The *Haftarah* reading, burdened by less restrictions than the Torah reading, became the vehicle for celebration of personal *simchas* (joyous occasions) such as bar and bat mitzvot.

Reform Judaism has eliminated the *Rosh Chodesh* prayers and all of the prayers for community well-being except for the *Mi-She'berach.* Orthodox Judaism does not permit girls to read the *Haftarah* or the Torah, have an *aliya,* or lead services upon becoming bat mitzvah.

read the excerpts from the Torah and Prophets that were going to be discussed, and was introduced with a prayer, called a *reshut*, asking the congregation's permission to interrupt the proceedings in his honor.

132 Sil
148 Art
456 AS
150 Sim
422 SmS
429 GP
429 GPS
146 NGP
146 NGS
432 KH
95 SS
112 SSS

Returning the Torah to the Ark
- *Ashrei* (Psalm 145)
- *Y'Hallelu Et Shem Adonai* (excerpts from Psalm 148)
- Psalm 29 (Psalm 24, on weekdays)
- *U'v'nucho yomar*
- *Eitz chayim hi*

With *Ashrei* (Psalm 145), excerpts from Psalm 148, and Psalm 29, we again use psalms to prepare our minds—on Sabbath and Festivals for the *Musaf* (Additional) *Amida*, and on weekdays for the *Kedusha D'Sidra*. We finish the verse from Numbers that was recited when we removed the Torah from the Ark. We are reinforced with admonitions from Proverbs not to forsake the ways of the Torah. Finally, we feel sadness as the Ark is closed, and we sing the final verse of Lamentations: "*Hashiveinu Adonai eilecha v'nashuva chadesh yameinu k'kedem*.

We move from community and intellectual discourse back into our own minds. We are trying to reinforce the changes in our state of mind that we have achieved through prayer as we prepare to conclude the service. We are sad as we close the Ark.

U'v'nucho Yomar picks up where we left off in Numbers in removing the Torah from the Ark. The complete passages reads: "When the Ark was to set out [*Va'yhi binsoa ha'aron*], Moses would say, 'Advance, O Lord! May Your enemies be scattered, and may Your foes flee before You!' And when it halted he would say [*U'v'nucho yomar*], "Return, O Lord, You who are Israel's myriads of thousands."

We signify in putting the Torah back into the Ark that this is just a temporary halt in reading the Torah, that we shall return to do so again.

The Reform *siddur, Gates of Prayer* (1975 ed.), omits *Ashrei* and *Y'hallelu et shem Adonai* as well as the excerpt from Numbers. One line from Psalm 29 is all that remains of the traditional prayers for replacing the Torah in the Ark. The 1994 edition of *Gates of Prayer* has restored some of them.

137 Sil
460 AS
428 SmS
—GPS
—NGS
—KH
115 SSS

Chatzi (Half) *Kaddish* (Sabbath and Festivals only)

We make a transition on Sabbath and Festivals to *Musaf*, the Additional service.

We complete the movement of the mind back to the *Amida*. We are about to again speak directly with God about our community needs and requests.

Omitted in the Reform service, which rejects *Musaf* as a vestige of sacrificial worship. Also omitted in the Reconstructionist service.

Musaf Amida (Sabbath and Festivals only) 137 Sil 460 AS 428 SmS —GPS —NGS —KH 115 SSS	We repeat the process of approaching God through the *Amida*, discussed above, with two differences: a preface to the middle blessing (beginning, *Tikkanta Shabbat*) in which we recite the rules regarding the additional sacrifice offered in the Second Temple on those days; and a special *Kedusha* recited when the *Musaf Amida* is repeated by the prayer leader. The special *Kedusha* includes the proclamation of the *Shema*, a memento of a ruse by which rabbis in fifth-century Persia duped the authorities who attempted to prohibit saying the *Shema*; they moved the *Shema* from early in the service to *Musaf*, by which time the guard posted to ensure compliance with the ban had departed.	There has been only a brief period of preparing the mind for the Additional *Amida*, because we are already in a transformed state of mind that we carried through the Torah service. All we should need now is a short "refresher" of psalms. If we are to benefit from *devekut*, our transformed mental state, in our daily lives, we must be able to preserve it through community activity and intellectual discourse, and still feel its effects sufficiently to be able to get close to God. The *Musaf Amida* is, in a sense, a test of whether our spiritual transformation earlier in the morning has been successful.	The *Musaf* service originated when prayer, specifically the *Amida*, was substituted for sacrifice after the Second Temple was destroyed in 70 c.e. It commemorated the extra sacrifice, the *korban musaf*, offered on the Sabbath and Festivals. The word *korban* (sacrifice) comes from the root *k-r-b*, meaning "to get close to." The idea of substituting prayer for sacrifice was that prayer was an equally valid means of "getting close to" God. The liturgy of Reform Judaism has excised all references to sacrifice, including *Musaf*.
Kedusha D'Sidra (*U'va L'Tzion Goel*) (weekdays only) 154 Art 156 Sim —GPS —NGP —NGS —KH 98 SS	This is a weekday substitute for an *Amida* after studying the Torah. Its structure parallels that of the *Amida*.	Our state of mind during *Kedusha D'Sidra* should be deeply focused, as it was in the *Amida* for which it is a substitute. Refrain from rushing through it, and take time after it for personal meditation.	
Kaddish Shalem (Complete *Kaddish*) 156 Sil 156 Art 464 AS 158 Sim 506 SmS —GP —GPS —NGP —NGS —KH 101 SS 127 SSS	Again the *Kaddish* marks a transition in the traditional service.	We pass again from deep focus to a sense of spiritual community as we move toward *Aleinu*, the "Jewish Pledge of Allegiance," which concludes public prayer.	

Prayer / References	Description		
Ein K'Eloheinu (Sabbath and Festivals only) 157 Sil 476 AS 508 SmS 730 GPS 159 NGS 442 KH 128 SSS	Ancient tradition holds that one should bless God one hundred times each day. Because the Sabbath and Festival *Amida* contains seven blessings compared to nineteen on weekdays, the resulting "blessing deficit" must be met, in part, by reciting *Ein K'Eloheinu.* This poem was arranged by students of Rashi so that it contains four acrostic blessings.	We rekindle community feeling with a joyous hymn in preparation for *Aleinu.*	
Talmud study and *Kaddish D'Rabbanan* (Orthodox liturgy; Sabbath and Festivals only) 480 AS 128 SSS	in the Orthodox liturgy, a brief talmudic study session follows *Ein K'Eloheinu.* The Scholar's *Kaddish,* the ancient prayer that ended a study session, is then recited.	We anticipate the first *mitzvah* we will perform in our transformed mind-state: comforting mourners. The study session at this point probably is related to the origin of the Mourner's *Kaddish* in study sessions held in honor of the deceased. *Kaddish* must follow a study session, so the Orthodox liturgy provides one.	The talmudic passages studied after *Ein K'Eloheinu* parallel *Aleinu.* One, pertaining to the burning of incense in the Second Temple, is symbolically retained at the end of the Conservative text of *Ein K'Eloheinu,* even though the Conservative liturgy has discarded the Scholar's *Kaddish* at this point.
Aleinu It Is Our Duty 158 Sil 158 Art 480 AS 160 Sim 510 SmS 615 GP 615 GPS 148 NGP 148 NGS 444 KH 102 SS 132 SSS	This prayer marks the conclusion of the service. Originally written for *Rosh HaShana,* it became part of every service in commemoration of the martyrdom of fifty-one Jewish men and women who were burned at the stake in Blois (France) by Crusaders in 1171. The martyrs, falsely accused of ritual murder, died chanting *Aleinu.*	*Aleinu* is a "Jewish Pledge of Allegiance." "It is a symbol of loyalty in the face of persecution. Through prayer we have achieved *devekut*; we have fortified our minds to observe the *mitzvot* and resist evil. Now we contemplate the example of people who used prayer to fortify their minds so powerfully that they resisted evil even on pain of death.	The 1975 edition of *Gates of Prayer* included four different versions of *Aleinu*; the 1994 edition has just one. References to Jews as the Chosen People and to God's kingship are deleted in the Reform version.
Kaddish Yatom (Mourner's *Kaddish*) 161 Sil 160 Art 482 AS 162 Sim 512 SmS 629 GP 629 GPS 154 NGP 154 NGS 450 KH 104 SS 133 SSS	The service is now over. As it ends, we comfort mourners in our spiritual community. In talmudic legend, the congregation's response, *Y'hei shmei rabba m'vorach,* had magical powers to help the dead to reach heaven.	In comforting mourners, we perform our first *mitzvah* in our transformed state of mind.	*Kaddish* is a prayer with no direct connection to death. It occurs a number of times in the traditional Morning service, this being the last, and is discussed further above. *Kaddish* marked the end of a study session. Life is, in a sense, a constant study session that ends only upon death.

161 Sil
162 Art
484 AS
22 Sim
514 SmS
729 GP
729 GPS
156 NGP
156 NGS
105 SS
135 SSS

Adon Olam Lord of the World (Sabbath and Festivals)

Psalm of the Day (weekday mornings)

An'im Z'mirot (Shir Ha'Kavod, Song of Glory)

We sing a joyful hymn to raise the spirits of the mourners. In the kabbalistic view, if we have been sufficiently transformed in spirit through prayer, our souls ascend to God.

Spiritually transformed, with joy and a feeling of fulfillment on having performed a good deed by comforting the mourners, we depart the spiritual community. We retain a sense of unity with that community until we meet again for prayer.

Traditional services may also end with the mystical prayer *An'im Z'mirot,* also known as *Shir Ha'Kavod* (Song of Glory). This is the end of a longer hymn known as *Shir Ha'Yichud* (Song of Unity), written by a twelfth-century German mystic, Rabbi Judah He'Chasid of Regensburg. It was believed by the Lurianic kabbalists to hasten *tikkun olam,* the restoration of the original harmony of the universe, and to aid the worshipper's soul in ascending to the higher spiritual realm. Now, just before we leave the synagogue, is our final opportunity of the morning to achieve sufficient *kavana,* concentration, to make the ascent.

Adon Olam originated as an ancient bedtime prayer. That is why it ends, "My soul I give to His care/Asleep, awake, for He is near/And with my soul and my body/God is with me, I have no fear."

Weekday morning services in Orthodox and Conservative liturgies conclude with the Psalm of the Day, the psalm which, according to tradition, was specially recited by the Levites on that day of the week. Some traditional congregations end on Sabbath with *An'im Z'mirot,* for which the congregation stands and the Ark is opened to symbolically aid the ascent of each person's soul. Some traditional congregations end on weekdays with Maimonides' Thirteen Articles of Faith, *Ani Ma'amin.*

Bibliography

Abrahams, Israel, *A Companion to the Authorized Daily Prayerbook* (printed London 1922; reprinted New York: Hermon Press, 1966)

Armstrong, A.H., *Classical Mediterranean Spirituality* (New York: Crossroad Publishing Co., 1986)

Arzt, Max, *Joy and Remembrance* (Bridgeport, Conn.: Hartmore House, 1979)

Ben-Or, Ehud, *Worship of the Heart* (Albany: State University of New York, 1995)

Biale, Rachel, *Women and Jewish Law* (New York: Schocken Books, 1984)

Bickermann, Elias, "The Civic Prayer for Jerusalem," *Harvard Theological Review*, vol. 55, p. 163 (1962)

Blidstein, Gerald J., "Kaddish and Other Accidents," 14 *Tradition* 80 (1974)

Blumenthal, David, *Understanding Jewish Mysticism, Vol. II* (New York: Ktav Publishing House, 1982)

Bokser, Ben Zion, "The Thread of Blue," 31 *Proceedings of the American Academy for Jewish Research*, p. 1 (1963)

Bonwick, James, *Egyptian Belief and Modern Thought* (Indian Hills, Colorado: Falcon's Wing Press, 1956)

Boyce, Mary, *Zoroastrians: Their Religious Beliefs and Practices* (London: Routledge & Kegan Paul, Ltd., 1979)

Bradshaw, Paul F. and Lawrence A. Hoffman (eds.), *The Changing Face of Jewish and Christian Worship in North America* (Notre Dame: University of Notre Dame Press, 1991)

————— , *The Making of Jewish and Christian Worship* (Notre Dame: University of Notre Dame Press, 1991)

Brody, Robert, "Morning Benedictions at Qumran?" 81 *Tarbiz* 493 (1982)

Caquot, A., and M. Sznycer, *Ugaritic Religion* (Leiden: E.J. Brill, 1980)

Cohen, Chayim, "Was the P Document Secret?" 1 *Journal of the Ancient Near Eastern Society* 39 (1969)

Cohen, Steven and Kenneth Brander (eds.), *The Yeshiva University Haggada* (New York: Yeshiva University, 1985)

Cohen, Jeffrey M., *1,001 Questions and Answers on Pesach* (Northvale, N.J.: Jason Aronson Inc., 1996)

————— , *Blessed are You: a Comprehensive Guide to Jewish Prayer* (Northvale, N.J.: Jason Aronson Inc., 1993)

————— , *Horizons of Jewish Prayer* (London: United Synagogue, 1986)

————— , *Prayer and Penitence: A Commentary on the High Holy Day Machzor* (Northvale, NJ: Jason Aronson, Inc., 1994)

Cohen, Naomi G., "The Nature of *Shim'on HaPekuli's* Act," 52 *Tarbiz* 547 (1983) (Hebrew)

Cumont, Franz, *The Oriental Religions in Roman Paganism* (New York: Dover, 1956) (reprint of 1911 original edition)

Donin, Hayim Halevy, *To Pray as a Jew* (New York: Basic Books, 1980)

Dreyfus, A. Stanley, "The *Gates* Liturgies: Reform Judaism Reforms Its Worship," in Paul F. Bradshaw and Lawrence Hoffman (eds.), *The Changing Face of Jewish and Christian Worship in North America* (Notre Dame: University of Notre Dame Press, 1991)

Elbogen, Ismar, *Jewish Liturgy: a Comprehensive History* (1913; translation by Raymond Scheindlin, Jewish Publication Society, New York, 1993)

————— , *Studies in Jewish Liturgy*, in Jakob Petuchowski (ed.), *Contributions to the Scientific Study of Jewish Liturgy* (New York: Ktav Publishing House, 1970)

Fine, Lawrence, *Safed Spirituality* (New York: Paulist Press, 1984)

Finkelstein, Louis, "The Birkat Ha-Mazon," 19 *J.Q.R.* 211 (1929)

————— , "The Oldest Midrash: Pre-Rabbinic Ideals and Teachings in the Passover Haggada," *Harvard Theological Review*, vol. xxxi (1938)

————— , "The Origin of the Hallel," *Hebrew Union College Annual*, vol. 23, p. 319 (1950)

————— , "The Origin of the Synagogue," *Proceedings of the American Academy of Jewish Research*, vol. 1, p. 49 (1928)

————— , "Pre-Maccabean Documents in the Passover Haggada," *Harvard Theological Review*, vol. xxxv (1942)

Fleischer, Ezra, "On the Beginnings of Obligatory Jewish Prayer" (Hebrew), *Tarbiz*, vol. 59, p. 397 (1990)

————, "The *Shemone Esre*—Its Character, Internal Order, Content and Goals," 62 *Tarbiz* 179 (1993)

Flusser, David, "Some of the Precepts of the Torah From Qumran (4QMMT) and the Benediction Against the Heretics," 61 *Tarbiz* 333 (1992)

Fraade, Steven, *From Tradition to Commentary; Tradition and Its Interpretation in the Midrash to Deuteronomy* (Albany: SUNY Press, 1991).

Freehof, Solomon, "Devotional Literature in the Vernacular," *Central Conference of American Rabbis* vol. 33 (1923)

————, "The Origin of the Tachanun Prayers," *Hebrew Union College Annual*, vol. 2 (1925), 339–350

Frye, Richard N., "Qumran and Iran: the State of Studies," in J. Neusner (ed.), *Christianity, Judaism, and Other Greco-Roman Cults* (Leiden: E.J. Brill, 1975)

Gandz, Solomon, "The Robeh or the Official Memorizer of the Palestinian Schools," 7 *Proceedings of the American Academy for Jewish Research* 5 (1935)

Garcia, Martinez, Florentino, *The Dead Sea Scrolls Translated* (Leiden: E.J. Brill and Grand Rapids: William B. Eerdmans, 1996)

Ginzberg, Louis A., *A Commentary on the Palestinian Talmud*, Vol. I (New York: Jewish Theological Seminary, 1941)

Gordon, Martin L., "*Netilat Yadayim Shel Shaharit:* Ritual of Crisis or Dedication?" 8 *Gesher* 36 (1981)

Gradwohl, R., "Eine Ueberfluessige Textanderung," *Tradition und Erneuerung*, vol. 40 (1976)

Greenberg, Moshe, *Biblical Prose Prayer as a Window to the Popular Religion of Ancient Israel* (Berkeley: University of California Press, 1983)

Grishaver, Joel L., *19 Out of 18* (Los Angeles: Torah Aura Productions, 1991)

Hammer, Reuven, *Entering Jewish Prayer* (New York: Schocken Books, 1993)

Handel, Yitzchak, "Educational Principles of the Haggada" ("Handel"), in Cohen & Brander, *The Yeshiva University Haggada, supra.*

Handy, Lowell K., *Among the Host of Heaven: the Syro-Palestinian Pantheon as Bureaucracy* (Winona Lake, Indiana: Eisenbrauns, 1994)

Haran, Menahem, "Priest, Temple, and Worship," 48 *Tarbiz* 175 (1978)

————, *Temples and Temple-Service in Ancient Israel* (Winona Lake, Indiana: Eisenbrauns, 1985)

Harlow, Jules (ed.), *Mahzor for Rosh Hashanah and Yom Kippur* (New York: The Rabbinical Assembly, 1972)

————, "Revising the Liturgy for Conservative Jews," in Paul F. Bradshaw and Lawrence A. Hoffman (eds.), *The Changing Face of Jewish and*

Christian Worship in North America (Notre Dame: University of Notre Dame Press, 1991)

————, *Siddur Sim Shalom* (New York: Rabbinical Assembly, United Synagogue of Conservative Judaism, 1989)

Heinemann, Joseph, *Prayer in the Talmud* (revised English version of *Ha'T'filla Bi'T'kufat Ha'Tanna'im V'Ha'Amora'im*) (New York: Walter de Gruyter, 1977).

Hertz, J.H. (ed.), *Pentateuch & Haftorahs* (2d ed.) (London: Soncino Press, 1980)

Heschel, Abraham Joshua, *The Sabbath: Its Meaning for Modern Man* (New York: Farrar, Straus & Young, 1951)

Hilvitz, A., *"Amirat P'sukei 'Ma Tovu' Lifnei Ha'T'filla,"* Sinai, vol. 78, p. 263 (1976) (Hebrew)

Hoffman, Lawrence A., *Beyond the Text: a Holistic Approach to Liturgy* (Bloomington: Indiana University Press, 1987)

————, *The Canonization of the Synagogue Service* (Notre Dame: University of Notre Dame Press, 1979)

————, *Gates of Understanding 2: Appreciating the Days of Awe* (New York: Central Conference of American Rabbis, 1984)

————, *"Jewish Liturgy and Jewish Scholarship,"* in Jacob Neusner (ed.), *Judaism in Late Antiquity* (Leiden: E.J. Brill, 1995), Part I, p. 239

————, *"Reconstructing Ritual as Identity and Culture,"* in Bradshaw and Hoffman, (eds.), *The Making of Jewish and Christian Worship, supra.*

Holtz, Barry W., *Finding Our Way: Jewish Texts and the Lives We Lead Today* (New York: Schocken Books, 1990)

Hooke, S.H., *The Origins of Early Semitic Ritual* (London: The British Academy, 1938)

Idel, Moshe, *Hasidim: Between Ecstasy and Magic* (Albany: State University of New York Press, 1995)

————, *Kabbalah* (New Haven: Yale University Press, 1988)

————, *"Secrecy, Binah and Derishah,"* in H.G. Kipperberg and G.G. Strousma (eds.), *Secrecy and Concealment: Studies in the History of Mediterranean and Near Eastern Religions* (Leiden: E.J. Brill, 1995), p. 311

————, *Studies in Ecstatic Kabbalah* (Albany: State University of New York Press, 1988)

Idelsohn, A.Z., *Jewish Liturgy and Its Development* (1932; reprinted, New York: Schocken Books, 1960)

Isaacs, Ronald H. and Kerry M. Olitzky (eds.), *Critical Documents of Jewish History: a Sourcebook* (Northvale, NJ: Jason Aronson Inc., 1995)

Jacobs, Louis, *Hasidic Prayer* (New York: Schocken Books, 1973)

Jacobson, B.S., *The Weekday Siddur: An Exposition and Analysis of Its Structure, Contents, Language and Ideas* (Tel Aviv: Sinai, 1973)

Jastrow, Morris, Jr., *Aspects of Religious Belief and Practice in Babylonia and Assyria* (New York: Benjamin Blum, Inc., 1971) (reprint of 1911 original edition)

Kamenetz, Rodger, *The Jew in the Lotus* (New York: HarperCollins, 1994)

Kaplan, Aryeh, *Jewish Meditation* (New York: Schocken Books, 1985)

———, *Meditation and the Bible* (Northvale, NJ: Jason Aronson Inc., 1995)

Katsh, Abraham, *Judaism in Islam* (New York: New York University Press, 1954)

Kaufmann, Yehezkel, *The Religion of Israel* (trans. and abridged by Moshe Greenberg; Chicago: University of Chicago Press, 1960)

Kimelman, Reuven, "The Daily *Amidah* and the Rhetoric of Redemption," 79 *J.Q.R.* 165 (1989)

Kipperberg, H.G. and G.G. Strousma (eds.), *Secrecy and Concealment: Studies in the History of Mediterranean and Near Eastern Religions* (Leiden: E.J. Brill, 1995)

Klein, Earl, *Jewish Prayer: Concepts and Customs* (Columbus: Alpha Publishing Co., 1986)

Kol HaNeshamah: Shabbat VeHagim (Wyncote, Pennsylvania: Reconstructionist Press, 1994)

Krauss, Samuel, "The Jewish Rite of Covering the Head," *Hebrew Union College Annual*, vol. 19, p. 121, 130 (1945–46)

Lamm, Norman, "Some Comments on Centrist Orthodoxy" (New York: Rabbinical Council of America, 1986), reprinted in Ronald H. Isaacs and Kerry M. Olitzky (eds.), *Critical Documents of Jewish History: a Sourcebook* (Northvale, NJ: Jason Aronson, Inc. 1995)

Leibowitz, Nehama, *New Studies in Shemot (Exodus)*, (Jerusalem: Ha-Omanim Press, 1993)

Lerner, Michael, *Jewish Renewal: a Path to Healing and Transformation* (New York: HarperCollins Publishers, Inc., 1994)

Liber, M., "Structure and History of the *Tefilah*," 40 *J.Q.R.* 347 (1950)

Liebreich, Leon J., "The Compilation of the Pesuke De-Zimra," *Proceedings of the American Academy for Jewish Research*, vol. 18, p. 255 (1949)

———, "The Intermediate Benedictions of the *Amidah*," 42 *J.Q.R.* 423 (1952)

Lowenthal, Marvin, *The Jews of Germany* (New York: Longmans, Green & Co., 1936)

Maher, Michael, "The Meturgemanim and Prayer," 44 *Journal of Jewish Studies* 220 (1993)

Millgram, Abraham, *Jewish Worship* (Philadelphia: Jewish Publication Society of America, 1971)

Moore, George Foote, *Judaism in the First Centuries of the Christian Era*, vol. I (Cambridge, MA.: Harvard University Press, 1927)

Muffs, Yohanan, "Joy and Love as Metaphorical Expressions of Willingness and Spontaneity in Cuneiform, Ancient Hebrew, and Related Literatures," in J. Neusner (ed.), *Christianity, Judaism, and Other Greco-Roman Cults* (Leiden: E.J. Brill, 1975)

————, "Love and Joy as Metaphors of Volition in Hebrew and Related Literatures, Part II: The Joy of Giving," *Journal of the Ancient Near Eastern Society*, vol. 11, p. 91 (1979)

Neusner, Jacob (ed.), *Judaism in Late Antiquity* (Leiden: E.J. Brill, 1995)

————, "The Rabbinic Traditions About the Pharisees Before A.D. 70: the Problem of Oral Transmission," 22 *Journal of Jewish Studies* 1 (1971)

Newsome, James D., *Greek, Romans, Jews: Currents of Culture and Belief in the New Testament World* (Philadelphia: Trinity Press International, 1992)

Nulman, Macy, *The Encyclopedia of Jewish Prayer* (Northvale, NJ: Jason Aronson Inc., 1996)

Orlinsky, Harry, et. al. (eds.), *Tanakh: A New Translation of the Holy Scriptures* (Philadelphia: Jewish Publication Society, 1985)

Petuchowski, Jakob (ed.), *Contributions to the Scientific Study of Jewish Liturgy* (New York: Ktav Publishing House, 1970)

Petuchowski, Jakob, *Prayerbook Reform in Europe* (New York: World Union for Progressive Judaism, 1968)

Posner, Raphael, et al., *Jewish Liturgy* (Jerusalem: Keter, 1975)

Raphael, Chaim, *A Feast of History: Passover Through the Ages as a Key to Jewish Experience* (New York: Simon & Schuster, 1972)

Reif, Stefan C., *Judaism and Hebrew Prayer: New Perspectives on Jewish Liturgical History* (Cambridge: Cambridge University Press, 1993)

Saffrey, H.D., "The Piety and Prayers of Ordinary Men and Women in Late Antiquity," in A.H. Armstrong, *Classical Mediterranean Spirituality* (New York: Crossroad Publishing Co., 1986)

Saggs, H.W.F., *The Encounter with the Divine in Mesopotamia and Israel* (London: The Athlone Press, 1978)

Sauneron, Serge, *The Priests of Ancient Egypt* (New York: Grove Books, Inc., 1960)

Schacter, Jacob (ed.)., *Reverence, Righteousness, and Rahmanut—Essays in Memory of Rabbi Dr. Leo Jung* (Northvale, NJ: Jason Aronson Inc., 1992)

Schaffer, Arthur, "The History of Horseradish as the Bitter Herb of Passover," 8 *Gesher* 217 (1981)

Scherman, Nosson (ed.)., The Complete Artscroll Siddur (Siddur Ahavot Shalom) (Brooklyn: Mesorah Publications, Ltd., 1984)

———— and Rabbi Meir Zlotowitz (eds.), Artscroll Haggada (New York: Mesorah Publications, 1977)

Scholem, Gershom, Major Trends in Jewish Mysticism (New York: Schocken Books, 1995)

————, "Merkabah Mysticism and Jewish Gnosticism," in idem., Major Trends in Jewish Mysticism, supra.

————, The Messianic Idea in Judaism and Other Essays on Jewish Spirituality (New York: Schocken Books, 1971)

Segal, M.H., "The Religion of Israel Before Sinai, 52 J.Q.R. 41 (1961)

Sender, Yitzchak, The Commentator's Siddur (Chicago: Sender, 1995)

Silverman, Morris (ed.), High Holiday Prayer Book (New York: United Synagogue, 1951)

Silverman, Morris (ed.), Sabbath and Festival Prayer Book (New York: Rabbinical Assembly of America, 1946)

The Soncino Talmud (CD-ROM edition, Chicago: Davka Corp., 1995)

Stern, Chaim (ed.), Gates of Prayer (The New Union Prayer Book) (New York: Central Conference of American Rabbis, 1975)

Stern, Chaim (ed.), Gates of Prayer for Shabbat and Weekdays: a Gender Sensitive Prayerbook (New York: Central Conference of American Rabbis, 1994)

Swartz, Michael D., "Alay Le-Shabbeah: a Liturgical Prayer in Ma'aseh Merkabah," 77 J.Q.R. 179 (1987)

Tabory, Joseph, Jewish Festivals in the Time of the Mishna and Talmud (Hebrew) (Jerusalem: Magnes Press, 1995)

————, "The Place of the Malkhiyyot Benediction in the Rosh Ha-Shana Additional Service," Tarbiz, vol. 48, p. 30 (1979)

Tarnor, Norman, A Book of Jewish Women's Prayers: Translations From the Yiddish (Northvale, NJ: Jason Aronson Inc., 1995)

Ta-Shma, Israel, "Some Notes on the Origins of the 'Kaddish Yathom' (Orphan's Kaddish)," 53 Tarbiz 599 (1984)

Ta-Shma, Isaac, "Two Sabbath Lights," Tarbiz, vol. 45, p. 128 (1975)

Urman, Dan, "The House of Assembly and the House of Study: Are they one and the same?" Journal of Jewish Studies, vol. 44, p. 236 (1993)

Weinfeld, Moshe, "Grace After Meals at the Mourner's House in a Text from Qumram," 61 Tarbiz 15 (1991)

————, "Instructions for Temple Visitors in Ancient Israel and in Ancient Egypt," Tarbiz, vol. 62, p. 5 (1992)

Wolf, Rabbi George, Lexical and Historical Contributions on the Biblical and Rabbinic Passover (New York, 1991)

Wolfson, Dr. Ron, *The Art of Jewish Living—The Shabbat Seder* (New York: Federation of Jewish Men's Clubs, 1985)

Wybrew, Hugh, *The Orthodox Liturgy* (Crestwood, NY: St. Vladimir's Seminary Press, 1990)

Zahavy, Tzvee, "The Politics of Piety: Social Conflict and the Emergence of Rabbinic Liturgy," in Bradshaw and Hoffman (eds.), *The Making of Jewish and Christian Worship, supra.*

——, "The Psychology of Early Rabbinic Prayer," in *idem., Studies in Jewish Prayer* (Lanham, MD: University Press of America, 1990)

——, *Studies in Jewish Prayer* (Lanham, MD: University Press of America, 1990)

Zeitlin, Solomon, "The Hallel," *Jewish Quarterly Review*, vol. 53, p. 22 (1962)

——, "The Origin of the Synagogue," *Proceedings of the American Academy of Jewish Research*, vol. 2, p. 69 (1930)

——, "The Temple and Worship," 51 *J.Q.R.* 209 (1960)

Zimmer, Eric, "Men's Headcovering: the Metamorphosis of This Practice," in Jacob Schacter (ed.), *Reverence, Righteousness, and Rahmanut— Essays in Memory of Rabbi Dr. Leo Jung* (Northvale, NJ: Jason Aronson Inc., 1992), p. 325

Zlotnick, Dov, "Memory and the Integrity of the Oral Tradition," 17 *Journal of the Ancient Near Eastern Society* 229 (1985)

The Zohar, trans. Harry Sperling and Maurice Simon (London, 1949)

2 *Encyclopedia Judaica*, "Aleinu Le'Shabbe'ah."

4 *Encyclopedia Judaica*, "Bread."

5 *Encyclopedia Judaica*, "Confession of Sins."

5 *Encyclopedia Judaica*, "Death."

6 *Encyclopedia Judaica*, "Etrog."

7 *Encyclopedia Judaica*, "Grace After Meals."

7 *Encyclopedia Judaica*, "Hakkafot."

7 *Encyclopedia Judaica*, "Hallel."

7 *Encyclopedia Judaica*, "Hanukkah."

7 *Encyclopedia Judaica*, "Hanukkah Lamp."

7 *Encyclopedia Judaica*, "Haroset."

7 *Encyclopedia Judaica*, "Hasidim."

8 *Encyclopedia Judaica*, "Hineni He'Ani Mi-Ma'as."

11 *Encyclopedia Judaica*, "Maror."

11 *Encyclopedia Judaica*, "Menorah."

12 *Encyclopedia Judaica*, "Music."

14 *Encyclopedia Judaica*, "Selihot."

14 *Encyclopedia Judaica*, "Shema."

15 *Encyclopedia Judaica,* "Sukkah."
15 *Encyclopedia Judaica,* "Sukkot."
15 *Encyclopedia Judaica,* "Tekhelet."
15 *Encyclopedia Judaica,* "Temple."

INDEX

281

About the Author

Arnold S. Rosenberg is an attorney in private practice in San Francisco, California. He grew up a Conservative Jew in Rochester, New York, where he learned much of what he knows about Judaism from Rabbi Abraham J. Karp, and Cantor Samuel Rosenbaum. After graduating from Cornell University, where he was elected to Phi Beta Kappa, he attended Harvard Law School and received his J.D. in 1976. Mr. Rosenberg spent the next four years as a poverty lawyer in a Mexican *barrio* in Chicago, Illinois. Following a stint as a labor lawyer in Chicago and New York, he moved to San Francisco, where he and his family have lived since 1983. He has been married to Nelly Reyes for 14 years. They have two children, Julian and Nina.